Remapping Global Politics

This book seeks to redraw our mental maps of global politics and to explain the shifting and accelerating forces that are shaping those maps. The authors build on the concept of "postinternationalism," focusing primarily on "political space" and "political identity" which, they argue, are the new frontiers of global political theory. They suggest that the state is losing capacity, legitimacy, and authority to remain the primary actor in world affairs and is giving way to a more complex postinternational universe characterized by diverse and overlapping polities. This book is the result of the authors' long-standing joint research into the nature and dynamics of global politics, a collaboration that has spanned over three decades. It makes an important contribution to the literatures on globalization and the future of international relations theory.

YALE H. FERGUSON is Professor of Political Science and Co-Director of the Center for Global Change and Governance, Rutgers University, Newark, and Honorary Professor, University of Salzburg.

RICHARD W. MANSBACH is Professor of Political Science, Iowa State University. Their previous co-authored books are: *The Web of World Politics: Nonstate Actors in the Global System* (with Donald E. Lampert, 1976), *The Elusive Quest: Theory and International Politics* (1988), *The State, Conceptual Chaos, and the Future of International Relations Theory* (1989), *Polities: Authority, Identities, and Change* (1996), and *The Elusive Quest Continues: Theory and Global Politics* (2003).

CAMBRIDGE STUDIES IN INTERNATIONAL RELATIONS: 97

Cambridge Studies in International Relations is a joint initiative of Cambridge University Press and the British International Studies Association (BISA). The series will include a wide range of material, from undergraduate textbooks and surveys to research-based monographs and collaborative volumes. The aim of the series is to publish the best new scholarship in International Studies from Europe, North America and the rest of the world.

CAMBRIDGE STUDIES IN INTERNATIONAL RELATIONS

Remapping Global Politics

History's Revenge and Future Shock

Yale H. Ferguson
and
Richard W. Mansbach

CAMBRIDGE
UNIVERSITY PRESS

PUBLISHED BY THE PRESS SYNDICATE OF THE UNIVERSITY OF CAMBRIDGE
The Pitt Building, Trumpington Street, Cambridge, United Kingdom

CAMBRIDGE UNIVERSITY PRESS
The Edinburgh Building, Cambridge, CB2 2RU, UK
40 West 20th Street, New York, NY 10011–4211, USA
477 Williamstown Road, Port Melbourne, VIC 3207, Australia
Ruiz de Alarcón 13, 28014 Madrid, Spain
Dock House, The Waterfront, Cape Town 8001, South Africa

http://www.cambridge.org

First published 2004

Printed in the United Kingdom at the University Press, Cambridge

Typeface Palatino 10/12.5 pt.   *System* LATEX 2$_\varepsilon$ [TB]

A catalogue record for this book is available from the British Library

Library of Congress cataloguing in publication data

ISBN 0 521 84059 7 hardback
ISBN 0 521 54991 4 paperback

To
Rhoda and Kitty

Contents

Preface

The authors have been pursuing a joint research collaboration and agenda for over three decades. Our first joint book, *The Web of World Politics* (1976) sought to analyze what we perceived to be the growing significance and proliferation of nonstate actors in the global system. Our second, *The Elusive Quest* (1988) focused on the evolution and normative foundation of theory and method in the field of international relations. Next, *The State, Conceptual Chaos, and the Future of International Relations Theory* (1989) pointed up the diversity of interpretations of "the state" as a concept that masked different views of its character and significance. In *Polities* (1996) we turned to historical case studies of six pre-Westphalian systems and elaborated what we still believe is a timeless framework for understanding authorities, identities, and change. We put the Westphalian State in historical perspective, noted the contemporary erosion of state capacity, and suggested that the future would probably be more like the past of multiple authorities than the era when the European nation-state model was preeminent. *The Elusive Quest Continues* (2003) updated trends in theory and method in the preceding fifteen years.

Remapping Global Politics now compares and contrasts two political worlds, one international and the other postinternational. This book seeks to do exactly what the title promises – redraw our mental maps of global politics and explain the forces shaping change. Recognition of the changing nature of political space and time takes us well beyond the two-dimensional cartographic representations that were deemed sufficient for centuries. Among the most important of the outcomes is to confirm the always important but increasingly salient role of identity in explaining behavior. There are also separate chapters on the global economy, war, and technology.

This book owes much to towering theorists ranging from Karl Deutsch, Ernst Haas, and Hedley Bull to Susan Strange and James N. Rosenau, who early on glimpsed a world beyond an unchanging state system. There is insufficient space to name them all, but their contributions to our field have been enormous. The field keeps reinventing the wheel by failing to recognize that "new theory" is too often recycled "old theory," but in every period there have been pioneers or "jailbreakers" as Rosenau likes to put it – and he himself, happily and most decidedly, still is.

Thankfully, our marriages have lasted even longer than our research collaboration – hence the heartfelt dedication of this book to our spouses, Rhoda Mansbach and Kitty Ferguson, for their constant love and support.

Acknowledgments

Parts of some chapters in this book draw on substantially rewritten parts of previously published articles or chapters: Yale H. Ferguson and Richard W. Mansbach, "History's Revenge and Future Shock: The Remapping of Global Politics," in Martin Hewson and Timothy J. Sinclair, eds., *Approaches to Global Governance Theory* (Albany, NY: State University of New York Press, 1999), pp. 197–238; Yale H. Ferguson and Richard W. Mansbach, "Global Politics at the Turn of the Millennium: Changing Bases of 'Us' and 'Them'," *International Studies Review* 1:2 (Summer 1999), pp. 77–107 and published simultaneously in Davis, B. Bobrow, ed., *Prospects for International Relations: Conjectures about the Next Millennium* (Malden, MA, and Oxford: Blackwell, 1999), pp. 77–107; Yale H. Ferguson and Richard W. Mansbach, "Technology and the Transformation of Global Politics," *Geopolitics* 4:3 (Winter 2000), pp. 1–28; Yale H. Ferguson and Richard W. Mansbach, "Reconstructing Theory in Global Politics: Beyond the Postmodern Challenge," in Darryl S. L. Jarvis, ed., *International Relations and the 'Third Debate': Postmodernism and its Critics* (Westport, CN: Praeger, 2002), pp. 147–164; Yale H. Ferguson and Richard W. Mansbach, "Remapping Political Space: Issues and Non-Issues in Analyzing Global Politics in the Twenty-First Century," in Yale H. Ferguson and R. J. Barry Jones, eds., *Political Space: The New Frontier of Global Politics* (Albany, NY: State University of New York Press, 2002), pp. 87–111; Richard W. Mansbach, "Changing Understandings of Global Politics: Preinternationalism, Internationalism, and Postinternationalism," in Heidi H. Hobbs, ed., *Pondering Postinternationalism* (Albany, NY: State University of New York Press, 2000), pp. 7–23; Yale H. Ferguson, "Postinternationalism and the Future of IR Theory" in Heidi H. Hobbs, ed., *Pondering Postinternationalism* (Albany, NY: State University of New York Press, 2000), pp. 197–215; Richard W. Mansbach,

Acknowledgments

"Deterritorializing Global Politics," in Charles Kegley, Jr., and Donald Puchala, eds., *Visions of International Relations* (Columbia, SC: University of South Carolina Press, 2002), pp. 101–118; Richard W. Mansbach and Franke Wilmer, "War and the Westphalian State of Mind," in Mathias Albert, David Jacobson, and Yosef Lapid, eds., *Identities, Borders, Orders* (Minneapolis: University of Minnesota Press, 2001), pp. 51–71; Peter Dombrowski and Richard W. Mansbach, "From Sovereign States to Sovereign Markets?" *International Politics*, 36 (March 1999), pp. 1–23. We are particularly grateful to Peter Dombrowski and Franke Wilmer for their personal permission to use material co-authored with Mansbach.

1   Postinternational politics

Remapping "political space" is the "new frontier" of global political theory. Like the title voice-over of the television series *Star Trek*, both the task of remapping and the shifting nature of contemporary global politics challenge us to go boldly where no one has gone before.[1] The task of remapping is a critical one, precisely because the "Westphalian moment" is passing. Moreover, it is increasingly obvious that that moment only very gradually and never fully "arrived" and, to the extent that it did, may well have been a historical anomaly. The end of the Cold War, present-day globalizing trends, the undermining of some of the state's familiar roles, the proliferation of nonstate actors, fears of apocalyptic terrorism, and a host of other developments make much of existing international relations (IR) theory seem hopelessly obsolete. It not only fails to illuminate but also actually obfuscates the main features of present-day global politics. In sum, most of traditional IR theory is bad theory.

Even those like ourselves who have abandoned traditional approaches are keenly aware of how rapidly things are moving and how little we really know. We sense the startling new-ness of the current world as well as how much it resembles the past, not only the European epoch of the Westphalian State[2] but also the vast stretches of human history

---

[1] The opening sentences of this chapter echo the opening of Yale H. Ferguson and Richard W. Mansbach, "Remapping Political Space: Issues and Nonissues in Analyzing Global Politics in the Twenty-First Century," in Yale H. Ferguson and R. J. Barry Jones, eds., *Political Space: New Frontiers of Change and Governance in a Globalizing World* (Albany, NY: State University of New York Press, 2002), pp. 87–111.

[2] Although the emergence of territorial states was a long-term process, we refer to them as Westphalian States because of their association with the 1648 peace of that name that brought an end to the Thirty Years War. That peace, consisting of the Treaties of Onasbrück and Munster, established the right of princes of the Holy Roman Empire to conduct their

going back to much earlier political forms. T. S. Eliot's opening lines in his *Four Quartets* capture the situation exactly and yet (paradoxically, as Eliot would appreciate) leave us to fill in the details: "Time present and time past/Are both perhaps present in time future/And time future contained in time past."[3] And, as the poet suggests, "we shall not cease from exploration."

This book is part of the authors' continuing examination of how people organize themselves for political ends and of the dynamics behind the changing nature of political association. Its foundation is our earlier work on nonstate actors and the "polities" framework for analyzing global politics that we developed in the course of research on pre-Westphalian patterns and advanced in our 1996 volume *Polities: Authority, Identities, and Change.*[4] However, it is interesting and significant that our polities approach, generated independently, has nonetheless increasingly converged with the work of James N. Rosenau. Rosenau coined the term "postinternationalism" to describe "an apparent trend in which more and more of the interactions that sustain world politics unfold without the direct involvement of nations and states."[5] He continues to use the words postinternational and postinternationalism but now appears to prefer to describe his own "paradigm" or "worldview" in dynamic terms as one of "turbulence" or "fragmegration." Our polities model similarly speaks of "integration" and "fragmentation" or "fusion" and "fission."[6] But postinternationalism still seems to us to be the best shorthand characterization of contemporary global politics.[7]

own foreign affairs and conclude treaties with other rulers. The earlier Peace of Augsburg (1555) declared that Lutheran princes might impose their religion on subjects regardless of the preferences of the Holy Roman Emperor. These agreements together constituted a giant step toward legitimating state sovereignty.

[3] Peter Dicken closes the last section of his book on the "global shift" in the world economy with the same lines from Eliot. Dicken, *Global Shift: Transforming the World Economy*, 3rd ed. (New York: Guilford, 1998).

[4] Yale H. Ferguson and Richard W. Mansbach, *Polities: Authority, Identities, and Change* (Columbia, SC: University of South Carolina Press, 1996).

[5] James N. Rosenau, *Turbulence in World Politics: A Theory of Change and Continuity* (Princeton: Princeton University Press, 1990), p. 6. See also James N. Rosenau, *Along the Domestic–Foreign Frontier: Exploring Governance in a Turbulent World* (Cambridge: Cambridge University Press, 1997), especially p. 38n; and his "Beyond Postinternationalism," in Heidi H. Hobbs, ed., *Pondering Postinternationalism* (Albany, NY: State University of New York Press, 2000), pp. 219–237. Rosenau continues to stress fragmegrative processes in his latest book: James N. Rosenau, *Distant Proximities: Dynamics Beyond Globalization* (Princeton: Princeton University Press, 2003), pp. 11–16.

[6] Ferguson and Mansbach, *Polities*, pp. 51–57, 383.

[7] See the authors' separate essays in Hobbs, *Pondering Postinternationalism*: Richard W. Mansbach, "Changing Understandings of Global Politics: Preinternationalism,

In the chapters that follow, we analyze and describe the gradual appearance of a *postinternational world* with respect to political forms, identities, economics, war, technology, and collective norms, and we contrast this world with the vanishing *international world* – as it is usually and significantly termed – of traditional Eurocentric IR theory.

International politics grew out of a tradition of interpretive scholarship dating back at least to Thomas Hobbes and Hugo Grotius that universalized and exaggerated Europe's post-Westphalian experience by positing that sovereign states and interstate relations are all we need to know about our political universe and that the central problem of that universe is the management of violence and war. Eurocentric IR theorists have viewed the study of interstate war as constituting the core of their tradition. Typical of this tradition is K. J. Holsti's observation that: "When thinking about war, we usually conjure up the image of two countries arraying their military forces against each other . . ."[8] And, as he avers, this image "derives from the post-1648 European experience."[9] These premises reflected the state's conquest of political rivals and subsequent control of historical meaning.

For several hundred years theorists and practitioners of global politics have been accustomed to regarding the sovereign state as the object of humanity's highest loyalties, the primary locus of political authority, and the source of important public values. During the epoch of European ascendancy, sovereign states claiming exclusive rights over territory and subjects/citizens within their boundaries, as well as freedom from external interference, "dominated" global politics. That general condition masked the fact that human beings have always lived in a variety of political communities, with varying degrees of autonomy, and had multiple identities and loyalties. In fact, identity hierarchies have been continually changing since the beginning of human association. All we can say without qualification is that the state for one major historical period established a very successful claim to preeminence.

If global change has recently been as extensive as we contend, then the ontology or assumed elements of international relations are increasingly misleading. "'Ontology'," according to David Dessler, "refers to the

---

Internationalism, and Postinternationalism," pp. 7–23; and Yale H. Ferguson, "Postinternationalism and the Future of IR Theory," pp. 197–215.

[8] K. J. Holsti, *The State, War, and the State of War* (Cambridge: Cambridge University Press, 1996), p. 1.

[9] *Ibid.* For a discussion of this tradition, see K. J. Holsti, *The Dividing Discipline: Hegemony and Diversity in International Theory* (Boston: Allen & Unwin, 1985), p. vii.

concrete referents of an explanatory discourse. A theory's ontology consists of the real-world structures (things, entities) and processes posited by the theory and invoked in the theory's explanations." For example, in "classical physics, the ontology consists of space, time, and matter, meaning that all the entities or processes to which a classical explanation refers are embodiments of our relations between space, time, and matter."[10] The state-centric theories and models that continue to prevail in our field, at best, account for only a small part of what happens in the world and, at worst, are edifices built on sand. That ontology relies on an anarchic system consisting of territorial states, whose citizens are united in a quest for security that pits them against the citizens of other states. By contrast, we begin with an ontology that consists largely of polities and identities (individual and collective) driven by interdependent processes of centralization (integration/fusion) and decentralization (disintegration/localization/fission) of political authority.[11]

To the extent that the territorial polities of Europe and North America extended their cultural, as well as military and political hegemony beyond their original boundaries, it is not surprising that state-centric theories – derived from European versions of concepts such as "power," "sovereignty," "territoriality," and "sovereign frontiers" – acquired global reach. Such concepts not only embodied what European theorists considered to be the most important "real" or structural factors in international politics but also reinforced what those theorists thought ought to be the dominant norms and practices of global life. The current erosion of state authority and capacity signals that the interstate epoch is drawing to a close, and invites us to reexamine old ideas and construct new ones that will both provide a better "fit" with observable reality and a more accurate guide to changing political patterns and attendant norms.

Conflicting stories of global politics: continuity and change, anarchy and order[12]

From time to time words are co-opted by various schools of theory and their former meaning is transformed in the process. "Story" is one

---

[10] David Dessler, "What's at Stake in the Agent–Structure Debate?" *International Organization* 43:3 (Summer 1989), p. 445.
[11] Ferguson and Mansbach, *Polities*.
[12] Some of this section appeared in an earlier form in Yale H. Ferguson and Richard W. Mansbach, "Stories of Global Politics: Continuity and Change, Anarchy and Order, Polities and Markets," paper delivered to 4th Pan-European Conference on International Relations, Canterbury, UK, 2001.

such word, "discourse" another, and "contradiction" yet a third. For postmodernists a "story" is always fiction of sorts, because it reflects the myopia and biases of the storyteller. "Discourse" is similarly the language expressing a particular way of seeing the world, almost a catechism, for example, the "discourse of modernity." "Contradiction" by contrast is not a word favored by postmodernists, ironically because, for extreme relativists, it is inherent in virtually all story telling or discourse. Contradiction had earlier been co-opted by Marxist analysts for whom it carried progressive ideological overtones initially derived from Hegel's Idealism.[13] However bright the outlook for capitalism at any given time, Marxists always presumed there were inevitable contradictions besetting that economic system that would eventually lead to its instability or even demise and thus to the triumph of socialism.

Although this book tells one essential story about postinternational polities, stories concerning the same subject may differ and more than one may be "true." Of course, some stories may be false, and not all "true" stories are necessarily *equally* true partly because of the selection of facts and differences in interpreting their meaning. Discourse should be regarded as a conversation, not a recitation of predetermined ideas and conclusions. Indeed, if there is any discourse in the sense of a conversation relevant to global politics, it is one of sheer complexity involving many voices, many readings of the "facts," and many normative predilections. Moreover, to begin to understand global politics is necessarily to accept contradictions and ambiguities as part and parcel of that complex "reality."

Contemporary debates about globalization illustrate some of the problems of getting at truth.[14] Consider economic globalization. First, there are the problems of conceptual consensus and clarity. In measuring economic globalization, it makes a good deal of difference if one is looking strictly at the growth of international trade and investment, which has been advancing in fits and starts for well over a century, at the pace and volume of international currency flows for speculative purposes, or at the proliferation of mergers, alliances, and networks among firms. If we limit "globalization" to the growth of international trade and investment, as does Paul Hirst,[15] we can conclude, as does Hirst,

---

[13] See Francis Fukuyama, *The End of History and the Last Man* (New York: Free Press, 1992).

[14] See, for example, Stanley Hoffmann, "The Clash of Globalizations," *Foreign Policy* 81:4 (July–August 2002), pp. 104–115.

[15] Paul Hirst, "The Global Economy – Myths and Realities," *International Affairs* 73 (1997), pp. 409–425. For a fuller exposition, see also Paul Hirst and Grahame Thompson, *Globalization in Question*, 2nd ed. (Cambridge: Polity, 1999).

that such "a process has been going on, punctuated by the interruptions of severe economic crises and wars, for well over a century." Hirst identifies "three major phases." The initial phase was "the *belle-époque* of 1870–1914, when world trade and output grew in parallel at an annual rate of 3.5 percent and 4.5 percent, respectively." Thus: "By the late nineteenth century, the whole world had become part of a developed and interconnected commercial civilization." A second period of growth extended from the end of World War II through the OPEC oil crisis of 1973, when trade grew annually at 9.4 percent and output at 5.3 percent. The final phase was 1973–79, when capital movements accelerated because of the deregulation of financial markets and floating exchange rates.[16]

The agenda behind Hirst's definition of globalization becomes apparent when he stresses that the first two periods did not "undermine the nation-state" and that, in fact, "many modern nation-states were forged during the *belle époque* and sustained by rapid industrial growth." And he argues that, between 1950 and 1973, supposedly the "heyday of autonomy in national economic policy and of Keynesian demand management," when governments cooperated, they could exercise a considerable amount of "supranational governance." So has nothing changed? Hirst acknowledges that direct merchandise trade has become much less significant as capital flows have increased, but he avoids asking whether the vast speculative flows of currency that characterize the present are unprecedented and does not address what impact they and other globalizing trends might have upon state autonomy and capacity. Are current capital flows global in scope? Hirst notes that over 90 percent of foreign direct investment still takes place between and among rich countries, representing just over a quarter of the world's population. His intention is twofold, first to demonstrate that much investment is not actually global but concentrated and, second, that as long as this is the case, the potential for the relatively small group of affected countries to design joint strategies for regulation remains high. He concludes that "governance [is] possible, given the political will and a measure of international consensus,"[17] thereby introducing a powerful qualification of his forecast. The claim that the spatial scope of globalizing trends is limited is also found in observations that much of global economic activity emanates from a few "world cities" or that it is more intense in particular bilateral relationships and/or in certain regions.

---

[16] Hirst, "The Global Economy," pp. 410–412.   [17] *Ibid.*, p. 425.

What about the spatial extent of transnational corporations (TNCs)? Are they globalized in terms of scope, structure, and market strategies? Hirst maintains that firms "are still multinational, not transnational; that is, they have a home base in one of the Triad [Europe, Japan, and North America] countries" and "are not footloose capital but are rooted in a major market in one of the three most prosperous regions of the world."[18] Yet TNC's have spatial characteristics – sales, customers, production facilities, and currency holdings – that distinguish them from national enterprises. Corporate leaders *are* designing transnational and sometimes global strategies, and production and management structures *are* increasingly being integrated across vast stretches of the planet. New corporate networks and alliances abound.

For Jan Aart Scholte, globalization is "the spread of 'supraterritorial' or 'transborder relations.'" This definition enables him to reach a very different conclusion than Hirst, even while accepting that relative levels of "cross-border trade, investment and migration a hundred years ago were roughly the same or higher than they are today." What Scholte finds "distinctive" about contemporary globalization is that it involves "a fundamental transformation of human geography" in which the world has "acquired a (rapidly growing) global dimension alongside the territorial framework of old" that is reflected in spheres such as telecommunications, marketing, and "transworld finance." As a result, Scholte concludes that "the territorialist assumptions which underpin modern understandings of 'international relations' have become untenable." "[B]orders are not so much crossed as *transcended*."[19] In sum, the global political and economic worlds are not entirely old or new; they are worlds in transition.

Closer to Scholte than Hirst, still others, including co-authors David Held, Anthony McGrew, David Goldblatt, and Jonathan Perraton,[20]

---

[18] *Ibid.*, p. 418. For a similar argument, see Louis W. Pauly and Simon Reich, "National Structures and Multinational Corporate Behavior: Enduring Differences in the Age of Globalization," *International Organization* 51:1 (Winter 1997), pp. 1–30; and Paul N. Doremus, William W. Keller, Louis W. Pauly, and Simon Reich, *The Myth of the Global Corporation* (Princeton: Princeton University Press, 1998).

[19] Jan Aart Scholte, "Global Capitalism and the State," *International Affairs* 73 (1997), pp. 429–430, 432. Emphasis in original. See also Jan Aart Scholte, *Globalization: A Critical Introduction* (New York: St. Martin's, 2000), especially ch. 2. In ch. 1, Scholte distinguishes between what he sees as five different definitions of "globalization": internationalization, liberalization, universalization, westernization (modernization), and deterritorialization (his own preference).

[20] See David Held, Anthony McGrew, David Goldblatt, and Jonathan Perraton, *Global Transformations: Politics, Economics and Culture* (Cambridge: Polity, 1999). One annual

view globalization as a multidimensional process or set of processes that involves not only the world economy and technology but also additional governance,[21] military, cultural,[22] demographic, human rights, and environmental dimensions. Moreover, whatever may be happening "globally" in any one of these dimensions, many analysts perceive that there are important local, country,[23] regional, subregional, bilateral, city-to-city,[24] and hegemonic patterns in the overall picture as well.

The way in which globalization is conceptualized is, then, evidently central to any assessment of whether the current era is novel historically. There were other periods in ancient history – for example, the ancient Mediterranean at the height of the Roman Empire – when at least a part of the world was highly integrated under a hegemon. During Europe's Middle Ages, before tribal and ethnic identities had hardened into full-fledged national identities, political boundaries were indistinct, and merchants, artisans, and clerics moved across the continent with little concern about legal frontiers. We might also recall the heyday of the colonial empires in the late nineteenth and early twentieth centuries, when the globe was divided up by a handful of major European powers. Strict mercantilism had given way to the growth of interdependence and international trade, a single gold standard prevailed from 1870 to 1914, and European society and civilization (despite rising nationalism) could with some justification regard itself as a "proud tower."[25]

Thus, wherever one turns in the analysis of global politics, multiple stories abound. There are no generally accepted benchmarks against

"Globalization Index" for countries measures four factors: political engagement, technology, personal contact, and economic integration. See "Measuring Globalization: Who's Up, Who's Down," *Foreign Policy* 134 (January–February 2003), pp. 60–72.

[21] For an overview of different approaches on the matter of governance, see especially Martin Hewson and Timothy J. Sinclair, eds., *Approaches to Global Governance Theory* (Albany, NY: State University of New York Press, 1999); and Craig N. Murphy, "Global Governance: Poorly Done and Poorly Understood," *International Affairs* 76:4 (October 2000), pp. 789–803. See also Rosenau, *Distant Proximities*, chs. 12–18; Robert O. Keohane and Joseph S. Nye, Jr., "Governance in a Globalizing World," in Robert O. Keohane, *Power and Governance in a Partially Globalized World* (New York: Routledge, 2002), pp. 193–218; and Rodney Bruce Hall and Thomas J. Biersteker, eds., *The Emergence of Private Authority in Global Governance* (Cambridge: Cambridge University Press, 2002).

[22] See Peter L. Berger and Samuel P. Huntington, eds., *Many Globalizations: Cultural Diversity in the Contemporary World* (Oxford: Oxford University Press, 2002).

[23] *Ibid.*

[24] Paul L. Knox and Peter J. Taylor, *World Cities in a World-System* (Cambridge: Cambridge University Press, 1995), and Saskia Sassen, *The Global City: New York, London, Tokyo* (Princeton: Princeton University Press, 1994). See also Saskia Sassen, ed., *Global Networks: Linked Cities* (New York: Routledge, 2002).

[25] See Barbara Tuchman, *A Proud Tower: A Portrait of the World Before the War 1890–1914* (New York: Ballantine Books, 1996).

which to measure change[26] and little agreement regarding the nature of the contemporary world or even what features of it are most important to consider. Accounts differ as to how far we need to depart from the "sovereign" psychology of recent centuries, and the research based on that psychology,[27] to redraw our own mental maps to take account of shifting patterns of governance as well as identities.

Against a muddy background of competing definitions and historical precedents – and for a further example of that competition – it is useful to highlight the different stories told by two theorists, Stephen D. Krasner and Rosenau, whose conclusions regarding the degree of continuity or change in global politics at the start of the twenty-first century stand in stark contrast to one another.

Rosenau examines "multiple contradictions" and anomalies in global politics in his work on "a new and wide political space" that he terms "the domestic–foreign frontier":

> The international system is less commanding, but it is still powerful. States are changing, but they are not disappearing. State sovereignty has been eroded, but it is still vigorously asserted. Governments are weaker, but they can still throw their weight around. At certain times publics are more demanding, but at other times they are more pliable. Borders still keep out intruders, but they are also more porous. Landscapes are giving way to ethnoscapes, mediascapes, ideoscapes, technoscapes, and finanscapes, but territoriality is still a central preoccupation for many people.[28]

Given accelerating change, he asks:

> How do we assess a world in which the Frontier is continuously shifting, widening and narrowing, simultaneously undergoing erosion with respect to many issues and reinforcement with respect to others? How do we reconceptualize political space so that it connotes

---

[26] See K. J. Holsti, "The Problem of Change in International Relations," in Ferguson and Jones, eds., *Political Space*, pp. 23–43.

[27] For example, Andreas Osiander argues that the idea that sovereignty was established during the Thirty Years War is false; he traces it to the nineteenth century and the period of industrialization. See "Sovereignty, International Relations, and the Westphalian Myth," *International Organization* 55:2 (Spring 2001), pp. 251–287. See also James A. Caporaso, ed., *International Studies Review*, special issue, *Continuity and Change in the Westphalian Order* 2:2 (Summer 2000). Similar dating is used by Eric Helleiner in "Historicizing Territorial Currencies: Monetary Space and the Nation-State in North America," *Political Geography* 18 (1999), pp. 309–339, as well as by Janice E. Thomson, *Mercenaries, Pirates, and Sovereigns* (Princeton: Princeton University Press, 1994) for state centralization of sovereign war power.

[28] Rosenau, *Along the Domestic–Foreign Frontier*, p. 4.

identities and affiliations (say, religious, ethnic, and professional) as well as territorialities? . . . Under what circumstances does authority along the Frontier accrue to like-minded states, to global regimes, to transnational organizations, to subnational entities, or to coalitions of diverse types of actors?[29]

In contrast to Rosenau's story of dramatic change, Krasner makes no secret of his fundamentally realist orientation. In Krasner's story, differences in national power and state interests continue to share star billing in explaining global outcomes. At root, little of fundamental importance has changed, including international institutions: "There are no constitutive rules that preclude rulers from contracting to establish whatever kind of institutional form might serve their needs." States remain in control as "[r]ulers, seeking to maintain their own position and promote the interests of their constituents, can choose among competing principles and, if they command adequate resources, engage in coercion or imposition. In a contested environment in which actors, including the rulers of states, embrace different norms, clubs can always be trump."[30] In Krasner, then, we get the outline of a persuasive story of globalization as the product of rules set by a few developed and developing states that retain the capacity to bring an end to the process if they wish to do so.

Krasner's story is an up-to-date and edited version of the classic realist tale that always begins with "once upon a time in Old Europe," either with Westphalia (which Krasner downplays as a watershed event) or the end of the Middle Ages. The realist story is one about absolutist divine-right monarchs who gradually succeed in gaining the upper hand over aristocratic rivals at home and external challengers with universalist ambitions. Over time, boundaries are secured and mapped; "hard-shell" territorial states become the dominant polities in global politics; the principle of sovereignty legitimizes the rulers of states and comes to symbolize a claim both to domestic authority and noninterference from abroad; kings monetarize local microeconomies and steadily increase their capacity to tax; national treasuries swell; the money is used to create an administrative bureaucracy and to make war, first usually with hired mercenaries and then a national military; the state provides reasonable security from foreign predators and from upstart nobles and bandits

---

[29] *Ibid.*, p. 5.
[30] Stephen D. Krasner, *Sovereignty: Organized Hypocrisy* (Princeton: Princeton University Press, 1999), p. 238.

near at hand; and that security, and more formalized legal systems, facilitate the development of internal markets and foreign trade.[31]

Krasner the realist focuses on the past, present, and likely future of "state sovereignty." His selection of facts and the links he makes among them are different from those in Rosenau's story. Hence, he sees change in a very different light than does Rosenau, insisting that those who argue that there has been an erosion of sovereignty in recent years are using a misleading benchmark. Westphalia did not inaugurate a new era of hard-shell territoriality; rather, nation-states in Europe emerged only through a meandering process of consolidation that took centuries. Sovereignty was never regarded as absolute authority over a state's own subjects and even less as an absolute deterrent to external interference; it has actually been, from the start, a form of "organized hypocrisy." "There has never been an ideal time during which all, or even most, political entities conformed with all the characteristics that have been associated with sovereignty – territory, control, recognition, and autonomy." There have been many violations of sovereignty in the past: "The European Union, the practices of international financial institutions, some minority rights agreements after Versailles, and treaties providing for religious toleration in Europe such as the Peace of Westphalia have all involved invitations to compromise Westphalian sovereignty." There have also been nonsovereign entities in the past: "Other institutional forms have been accorded international recognition, including even entities without territory." "Colonies have signed international agreements and been members of international organizations."[32]

As for the present, Krasner contends, states are adapting and adjusting rather than declining: "The reach of the state has increased in some areas but contracted in others."[33] Nongovernmental organizations (NGOs) are gaining some influence but still have less clout than governments and interstate organizations. The European Union, Krasner admits, does not fit his story, but it is a unique case and definitely not a model for other parts of the world.[34]

At first glance, it is almost as though Rosenau is looking at an entirely different political universe when he narrates his story of change

---

[31] See Michael Mann, *States, War and Capitalism: Studies in Political Sociology* (Oxford: Basil Blackwell, 1988).

[32] Krasner, *Sovereignty*, pp. 238, 237.

[33] Stephen D. Krasner, "Sovereignty," *Foreign Policy* 122 (January–February 2001), p. 24. This is a conclusion shared by Georg Sørensen, *The Transformation of the State* (London: Palgrave, 2004).

[34] Krasnner, "Sovereignty," pp. 26, 28–29.

in global politics. Rosenau acknowledges historical precedents of dispersed authority such as the Medici family and the Hanseatic League; widespread diseases like the bubonic plague; and the information impact of the printing press, wireless, and telephone. But for him "there are at least three major dimensions of the present era that have led to differences in kind and not just in degree when compared with earlier times."[35]

The first "concerns the structures that sustain the politics of the Frontier." Arguing that the role of territory and territorial boundaries has been attenuated, Rosenau quotes David Held (echoing John Burton):

> While in the eighteenth and nineteenth centuries trade routes and empires linked distant populations together through quite simple networks of interaction, the contemporary global order is defined by multiple systems of transaction and coordination, which link people, communities and societies in highly complex ways and which, given the nature of modern communications, virtually annihilate territorial boundaries as barriers to socio-economic activity and relations, and create new political uncertainties.[36]

The second and third dimensions are, respectively, "the structures of the globalized world economy" and "the time frame within which events and trends unfold." Asserting the globalization of economic forces, Rosenau cites Stephen J. Kobrin on the scale of technology that makes national markets "too small to be meaningful economic units," the "explosion of transnational strategic alliances," and integration "through information systems and information technology rather than hierarchical organizational structures."[37]

In sum, Rosenau tells the story of a world where history is speeding up, a world characterized by a bifurcation of global structures, the proliferation of actors, technological revolutions, the globalization of economic exchange, the presence of interdependence/collective goods issues, the weakening of state authority, subgroupism, increasingly skilled individuals, and a widening income gap both within and across countries that reflects those who are benefiting from globalization and those who are not.[38] For Rosenau, one of the central consequences of change is a dramatically altered array of "global governance" that "encompasses the activities of governments [at various levels, but also

---

[35] Rosenau, *Along the Domestic–Foreign Frontier*, pp. 22–23.
[36] *Ibid.*, pp. 22–23.   [37] *Ibid.*, p. 23.   [38] *Ibid.*, pp. 56–77.

includes] the many other channels through which 'commands' flow in the form of goals framed, directives issued, and policies pursued."[39]

"Viewed on a global scale," he declares, "governance is the sum of a myriad – literally millions – of control mechanisms driven by different histories, goals, structures, and processes."[40] These mechanisms are "not synonymous with government" and lack the backing of "police powers." Instead, in words that previewed later constructivism, Rosenau in 1992 defined global governance as "a system of rule that is as dependent on intersubjective meanings as on formally sanctioned constitutions and charters."[41] Governance consists of "numerous patterns that sustain global order." These unfold "at three basic levels of activity" – intersubjective, behavioral, and "the aggregate or political level where . . . rule-oriented institutions and regimes enact and implement the policies" produced at the other levels.[42] Governance includes decisional activities ranging from individual market choices to "world civic politics,"[43] international regimes, and customary law. This is why, despite the growing incapacity of states, things still get done, often efficiently and effectively, in the postinternational world. For Rosenau:

> [T]he world is not so much a system dominated by states and national governments as a congeries of spheres of authority (SOAs) that are subject to considerable flux and not necessarily coterminous with the division of territorial space. SOAs are, in effect, the analytic units of the new ontology. They are distinguished by the presence of actors who can evoke compliance when exercising authority as they engage in activities that delineate the sphere. The sphere may or may not correspond to a bounded territory: those who comply may be spread around the world and have no legal relationship to one another, or they may be located in the same geographic space and have the same organizational affiliations.[44]

Krasner's and Rosenau's stories may appear to be – and actually are in some respects – polar opposites. But both are substantially "true" insofar as they highlight contradictory aspects of observable global political

---

[39] James N. Rosenau, "Governance in the Twenty-first Century," *Global Governance* 1:1 (Winter 1995), pp. 13–43.
[40] Rosenau, *Along the Domestic–Foreign Frontier*, p. 115.
[41] James N. Rosenau, "Governance, Order, and Change in World Politics," in Rosenau and Ernst-Otto Czempiel, eds., *Governance Without Government: Order and Change in World Politics* (Cambridge: Cambridge University Press, 1992), p. 4.
[42] *Ibid.*, p. 14.
[43] See Paul Wapner, "Politics Beyond the State: Environmental Activism and World Civic Politics," *World Politics* 47:3 (April 1995), pp. 311–340.
[44] Rosenau, *Along the Domestic–Foreign Frontier*, p. 39.

"reality" and reflect the very different values of the story tellers. Together, they constitute something of a conversation about past and present in global politics, and the potential for and possible limits of change. These divergent stories each represent the tip of different icebergs. Sustaining each of them are a variety of other stories that are subplots in the two mega-chronicles.

Despite our affinity for Rosenau, Krasner's contention that the intersubjective understandings and practice of sovereignty continually evolve is largely correct. Like the present authors, Krasner is not wedded to international law or the legal claim that what sovereignty actually guarantees cannot vary or be partial. In this, Krasner is historically more attuned than Rosenau, but Rosenau does address some perils of relying on history: "[W]hile there often appears to be nothing new in history, the speed, simultaneity, and scope of events infuse new meanings and structures into seemingly familiar patterns. Accordingly, one can be misled by the past if in the present context one fails to allow for the dynamics of transformation."[45]

In the end, once we agree with Krasner that sovereignty in a practical sense can evolve and indeed has, the issue that remains – and it is a crucial one – is interpreting the implications of such change. And here we diverge from Krasner and find ourselves far more at home with Rosenau. For this reason, we return to Rosenau's story.

James Rosenau: from international to postinternational politics[46]

Rosenau's "postinternational" label was part of an effort to break free of the shackles of statist assumptions. "[P]ostinternationalist politics" he declared, is the result of dramatic changes in global politics just as the social sciences more generally are "marked by analyses of postcapitalist society, postcivilized era, postcollectivist politics, posteconomic society, posthistoric man, postideological society, postliberal era, postliterature culture, postmarket society, post-Marxists, postmaterialist value system, postmaturity economy, postmodernism, postorganization society, post-Christian era, postscarcity society, postsocialist society, posttraditional

---

[45] *Ibid.*, p. 24.
[46] Some of what follows appeared in an earlier version in Richard W. Mansbach, "Changing Understandings of Global Politics," in Hobbs, ed., *Pondering Postinternationalism*, pp. 7–23.

society, and postwelfare society, as well as postindustrial society. . . ."[47] "International" only describes relations and interactions among a subset of collective actors called "states," and that is less and less the defining characteristic of what we study. Instead, politics is a seamless web extending from individuals in families and other communities all the way to global structures, and what has been called "international relations" is neither a distinctive field nor discipline.

Rosenau's path from international to postinternational politics was evolutionary rather than revolutionary. The distance traveled from the rigorous state-centric positivist of the late 1960s to the somewhat less robust advocate of "potential observability"[48] and occasionally reflexive postinternationalist is immense. Over four decades ago, when he and Klaus Knorr declared that "both theory and research are aspects of the scientific enterprise,"[49] Rosenau was a prophet of science and a foe of mixing facts and values. The patterns of behavior of any human institution were, he then believed, as susceptible to rigorous empiricism as "the characteristics of the electron or the molecule."[50] Although Rosenau no longer insists upon strict science, he remains determined to develop a vocabulary and analytic framework to account for a dramatically changed reality, and to stay within an empirical tradition[51] despite the proliferation of "dissident" and "guerrilla" analyses that reject objectivity, lionize relativism, and obfuscate ideas.

The postinternational enterprise seems light-years away from the concerns of Rosenau the scientist, who confidently declared that "the nation-state is no different from the atom or the single cell organism." Nevertheless, there is more than an echo of the scientist in his current preoccupation with complexity theory and frequently expressed hope that advances in computer technology may eventually allow us to build "agent-based feedback processes into models that simulate the dynamics of change, fragmegration, and micro-macro

---

[47] James N. Rosenau, "Global Changes and Theoretical Challenges: Toward a Postinternational Politics for the 1990s," in Ernst-Otto Czempiel and Rosenau, eds., *Global Changes and Theoretical Challenges: Approaches to World Politics for the 1990s* (Lexington, MA: Lexington Books, 1989), pp. 2–3.

[48] *Ibid.*, pp. 27–33.

[49] Klaus Knorr and James N. Rosenau, "Tradition and Science in the Study of International Politics," in Klaus Knorr and James N. Rosenau, eds., *Contending Approaches to International Politics* (Princeton: Princeton University Press, 1969), p. 17.

[50] James N. Rosenau, *The Scientific Study of Foreign Policy* (New York: Free Press, 1971), p. 21.

[51] For a stronger statement of this position, see Nicholas Onuf, "Writing Large: Habit, Skill, and Grandiose Theory," in Hobbs, ed., *Pondering Postinternationalism*, pp. 99–113.

interactions."[52] Furthermore, despite the evolution in his thinking, throughout his career Rosenau has returned over and over again to many of the same puzzles, notably the relationship of wholes and parts, the links between domestic and foreign factors (the generic problem of "inside/outside"), and the interdependent fates of individuals and communities. What facilitated the evolution in his thinking was that he never was a realist or neorealist. Unlike neorealists like Kenneth Waltz, Rosenau was never an advocate of structural determinism and found a place for all levels of analysis in his models, a fact perhaps best exemplified in his analyses of the comparative study of foreign policy. He was never overly troubled by mixing Waltzian "images" or what Rosenau would later call "micro/macro." In some ways, his early interest in the "micro" aspects of political life anticipated the later constructivist emphasis on voluntarism.

Rosenau never fully accepted that states could be treated as "billiard balls" or "black boxes," or that the boundary between "inside" and "outside" was anything other than porous. Initially, his examination of the links between the domestic and international realms took the form of efforts to explore the ways in which domestic political processes and structures condition foreign policy. In the course of this exploration, the concepts of national interest and state sovereignty began to dissolve. "Perhaps never before," he declared in 1967, "have the domestic sources of foreign policy seemed so important."[53] From this point, it is a straight path to dismissing the idea that a state can be treated "as an actor whose nature, motives, and conduct are so self-evident as to obviate any need for precise conceptualizing." "Such a usage takes macro analysis back to unitary actors and reified collectivities."[54] This stream of theorizing led Rosenau to question the nature and role of the sovereign state in global politics more generally, ultimately moving him to identify actors or agents as generic "spheres of authority (SOAs)" and to extend the notion of government to that of "governance," that is, "mechanisms for steering social systems toward their goals."[55]

Rosenau's early emphasis on the role of individuals and on the porous nature of sovereign frontiers derived from his recognition that people, even those geographically remote from one another, increasingly share

---

[52] Rosenau, *Distant Proximities*, p. 47.
[53] James N. Rosenau, "Introduction," in Rosenau, ed., *The Domestic Sources of Foreign Policy* (New York: Free Press,1967), p. 2.
[54] Rosenau, *Turbulence in World Politics*, p. 117.
[55] Rosenau, *Along the Domestic–Foreign Frontier*, pp. 39, 41.

common fates. In a frequently cited passage, he declared: "Almost every day incidents are reported that defy the principles of sovereignty. Politics everywhere, it would seem, are related to politics everywhere else."[56] The focus in his latest book is on the "enormous diversity in the way people experience the distant proximities of which their lives are composed."[57]

Nevertheless, it merits noting that Rosenau's work also initially evinced a certain reluctance to abandon the sovereign state as his principal unit of analysis. "Transnational polities," he argued in 1969, "are a long way from supplanting national politics and, if anything, the world may well be passing through a paradoxical stage in which *both* the linkages and the boundaries among polities are becoming more central to their daily lives."[58] He was still a "foreign-policy" theorist, with at least a fig leaf separating the foreign and domestic arenas of political life. Only later did he decide that in order "to break out of the conceptual jails in which the study of world politics is deemed to be incarcerated,"[59] it was necessary to take cognizance of the "vast increase in the number and type of collective actors whose leaders can clamber onto the global stage and act on behalf of their memberships."[60] In other words, a gradual recognition that the conventional model of an interstate system no longer reflected his understanding of global politics persuaded Rosenau to abandon that model.

What follows is our version of the basic elements of what Rosenau called postinternational thinking. Although we are not entirely in agreement with him on some points, we celebrate his effort to escape "the conceptual jails" in which many international relations theorists remain "incarcerated."

The hallmarks of postinternational theorizing

Postinternational theory represents a break with realism and neorealism in the analysis of global politics. It seeks to account for anomalies

---

[56] James N. Rosenau, "Introduction: Political Science in a Shrinking World," in Rosenau, ed., *Linkage Politics* (New York: Free Press, 1969), p. 2. Rosenau's analysis of linkages anticipated the growing interest in the 1970s in "transnational politics" and "international regimes."
[57] Roenau, *Distant Proximities*, p. 5.
[58] James N. Rosenau, "Toward the Study of National–International Linkages," in Rosenau, ed., *Linkage Politics*, p. 47. Emphasis in original.
[59] Rosenau, *Turbulence in World Politics*, p. 22. Rosenau's shift from writing about "international" politics to "world" politics was more than a matter of semantics.
[60] Rosenau, *Along the Domestic–Foreign Frontier*, p. 67.

unexplained by the various theoretical islets into which the international relations field has been divided and subdivided in recent decades. While the vocabulary and conceptual elements of postinternational thinking perform the critical function of "pointing to" a different set of factors (and, therefore, a changed ontology) in order to understand global politics, it has not yet acquired anything like complete explanatory or predictive power. In this sense, postinternational reasoning is yet another "pre-theory," framework, or approach to understanding.[61] But, we insist, it has come a long way and is on the right track, in powerful contrast to theories that describe a state-centric world that never fully was, does not exist now, and almost certainly never will exist. Like Rosenau's earlier pre-theory, the postinternational enterprise seeks to encourage communication among theorists in order to recommence the quest for grand (or at least grander) theory.[62] What then are the main tenets of postinternational thinking?

History's revenge and future shock

The first feature of postinternational theorizing is its emphasis on continuous change – though at different rates in different contexts – and a rejection of the relatively static premises of neorealism and other forms of structural determinism. For Rosenau, the concept of postinternational "suggests flux and transition" and "allows for chaos."[63] Older formulations do not suffice because change "is so pervasive in both the internal and external lives of communities and nation-states."[64] Change, of course, is relative. In some cases, change is little more than an additive extension of existing patterns, not necessarily obliterating all that has gone before. At the other extreme, change may be transformative,

---

[61] James N. Rosenau, "A Pre-Theory Revisited: World Politics in an Era of Cascading Interdependence," *International Studies Quarterly* 28:3 (September 1984), pp. 245–305.

[62] Postinternational thinking is not a "paradigm" in the Kuhnian sense any more than was realism or neorealism, even though it reflects a subject marked by intellectual discontinuity and dramatic shifts in cognitive evolution. Rosenau himself retains the language of paradigms but makes fewer demands on them as instruments than did Kuhn. "The world is too murky and uncertain for . . . knowledge claims to approach irrefutable truth. . . . [T]here is no magic to the paradigms we employ to comprehend the course of events." "Multilateral Governance and the Nation-State System: A Post-Cold War Assessment," paper for the first meeting of a Study Group of the Inter-American Dialogue, Washington, DC, April 24–25, 1995, p. 5.

[63] Rosenau, "Global Changes and Theoretical Challenges," p. 3.

[64] James N. Rosenau, "Before Cooperation: Hegemons, Regimes, and Habit-driven Actors in World Politics," *International Organization* 40:4 (Autumn 1986), pp. 849–850.

producing qualitative as well as quantitative alterations in the nature of political life.[65] Is a new global order resting on new systemic foundations emerging, or is the existing system simply reconstituting itself to reflect shifting technological, economic, and political realities? Rosenau focuses on transformative change reflected by "the diminished competence of states, the globalization of national economies, the fragmentation of societies into ethnic, religious, nationality, linguistic, and political subgroups, the advent of transnational issues that foster the creation of transnational authorities, and the greater readiness of citizenries to coalesce in public squares."[66]

Yet, as the contrast between Rosenau and Krasner reveals, we may come to different conclusions about the nature of change even when looking at identical phenomena. Recognizing this, Rosenau argues that there seem to be different "temperaments" at work in theory.[67] Some theorists are predisposed to look for continuities, while others are inclined to emphasize the degree to which the present is different from the past and point to discontinuities between epochs. This is an uncharacteristically postmodern observation for Rosenau, albeit correct as far as it goes. It is possible that we are all being bamboozled or are simply incapable of achieving sufficient distance because of overfascination with current events.

Herein lies the critical importance of history, with all the subjectivity so admired by constructivists that is inevitably involved in its interpretation. At the end of the day, the present is the same and similar to the past in some respects and different in others. So, *exactly how is the present both similar to the past and also different*? If all theorists were obliged to answer both questions and marshal evidence before writing anything else, we should have a substantive and constructive debate on the issue of change. Rosenau himself was reluctant to sever all ties between the international and postinternational worlds, retaining a "state-centric" world, alongside another "multicentric" one.[68] And his use of the terms "subgroupism" and "subsystem" to denote "ethnic, religious, linguistic, racial, nationality" polities suggests that these are somehow dependent

---

[65] Holsti, "The Problem of Change in International Relations."

[66] Rosenau, "Government, Order, and Change in World Politics," p. 23. See also Rosenau, *Turbulence in World Politics*, ch. 10.

[67] James N. Rosenau, "NGOs and Fragmented Authority in Globalizing Space," in Ferguson and Jones, *Political Space*, pp. 261–279.

[68] Rosenau, *Turbulence in World Politics*, p. 11.

on territorial states.[69] This, he admits, does not entail "a thoroughgo-ing jailbreak," but only "an escape hatch through which to beat a hasty retreat back to the neorealist paradigm in the event the multi-centric world proves too chaotic for incisive theorizing."[70] However, in our view, acknowledging multiple authorities and bewilderingly complex interactions is the only road to reasonable comprehension.

Overall, postinternational theory *does* emphasize fundamental change in global politics tempered by historical inheritance. It breaks sharply and self-consciously with static models, which claim to be timeless and universal.[71] Postinternational change is the product of simultaneous processes of fusion and fission of authority. The first process is reflected in the growth of regional, global, and less-well-defined authority net-works that connect and govern persons "remote" from one another. Remoteness, of course, is a function of physical distance, technology, and, most important, mindset. Ancient empires were almost impossible to control from a distant center owing to the limits of transportation and communication technologies, and contemporary networks would be inconceivable in the absence of much more advanced technologies. The second tendency consists in the fracturing of existing political units into ever smaller pockets of self-identification that localize and often specialize authority and encumber efforts to provide answers to collec-tive goods dilemmas.

Thus, some associations are falling apart even as others come together; "some norms are spreading and others are receding; some multilateral projects are utter failures and others are remarkable successes."[72] "The seeming contradictions between the forces spreading people, goods, and ideas around the world and those that are impelling the contraction of people, goods, and ideas within narrowed or heightened geographic boundaries"[73] are engines of change in the postinternational model or what Rosenau describes as fragmegration. The "central argument" of his latest book is that "the best way to grasp world affairs today requires viewing them as an endless series of distant proximities in

---

[69] Rosenau, *Along the Domestic–Foreign Frontier*, p. 311. The title of this book itself maintains the two worlds, even as the boundary between them is characterized as an increasingly fuzzy frontier.

[70] Rosenau, *Turbulence in World Politics*, p. 247.

[71] For example, Robert Gilpin, *War and Change in World Politics* (Cambridge: Cambridge University Press, 1981), p. 7.

[72] James N. Rosenau, "Multilateral Governance and the Nation-State System: A Post-Cold War Assessment," paper for the first meeting of a Study Group of the Inter-American Dialogue in Washington, DC, 1995, p. 3.

[73] *Ibid.*

which the forces pressing for greater globalization and those inducing greater localization interactively play themselves out."[74]

The normative implications of these processes remain decidedly confused. Political, economic, and cultural integration overcomes collective dilemmas, but may consign fragmented and less competitive parts of the world to permanently lower living standards. Disintegration preserves local culture and reinforces the psychological efficacy of smaller units, yet it may also result in marginalization and ethnic strife over pitifully insignificant battlefields like Kosovo or East Timor. The two processes of change are related. Centralization produces a desire for recognition of and respect for social, cultural, and political heterogeneity and spurs efforts to decentralize authority. Decentralization produces demands for greater functional capacity, efficiency, and economies of scale that can only be realized through authority on a greater scale. The result is a complex world of local, regional, and global authority structures that we term "polities," and Rosenau, SOAs. Polities sometimes coexist, sometimes cooperate, and sometimes clash.

The decline of the territorial state

Postinternational theory recognizes that the parsimonious model of a state system is no longer adequate to describe or explain the complexities of global life. Rosenau "self-consciously breaks with" the state-is-still-predominant "tendency," and he regards the state as "less coherent and effective" than in the past and as only one of several types of collective "macro actors."[75] As Westphalian States erode and reveal themselves as incapable of meeting citizens' basic needs and demands, their authority diminishes. And as state authority diminishes so does state capacity, thereby producing a downward spiral in which citizens come to identify with other authorities who claim that they are able to cope where states cannot. Today, there are vast areas with crucial impact on the welfare of citizens that most governments do not control or even influence to any major degree. "Politicians everywhere," claims Susan Strange,

> talk as though they have the answers to economic and social problems, as if they really are in charge of their country's destiny. People no longer believe them. Disillusion with national leaders brought down the leaders of the Soviet Union and the states of central Europe. But the disillusion is by no means confined to socialist systems. Popular contempt for ministers and for the head of state has grown in most of

[74] Rosenau, *Distant Proximities*, p. 4.   [75] Rosenau, *Turbulence in World Politics*, p. 97.

the capitalist countries . . . Nor is the lack of confidence confined to those in office; opposition parties and their leaders are often no better thought of than those they wish to replace.[76]

As the boundaries of states become more porous and states are forced to bargain over and share citizens' loyalties with other authorities, additional boundaries come to demarcate "inside/outside."[77] In the process, the dichotomy between the domestic and foreign arenas, so important in the development of Western political philosophy and international relations theory, is largely transcended. The answer to what is "inside" and what is "outside" comes to depend on the issue at hand and the identity hierarchies in place.

Furthermore, the beginning of wisdom about the "modern" state system is that there is an almost infinite variety among the 200 or so members of the sovereign state club. About all they have in common is reciprocal recognition by other club members that all are legally "independent" and sovereign – and that is where the similarity stops. Given states' very different histories, cultures, and economies, the tremendous variation to be found within this single polity form is hardly surprising. Rwanda is "tribal," even as Singapore is a "global city" and Iran has been a "theocracy."

As fission and fusion continue, the search for new identities and the revival of old ones that can provide coherent collective norms intensify. These processes involve instability in human loyalties, and the movement "away from loyalties focused on nation-states and toward variable foci."[78]

Multiple identities and loyalties

Another characteristic of postinternational thinking is renewed emphasis on individuals as units of analysis and recognition of multiple individual and collective identities and loyalties. Rosenau writes of "four levels of aggregation – the micro level of individuals, the macro level of public and private collectivities, the macro-macro level of the interaction among collectivities, and the micro-micro level wherein individuals at

---

[76] Susan Strange, *The Retreat of the State: The Diffusion of Power in the World Economy* (Cambridge: Cambridge University Press, 1996), p. 3.
[77] For the distinction between self-defined "boundaries" and political "borders," see John Armstrong, "Nations before Nationalism," in John Hutchinson and Anthony D. Smith, eds., *Nationalism* (New York: Oxford University Press, 1994), pp. 140–147.
[78] Rosenau, *Turbulence in World Politics*, p. 335.

the micro level shape and are shaped by their collectivities at the macro level."[79] Depending on context and issue, individuals may serve several and even many masters. Citizenship and nationality hardly begin to define who we are and where our loyalties lie, and those allegiances may lie far down our identity/loyalty hierarchy. The question of who is inside and who is outside the boundaries of civic and moral obligation is regaining an importance for political theory and global politics not seen since the birth of the Westphalian State.

A variety of features, new and old, real and invented, may serve as the bases of self-identity. Most identities are insufficiently stable or salient to provide clear political cues or durable boundaries between political communities. Any definition of self is multidimensional and fluid, and for each individual the ranking of identities and therefore the intensity of loyalties will be different. That hierarchy will change and new identities may be created as the significance attached to political relationships with others is altered and as context shifts. Identities are rarely, if ever, fully primordial, however significant it also is that bits and pieces of the past are often assembled in their construction. Few Bosnians, for example, would have thought of religion as their dominant identity until Bosnian "Muslims" were subjected to collective persecution. Just as the identities of subjects and, later, citizens were manipulated by kings and nationalist revolutionaries to sanctify the state, so today do mullahs and nationalists manipulate identities to undermine the states in which they reside.

In contrast to the linking of national and subject/citizen identities in the late eighteenth and early nineteenth centuries, the last decades of the twentieth witnessed their decoupling. State fragmentation and "neotribalism" are especially prevalent in Africa, the Balkans, Southeast Asia, and along Russia's periphery. Identities and loyalties that colonial authorities and commissars suppressed have resurfaced, adding to the artificiality of sovereign boundaries.[80] In this sense, ethnic conflict is a problem of shifting identity boundaries in a state system constructed by Europeans in non-European settings. The governments of many of these states, far from being the outcome of social contracts, impartial arbiters of social conflicts, or surrogates for a "national interest," represent the privileges of tribal, family, regional, or military factions. They suffer an absence of legitimacy, enjoy no more coercive capability than

---

[79] Rosenau, *Distant Proximities*, p. 47.
[80] Similar relations between colonizers and the colonized existed long before the interstate system was born. See Donald J. Puchala, *Theory and History in International Relations* (New York: Routledge, 2003), pp. 143–163.

adversaries, and lack any sense of responsibility to the community called the nation-state.

We term the institutional expressions of collective identities, whether sovereign or not, "polities." Polities are collectivities with a measure of identity, hierarchy, and capacity to mobilize followers for political purposes (that is, value satisfaction or relief from value deprivation). As we have noted, polities routinely not only coexist and cooperate but also conflict. Some polities conquer or incorporate others, much as European states did the tribal and imperial polities in the Americas, Africa, and the Middle East – but that is almost never the end of the matter. The process by which some polities are encapsulated by others and embedded within them we call "nesting." In this dialectical-like process, a dominant polity is modified and may assume some of the characteristics of the polity it has partly digested. Old identities and loyalties rarely vanish completely in the course of conflict but instead lie dormant, ready to be resurrected or reconstructed perhaps centuries later. The post-Cold War explosion of tribal, ethnic, religious, and racial identities entails the revival of such identities and memories, often mobilized against venerable state institutions and borders. For example, in Chiapas and Guatemala "Mayan" identities have been mixing with Marxism and liberation theology to challenge the primacy of the Westphalian State. "It is not that someone is speaking on our behalf, defending us," declared Demetrio Cojtí, a Maya social scientist, "but that we ourselves are developing visions of our own identity, from a colonialist church to our relationship with the state."[81]

The decline of state authority and the unmooring of individual loyalties from traditional institutions produce what Susan Strange memorably labeled "Pinocchio's problem." Once Pinocchio became a real boy, he no longer had his puppet strings to guide him and, therefore, no authority to command his behavior. Strange underlines the dilemma:

> If indeed we have now, not a system of global governance by any stretch of the imagination, but rather a ramshackle assembly of conflicting sources of authority, we too have Pinocchio's problem. Where do allegiance, loyalty, identity lie? Not always, obviously in the same direction. Sometimes with the government of a state. But other times, with a firm, or with a social movement operating across territorial frontiers. Sometimes with a family or a generation; sometimes with fellow-members of an occupation or a profession . . . [T]here is a new

---

[81] Cited in Larry Rohter, "Maya Renaissance in Guatemala Turns Political," *New York Times*, August 12, 1996, p. A5.

24

absence of absolutes. In a world of multiple, diffused authority, each of us shares Pinocchio's problem; our individual consciences are our only guide.[82]

In other words, there is no single substitute for the role of the West-phalian State and no institution that can command authority or demand loyalties across the board. Instead, different authorities must compete for those loyalties, and individuals will look for guidance and rewards from a variety of institutions depending upon issue and context.

An expanding cast of important global actors

When Rosenau admitted that his "Pre-Theory was a static product of a static era," he insisted that "we need to return to fundamentals,"[83] one of which is the cast of actors on which our attention should be focused. In a dramatic break with the prevailing Eurocentric conception of the international system, Rosenau turned upon the Westphalian State itself, blaming the "static conception of authority structures, both within and between societies" that "treated the world as frozen into a structure comprised of nation-states"[84] for shortcomings in his original prethe-ory concerning the comparative study of foreign policy. He went on to identify six "macro changes" in global politics: (1) resource scarcities; (2) demands for redistributing global wealth; (3) breakdown of authority in nation-states; (4) fragmentation of ties among states; (5) the growing importance of "unfamiliar" socioeconomic issues; and (6) the microelec-tronics revolution – as having fundamentally altered global politics and as having made obsolete the Eurocentric model of a state system.[85] A "worldwide crisis of authority" had "so thoroughly undermined the prevailing distribution of global power as to alter the significance of the State as a causal agent in the course of events." So profound was the impact of "skillful publics" and "subgroupism," that "it no longer seems compelling to refer to the world as a State system."[86]

These changes, Rosenau argued, heralded the emergence of new authoritative "sovereignty-free actors" – "multinational corporations, ethnic groups, bureaucratic agencies, political parties, subnational gov-ernments, transnational societies, international organizations, and a host of other types of collectivities"[87] – that could play important roles in "governance." "Governance," for Rosenau, as we saw earlier, does

---

[82] Strange, *The Retreat of the State*, pp. 198–199.
[83] Rosenau, *Turbulence in World Politics*, pp. 246, 247.
[84] *Ibid.*, p. 251.   [85] *Ibid.*, pp. 253–255.   [86] *Ibid.*, pp. 263–264.   [87] *Ibid.*, p. 36.

not require "government" or "hierarchy"; "systems of rule can be maintained and their controls successfully and consistently exerted even in the absence of established legal or political authority."[88] As Benjamin Cohen stresses, governance may not "even call for the presence of explicit actors . . . To suffice, all that governance really needs is a valid social consensus on relevant rights and values." "In fact," he argues, "authority may be manifested through any number of channels of de facto control . . . By no means is it true, therefore, that we are left with a 'yawning hole of non-authority' just because power in the world economy has shifted away from national governments. Market forces may be impersonal, but that does not make them any less capable of governance."[89] In Rosenau's description:

> a new form of anarchy has evolved in the current period – one that involves not only the absence of higher authority, but also encompasses such an extensive disaggregation of authority as to intensify the pace at which transnational relations and cross-border spill-overs are permeating the [domestic–foreign] frontier, even as it also allows for much greater flexibility, innovation, and experimentation in the development and application of new control mechanisms.[90]

As he sees it:

> an SOA can be an issue regime, a professional society, an epistemic community, a neighborhood, a network of the like-minded, a truth commission, a corporation, business subscribers to codes of conduct (e.g., the Sullivan principles), a social movement, a local or provincial government, a diaspora, a regional association, a loose confederation of NGOs, a transnational advocacy group, a paramilitary force, a credit-rating agency, a strategic partnership, a transnational network, a terrorist organization, and so on across all the diverse collectivities that have become sources of decisional authority in the ever more complex multi-centric world.[91]

The postinternational universe, then, is inhabited by a vast range of actors and authorities, reflecting different identities, differentially engaged in countless issues, and vested with authority in selected contexts. In this world, the state plays "its" games within and without, as do a wide variety of other authorities. Hosts of outcomes are shaped

---

[88] Rosenau, *Beyond the Domestic–Foreign Frontier*, pp. 146–47.
[89] Benjamin J. Cohen, *The Geography of Money* (Ithaca, NY: Cornell University Press, 1998), p. 145.
[90] *Ibid.*, pp. 151–152.   [91] Rosenau, *Distant Proximities*, p. 295.

not only by broad trends in the world that affect most issues but also by individuals at the micro level and groups, and as chaos and complexity theorists remind us, sometimes by the smallest of actions and developments ("the butterfly effect").

The declining role of distance and acceleration of history

The postinternational world emphasizes the growing gap between physical and psychological distance, the accelerating pace of change, the increasing impact of mass media, and the technologies associated with all of the foregoing. Territory, while still critical in many cases like the Israeli–Palestinian dispute, overall is no longer the dominant stake in global rivalries as it often was in the past. The speed and extent to which persons, things, and ideas move are unprecedented. Microelectronic technologies such as computers, e-mail, fax machines, and space satellites have made it possible to move messages and funds almost instantaneously, and such technologies have significantly eroded the distinction between "short term" and "long term."[92] Polities have always occupied some of the same political space, and the new deterritorializing technologies are making it even easier for them to do so.

The participation explosion

Consonant with its liberal bias, postinternational theory places the individual rather than the state at the center of analysis. The role of people, organizing and reorganizing their political communities, is expanding often at the expense of state authority. Rosenau argues that the revolutions in transportation, information, and communication, combined with the progress of education in much of the world, are having a profound impact at the micro level.[93] He insists that there is no necessary convergence around values like democracy or capitalism, rather that people are becoming more "skilled in terms of their culture."[94] In some countries, irreverent investigative media give them exactly the "facts" they need to find out whether their interests are being sacrificed to those of national governments that are often incompetent, definitely expensive, and sometimes venal. For Rosenau, the acquisition of new skills

[92] See Susan Strange, *Mad Money: When Markets Outgrow Governments* (Ann Arbor, MI: University of Michigan Press, 1998), pp. 24–29.
[93] Rosenau, *Distant Proximities*, chs. 10–11. Ernest Gellner provides an excellent analysis of the role of education in the rise of nationalism in an earlier epoch. Ernest Gellner, "Nationalism and Modernization," in Hutchinson and Smith, eds., *Nationalism*, pp. 55–63.
[94] Rosenau, *Distant Proximities*, p. 245.

and orientations by individuals is accompanied by a growing sense of self-efficacy: "People may be experiencing uncertainty over where their lives are headed, and they may have a greater sense of remoteness from the centers of decision, but they nonetheless seem ready to act on their convictions."[95]

At the same time as the fates of people everywhere have become linked, citizens' expectations are expanding, and the demands they place on institutions are multiplying. Fewer and fewer people meekly accept the status and destiny that come with birth. Expanding demands tax existing national and global institutions, pressuring them to find new ways to cope with burgeoning claims from below. Modern citizens enjoy advantages that were unavailable to their ancestors, but their expectations have risen even faster. As a result, their *relative* satisfaction may decline even as their absolute well-being grows, further testing the legitimacy of existing authorities.

Whether as consumers, activists, or protesters, individual citizens collectively create global constraints and opportunities. Thus, Strange declares that "the perceptions of ordinary citizens are more to be trusted than the pretensions of national leaders and of the bureaucracies who serve them; the commonsense of common people is a better guide to understanding than most of the academic theories being taught in universities."[96]

Changing sources of security and insecurity

Individual, state, and global security are merging, because in the complexly interdependent postinternational world the conditions for well-being and happiness for most people beg for a high degree of collective action that, unfortunately, all too often is not achieved. Most individuals cannot by their own efforts meet their needs for food, shelter, health, and old age as some of their ancestors did, and many individual states can neither shield citizens from threats nor cope with globalized challenges.

States initially acquired their special status in part because of their relative effectiveness in organizing military force to defend their own boundaries from external attack. A pervasive "security dilemma" defined largely in terms of defense against a potential military attack was a major feature of the "international" era of global politics. Ironically,

---

[95] *Ibid.*, p. 249.   [96] Strange, *The Retreat of the State*, p. 3.

such a realist or power turn of mind[97] was especially pervasive in the very Cold War period when two rival empires and ideologies were more important than individual states and everyone had to live under the shadow of a possible nuclear holocaust. By contrast, the postinternational era reflects a more liberal turn of mind and a far more flexible and diffuse, although no less disturbing, sense of threat. As Stanley Hoffmann observes: "The [September 11] attacks also showed that, for all its accomplishments, globalization makes an awful form of violence easily accessible to hopeless fanatics. Terrorism is the bloody link between interstate relations and global society. As countless individuals and groups are becoming global actors along with states, insecurity and vulnerability are rising."[98] Okwui Enwezor, the director of one of the world's leading exhibitions of contemporary art (Documenta II in Kassel), comments: "Globalization means the terrible nearness of distant places."[99] Economic columnist Robert J. Samuelson writes that "we have gone (it seems) from a world of small and understandable risks to a world of huge and imponderable dangers." "[A]mong economic elites, there's a foreboding that something – terrorism, corporate scandals, a 'dollar crisis,' a 'Japan crisis' – is leading us to we know not where." He quotes Peter Bernstein on the point: "Uncertainty is something we cannot quantify, we do not know what is going to happen, we don't know what the probabilities are."[100]

The liberal bias of postinternational thinking

Postinternational thinking has a bias toward individual "agency" at the expense of "structure," while recognizing that structural impediments and opportunities are always present. At a minimum, individuals are transforming global politics into a participant sport. Whether as demonstrators in Seattle, Leipzig, and Jakarta; terrorists in Kandahar, Jerusalem, or Bali; investors in New York and London; or purchasers of goods in any city, individuals are imposing their preferences on leaders, often in unorthodox and sometimes violent ways.

Nevertheless, we must be cautious. However much individuals are increasingly empowered at the micro level, they remain anchored by

---

[97] See Yale H. Ferguson and Richard W. Mansbach, *The Elusive Quest Continues: Theory and Global Politics* (Saddle River, NJ: Prentice-Hall, 2002), ch. 4.
[98] Hoffmann, "Clash of Globalizations," pp. 104–105.
[99] Quoted in *Newsweek* (June 24, 2002), p. 84.
[100] Robert J. Samuelson, "The Erosion of Confidence," *Newsweek*, June 17, 2002, p. 45.

existing identities and the loyalties those identities produce. Consequently, the choices individuals make will not be strictly voluntary ones, and this marks a key limit for liberal individualism. Competing authorities are bidding for individuals' allegiance and also simultaneously establishing their control and influence over them.

Like liberals more generally, the authors applaud most norms of the world they are describing. Nevertheless, we must remain deeply skeptical about presumed democratic implications in the idea of a participation explosion. As we shall see later, there is another side to this phenomenon that may work against democratic norms. Skills and knowledge acquisition are markedly uneven[101] – not least between North and South, and indeed between rich and poor in any society – and manipulation of identities everywhere further reduces individual choice. Although everyone acquires *some* additional skills, a managerial and technocratic class is emerging that is linked globally by language (English and "techno-jargon"), airplanes, satellite cellphone, e-mail, and video-conferencing. Democracy in a traditional political sense may actually be eroded by the fact that new communications technologies make it easier to create and maintain globe-spanning collectivities and closed epistemic communities.

Postinternational theory and history

The combination of individuals' greater skills, the revolutions in space and time, market globalization, the breakdown of authority structures and erosion of sovereign boundaries, the incapacity of states to cope with collective challenges to citizens' welfare and survival, and the proliferation of nonstate identities led Rosenau to conclude that the postinternational world is so unique "that the lessons of history may no longer be very helpful," and this leaves "observers without any paradigms or theories that adequately explain the course of events."[102] For Rosenau, perhaps, a more extensive historical investigation would reveal enduring and cyclical political patterns as well as dark currents that might erode his liberal conviction that history is headed in some discernibly positive direction.

Although, by emphasizing change *per se*, Rosenau is light years in advance of those with a "1648-and-All That" outlook, his view implies,

---

[101] *Ibid.*, p. 102. See also Robert B. Reich, *The Work of Nations: Preparing Ourselves for 21st-Century Capitalism* (New York: Alfred A. Knopf, 1991), pp. 177–180.
[102] Rosenau, *Turbulence in World Politics*, p. 5.

mistakenly in our opinion, that the features of the postinternational world are so novel that history is irrelevant. As we shall explain in the next chapter, just the opposite is the case. A richer understanding of history suggests that there is more to global politics than a few centuries of European experience and that history does *not* move in a predictable direction. Few have cared to ponder the world before 1648 or in a non-European context, a significant omission at a time when old historical political forms and ideas are being resurrected or reinvented around the world. In such settings especially, politicians and theorists engage in contests for control of historical meaning – shaping and reshaping the meaning of the past to legitimate interpretations and policies for the present.

In sum, just as we must consider the "international" world to make sense of postinternational thinking, so we must go further back and identify a preinternational world that may provide greater perspective on the present and clues to the future. Indeed, in some respects, a preinternational world may have more in common with a postinternational one than with the relatively brief epoch in which European states were so prominent.[103] Careful attention to history reveals not only that the postinternational world has precedents but also that Europe's interstate system was limited both temporally and spatially.

Conclusion: remapping global politics

The Eurocentric world of international politics is giving way to a universe more plainly characterized by diverse and often overlapping polities, and processes of fission and fusion. States are becoming more and more functionally dissimilar. Only a relatively few sovereign states continue to dominate or successfully co-opt important groups that lie within or, increasingly, cross or transcend their boundaries. And even the most successful face serious competition from the forces of integration and fragmentation.

Many of the world's states find it difficult to cope; some are in a condition of outright civil war and/or near collapse; and a few have actually "failed" to such a drastic extent that they have ceased to exist except on increasingly deceptive maps. We are too accustomed to looking at maps of neat state boxes, assuming that these provide an adequate picture of the principal units and "containers" in global politics, and that

---

[103] Ferguson and Mansbach, *Polities.*

their boundaries define what is "national" versus "international." When necessary, we redraw the boxes, less interested (strangely) in explaining how a supposedly sovereign unit like the USSR or Yugoslavia could somehow be reduced or disappear, than in asserting that nothing really has changed because the new box also enjoys a sovereign label.

Recent decades have witnessed a recrudescence of identities and ideologies that clash with the loyalties and obligations of individuals as citizens of sovereign states. In some instances, this phenomenon constitutes a genuine reawakening of earlier ideas and forms; in others a reinvention of the past; and sometimes the appearance or at least recognition of a new identity or ideology. For example, capitalism is virtually global in scope; industrial and financial capital (as Karl Marx predicted) have been united; yet Marxist ideas – unfashionable since the end of the Cold War – are still influential among numerous intellectuals and activists.

On the one hand, the role and implications of sovereign states have traditionally been grossly overrated; and, on the other hand, contemporary trends make that story of global politics more misleading than ever. The question is not whether sovereign states exist and continue to matter. Of course they do. Some may even increase their capacity in particular fields. Rather, the question is what does the state-centric/interstate model of global politics fail to tell us that is important, or, worse, what does that model distort and obscure? States are an exceedingly mixed bag, and it is hardly an exaggeration to suggest that the differences among them are far more numerous and significant than the characteristics they share. Political boundaries have never been immutable; rather they have changed to a greater or lesser extent, sometimes quickly and more often slowly and incrementally, throughout history. If they appear to be more stable today than often in the past, it is because they matter less and less – they are so easily transcended. Interstate wars (see Chapter 7) are fewer in number because the cost of war has risen while the value of (most) territory has declined.

Why have so many observers of international relations accorded observations like these only marginal significance? One reason is the legalistic bias that is another aspect of the European tradition. The only "true" authorities are those that are sanctified by law, and states are the only legal sovereigns. Sovereignty entitles states to privileges whether or not they can enjoy them. Yet from the outset, sovereignty, in practical terms, was (as Krasner observes) never more than a *claim* to and *justification* of authority, which, to be sure, was and continues to be realized in varying degrees. For many, state sovereignty is rather like the fancy titles of dispossessed royalty: it guarantees admission to the club but will not necessarily help pay the dues or keep away creditors. For some, it merely denotes a national treasury ready for plundering.

Historians and international relations theorists have tended to perpetuate Eurocentric myths instead of engaging in small-r "realistic" analysis. Most historians and students of comparative politics have contented themselves with being specialists on one or two countries. Many political scientists for years embraced state-centric theories and employed their own versions of state boxes for number-crunching purposes. Many insisted on maintaining a strict inside/outside divide, arguing that "international relations" is a state-to-state realm that should be an entirely autonomous field of study. International lawyers, who might have been expected to be narrowly legalistic, actually have done more than most of their social scientist counterparts to highlight the growing role of international organizations as well as emerging norms affecting matters like human rights and peacekeeping.

Mesmerized by the state, almost everyone except a few neo-Marxists and economists long tended to neglect "economic" actors like transnational enterprises. "Civic society" was deemed the sole purview of sociologists and specialists on domestic politics. Historians who "discovered" economic and cultural history thought they were offering an alternative to "political" history. As for international business and finance, the assumption seemed to be that such "private sector" subjects belonged strictly in business schools; clearly, they were beyond the pale of "public sector" investigators like political scientists and diplomatic historians. A few scholars were concerned about changing technology but only as it affected the balance of terror – missiles and arms control – and the race for space. Ethnicity was seen as a quaint leftover from "tribal" times that modern governments were inexorably educating out of existence.

Now, after the events of recent decades, it appears that citizens and scholars alike were remarkably naïve, caught in an intellectual time-warp. Even today, unfortunately, state-centrism is deeply embedded in the traditional disciplines.[104] Academics may be the last to address the "real world" because they have such an investment in familiar models and theories. The field of "international relations," with its woeful

---

[104] John Agnew, "Spacelessness Versus Timeless Space in State-Centered Social Science," *Environment and Planning* 28:11 (1996), p. 1930.

name, is – in the most charitable assessment – in considerable disarray. It is split among numerous coteries and cliques that rarely speak to one another and, when they do, sometimes intentionally hinder communication by subverting the language they use. Nonetheless, the growing diversity of approaches may actually portend eventual progress, and there are more and more scholars and policymakers who are aware that a postinternational world requires new ways of thinking.

A central question for scholars of global politics in this new millennium is what will be the long-range impact of what Strange termed "the retreat of the state."[105] Individuals face growing uncertainty as to where our allegiances should and will lie. When the opportunities arise, as they surely will in a fluid environment, will we resurrect or refurbish old identities and loyalties, or establish new ones? Our conceptions of ourselves and others will be continually changing, or sometimes will be ages old, and the task for us is to explain what the limited range of choices are, which are likely to prevail – and, again as always, why?

---

[105] Strange, *The Retreat of the State.*

2   Theory and method

With what theoretical tools should we approach the postinternational enterprise? Theorists' visions of the world around them are filtered through and colored by their own preferences and perceived interests, expectations, normative commitments, and personal experiences and memories. Theory also entails strategic simplification, a process through which brute "facts" are refined. Facts themselves have no meaning until the theorist has organized them into patterns that themselves may not exist apart from the theorist's own imagination. The essential tasks for the theorist are to point out what it is necessary to explain and why, and what phenomena are likely to provide the desired explanation(s). Such recognition is intuitive, a product of our inner eye rather than of some external "reality." In the end, then, it is the theorist who, by the constant interaction of induction and deduction, imposes logic on events, "sees" patterns in them, and "labels" them. The result is never more than a single and necessarily partial version of reality.

Theorizing, then, is an act of creation, imagination, and insight. "Eureka, I see what all this means! I see how the facts are related! I see the elements of cause and effect in the patterns that are emerging in my consciousness." In a very real sense, such acts of creative imagining are what we associate with and expect from the dramatist, the novelist, the musician, or the painter, and it is that same recognition that leads us to condemn extreme "relativism." Successful theorists enlarge and deepen our vision of the world around us, much as did Eugène Delacroix when he allowed action to continue outside the frames of his painted epics. Bad theory narrows our vision and confuses more than it clarifies, either by producing a severely distorted caricature of observable reality or through intentional obfuscation.

Despite the dramatic changes in global politics, as we have observed, international relations theorists have been slow to change, and that perhaps is not surprising. In Steve Smith's words: "Once established as common sense, theories become incredibly powerful since they delineate not simply what can be known but also what it is sensible to talk about or suggest."[1] Moreover, theory-building evokes genuine passions and elicits defensive pride on the part of combative international-relations scholars. Questions of "how" and "what" to analyze are provocative not only because they are often interesting and important in themselves but also because they have implications for such personal and professional concerns as academic jobs, research funding, journal acceptances, and disciplinary status. Indeed, the dramatic rise of "science" in US approaches to international relations, starting in the 1960s, owed much to Washington's willingness to provide largesse for such research.

As a field of scholarship, global politics is perpetually reexamining its epistemological, ontological, methodological, and conceptual underpinnings.[2] Yet, theory in that field is only very slowly coming to grips with a postinternational world that is more complex and dynamic than the traditional ideal-type interstate system. On the one hand, there is a widespread aversion to accepting complexity and change because to do so would presumably be too "messy" (Rosenau's term), lacking in parsimony. On the other hand, postmodernity's extreme relativists overreact in the opposite direction, celebrating the obstacles to "knowing" anything. Many postmodernists "think that there is nothing beyond language as a social construction" in contrast to "constructivists who think that language is indispensable to social construction."[3]

The not-so-great debates

Despite the so-called great debates that have enlivened the study of global politics in recent decades, there has been a remarkable underlying

---

[1] Steve Smith, "Positivism and Beyond," in Smith, Ken Booth, and Marysia Zalewski, eds., *International Theory: Positivism and Beyond* (Cambridge: Cambridge University Press, 1996), p. 13. This recalls a key argument in Yale H. Ferguson and Richard W. Mansbach, *The Elusive Quest: Theory and International Politics* (Columbia, SC: University of South Carolina Press, 1988) and Ferguson and Mansbach, *The Elusive Quest Continues.*

[2] Yosef Lapid, "The Third Debate: On the Prospects for International Theory in a Post-Posivitist Era," *International Studies Quarterly* 33:3 (September 1989), pp. 235–254.

[3] Nicholas J. Onuf, "The Politics of Constructivism," in K. M. and K. E. Jörgensen, eds., *Constructing International Relations: The Next Generation* (London: M. E. Sharpe, 2001), p. 246.

consensus about what to study and how to study it. The "realist–idealist" debate of the 1950s was less a theoretical dialogue than a critique of interwar foreign policy in the West and a reaffirmation of the Eurocentric tradition of power politics.[4] The debate between "traditionalists" and "scientists" in the 1960s and 1970s was also something of a non-debate because both sets of theorists were committed empiricists and, for the most part, realists as well.[5] The "traditionalists" were not enemies of empiricism. Hans Morgenthau, for example, while insisting on a role for "unique occurrences," wrote proudly of "the science of international politics" and never questioned the reliability of empirical observation. Like any good empiricist, he set himself the task of understanding causality in the political universe, his principal aim being "to detect and understand the forces that determine political relations among nations, and to comprehend the ways in which these forces act upon each other and upon international political relations and institutions."[6] Instead of revolving around genuine theoretical or epistemological differences, the tradition/science debate actually focused on methodology.

As realists (later, as neo-realists) themselves, the scientists started with a state-centric orientation. Indeed, one of the reasons why the scientific study of the central problem of war has to date provided few coherent explanations, as John Vasquez suggests, "may be that the dominant realist perspective . . . has simply not been up to the task."[7] Reification of the state and the exclusion of nonstate actors appealed to empiricists because that approach permitted parsimony and comparison. The "elegance" of the explanations produced was its own reward, never mind that they were simple-minded reductions of a far more interesting and complicated political universe. The paradox is, as Richard Ashley argues, "the state-as-actor assumption is a metaphysical commitment prior to science and exempted from scientific criticism."[8]

---

[4] E. H. Carr, *The Twenty Years' Crisis, 1919–1939* (New York: Harper & Row, 1964).

[5] John A. Vasquez, *The Power of Power Politics: A Critique*, rev. ed. (Cambridge: Cambridge University Press, 1998). Nevertheless, in another sense, the realist Hans Morgenthau was also skeptical of science because he viewed the world as ultimately tragic. See Morgenthau, *Scientific Man vs. Power Politics* (Chicago: University of Chicago Press, 1946).

[6] Hans J. Morgenthau, *Power Among Nations: The Struggle for Power and Peace*, 6th ed., rev. by Kenneth W. Thompson (New York: Knopf, 1985), pp. 20, 18.

[7] John A. Vasquez, *The War Puzzle* (Cambridge: Cambridge University Press, 1993), p. 3.

[8] Richard K. Ashley, "The Poverty of Neorealism," in Robert O. Keohane, ed., *Neorealism and its Critics* (New York: Columbia University Press, 1986), p. 270. Neoliberal institutionalists are also largely state-centric though there is some room for the impact of institutions on state behavior.

"Scientists" preached the gospel that we could know nothing about X unless we could somehow quantify how much of X there was. Theorists turned from issues of understanding and meaning to gathering and coding data, and their enterprise almost inevitably supported the realist map of the world. States were ready-made sources for numbers about population, military spending, and so on, but the coders would count almost anything that had a number: bodies, megatons, votes, answers on public opinion polls, whatever. And at the end of the day, we knew little more than we did at the outset. And neither rational choice nor second-generation game/expected utility theory have measurably improved the payoffs. The emphasis is still on elegance and parsimony, most recently games for the gamers.

Thus, in retrospect, the second great debate between "science" and "traditionalism" was also not all that "great." At root, the "scientists" ignored theory while focusing on method. And since parsimony and statistical comparability were goals, "scientists" desired to retain a model of global politics based on functionally homologous and exclusive units (territorial states) for which there seemed to be plentiful data. In addition, each territorial state unit occupied an exclusive space so as to prevent the sort of messy "medieval" overlap that would complicate comparison. And, as the years passed, statistical techniques became more and more sophisticated, and the search continued for a talisman and "magic bullet"[9] that never seemed to materialize.

For the most part, the participants in these debates turned a blind eye to the dynamic aspects of global politics and shared what Ashley calls "a historicism that freezes the political institutions of the current world order."[10] In the end, the scientists were much the same as the theorists described by geographers John Agnew and Stuart Corbridge:

> [Among the contextual factors that] have interacted to reproduce the dominant view about state territoriality found in such apparently different works as those of Waltz and Keohane . . . is the preference for abstract and "closed-system" thinking among advocates of a scientific (positivist) approach to international relations. . . . From this perspective a "state" is an ideal-type or logical object rather than any particular state and, thus, states can be written about without reference to the concrete conditions in which they exist. If the system of international

---

[9] The spirit of the times is superlatively reflected in the "magical" role played by "psychohistory" as "the science of human behavior reduced to mathematic equations," in Isaac Asimov, *Foundation's Edge* (Garden City, NY: Doubleday & Co., 1982), p. ix.
[10] Ashley, "The Poverty of Neorealism," p. 289.

relations is thought of as an "open system", such abstract (ahistorical and aspatial) theorizing becomes impossible. Causal chains would form and dissolve historically and geographically. They could not be reduced to a set of primitive terms that would hold true across space and through time. Essential state sovereignty is such a primitive term.[11]

Notwithstanding their limited accomplishments, the scientists continued to dominate the study of global politics, especially in the United States, for several decades. However, as it became clearer that the strict observations required by positivism (a term that has gradually replaced empiricism with the onset of "reflexivism")[12] were hardly the same as theory and that much of what we think we "know" about global politics diverged from such observations, new names began to be heard by the late 1980s – Wittgenstein, Derrida, and Foucault. So began what Yosef Lapid labeled the "Third Debate."[13] The rigorous demand for facts-through-observation was almost entirely abandoned by the challengers in the belief that only insight and imagination could produce genuine theory. One cannot directly observe "assumptions," and, except for the scientific method itself, much of the empirical movement of the 1960s to the 1980s avoided confronting or even openly stating assumptions. Even the field's simplest concepts such as "state" and "power," out of which our main theories have been constructed, are abstractions and are not directly observable. *The concepts needed to build theory, necessarily had to be defined by theorists themselves.* At best the positivists could look at artifacts or what they believed to be valid indicators of what could not be seen. And of what could be unequivocally observed and measured, little seemed to be terribly important. Finally, limiting understanding to observation meant there was no (acknowledged) place for norms or values. "Modernists,"[14] in the words of positivist J. David Singer, were "often indifferent" to the normative concerns of philosophy.[15]

[11] John Agnew and Stuart Corbridge, *Mastering Space: Hegemony, Territory and International Political Economy* (New York: Routledge, 1995), p. 83.

[12] Like empiricism, positivism denotes knowledge derived solely from sensory perceptions or the tools that extend those perceptions. A positivist ignores metaphysics and knowledge gained through reasoning and reflection.

[13] Lapid, "The Third Debate," pp. 235–254.

[14] Martha Finnemore and Kathryn Sikkink, "International Norm Dynamics and Political Change," *International Organization* 52:4 (Autumn 1998), p. 889. The authors go on to argue that, far from maintaining the separation of facts and values, "contemporary empirical research on norms is aimed precisely at showing how the 'ought' becomes the 'is'" (p. 916).

[15] J. David Singer, "The Incompleat Theorist: Insight Without Evidence," in Klaus Knorr and James N. Rosenau, eds., *Contending Approaches to International Politics* (Princeton: Princeton University Press, 1969), p. 80.

Dissidence and relativism

Where then could norms and values be "observed," and how could they be reunited with facts? One answer was language because it reflects human biases and enters into the problems we seek to study, the ways we address them, and the conclusions we reach. This argument was a gauntlet thrown in the faces of positivists, and the attacks on social science quickly found favor in Europe, where many scholars had never accepted the premises of the positivists (often associated with US intellectual imperialism) in the first place. This opened the floodgates in IR to "postpositivism," "poststructuralism," "postmodernism," and their less-radical competitors and sometime fellow-travelers including "critical theory" and "constructivism."[16]

Many empiricists and not just strict scientists, especially in the United States, loathed all the resulting stuff about hermeneutics and "the other." For Peter Katzenstein, Robert Keohane, and Stephen Krasner, "postmodernism falls clearly outside of the social science enterprise, and in international relations research it risks becoming self-referential and disengaged from the world, protests to the contrary notwithstanding."[17] The extreme relativists were engaged not in making sense of the real world, but in games of another non-scientific sort, language games, with double entendres and other clever word-play in which all interpretations were equally valid.[18]

Like scientific jargon, language itself is a casualty in the writings of some of the participants in the Third Debate. For the more extreme of postmodernists, declares Charles Hostovsky, "plainly expressed language is out of the question" because it is "too realist, modernist and obvious": "Postmodern language requires that one use play, parody, and indeterminacy as critical techniques to point this out. Often this is quite a difficult requirement, so obscurity is a well-acknowledged substitute." Sometimes a writer will not have time to "muster even the minimum number of postmodern synonyms and neologisms to avoid public disgrace," hence one strategy is "to use as many suffixes, prefixes,

---

[16] Some of the material in this chapter draws upon our earlier critique of postmodernism in Yale H. Ferguson and Richard W. Mansbach, "Reconstructing Theory in Global Politics: Beyond the Postmodern Challenge," in Darryl S. L. Jarvis, ed., *International Relations and the "Third Debate": Postmodernism and its Critics* (Westport, CT: Praeger, 2002), pp. 147–164.
[17] Peter J. Katzenstein, Robert O. Keohane, and Stephen D. Krasner, "*International Organization* and the Study of World Politics," *International Organization* 52:4 (Autumn 1998), p. 678.
[18] Martin Hollis, *The Philosophy of Social Science: An Introduction* (Cambridge: Cambridge University Press, 1994), p. 241.

hyphens, slashes, underlinings and anything else your computer . . . can dish out." Top it all off by inserting "a few names [e.g., Continental European theorists] whose work everyone will agree is important and hardly anyone has had the time or inclination to read [as in de/gendered-Baudrillardian discourse]";[19] then hope that someone will not actually ask what you are talking about, in which case you can always reply with more postmodern-speak. Hostovsky is wickedly close to the mark.

Disappointment with the fruits of science thus prepared the ground for various Third Debate currents that collectively rejected strict science, and emphasized the subjective and normative dimensions of knowledge. In addition, the scientific tradition was, arguably, harmful to theory construction because it confused positivism with theory, thereby conflating theory and method. The international relations positivists were not only *empirical* but also focused on and investigated *objective* and easily measurable phenomena. What is often inadequately understood is that supposedly subjective phenomena like ideas, norms, or principles are as accessible *in principle* to observation as are objective phenomena, although in practice, given current tools, they are more difficult to "observe" or measure. Normative theorists, then, can be serious empiricists. With this in mind, postmodernism is *simultaneously* non-empirical and preoccupied with subjective phenomena. Constructivism is preoccupied with subjective phenomena, but it is empirical. Rational choice/expected utility theorists deal with both objective and subjective phenomena but are largely non-empirical.[20]

The growing postpositivist initiative in global politics also involved skepticism about the power tradition and grand theory more generally, and reflected and contributed to the ensuing anarchy that characterizes theory in the field today. Postmodernists have deconstructed and helped to undermine traditional theories, which in some respects has been all to the good, and it is also healthy that they have made most of us more self-conscious about our own biases. But postmodernism in all of its manifestations, despite reopening crucial issues of understanding and knowing, has not yet provided a constructive foundation upon which to build (re-construct) theories of global politics, and indeed such a positive

---

[19] Charles Hostovsky, "How to Speak and Write Postmodern," hostovsk@GEOG. UTORONTO.CA.

[20] Yet another confusion stems from use by almost all schools of theory of the concept of "interests." In realism and neorealism, interests are objective and unchanging, except when the distribution of power is altered. Constructivists regard interests as subjective and malleable, a reflection of identity rather than power or rank. For rational choice/ expected utility theorists, interests are strictly goals of players in the game at hand.

enterprise would run directly counter to what most postmodernists are about.

Postmodernism is in truth (pun intended) not one but a cluster of approaches that share a belief that "knowledge" is less a consequence of impartial enquiry than an expression of power relations in particular social and cultural contexts. Far from being a neutral seeker after "truth," the scholar, in Steve Smith's words, "is always caught up in a language and mode of thinking which, far from interpreting a world, instead constructs it."[21] "[P]ostmodernism is essentially a 'contrast concept',," declares Krishan Kumar. "It takes its meaning as much from what it excludes or claims to supersede as from what it includes or affirms in any positive sense. The primary, or at least initial, meaning of post-modernism must be that it is not modernism, not modernity. Modernity is over." Well, yes, except that there remains some debate about in what sense postmodernism is "post." Have we gone "beyond" modernism? Kumar again:

> The "post" of post-modernity is ambiguous. It can mean what comes after, the movement to a new state of things, however difficult it might be to characterize that state in these early days. Or it can be more like the post of *post-mortem*: obsequies performed over the dead body of modernity, a dissection of the corpse. The end of modernity is in this view the occasion for reflecting on the experience of modernity; post-modernity is that condition of reflectiveness. In this case there is no necessary sense of a new beginning, merely a somewhat melancholy state of an ending.[22]

But what is or was "modernism"? Once again, we confront ambiguity. As Kumar points out, "modernity" and "modernism" are often used interchangeably and also might be different. He prefers to use "modernity" to mean "all of the changes – intellectual, social and political – that brought into being the modern world" and to reserve "modernism" for the late nineteenth-century cultural movement in the West that was actually partially a reaction against modernity. The first meaning is the one most postmodernists adopt, although the second is useful as a reminder that – as we will note shortly – contemporary postmodernism has antecedents, so in some respects it is not so much post as reprise.

[21] Smith, "Positivism and Beyond," in Smith, Booth, and Zalewski, eds., *International Theory*, p. 30.
[22] Krishan Kumar, *From Post-Industrial to Post-Modern Society: New Theories of the Contemporary World* (Oxford: Blackwell, 1995), pp. 66–67.

Neither modernism nor postmodernism has meaning in the absence of "premodernism" – and what, then, is that? A world of primordial and overlapping identities, "tribalism," and variable political forms from cities to leagues and federations to empires antedate the modern era. So, too, do intellectual attitudes other than Aristotle's, some of which bear an intriguing resemblance to postmodernism. Felipe Fernández-Armesto observes that Protagoras's "guiding maxim" was that man "is the measure of all things that are and the non-existence of the things that are not." Socrates found that idea profoundly disturbing. "Is this not roughly what [Protagoras] means," he said, "that things are for me such as they appear to me, and for you such as they appear to you?" Socrates was sure Protagoras "was wrong but got baffled in the attempt to disprove him." Reports Fernández-Armesto: "He confessed to 'vexation and actual fear . . . for what else could you call it when a man drags his arguments up and down because he is so stupid that he cannot be convinced and is hardly to be induced to give up any one of them?' After whirling all day in a vortex of circular arguments, Socrates dismissed them all as 'wind' and postponed the discussion to a morning which, in surviving texts, never comes."[23]

Modernity, in the sense of "the modern world," began in the West with the medieval transition from "the ancient world" and continued through the Renaissance and Westphalia into the second half of the twentieth century. States enhanced their legitimacy by constructing the notion of popular sovereignty, thereby making "subjects" into "citizens" who now were part owners and part property of the territory in which they resided. This sharp shift in collective identity provided the human energy (read "nationalism") that fostered Europe's nineteenth-century imperialism and the later world wars.

Economically, the same timeframe saw the widespread expansion of capitalism, steady industrialization, increasing trade before and after the Great Depression, and the eventual emergence of a world economy. Society became more complex, with a growing middle class, proletariat, and, as always, an underclass of the poor. The gap between rich and poor found an echo at another level in a global pattern of "haves" and "have nots" between and within countries. Intellectually, beginning with the Renaissance, there was more emphasis on the individual and a belief in the inevitability of human progress. Organic interpretations of the state

---

[23] Felipe Fernández-Armesto, *Truth: A History and a Guide for the Perplexed* (London: Bantam, 1997), p. 204.

43

and growing interest in the biological sciences, especially evolution, in the nineteenth century fed a less benign stream of identity with ugly Social Darwinian properties, and ideas of progress and the individual were combined in some cases into self-realization through the state (for example, National Socialism). The Renaissance and later the Enlightenment also ushered in an increasing secular faith in human reason and especially positivism or science as the key to knowledge, and an engine of progress, that often seemed to conflict with religious faith and church doctrine. In sum, "modernity" is an ambivalent idea, which has been defined and redefined and attacked and defended for a long, long time.

There are, of course, a variety of postpositivists and postmodernists. Some are extreme relativists and others insist that language can *only* be understood, at best, in particular contexts. For Derrida the context is individuals; for Foucault social (power relations); and for Wittgenstein the rules of a particular "game" in which language is engaged. Since language has no dependable meaning and yet we can describe the world only through language, our views of the world are undependable and fundamentally incommunicable to others. Theories must be value-laden and reflect the distribution of social power by "privileging" some meanings over others. Language and its visual counterpart in the media images of a technological age should be continually "deconstructed" and their "genealogies" explored to reveal the different versions of the reality ("discourses") they reflect. There is no such thing as a better epistemology, only hermeneutics or the philosophical concern with understanding and interpretation. There is no hope for genuine human progress, only the inevitable "alienation" and "exile" encountered in an essentially meaningless universe.

The combination of a normative focus with relativism is particularly disturbing. Relativism makes it virtually impossible to make and sustain value judgments. What is "right" and "wrong" is contextual at best. Just as the adulation of Bach, Shakespeare, and da Vinci "empowers" selected elites, so does insistence on a particular set of value claims that can be dismissed as "privileging" the bourgeoisie, the Judeo-Christian West, and so forth. This produces the paradox of a profoundly normative group of scholars – the postmodernists – impeding their hidden egalitarian and anti-elitist preferences by the very relativism that allows them to deny the validity of normative or prescriptive claims. For liberals (like the authors) who are profoundly convinced of the need for genuine citizen participation in political systems and of the equality of women and men as a universal claim, relativism is both a threatening and pitiable perspective.

However, a valuable aspect of postmodernism, which we accept and encourage, is a focus on identities broadly speaking,[24] as emphasized by the familiar postmodernist notions of "the self" and "the other." As R. B. J. Walker observes:

> The usual categories and valorizations – of cultures and nations, of passions and Balkanizations – remain with us. Even so, a sense of novelties and accelerations is also pervasive. . . . [A] common identity is precisely what we do not have. . . . Modern political identities are fractured and dispersed among a multiplicity of sites, a condition sometimes attributed to a specifically postmodern experience but one that has been a familiar, though selectively forgotten, characteristic of modern political life for several centuries.[25]

It is this focus that also attracts feminist theorists. Gender, as an identity, appears to have been omitted from history; and as J. Ann Tickner argues, both men and women assign "a more positive value to masculine characteristics" in a world in which gender relations "affect every aspect of human experience," including global politics.[26] How did this come to be? "While many feminists do see structural regularities, such as gender and patriarchy, they define them as socially constructed and variable across time, place, and cultures, rather than as universal and natural." In her view, "feminists cannot be anything but skeptical of universal truth claims and explanations associated with a body of knowledge from which women have frequently been excluded as knowers and subjects."[27]

In the end, postmodernists have refused to try and replace what they seek to destroy. "Dissidents" freely admit they wish to shatter the little theoretical consensus that exists in the name of "an ethics of freedom," even as they deny any responsibility to provide an alternative: "[D]issident scholars," write Ashley and Walker, "have persistently

---

[24] See, for example, Yale H. Ferguson and Richard W. Mansbach, "Global Politics at the Turn of the Millennium: Changing Bases of 'Us' and 'Them'," in Davis B. Bobrow, *Prospects for International Relations: Conjectures about the Next Millennium*, special ed., *International Studies Review* 1:2 (Summer 1999), pp. 77–107. Constructivists are also highly interested in identity formation.

[25] R. B. J. Walker, *Inside/Outside: International Relations as Political Theory* (Cambridge: Cambridge University Press, 1993), p. 161.

[26] J. Ann Tickner, "You Just Don't Understand: Troubled Engagements Between Feminists and IR Theorists," *International Studies Quarterly* 41:4 (December 1997), p. 614.

[27] *Ibid.*, p. 629.

refused to do what many insist they are obliged to do. . . . They have not offered a new paradigm. . . . Indeed, to read almost any dissident text is to find not only a formal refusal or paradigmatic conceit but also a series of textual moves that function to disrupt any attempt to conduct a memorializing reading and turn a text into a paradigm of any sort."[28] Indeed, postmodernism's "central tenet," according to Steve Smith, "is one which seeks nothing less than the overthrow of virtually all preceding positions on epistemology."[29]

Postmodernists are surely correct in arguing that theory reflects and reinforces power relations among and within institutions, societies, and cultures, and that research is a value-laden undertaking. Undermining traditional theories and opening up "thinking space" are contributions in themselves. Postmodern critiques are important correctives to the unalloyed positivism adopted early on by the scientists and still insisted upon by many in the field, but postinternational thinkers like ourselves are not prepared to abandon empiricism, lock, stock, and barrel. It precludes both understanding and prescribing to believe that there is "no logical basis, even in positivism's own terms, for the proposition that knowledge of reality is directly derived from an independent world 'out there',"[30] or that "nothing exists outside of discourse."[31] Otherwise, empiricism *itself* would be the victim of postmodern scholarship, and truth would no longer be accessible beyond individual understanding and reflection.

With what could we replace empiricism unless we concede that "knowing" is impossible and are content to remain irresponsible critics? Although theorists of global politics have often ignored the subjective and normative dimensions of what they do,[32] that does not doom empiricism. It certainly does not mean that we cannot acquire useful knowledge about global politics independent of the language we use

---

[28] Richard K. Ashley and R. B. J. Walker, "Reading Dissidence/Writing the Discipline: Crisis and the Question of Sovereignty in International Studies," *International Studies Quarterly* 34:3 (September 1990), p. 398. This article appeared in a "special issue" of *ISQ* that is taken as additional evidence of "ghettoizing" by "dissidents" whose work appeared in it.
[29] Smith, "Positivism and Beyond," in Smith, Booth, and Zalewski, eds., *International Theory*, p. 29.
[30] Jim George, *Discourses of Global Politics: A Critical (Re)Introduction to International Relations* (Boulder, CO: Lynne Rienner, 1994), p. 53.
[31] David Campbell, *National Deconstruction: Violence, Identity, and Justice in Bosnia* (Minneapolis: University of Minnesota Press, 1998), pp. 24–25.
[32] We welcome the recent return of overtly normative approaches to the field. Cf. Chris Brown, *International Relations Theory: New Normative Approaches* (New York: Columbia University Press, 1993).

or cannot distinguish between an observer and that which is observed. With no standards for evidence, indeed, why should an observer accept the postmodernist perspective more than any other?

As constructivists and others rightfully remind us, our understanding of facts is conditioned by context and norms and is, therefore, constantly changing *in some respects*.[33] The selection of facts and their arrangement – among the most important tasks for a theorist – is a tricky business. Both are conditioned by inevitable though not always conscious prejudices arising from normative premises. We perceive what we look for and sometimes miss what is in front of our noses. *Meaning* is what matters, and meaning is given to facts partly as a result of normative and political commitments, so it is important to study those facts from a variety of perspectives. In that regard, theoretical pluralism is to be applauded.

It is commonly overlooked that there is a division between empiricists who are reluctant to confront subjective factors and those who forgo strict measurement in order to engage a broader range of factors. Despite the ambiguity of most key concepts, there *are* "facts" independent of the observer about which intersubjective agreement is possible even though meaning is attached to them by the observers themselves. Facts, along with reason, provide the elements for what Michael Nicholson calls "moderate positivism"[34] which is akin to what Rosenau has in mind when he speaks of "potential observability."[35] "In this procedure," Rosenau declares, "each step in the construction of a model is taken only after a determination of whether its components are at least theoretically susceptible to being observed, even if some innovation in observational techniques must first be made."[36] This version of empiricism has to sacrifice a substantial degree of parsimony and abstraction, but historical analysis (in particular) sensitizes the theorist to the costs of parsimony. Parsimony may be desirable but is hardly an end in itself. The Nicholson/Rosenau version of empiricism allows for the reunification of facts and values in a manner that recalls John Dewey's less demanding

---

[33] The impact of changing norms on institutions in global politics and the ways in which research can have an effect on political reality are highlighted in Margaret Keck and Kathryn Sikkink, *Advocates Beyond Borders: Advocacy Networks in International Politics* (Ithaca, NY: Cornell University Press, 1998).

[34] Michael Nicholson, "The Continued Significance of Positivism?" in Smith, Booth, and Zalewski, eds., *International Theory*, pp. 130–134.

[35] See his own "dialogue" with the postmodernists in Rosenau, *Distant Proximities*, ch. 19.

[36] Rosenau, *Turbulence in World Politics*, p. 27. The way in which Martha Finnemore and Kathryn Sikkink approach research on norms also reflects a less demanding empiricism. See their "International Norm Dynamics and Political Change," p. 892.

and more philosophical version of empiricism as problem-solving pragmatism, infused by socially conditioned norms.[37] For postinternational thinkers, as for Dewey, universal truth is suspect; instead, knowledge like the postinternational world itself is contextual, contingent, and subject to change depending on time and place.[38] And even if theory is "wrong," it may serve substantial social and political purposes.

Reliable data *does* buttress insightful theory, but which data we need to collect is unclear. Fact selection and interpretation again occupy center stage. Not everything we "know" or wish to "know" is as subjective as postmodernists claim it to be. Any phenomenon of interest can be seen in different lights and acquire a variety of partly correct interpretations. *But there are only a limited number of interpretations that can reasonably be allowed.* In the end we cannot escape dealing with questions for which more than one legitimate answer exists; this is the issue of a multiplicity of partly true stories with which we began this book. Thus, we can tell plausible stories about how the Cold War was a realist struggle for power, a war between two incompatible political and economic ideologies, a clash of cultures, a reflection of key personalities like Stalin or Dulles, a result of mirror images or misperceptions, and so on.[39] Together, like a cubist painting, we may have a composite that is more revealing than any of its parts alone.

Although there may be no "absolute truth" in a changing universe, there is often at least a sufficient amount of intersubjective consensus to make for a useful conversation[40] arising out of common identity, norms, and culture that produce common expectations about legitimate behavior. That conversation may not lead to proofs that satisfy scientists, but it can be illuminating. As we shall see shortly, constructivists argue that norms may produce action by actors that actually creates or "constitutes" identities and interests, and simultaneously gives meaning to that action. In this way, we gain a degree of useful "understanding" about the things we need to "know."

---

[37] See, for example, John Dewey, *Characters and Events: Popular Essays in Social and Political Philosophy*, vol. II (London: Allen & Unwin, 1929).

[38] Some of this material appears in an earlier version in Richard W. Mansbach, "Deterritorializing Global Politics," in Charles W. Kegley, Jr. and Donald Puchala, eds., *Visions of International Relations* (Columbia, SC: South Carolina University Press, 2002).

[39] See Yale H. Ferguson and Rey Koslowski, "Culture, International Relations Theory, and Cold War History," in Odd Arne Westad, ed., *Reviewing the Cold War: Approaches, Interpretations, Theory* (London: Frank Cass, 2000), pp. 149–179.

[40] On this point, see Hollis, *The Philosophy of Social Science*, pp. 240–247; and Fernández-Armesto, *Truth*, ch. 6.

The constructivist turn: individuals, identities, and human autonomy

The anti-empiricism of postmodernists limits the usefulness of their focus on identity in contrast to recent theory generically called "constructivism." One stream of constructivism is especially attractive because of its preoccupation with rules, norms, and perceptions of decisionmakers in global politics. In essence, constructivists maintain that we as agents act in the world (subjectively) in accordance with our perceptions of that world, that the world as it is (objectively) helps to shape (but may not be the same as) those perceptions, and that both perceptions and actions in turn have an impact on the objective nature of the world.

In Chapter 1, we suggested that a postinternational perspective tilted in the direction of people rather than states as units of analysis. Three decades ago, the levels-of-analysis problem was a burning issue, not least because it reflected empirical and, more importantly, (unspoken) normative differences among theoretical perspectives in a young discipline. Conservative realists saw a world of autonomous states as actors constrained by the structural attributes of a global system; liberals focused on individual decisionmakers and citizens. Overall, conservatism triumphed, and those who viewed individuals as autonomous units of analysis whose happiness and welfare were the legitimate ends of global politics were termed "utopians" and "idealists" and largely purged from higher education.

The general constructivist position in what is today called the "agent/structure problem"[41] is largely compatible with older liberal belief in the role of individuals as units of analysis in global politics. For constructivists, individual agents' perceptions of their environment, including structures, influence their actions, which in turn affect the environment/structures in which they are engaged, and then these same structures in a giant feedback loop return to influence the perceptions and behavior of agents. In fact, it is difficult to see how "agent" and "structure" can be separated in that each conditions and "constitutes" the other in a continuous process. The identities and interests of agents are not exogenous factors but are constituted by practices and inter-subjective agreement, or, as Hall puts it: "[C]hanges in the collective

---

[41] See Alexander E. Wendt, "The Agent–Structure Problem in International Relations Theory," *International Organization* 41:3 (Summer 1987), pp. 335–370; Dessler, "What's at Stake in the Agent–Structure Debate?"; and Walter Carlsnaes, "The Agent–Structure Problem in Foreign Policy Analysis," *International Studies Quarterly* 36:3 (September 1992), pp. 254–270.

identity of societal actors transform the interests of relevant collective actors." He continues: "Group interests are strongly conditioned by the self-identifications of members of these groups with respect to other groupings."[42] All actions and decisions take place within some context, and actors (along with their perceptual and normative baggage) and structures necessarily are part of that context. Real behavior, then, reflects a mix of voluntarism and determinism.

As for the *degree* to which agent and structure influence each other, that must surely require consideration of context, varying according to factors such as nature of polity, systemic distribution of capability and attitudes, and personality of leaders. The debate about global structures harks back to the fundamental puzzle of how the whole and its parts are related. The agent/structure literature raises, but by no means resolves, the issue either for a single society or for the global system as a whole. At one extreme is Waltz's parsimonious model in which the overall distribution of states' power capabilities supposedly accounts for everything of importance. Almost as parsimonious are contests among putative "civilizations" and Gramscian models of hegemonic elites. Yet any system can be "reduced" to its component parts, not only the global system but also particular states and countless groups – to individual actors.

Postinternational thinking neither ignores structure nor assumes that agents are omnipotent. Rather, as in the constructivist view that agent and structure are inseparable, postinternational theory claims that the situation changes from issue to issue and even by case: an agent in one issue or case may be part of structure in the next or may even be irrelevant.

In the end, it is fair to ask not only what are the major issues and trends in global politics, but also what types of actors/agents seem to be gaining and losing, both overall and in particular respects with regard to the issue contests observed. Constructivists have so far offered little enlightenment on such subjects. Like postmodernism, constructivism, as Ruggie declares, "is not itself a theory of international relations . . . but a theoretically informed approach to the study of international relations."[43] Unlike postmodernists, however, constructivists do see themselves as obliged to build theory.

---

[42] Rodney Bruce Hall, *National Collective Identity: Social Constructs and International Systems* (New York: Columbia University Press, 1999), p. 5. Emphasis omitted.
[43] John Gerard Ruggie, "What Makes the World Hang Together? Neo-utilitarianism and the Social Constructivist Challenge," *International Organization* 52:4 (Autumn 1998), pp. 879–880.

The constructivist focus on "identities, norms, knowledge, and interests."[44] is entirely compatible with the postinternational emphasis on identities and identity change. And, according to Katzenstein, Keohane, and Krasner: "Since they emphasize how ideational or normative structures constitute agents and their interests, conventional constructivists differ sharply from rationalists on questions of ontology."[45] Like liberals, constructivists "insist on the importance of social processes that generate changes in normative beliefs, such as those prompted by the antislavery movement of the nineteenth century, the contemporary campaign for women's rights as human rights, or nationalist propaganda."[46]

However, not all constructivism is equally useful for postinternational politics. For example, Alexander Wendt's "thin constructivism" that he hopes will lead to a "principled middle way" between positivism and postmodernism[47] is unabashedly state-centric.[48] However different Wendt's branch of constructivism may be in highlighting the role of ideas and perceptions in shaping behavior, it shares the conservative realist story of state primacy. Wendt writes: "It may be that non-state actors are becoming more important than states as initiators of change, but system change ultimately happens *through* states. In that sense states are still at the center of the international system, and as such it makes no more sense to criticize a theory of international politics as 'state-centric' than it does to criticize a theory of forests for being 'tree-centric.'"[49]

In Wendt's constructivism, "anarchy" in the modern world is still what "*states* make of it." Wendt admits to sharing central realist assumptions, for example, that the international system is anarchic and that states wish to survive and are rational, as well as "a commitment to states as units of analysis, and to the importance of systemic or 'third image' theorizing."[50] Perhaps the fact that one can be a realist and a neorealist and just a little bit postmodern, too, helps account for the wide appeal of Wendt's constructivism.

---

[44] Katzenstein, Keohane, and Krasner, "*International Organization* and the Study of World Politics," p. 678.

[45] *Ibid.*, p. 675. Ruggie defines ontology as "the real-world phenomena that are posited by any theory and are invoked by its explanations" (Ruggie, "What Makes the World Hang Together? p. 879).

[46] *Ibid.*, p. 682. See also pp. 867–868.

[47] Alexander E. Wendt, *Social Theory of International Politics* (Cambridge: Cambridge University Press, 1999), pp. 1–2.

[48] *Ibid.*, pp. 193–245.   [49] *Ibid.*, p. 9. Emphasis in original.

[50] Alexander E. Wendt, "Constructing International Politics," *International Security* 20:1 (Summer 1995), p. 75. Emphasis added.

There is another more sophisticated stream of constructivism that is less tied to realism and is much more useful in understanding the postinternational world. It acknowledges debts to Durkheim and Weber, and evolved through the work of Giddens,[51] Nicholas Onuf,[52] Friedrich Kratochwil,[53] and John Gerard Ruggie.[54] This stream also accepts what might be termed the "subjective" aspect of decisionmaking and the impact of actors' behavior upon structures and trends (and vice versa)[55] – but there is much more. The actors that make up the global system are themselves changing as they evolve "new conceptions of identity and political community." For example, the rise of modern nationalism in Europe significantly transformed the character of "states." Similarly, new conceptions of identity and political community may result in different rules and structures at the international level.[56]

Ruggie was an early exponent of this branch of constructivism, and his emphases on identity and agent are reflected in his definition of episteme, which he admits owes much to Foucault. Ruggie uses the term to emphasize the importance of the intersubjective construction of meaning. Epistemes, he wrote, "refer to a dominant way of looking at social reality, a set of shared symbols and references, mutual expectations and a mutual predictability of intention. Epistemic communities may be said to consist of interrelated roles which grow up around an *episteme*; they delimit, for their members, *the* proper construction of social reality."[57]

---

[51] Anthony Giddens, *The Constitution of Society: Outline of the Theory of Structuration* (Cambridge: Polity, 1984). See also E. Adler, "Seizing the Middle Ground: Constructivism in World Politics," *European Journal of International Relations* 3:3 (1997), pp. 319–363.

[52] See Nicholas J. Onuf, *World of Our Making: Rules and Rule in Social Theory and International Relations* (Columbia, SC: University of South Carolina Press, 1989); "Levels," *European Journal of International Relations* 1:1 (March 1995), pp. 35–58; and "Constructivism: A User's Manual," in Vendulka Kubálková, Nicholas Onuf, and Paul Kowert, *International Relations in a Constructed World* (Armonk, NY: M. E. Sharpe, 1998), pp. 58–78.

[53] See especially Friedrich V. Kratochwil, *Rules, Norms, and Decisions: On the Conditions of Practical and Legal Reasoning in International Relations and Domestic Affairs* (Cambridge: Cambridge University Press, 1989).

[54] Cf. Friedrich V. Kratochwil and John Gerard Ruggie, "International Organization: A State of the Art on the Art of the State," *International Organization* 40:3 (Autumn 1986), pp. 753–775.

[55] Onuf, *World of Our Making* (p. 142) "denies ontological priority" to either agency or structure.

[56] Reynold Koslowski and Friedrich V. Kratochwil, "Understanding Change in International Politics: The Soviet Empire's Demise and the International System," *International Organization* 48:2 (Spring 1994), p. 136.

[57] John Gerard Ruggie, "International Responses to Technology: Concepts and Trends," *International Organization* 29:3 (Summer 1975), pp. 569–570. Emphasis in original.

Like Ruggie, Onuf emphasizes the continuous and reciprocal relationship between people and society, mediated by rules that include, but are not limited to, legal rules. Similarly, Kratochwil stresses the evolving nature of "moral facts" and he offers a powerful defense of the role of international law.[58]

Constructivists of this mindset are especially interested in formal and less-formal international regimes, forms of governance which they see as necessary and natural, rather than directly traceable to calculated (what Ruggie calls "neoutilitarian"[59]) state interests as in Robert Keohane's neoinstitutionalist world[60] or even the slightly more venturesome vision of international society propounded by Hedley Bull.[61] As Onuf expresses it, rules form institutions, institutions form societies, and rules yield rule (what others might describe as patterns of governance). This is an important theoretical insight for those who see a world of declining states and proliferating forms of authority.

Constructivism in this vein is also conducive to restoring a dynamic dimension to global politics. Core concepts acquire meaning through how people act, and that meaning evolves through additional action and belief. For constructivists and realists alike, sovereignty is a key constitutive rule that purports to decree who may play the game of global politics and keep out interlopers.

The critical role of history

Facts, as well as values, have a role in the postinternational enterprise, and the bulk of those facts are historical. Both change and continuity acquire empirical meaning in historical context, a point that becomes doubly important if we are to make sense of a postinternational political

[58] Kratochwil, *Rules, Norms, and Decisions*, pp. 124, 61–64.
[59] Ruggie, "What Makes the World Hang Together?" p. 855.
[60] Robert O. Keohane, *After Hegemony: Cooperation and Discord in the World Political Economy* (Princeton: Princeton University Press, 1984), especially pp. 78–80. Keohane seemed to have moved toward a constructivist position when, with Judith Goldstein, he wrote that "ideas *as well as* interests have causal weight in explanations of human action" and that researchers should "investigate not just what strategies are devised to attain interests but how preferences are formed and how identities are shaped." Goldstein and Keohane, "Ideas and Foreign Policy: An Analytical Framework," in Goldstein and Keohane, eds., *Ideas and Foreign Policy: Beliefs, Institutions, and Political Change* (Ithaca, NY: Cornell University Press, 1993), pp. 4, 6. Emphasis in original. Ruggie argues, however, that in the end Goldstein and Keohane retreat back into neoutilitarianism (Ruggie, "What Makes the World Hang Together?" pp. 866–867).
[61] Hedley Bull, *The Anarchical Society: A Study of Order in World Politics* (New York: Columbia University Press, 1977).

universe. In other words, today's shift to a postinternational world only makes sense in the context of tomorrow and yesterday. As noted earlier, history is not linear, and the present and future consist of elements from the past as well as genuinely novel factors. Indeed, there are cyclical aspects to our view of history as revealed in the discussion of fission and fusion.[62]

No contemporary phenomena, including the elements of the postinternational universe, lack historical roots or, at least, analogies. As Donald Puchala observes regarding Europe's Middle Ages and the present:

> [M]any aspects of the *modern* world were by the late 1980s beginning to look somewhat *medieval*. Structures and processes that identified twentieth-century international relations were reappearing in modern contexts. For one thing ethnic frontiers in our contemporary world were beginning to obscure political frontiers – just, perhaps, as in medieval times: "-lands," "-marks," and "-stans" were better defined and sometimes politically more important than the "-doms" of the kings.

Puchala then raises the key questions: "If such 'medievalization' can be observed today, how can it be explained? More intriguing, is periodic medievalization a recurrent feature of international history? If so what typically causes it and what typically comes after?"[63]

Historical facts alone, like dictionaries or telephone books, have little meaning outside of context and the patterns imposed upon them by theorists. Interpretation permits theorists to make connections among facts and impose patterns on them, and to evaluate them normatively. Since interpretation depends on the theorist's location in time and space, truth becomes at best a moving target. As students of global politics, we are not so much concerned with the facts themselves as with the broader context in which they fit and the degree to which the patterns imposed upon them are applicable to other places and other times. Thus, theory shapes history as much as history shapes theory.

Theory should account for the past systematically, rather than ransacking it as do realists and neorealists who reject claims of change. And we accept, as does Rodney Bruce Hall, that it is a complex business: "I cheerfully and consciously surrender parsimony for richer and more

---

[62] For more on cyclical approaches to history, see Puchala, *Theory and History of International Relations*, pp. 51–72.
[63] *Ibid.*, pp. 2, 3.

nuanced characterization of the societies and systems I wish to study. Social reality is complex. It always has been. Thus we cannot expect to apprehend the evolution of social reality without a serious foray into history."[64]

Dealing with historical fact constitutes a different order of empiricism than do laboratory experiments because history is not directly observable by contemporary analysts. It must *always* be "seen" through the eyes of others. Thus, what is "sensed" by the investigator has previously been interpreted and often reinterpreted. Even those who may actually have witnessed the events in question may have delivered a highly inaccurate or deliberately biased account. As Fernández-Armesto readily acknowledges: "Historians like me know, at least as well as practitioners of any other discipline, how elusive objectivity is. Even if we perform miracles of self-immolation, we are left with sources which derive from other hands and bear the imprint of other subjects – witnesses, reporters, compilers of data and hearsay."[65]

Historical facts then come to us not directly as do scientific facts but through the philosophical preferences, political and personal interests, and theoretical positions of others. There are not only unknown facts to be ascertained, but also there are many layers of accumulated meaning to be scraped away. Thus, we know as facts that Scotland's "Bonnie Prince Charlie," the Stuart pretender to the throne of Great Britain, returned to Scotland and with a force of Scottish Highlanders and French and Irish soldiers, sought to regain his patrimony until defeated at Culloden in 1745. But what matters is how to sort out the various meanings assigned to the individual and the event by axe-grinding historians. Was Prince Charles the unpopular drunken rebel with only a small following who served the cause of French hostility to Britain, as depicted by one generation of historians? Or, was he the dashing hero who supported legitimacy against a German Hanoverian interloper, as depicted by another generation? Was he a Scottish nationalist and patriot, or was he dynast pure and simple? The answers to such questions are critical not only in assigning meaning to Charles but, more importantly, in making sense of the broader sweep of European politics at the time.

Understanding contemporary polities needs a historically sensitive approach in order to recognize that the territorial state joined the march of history quite late – and perhaps, it may yet prove, only for an extended

---

[64] Hall, *National Collective Identity*, p. xii.   [65] Fernández-Armesto, *Truth*, p. 227.

"Westphalian moment." This insight makes it easier to appreciate the tentativeness – indeed, almost "accidental" or serendipitous nature – of the process by which sovereign states actually emerged, and it highlights the perennial importance of a host of other polities, identities, and loyalties. Any way we look at it, the era of the sovereign state really has been a small sliver of time in the vast reaches of human history, let alone, of course, a future that is yet to unfold. Hendrik Spruyt rightly hastens to deny that his conclusion about the efficiency of the early-modern state for the purpose of war should "be understood as introducing an element of teleological development into my view of institutional evolution." Indeed, he adds: "Had the institutional form of the sovereign state not emerged – and it did not outside Europe – then the selective process might have operated between city-states and city-leagues. Moreover, with another dramatic transformation, the contemporary 'winner' of this process of selection and empowerment – that is, sovereign, territorial authority – might prove to be susceptible to change itself."[66]

Too often theorists have used history as a ready source of persuasive examples for rhetorical ends, and even today much theory reflects the dominance of Europe's control over historical meaning. Even the term "neomedieval" betrays an unfortunate European bias. Few scholars of international relations in recent decades have utilized history systematically. Rosenau seems to argue that the "centralizing and decentralizing" processes he identifies are recent. In fact, such processes, though now arising from several (not all) unprecedented sources, have always characterized global politics. While fusion and fragmentation are more apparent in transitional epochs, when some political forms dramatically change their relationship to others, those processes are present at all times. The birth of extensive imperial political forms in Mesopotamia and China, the emergence of city-states in classical Greece, the period leading to the Peace of Westphalia in Europe and the decline of universal contenders for authority like the Holy Roman Empire, and the triumph of Westphalian polities over indigenous tribal forms during Europe's global expansion marked transitional epochs. The central question for our times is whether we are in another such epoch, and the answer seems to be almost certainly yes.

---

[66] Hendrik Spruyt, *The Sovereign State and its Competitors* (Princeton: Princeton University Press, 1994), p. 179.

In retrospect, it seems odd that few international-relations scholars followed the path blazed by Adda Bozeman's brilliant analysis of pre-Westphalian and non-Western civilizations.[67] Bozeman sought to show the variety in political organization, political ideas, and "international" behavior prior to Europe's ascendancy and the spread of European institutions and ideas into other regions. "Most of these indigenous patterns of life and thought became blurred during the centuries of European supremacy, when they were being integrated in the Occidental scheme of things," but, "it became increasingly apparent that the Western ideas were not the exclusive mainsprings of their political attitudes and actions."[68] Then, in a remarkably prescient rejection of an aspect of Francis Fukuyama's "the end of history" thesis, she observed:

> One of the basic concepts in modern international politics is the sovereign democratic nation-state which acquired its connotations in the histories of Western Europe and America. Since groups of people in all continents have willingly identified their collective aspirations with this norm of organization by claiming the right to self-determination . . . it was generally understood that the modern state had actually superseded older, local forms of government. In the prevailing climate of egalitarian thinking, it is easy to forget that most communities in the Balkan and Black Sea regions had matured under the political tutelage of the monolithic Byzantine Empire, whose tenets of rule were quite at variance with those developed in the West. . . .[69]

Bozeman pointed out that neither Indian nor Chinese political history had analogues to modern democracy. Islam lacked the secular legal experience necessary to derive civic rights, and West Africa lacked both the common culture and the language that underpinned some European states. In all this, Bozeman's preinternational world also appeared to foreshadow the world of competing civilizations that Huntington described over three decades later.

There are additional theoretical developments emanating from various other history-based approaches that seem to us to be moving in the direction of a postinternational map of global politics. Among neorealists, for example, Barry Buzan, Charles O. Jones, and Richard Little

---

[67] Adda B. Bozeman, *Politics and Culture in International History* (Princeton: Princeton University Press, 1960).
[68] *Ibid.*, p. 5.
[69] *Ibid.*, p. 6; Francis Fukuyama, *The End of History and the First Man* (New York: Free Press, 1992).

have argued that Waltz's conception of overarching international system structure (bipolar, multipolar, and so on) is so parsimonious as to obscure a significant "deep structure" of various actors, institutions, and processes. The timeframe of the initial study began before the Westphalian era in Europe,[70] and Buzan and Little have now continued their project to elaborate an analytical framework and to encompass even more historical "international systems."[71] Sympathetic as we are to their pioneering work, we regard Waltzian neorealism as a poor foundation and reject their notion that different historical periods necessarily involve a *succession* of *dominant political forms*. To be sure, we recognize that the state model gained primacy in Europe in the Westphalian era and was later carried on the banners of European empires. But other polities not only continued to coexist with the state but also actually often remained equally or more "authoritative" within their respective domains. Put another way, whatever the state's claim to absolute authority, it was not dominant – had very little control over or, indeed, any particular interest in controlling – many important aspects of social life. And in the colonial world, especially, the veneer of state control was often extremely thin, while the likes of tribal chiefs and religious authorities held much of the real power on the ground.[72]

Other systems-level approaches include world-systems theory, associated with Immanuel Wallerstein,[73] and a relative newcomer, world-system history.[74] The former has traditionally suffered from its narrow neo-Marxist definition of international structure as the distribution of economic capabilities. World-system history, by contrast, appears to be a more eclectic perspective that is able to accommodate a broader range of systemic variables, polities, and research methodologies.

---

[70] Barry Buzan, Charles Jones, and Richard Little, *The Logic of Anarchy: Neorealism to Structural Realism* (New York: Columbia University Press, 1993).

[71] Barry Buzan and Richard Little, *International Systems in World History: Remaking the Study of International Relations* (Oxford: Oxford University Press, 2000). See also Buzan's and Little's summary of their views about the present-day international structure, entitled "One World or Two?" in Yale H. Ferguson and Richard W. Mansbach *et al.*, "What Is the Polity? A Roundtable," *International Studies Review* 2:1 (Spring 2000), pp. 17–21.

[72] See also Richard Little, "Reconfiguring International Political Space: The Significance of World History," in Ferguson and Jones, *Political Space*, pp. 45–60. Little makes an eloquent case for the use of history and also comments on the Ferguson/Mansbach "polities" framework.

[73] Cf. Immanuel Wallerstein, *The Politics of the World-Economy: The States, the Movements, and Civilization* (Cambridge: Cambridge University Press, 1984).

[74] Robert A. Denemark, Jonathan Friedman, Barry K. Gills, George Modelski, eds., *World System History: The Science of Long-Term Change* (London: Routledge, 2000).

Some of the most historically informed analyses of global politics have emerged from historical sociology and, in particular, the work of Michael Mann. Mann spent much of his early career explaining how the "autonomous power of the state" evolved, especially through connections with war and capitalism.[75] The historical reach of his planned trilogy on *The Sources of Social Power*[76] extends to ancient Mesopotamia, encompassing a much wider array of social actors than the modern state alone. More recently, he has been probing the tension between nation-states and globalism (the ideology of globalization), with particular attention to relationships and institutions that are essentially neither. He writes: "To endorse 'globalism' would be to repeat the mistake of 'nation-statism'. We must reject any view of societies as singular bounded systems." "[S]ocieties have never been unitary. They have been composed of a multiplicity of networks of interaction, many with differing, if overlapping and intersecting, boundaries. This has been true of all prehistoric and historic periods . . . It remains true today." Mann identifies five "sociospatial levels of social interaction": local, national, international, transnational, and global. All five, as he sees it, are "entwined yet partially autonomous."[77]

Realists and neorealists are among the most pernicious ransackers of history as they try to transform messy historical reality into a story of how sovereign states are virtually universal political communities. Bits of history are trotted out to show that states remain multifunctional, to deny that the system has become hierarchical, and to insist on the dominance of structure. Therefore does Robert Cox argue that Kenneth Waltz and other neorealists adopt a "fixed ahistorical view,"[78] and well might Ruggie claim that "a dimension of change is missing from Waltz's model."[79] "Waltz's theory of 'society' contains only a reproductive logic, but no transformational logic," and "continuity . . . is a

---

[75] Cf. Mann, *States, War and Capitalism*.

[76] See especially Michael Mann, *The Sources of Social Power: A History of Power from the Beginning to A.D. 1760*, vol. I (Cambridge: Cambridge University Press, 1986).

[77] Michael Mann, "Neither Nation-State nor Globalism," *Environment and Planning* 28:11 (1996). For a contrast between the present authors' polities framework and Mann's view of the continued importance of the state, see his "States and Other Rule Makers in the Modern World," in Ferguson and Mansbach *et al.*, "What Is the Polity?" pp. 24–29.

[78] Robert W. Cox, "Social Forces, States and World Orders: Beyond International Relations Theory," in Keohane, ed., *Neorealism and its Critics*, p. 211. Waltz's metaphors are rarely historical. Rather, like his use of "firm," they tend to derive from microeconomics.

[79] John Gerard Ruggie, "Continuity and Transformation in the World Polity: Toward a Neorealist Synthesis," *World Politics* 35:2 (January 1983), p. 273. Ruggie argues that Waltzian neorealism lacks any mechanism for system transformation.

product of premise even before it is hypothesized as an outcome."[80] In the United States, the triumph of realists-as-scientists precluded serious historical analysis. As Ole Waever writes: "The millennial belief in American exceptionalism exempted the United States from qualitative change, and the historicist threat to this ideology was kept at bay with the assistance of a naturalistic social science containing change within the categories of progress, law, and reason. This historical consciousness adapted and survived dramatic challenges and thus sustained . . . a more abstract and 'scientific' social science, divorced from history."[81]

In fairness, there are some in the realist tradition who see the need for greater historical consciousness in order to allow for system transformation. Although E. H. Carr thought it difficult "even to imagine a world in which political power would be organised on a basis not of territory," he recognized that "[f]ew things are permanent in history; and it would be rash to assume that the territorial unit of power is one of them."[82] More recently, Buzan, Jones, and Little declared that neorealists do not deny the relevance of history or the potential for change in international politics.

> But they do assert that there are important features of international politics . . . that have occurred throughout the history of the international system and that need to be accounted for in terms of an unchanging systemic structure. It is this claim that analysts imbued with historicism wish to deny. . . . [T]he historicists insist that distortion will inevitably occur if it is presupposed that these practices always play an identical role in the international system or that they always carry the same subjective meaning simply because they are identified by a common label.[83]

Few historians and certainly not the present authors would quarrel with such a claim.

[80] John Gerard Ruggie, "Continuity and Transformation in the World Polity: Toward a Neorealist Synthesis," in Keohane, ed., *Neorealism and its Critics*, p. 152. Waltz disagrees, declaring that "structure is a generative notion, and the structure of a system is generated by the interactions of its principal parts" (Kenneth Waltz, "Reductionist and Systemic Theories," in Keohane, ed., *Neorealism and its Critics*, p. 61).

[81] Ole Waever, "The Sociology of a Not So International Discipline: American and European Developments in International Relations," *International Organization* 52:4 (Autumn 1998), p. 712.

[82] Carr, *The Twenty Years' Crisis*, p. 229.

[83] Buzan, Jones, and Little, *The Logic of Anarchy*, p. 85. See also Barry Buzan and Richard Little, "Reconceptualizing Anarchy: Structural Realism Meets World History," *European Journal of International Relations* 2:4 (December 1996), pp. 403–438; and *International Systems in World History*. In addition, see Richard Little, "Reconfiguring International Political Space," pp. 45–60.

The past is part of any present context, because the present has been at least partly shaped by the past and because many existing processes, political forms, and ideas remain embedded in the present. Although ours is a turbulent world and much that catches our eye seems to be unprecedented, it would be mistaken to think only in the present or to conclude that history is headed toward some fated destination. Certainly, the present *is* different *in some respects* from anything that came before and can be studied on its own terms, but features such as the ebb and flow of political communities and their fission and fusion have been characteristic of global politics almost literally forever.[84] Some things have hardly changed at all, and the past is a rich source of clues about what to look for in the present – and to help us speculate about the future. The sheer pace of change has accelerated, but we should not make too much of this. The mighty Assyrian empire collapsed in only thirty years, and the Aztecs (with a little help from the Spaniards) about as fast as the Soviet Union. Chaos and complexity have been with us since the Big Bang, and there have been many eras of extreme instability. Some of the sources of instability are also strikingly different today from what they were, say, in ancient Egypt or the Roman Empire at its height, but many such sources – for example, nested polities and multiple identities – are not different.

As argued in Chapter 1, theorists should be obliged to specify the extent to which the *present is not only different from but also similar to the past*. The pre-Westphalian experience may be more relevant to our understanding of the present and future than the relatively brief era of interstate politics. Global politics today is in some ways coming to resemble politics as it was before the onset of the European era of sovereign states, itself punctuated by major changes and always involving many local variations. Thus, no contemporary territorial state is like those with which Metternich was familiar (and about which Henry Kissinger wrote his doctoral dissertation). Virtually *all* modern states reflect the peculiarities of their own past. For Arab states, that past combines tribal traditions and the effects of an imperial unity based on Islam. For the

---

[84] Ferguson and Mansbach, *Polities*. See also Yale H. Ferguson and Richard W. Mansbach, "History's Revenge and Future Shock: The Remapping of Global Politics," in Hewson and Sinclair, *Approaches to Global Governance Theory*, pp. 197–238. This article was a revised version of a paper presented January 30, 1996, in the Research Seminar at the Norwegian Nobel Institute, Oslo, Norway, when Ferguson was Senior Fellow at the Institute. Especially since the title of the paper obviously prefigured that of this book, we gratefully acknowledge the support of the Norwegian Nobel Institute.

Chinese state, the present bears the imprint of the Middle Kingdom and the cultural continuity of millennia. Mexico and Central America still bear the scars of the collision between European Spain and the Aztecs, Mayas, and other indigenous tribal peoples. And some of Africa's states are crumbling before the onslaught of older tribal and ethnic identities. And so it goes.

For the most part, theorists are unaware of the historical sources of what they are examining. Or, they borrow indiscriminately from history and mythologize selected events, thereby *appearing* to acknowledge those historical sources. The contingent nature of knowledge, along with the suspicion that timeless and universal concepts like "state" are neither timeless nor universal make it urgent to make research historical and cross cultural. How else can we recognize not only continuities but also the contingent and contextual nature of what we take for granted? An historical perspective also helps us recognize the dynamic nature of our enterprise, making us skeptical of any unqualified assertion "that the fundamental nature of international relations has not changed over the millennia."[85]

However, to the extent that social scientists try to emulate natural scientists, there is little room for historical variation and sympathy for analyses that limit theory's capacity to generate timeless concepts and generalizations. Instead of demanding parsimony, we will do far better to follow historical sociologists like Mann, who describes a rich political universe in which the role of key social forces and institutions in shaping global politics varies by time and place.[86] For Mann, "real human societies" constitute a "mess" strewn with "many mistakes, apparent accidents, and unintended consequences."[87] This allows for a degree of causal and descriptive complexity that violates parsimony but emphasizes the impact of context on and the dynamic nature of global politics. The Westphalian State was not only historically contingent,[88] but its functions and capacity also evolved historically and flowered in conditions that to a large extent no longer exist.

---

[85] That comment comes from realist Robert Gilpin, *War and Change in World Politics*, p. 7. See also Kenneth N. Waltz, *Theory of International Politics* (Reading, MA: Addison-Wesley, 1979), p. 66.

[86] Mann, *The Sources of Social Power*, vol. I.

[87] Mann, *The Sources of Social Power*, vol. II, *The Rise of Classes and Nation-States, 1760–1914* (Cambridge: Cambridge University Press, 1993), pp. 2, 3.

[88] See, for example, Spruyt, *The Sovereign State and its Competitors*, and Charles Tilly, *Coercion, Capital and European States, AD 990–1990* (Oxford: Basil Blackwell, 1990).

We must acknowledge that historical analysis has its own perils. As we have noted, objectivity is no easier for an historian than for a social scientist. However, in the end it would be foolish to stand paralyzed and ignore history because historical research is partly theory-dependent and partly subjective. We have to accept the fact that there are few givens or certainties in the historical record, rather mainly probabilities and sometimes only possibilities. We have to live with ambiguity and proceed as best we can. Perhaps the most we can hope for is for our investigations to provide a more useful or convincing view of reality than other constructions.

Finally, we must at all costs avoid the fallacy of believing that history is going somewhere. Fukuyama is wrong here too. There is no grand historical plan and no destination. History, far from "ending," is forever being revived and reconstructed and at least partially re-lived. Contemporary global politics in substantial part *does* reflect history's revenge. As Stephen Kobrin reminds us, we should avoid "the very modern assumption that time's arrow is unidirectional and that progress is linear."[89] We reiterate: any satisfactory analysis has to establish what remains the same, what is changing, and the approximate rate of change.

Conclusion: retrieving reality

There is an urgent need to rethink theory in global politics in light of the failed promises of strict empiricists, but it would be an error to go from one extreme to the other. Those failed promises encouraged postmodern monastic movements in global politics that have abandoned empiricism almost entirely for communal rites and their own liturgy. By turning their backs on normative issues, wrestling with parochial research questions, and adopting arcane methodologies, positivists were largely responsible for "alienating" "the other," that is, the field's self-proclaimed "dissidents." Happily, we are becoming more conscious of the normative implications of theoretical choices even as the pages of journals remain cluttered with research results that seem almost irrelevant to our exciting and complex postinternational world.

Many of today's theoretical debates, such as what are the relative merits of neorealism and neoliberal institutionalism, are timid

---

[89] Stephen J. Kobrin, "Back to the Future: Neomedievalism and the Postmodern Digital World Economy," *Journal of International Affairs* 51:2 (Spring 1998), p. 364.

hair-splitting exercises.[90] The shared conservatism of realism, neorealism, institutionalism, and state-centric constructivism is apparent in a 1995 mini-symposium in *International Security*. How different are institutionalists from neorealists when Robert Keohane and Lisa Martin acknowledge that John Mearsheimer "correctly asserts that liberal institutionalists treat states as rational egoists operating in a world in which agreements cannot be hierarchically enforced, and that institutionalists only expect interstate cooperation to occur if states have significant common interests"?[91] How dramatic an advance is state-centric constructivism when Wendt affirms that he shares "all five of Mearsheimer's 'realist' assumptions."[92]

Consider for a moment how much those "shared assumptions" diminish novelty. (1) International politics is anarchic. This is the principal claim of Eurocentric international relations, yet in the absence of a world government, there nonetheless is a great deal of order in the world. Much of it is produced by polities other than states. (2) States have offensive capabilities. Do not most polities? (3) States cannot be 100 percent certain about others' intentions. Is that not true of all polities? (4) States wish to survive. States don't "wish" anything, but, if they did long to survive, we would have to conclude that in cases such as Yugoslavia, the Soviet Union, East Germany, and Somalia they do not make a very good job of making their wish come true. (5) States are rational, and that rationality links structure and behavior. That assertion would be denied by almost all theorists other than realists or rational-choice advocates. States are no more "rational" than they are "wishers" upon stars or anything else.

What then are *our* assumptions in this book? (1) Theory need not be falsifiable or testable to the extent demanded by strict scientists, but it should have some link to intersubjective "reality," and we should strive to make our claims as falsifiable as possible. Empiricists should acknowledge the normative concerns that guide the questions they raise and their analyses, and the normative implications of theories should be fully explored. (2) Grand theory is desirable and possible if it is relieved of overly restrictive empirical requirements. Parsimony is not an end in itself. Induction and correlative thinking limit us to what can be tested

---

[90] See Richard W. Mansbach, "Neo-This and Neo-That: Or, 'Play It Sam' (Again and Again)," *Mershon International Studies Review* 40 (April 1996), pp. 90–95.
[91] Robert O. Keohane and Lisa Martin, "The Promise of Institutionalist Theory," *International Security* 20:1 (Summer 1995), p. 39.
[92] Wendt, "Constructing International Politics," pp. 71–75.

using existing data and methods; data and method tend to drive theory rather than, properly, the reverse. (3) Language is, as postmodernists insist, inherently ambiguous, but it can be used to communicate rather than to obfuscate or obscure. Deconstruction can be helpful in revealing layers of meaning, yet the ultimate goal should be clarification and acquisition of a common stable of concepts. (4) Global politics is not a separate field; "the subject is politics."[93] (5) Structure conditions behavior but does not determine it. Broad global as well as less-encompassing trends and institutions at many levels and of various types shape the perceptions and constrain the choices that individuals have. However, people – in the streets, in voting booths, in stores, and elsewhere – are the wellsprings of the patterns we construct. (6) Westphalian States are only one of many types of polities, and global politics has always encompassed numerous layered, overlapping, and interacting polities (from families to empires) that coexist, cooperate, compete, and conflict. (7) Political communities are constantly undergoing change ("becoming"), subject at the same time to forces that would fracture them or embed them in still larger communities. (8) Territory is only one of many ways to define political space.

Finally, one of the most important lines of contemporary inquiry is one that we share with many postmodernists and constructivists: a focus on changing identity and changing patterns of authority.[94] Identity formation and competition are the engines of historical change. The meaning and content of the essential concepts we use also evolve. Just as the eighteenth-century European state was a far cry from most contemporary states, so ideas like "power" and "sovereignty" have different meanings in different places and at different times. Theory and the concepts with which it is constructed have both normative and political roots, and cannot help but reflect shifts in norms and political outcomes. Krasner captures some of this in his discussion of sovereignty: "[T]he actual content of sovereignty," was repeatedly "contested" and "persistently challenged" by other "institutional forms," and "the exercise of authority within a given territory, generally regarded as a core attribute of sovereign states, has been problematic in practice and contested in theory."[95]

---

[93] The title of ch. 2 in Ferguson and Mansbach, *Polities*.

[94] See Mansbach and Ferguson, "Global Politics at the Turn of the Millennium."

[95] Stephen D. Krasner, "Westphalia and All That," in Goldstein and Keohane, *Ideas and Foreign Policy*, pp. 235, 237. See also Stephen D. Krasner, "Abiding Sovereignty," *International Political Science Review* 22:3 (July 2001), pp. 229–251.

One of the hallmarks of the postinternational world is the declining role of territoriality. During the growth and institutionalization of Europe's states, territory was the basis of security, wealth, and prestige; and it characterized virtually every aspect of the international world. Much of this is changing in the postinternational world, as we shall see in Chapter 3.

3   Political space and time

The confusion of territory with political space by international relations theorists has seriously limited their recognition of profound changes in global politics. *Political space refers to the ways in which identities and loyalties among adherents to various polities are distributed and related, and territorial space is only one of the possibilities.* Conceptualizing space as exclusively territorial and contemplating time as though it were distinct from space reflect what Jonathan Boyarin calls "close genealogical links between the 'Cartesian coordinates' of space and time and the discrete, sovereign state, both associated with European society since the Renaissance. These links include relations of mapping, boundary setting, inclusion, and exclusion."[1]

Political space can actually be organized in many other ways than territory, and new technologies are facilitating reorganization. During Europe's Middle Ages, as well as in the run up to the Treaties of Augsburg and Westphalia, political, military, and economic power was tied to landed holdings. This fact, plus the presence of a large number of independent states in a relatively small area, help explain why the continental power tradition flourished in both theory and practice. As its connection with actual land decreased in importance, the concept of space also changed, until today territory remains only one of many ways to define the extent of a polity's domain, that is, the political space that it occupies.

[1] Jonathan Boyarin, "Space, Time, and the Politics of Memory," in Jonathan Boyarin, ed., *Remapping Memory: The Politics of Time Space* (Minneapolis: University of Minnesota Press, 1994), p. 4.

The parting of space and time

Consider what the following have in common or, as Rosenau asks with regard to individual cases, "of what is this an instance?"[2] – a speculative assault on the Russian ruble, a nuclear submarine silently making its way under the Arctic icepack, a computer espionage probe of the Lawrence Livermore National Laboratory,[3] satellite surveillance of military targets in Afghanistan, a cyberattack on the California power grid, the use of electronic cash in Korea, an Arab-language television broadcast of an Osama bin Laden diatribe, and a cyberspace "meeting" of exiled Burmese opposition leaders? The answer is twofold. First, all reflect the declining significance of physical distance in limiting influence or effective control. Until recently, it was assumed, in Kenneth Boulding's construction, "that each nation's strength is a maximum at its home base," called "its home strength." Boulding expressed this idea in his a "law of diminishing strength," summarized as "the further, the weaker; that is, the further from home any nation has to operate, the longer will be its lines of communication, and the less strength it can put in the field."[4] Herman M. Schwartz concludes that until the use of railroads, "virtually all economic, social, and political life" took place within about 20 miles of market towns, and he cites Charles Tilly's observation that in 1490 the average radius of most European polities was only 50 miles or about the distance a band of men on horse could travel in a day.[5] By contrast, the 9/11 terrorist attack on the United States and the economic meltdown that began in 1997 in Southeast Asia and soon thereafter infected Hong Kong and Korea, spread to Russia, and even reached the Western Hemisphere bear witness to the declining protection offered by physical distance or sovereign frontiers in a postinternational world.

Depending upon the distance from the center to the periphery of any polity or system, it was assumed there was an almost inevitable time lag between when events took place, the transmission of news of such events, and the generation of authoritative commands back and forth

---

[2] James N. Rosenau and Mary Durfee, *Thinking Theory Thoroughly: Coherent Approaches to an Incoherent World* (Boulder, CO: Westview Press, 1995), p. 3.

[3] On the Livermore Laboratory attack and that upon the California grid, see Richard A. Love, "The Cyberthreat Continuum," in Maryann Cusimano Love, ed., *Beyond Sovereignty: Issues for a Global Agenda* (Belmont, CA: Wadsworth/Thomson, 2003), pp. 195–217.

[4] Kenneth E. Boulding, *Conflict and Defense: A General Theory* (New York: Harper & Row, 1962), pp. 230, 231.

[5] Herman M. Schwartz, *States Versus Markets*, 2nd ed. (New York: St. Martin's, 2000), p. 13. For an analysis of why "most warmaking on land" was until recently a "short-distance activity," see John Keegan, *A History of Warfare* (New York: Alfred A. Knopf, 1993), pp. 301–315.

between center and periphery. The fact that political change at the periphery outpaced communication with the center is why decisions often had to be taken by officials on the spot (as in British India and South Africa), whether reluctantly or not. Today, as the relationship between space and time shifts and such lags become shorter and shorter, theorists must grapple with the implications of the "dislocation of space from time," as Giddens describes it.[6] In the present era, technology has redefined what Boyarin expresses as "our possible experiences of 'proximity' and 'simultaneity'."[7]

The fact of physical distance placed limits on central authority structures and imperial expansion and provided opportunities for and sometimes even compelled local polities to exercise autonomy. It also facilitated construction of local institutions able to resist or dilute externally imposed cultural hegemony. The extent to which a polity could overcome the inherent limits of distance – as Rome did through its complex network of imperial roads and waterborne transport – helped determine its long-term viability and capacity for growth. Today, however, the once close link between physical distance and time is weakening.

Like physical distance and time, geographic and psychological distances were historically closely related, but the two conceptualizations of distance are *not* the same. *Psychological distance is the degree of dissimilarity between cognitive frameworks or ways of looking at, assigning meaning to, and coping with the world* regardless of geographic distance. Where there is great psychological distance, the probability of misperception or misunderstanding and, therefore, conflict, is high, and the prospect for forming and sustaining a moral community is low. Today, it can no longer be assumed that perceptions of difference and the absence of empathy increase with physical distance and decrease with proximity. Technological change and the advent of globalized economic and cultural systems make it possible to maintain relative intimacy even at great physical distance. It is both the material and psychological dimensions of this situation to which Wallerstein is alluding when he observes that: "Coreness and peripherality, being relational, are not always geographically separated. The two kinds of activity may well coexist within the same square mile."[8]

---

[6] Anthony Giddens, *The Consequences of Modernity* (Stanford, CA: Stanford University Press, 1990), p. 19.
[7] Boyarin, "Space, Time, and the Politics of Memory," p. 13.
[8] Immanuel Wallerstein, "The Inter-state Structure of the Modern World-system," in Smith, Booth, and Zalewski, eds., *International Theory*, p. 88.

Psychological distance is as much a product of time as of space, and psychological distance can be lengthened by time alone, regardless of geography. In the postinternational era, time is effectively speeding up. French historian Fernand Braudel distinguished three types of change over time. The fastest consisted of day-to-day events in the lives of individuals; the second, slower than the first, entailed economic and political change that is the result of aggregating daily events; and the slowest, which was almost imperceptible in past centuries, included basic changes in the way people live.[9] Today, it is ever more difficult to maintain this distinction as the three merge, especially and importantly the last two. As Rosenau suggests, Braudel might today have to "differentiate immediate events in terms of days and weeks, conjunctural trends in terms of months and years, and the *longue dureé* in terms of decades."[10]

Until the late twentieth century, people could expect that the world into which they were born would remain much the same during their lives. The world of children, including even the potential for cataclysmic events, tended to resemble that of parents and grandparents. Generation "gaps," if they existed at all, were relatively modest. By contrast, today, the lengthening of life and the acceleration of change mean that a newborn child can anticipate not one but several generation gaps in his/her lifetime. Such gaps provide additional sources of potential identity and societal cleavages.

Moreover, different demographic patterns, combined with relative ease of migration across long distances, have led to vastly increased movements of persons from densely populated and impoverished societies with surpluses of young people to highly developed societies with slowing population growth rates and aging citizens. Such movements have already had profound consequences for Europe and North America in a variety of ways – growing social heterogeneity, cultural collisions and cultural dilution, remittances back home, "people smuggling," political battles over immigration policies, and so forth.

Global socioeconomic processes produce enormous cognitive gaps not only between generational and age cohorts but also between "modern" and "traditional" segments of society. At any moment, different societies or social segments are located at different historical points, with

---

[9] Fernand Braudel, *On History*, trans. Sarah Matthews (Chicago: University of Chicago Press, 1980), p. 3ff.
[10] Rosenau, *Along the Domestic-Foreign Frontier*, p. 24.

institutional forms and identities from various epochs. Thus, some societies and their institutions retain features from medieval Europe, tribal America, or even prehistory even while other segments have been globalized by modernity. Just as major cities (despite their internal diversity) have become islands of relative modernity and postmodernity, so every continent is dotted with peoples and places living in premodern settings and "off the grid." And the psychological distance between premodernity and postmodernity is infinitely greater than that between peoples from different cultures who are living at the same developmental moment.

Some of the biggest gaps and, therefore, the greatest psychological distances separate modernized urban elites from traditional agrarian peasants (many of whom are living in transition in urban shanty towns) within the *same* societies. In China, for example, political and social tensions are intensified by the presence of a modernizing and entrepreneurial elite in coastal cities such as Shanghai and Hong Kong amidst what remains a largely agrarian country. Increasingly, psychological distance also separates the ideas and norms of communist party leaders in Beijing from those of neoliberal communists to the south. And in Turkey, secular and urbanized "European" Muslims in Istanbul look westward, even as masses of peasants in Anatolia turn their eyes in the other direction.

The tastes and norms of new urban elites, integrated in the global economy – whether in Caracas, New York, or Karachi – have little in common with the much larger and poorer underclass that has grown throughout the course of massive urbanization. The elites can sometimes see that underclass from their office windows and cannot avoid viewing it through car or taxi windows or bumping up against it on crowded sidewalks. When peasants stream into urban centers like Rio de Janeiro and Mexico City, modernity and traditionalism come face to face, a situation that engenders endemic crime or civil violence. Under these conditions, physical distance no longer easily translates into psychological distance. In sum, people living within sight of one another in cities may – owing to age, education, or earnings – be psychologically remote, even as elites living around the world may – owing to modern technology, education, and norms – feel psychologically proximate.

Second, the examples with which we began this chapter reflect the declining relevance of territory more generally in global politics and the proliferation of alternative conceptions of political space. Put bluntly, territory is not as important as it once was, especially in economically and technologically advanced regions of the world. It still matters most in less advanced regions, especially a few unique concentrations of natural resources (for example, oil-rich Kuwait), durable strategic locations like the Golan Heights, and the putative "homelands" of ethnic minorities such as Palestine. And the latter is really more a matter of identity and psychological longing than it is material welfare, and such minorities regularly challenge sovereign authority and boundaries.[11]

Yet the widespread belief that Westphalian States are somehow special among polities owes much to the belief that their territoriality and the "mutually agreed upon spatial parameters, that is, borders"[12] that enclose them and are guaranteed by sovereignty give them a unique status. Along with hierarchy in which government acts as an authoritative surrogate for subjects or citizens, exclusive control of territory is the defining attribute of the Westphalian State.[13] For Ruggie, the "central attribute of modernity in international politics has been a peculiar and historically unique configuration of territorial space";[14] for Rosenau, "citizenship is rooted in territoriality";[15] and, for Agnew and Corbridge: "The merging of the state with a clearly bounded territory is the geographic essence of the field of international relations."[16] The declining role of territory is, therefore, essential to the transformation of the international world into a postinternational one, especially in producing new identities and redefining old ones.

However clear some of their frontiers were, most pre-Westphalian polities were not constrained by a fixed territory. Ruggie declares: "Writing of Mongol tribes, [Owen] Lattimore pointed out that no single pasture would have had much value for them because it soon would have become exhausted."[17] Mongolia remains much the same even today, with most Mongolians opposing privatization of land even after the end of Marxist rule in that country. Territory also played a relatively small role in the Islamic Empire that flourished between the seventh and eleventh centuries AD. That empire, described by Adda Bozeman

---

[11] We must distinguish between irredentism (claims to lost lands) and secession (withdrawal from an existing polity). See James Mayall, *Nationalism and International Society* (Cambridge: Cambridge University Press, 1990), pp. 55–69.

[12] Spruyt, *The Sovereign State and its Competitors*, p. 17.   [13] *Ibid.*, p. 38.

[14] John Gerard Ruggie, "Territoriality and Beyond: Problematizing Modernity in International Relations," *International Organization* 47:1 (Winter 1993), pp. 143, 144.

[15] Rosenau, *Along the Domestic-Foreign Frontier*, p. 276.

[16] Agnew and Corbridge, *Mastering Space*, p. 80.

[17] Ruggie, "Territoriality and Beyond," p. 149.

as an "empire-in-motion" and "the greatest of all caravans,"[18] was, like the later Mongol and Ottoman Empires, a "tribal empire."[19]

Changes in the role of territory did not happen overnight. Transnationalism and interdependence have been thickening in recent centuries, with backsliding during times of war and economic crisis. The decline in transportation costs after the late nineteenth century began to link national economies closer and closer together.[20] Today, "globalization" is the somewhat vague buzzword used to refer to these trends collectively, pointing to features like microelectronics technology,[21] that bind peoples around the world regardless of state boundaries. It points, too, to features that touch everyone's life through such consequences as pollution, disease, changing identities and values, aroused and alienated citizenries, and differential human welfare. Whatever the precise definition of globalization, it emphasizes the nonterritorial aspects of global life.[22]

Before leaving this topic, it should be noted that implicit in this conception of globalization is the idea that globalization is independent of and perhaps even to some extent in opposition to the preferences and efforts of states. However, there is a very different story in which the features of globalization are actually the fruit of the preferences and efforts of at least *some* states such as the United States and other modernizers.

Alternative conceptions of political space

Those who regard global politics as synonymous with international politics – that is, no more than a system of sovereign states – tend to confuse political space with territory. Territory no more exhausts the possible ways of delineating political space than the state exhausts the ways we organize ourselves for political ends. "[S]ystems of rule," as Ruggie suggests, "need not be territorial at all ... [E]ven where systems

---

[18] Bozeman, *Politics and Culture in International History*, p. 366.

[19] Michael W. Doyle, *Empires* (Ithaca, NY: Cornell University Press, 1986), pp. 105–108.

[20] Thomas L. Friedman, *The Lexus and the Olive Tree* (New York: Farrar, Straus and Giroux, 1999), pp. xv–xvi.

[21] See Richard Langhorne, *The Coming of Globalization: Its Evolution and Contemporary Consequences* (New York: Palgrave, 2001).

[22] For a skeptical view of the idea that the erosion of territoriality produces "the primacy of transnational arrangements and global identities in relation to states" (p. 391), see Edward Comor, "The Role of Communication in Global Civil Society: Forces, Processes, Prospects," *International Studies Quarterly* 45:3 (September 2001), pp. 389–408.

of rule are territorial . . . the prevailing concept of territory need not entail mutual exclusion."[23]

As we shall see in Chapter 5, individuals have multiple identities and under suitable conditions may develop loyalties to a variety of authorities. Political space is, for political philosopher Sheldon Wolin, that area "where the plans, ambitions, and actions of individuals and groups incessantly jar against each other – colliding, blocking, coalescing, separating."[24] In other words, political space is composed of varied patterns of authority that shape and determine value allocation. It delineates what is "inside" political communities from what is "outside," but it does more than that. Marx, for example, thought of political space in terms of class. Like class, caste, ethnicity, gender, and other potential categories of identity are largely nonterritorial conceptions in which members or adherents can occupy the same geographic location and in which identities, loyalties, and authorities can and often do overlap. Those identity categories that develop sufficient institutionalization and capacity to mobilize adherents may become polities.

Multiple identities, the proliferation of nonterritorial authorities, the porosity of state boundaries, and the increasingly diffuse nature of threats all contribute to diminishing the role of territoriality in global politics, and to fostering a growing gap between the distribution of effective authority in global politics and the map of a world divided into territorial boxes. The boundaries that separate territorial states from one another increasingly *do not* demarcate political spaces based on economic, social, or cultural interests. Each of these has its own boundaries that in the face of localization and globalization are less and less compatible with the border of states. Indeed, the boundaries that separate advanced elites that are tied into the global economy and culture from the poor in ever-expanding *favellas* within the same urban centers are probably more difficult to cross than those that separate citizens of the same class or profession in different states from one another.

The manner in which political space is organized has important theoretical implications. Thus, the conception of political space as largely synonymous with territory poses a barrier to theory-building in global politics today, rather like, according to Wolin, identification of politics with the Greek *polis* posed a problem for Roman political thinkers when they sought to apply Greek ideas based on a system of small city-states

---

[23] Ruggie, "Territoriality and Beyond," p. 149.
[24] Sheldon Wolin, *Politics and Vision: Continuity and Innovation in Western Political Thought* (Boston: Little, Brown, 1960), p. 16.

to a growing imperial polity. "[I]n Greek thought," he writes, "the concept of the political had become identified with the determinate spatial dimension of the *polis*."

> The rigid limits that Plato and Aristotle had set for the size and population of their ideal cities and the detailed attention that they devoted to matters of birth control, wealth and commerce, colonial and military expansion were part of their belief that the life of the *polis*, which they considered synonymous with its political character, could be articulated only within the narrow confines of the small city-state . . . This total absorption with a small, highly compact community imparted to Greek political thought a nervous intensity which contrasts sharply, for example, with the mood of later Stoicism which leisurely . . . contemplated political life as it was acted out amidst a setting as spacious as the universe itself.[25]

And theory about Europe's multipolar world of sovereign states, like Plato's theory about Greece's world of city-states, was "shaped to overcome the jostling anarchy unendurable in a crowded political condition."[26] However, the linking of political space to the nature of political life is nowhere more vividly described than in Wolin's characterization of Machiavelli's Italy in which ascriptive medieval identities of older elites were losing their legitimacy: "Minds that knew no repose, ambitions that were boundless, an insatiable pride, a restless species of political man . . . all of these considerations conspired to shrink political space, to create a dense and overcrowded world. A terrain with few areas open for unrestricted movement left one course for the politically ambitious: to dislodge those already occupying specific areas."[27]

Political space and medieval Europe

Perhaps the most widely discussed spatial alternative to Westphalian territoriality is Europe's medieval "system of segmented territorial rule," described by Ruggie, as having "none of the connotations of possessiveness and exclusiveness conveyed by the modern concept of sovereignty . . . a heteronomous organization of territorial rights and claims – of political space."[28] Unlike the interstate world, that system

---

[25] *Ibid.*, p. 72.   [26] *Ibid.*   [27] *Ibid.*, p. 218.
[28] John Gerard Ruggie, "Continuity and Transformation in the World Polity: Toward a Neorealist Synthesis," *World Politics* 35:2 (January 1983), p. 275. See also Bruce Cronin and Joseph Lepgold, "A New Medievalism? Conflicting International Authorities and Competing Loyalties in the Twenty-First Century," paper delivered at February 1995 Annual Meeting of the International Studies Association.

"reflected 'a patchwork of overlapping and incomplete rights of government,' which were 'inextricably superimposed and tangled,' and in which 'different juridical instances were geographically interwoven and stratified, and plural allegiances, asymmetrical suzerainties and anomalous enclaves abounded'." Thereafter: "The rediscovery from Roman law of the concept of absolute private property and the simultaneous emergence of mutually exclusive territorial state formations, which stood in relation to one another much as owners of private estates do"[29] produced "a 'legitimation crisis' of staggering proportions."[30] Thus, the shift from medieval to territorial polities, like the erosion of the latter in recent decades, was accompanied by what Rosenau calls a "turbulent environment"[31] and "*a world crisis of authority.*"[32] Such crises may take place and medieval structures may emerge, argues historian Joseph Strayer, when large political units no longer provide adherents with psychological or economic satisfaction;[33] that is, the result of fission.

Like the postinternational world, Europe's Middle Ages lacked a clear distinction between a "domestic" and "foreign" realm (or "inside" and "outside"), the absence of which made it impossible to distinguish clearly between public and private property, private and "national" interests, or between war and crime. Political life featured complex jurisdictions, shared loyalties, and competing identities, the absence of perceptions of "exclusive" authority. It lacked a clear distinction between public and private spheres and goods.[34] Multiple loci of authority produced a system that was "decentralized even by the standards of similar regimes elsewhere,"[35] even at a time when the mythology built on an ideal of a "Christian community" produced a sense of cultural and

---

[29] Ruggie, "Continuity and Transformation in the World Polity," pp. 274, 276. Ruggie is citing Perry Anderson, *Lineages of the Absolutist State* (London: New Left Books, 1974), pp. 37–38.

[30] Ruggie, "Continuity and Transformation in the World Polity." We must be careful about following Ruggie too closely on the relationship between "property" and "sovereignty" because there are differences in the Anglo-American and Continental traditions of defining private property. Continental thinkers have often viewed "private" property as owned and managed by the state, whereas Anglo-American scholars have emphasized a traditional of individual ownership. These differences have important implications for discussing the future of sovereignty in a postinternational world.

[31] Rosenau, *Turbulence in World Politics*, p. 59.

[32] Rosenau, "A Pre-Theory Revisited," p. 246. Emphasis in original.

[33] Joseph Strayer, *On the Medieval Origins of the Modern State* (Princeton: Princeton University Press, 1970), p. 14.

[34] Spruyt, *The Sovereign State and its Competitors*, p. 35.

[35] Martin van Creveld, *The Rise and Decline of the State* (Cambridge: Cambridge University Press, 1999), p. 59.

ideological solidarity, at least among elites.[36] When Rome collapsed, political and economic space again became largely local. Organizational forms, declares Michael Mann, "were confined within the intense local relationships of the village or tribe, plus a loose and unstable confederation beyond," and economic relations were limited largely to "small-scale, decentralized units of production, controlled by a lord using the labor of dependent peasants."[37] The medieval Church was an exception to this; its "law and morality represented long-distance regulation" that "was particularly important for trade,"[38] and, in Harold Berman's felicitous phrase, its clergy were "the first translocal, transtribal, transfeudal, transnational class in Europe to achieve legal and political unity."[39]

Like the postinternational world, the medieval system was home to a wide variety of polity types. Within the Holy Roman Empire, even after 1648, there were, according to Krasner, at least four additional types of polities – "ecclesiastical states, imperial cities, estates of imperial counts and knights, and secular states."[40] Lacking a fully territorial conception of space, Europe's feudal system was, as Spruyt argues, "rule over people rather than land," and "rule was reinforced by the special legal status of nobility and by the particular legitimation of their authority."[41] So too was precolonial Africa, which Jeffrey Herbst likens to medieval Europe. Herbst maintains that it was folly to assume that "the new states would take on features that had previously characterized sovereignty, most notably unquestioned physical control over the defined territory, but also an administrative presence throughout the country and the allegiance of the population to the idea of the state." In contrast to Europe's Westphalian epoch (but similar to the medieval situation), in precolonial Africa "control tended to be exercised over people rather than land," and "sovereignty tended to be shared."[42]

---

[36] Duality of loyalty was evident in the third Crusade when England's King Richard and France's King Philip were forced to march together to the Holy Land because they feared what the other might do if left alone in Europe.

[37] Mann, *The Sources of Social Power*, vol. I, pp. 337, 336.   [38] *Ibid.*, p. 337.

[39] Harold Berman, *Law and Revolution: The Formation of the Western Legal Tradition* (Cambridge, MA: Harvard University Press, 1983), p. 108.

[40] Krasner, "Westphalia and All That," p. 247.

[41] Spruyt, *The Sovereign State and its Competitors*, p. 40. He adds: "One speaks, therefore, of the king of the English (Rex Anglorum) in the twelfth century, rather than the king of England (Rex Anglie)."

[42] Jeffrey Herbst, "Responding to State Failure in Africa," *International Security* 21:3 (Winter 1996/97), pp. 121–122, 127, 128. This description could apply today to most nonstate polities as well.

The similarity between medieval Europe and the world that is emerging today makes it fashionable to suggest that we are experiencing a sort of "new medievalism." All five of the trends that Hedley Bull identified in 1977 as possible harbingers of a "new medievalism" – regional integration of states, disintegration of states, restoration of private international violence, transnational organizations, and technological unification of the world[43] – have become plainly visible. Like medieval Europe, today's world is a crazy-quilt of polities in continual evolution; and, like medieval Europe, "the distinction between 'internal' and 'external' political realms, separated by clearly demarcated 'boundaries'"[44] makes little sense. The resulting turbulence – whether pitting state authorities against ethnic or tribal entities, corporate or financial institutions, local authorities, or even regional polities – provides, as Krasner says of the era during which the modern Westphalian polity took shape, "a political and geographic space within which a new political form" can emerge.[45] With the erosion of "mutually exclusive territorial state formations" that distinguished Westphalian from medieval Europe, the idea of a new medievalism has put down deeper roots. Thus, Stephen Kobrin cites the declining relevance of "the idea of geography as a basis for the organization of politics and economics" as one of six changes in the international political economy that augur such a new medievalism.[46]

Nevertheless, we must be cautious about accepting the medieval metaphor because it is misleading in at least two important respects. First, it seems to suggest (once again) that the Europeans were somehow "special," when most of the segmentary political patterns that characterized that era were present everywhere – to differing degrees, of course, in different areas and eras – throughout much of history. For thousands of years, polities of various types around the world have expanded and contracted; layered and nested; and coexisted, cooperated, competed, and conflicted. They have competed not only through the exercise of

---

[43] Bull, *The Anarchical Society*, pp. 264–276.
[44] Ruggie, "Continuity and Transformation in the World Polity," p. 274.
[45] Krasner, "Westphalia and All That," p. 253.
[46] Stephen J. Kobrin, "Back to the Future: Neomedievalism and the Postmodern Digital World Economy," *Journal of International Affairs* 51:2 (Spring 1998), p. 369. The six changes he cites are in "space, geography and borders," "the ambiguity of authority," "multiple loyalties," "transnational elites," "distinctions between public and private property," and "unifying belief systems and supranational centralization" (p. 366). Gidon Gottlieb offers the medieval analogy as an alternative to a territorially organized world. *Nation Against State: A New Approach to Ethnic Conflicts and the Decline of Sovereignty* (New York: Council on Foreign Relations Press, 1993), pp. 37–38.

coercion but also through ideological appeals and the provision of material and psychological benefits to adherents.

Second, the idea of a new medievalism stresses the differences between the medieval period and the interstate era that followed, when we might equally emphasize the continuity and similarities that make Krasner cautious about not overestimating Westphalia or sovereignty. *In a very real sense – given the extent to which governance, as a practical day-to-day matter, is inherently decentralized (in the sense it is always exercised by a great variety of polities), it may be a mistake ever to search for a dominant polity or polity type.* Moreover, insofar as numerous authorities exercise control or influence – that is, "govern" – in their respective and sometimes overlapping realms, there has virtually never been an absence of "order" and "rules." *Anarchy* is an inappropriate description of global politics in *any* era, unless one is making the obvious point that there is no world government. By contrast, there has always been governance, although not until recently has it begun to be in some limited respects genuine global governance.

In addition, it is important to reiterate that when the medieval system eroded, Europe's political architecture was contingent, not inevitable, and there were a variety of alternative spatial arrangements available. The Westphalian State, as Spruyt observes, "arose because of a particular conjuncture of social and political interests in Europe"[47] during and after the Middle Ages and weathered the challenge of other polities – Italian city-states and the Hanseatic city league – because its territorial logic mobilized societies more effectively and organized relations among units more efficiently than did its rivals.[48] Unlike medieval political and economic space, which was essentially local, Westphalian States extended their territorial reach by institutionalizing hierarchy and pacifying the king's adversaries and competitors. The state also provided a definition of "us" based on residence in a common territory rather than "blood" kinship as in tribes in Africa, the Americas, and the Middle East, or lineage as in medieval Europe and China.

Political space and the Westphalian epoch

Had either the Roman Church or Holy Roman Empire triumphed in their long feud with each other, an imperial political form similar to that which evolved in China following the warring states era might have emerged, instead of the system of competing territorial states that

---

[47] Spruyt, *The Soviereign State and its Competitors*, pp. 18–19.   [48] *Ibid.*, p. 28.

actually did emerge. Nevertheless, there were moments, as during the Crusades or the formation of alliances to fight Turk and Tartar, during which a conception of Europe as a unified cultural construct temporarily dominated the territorial state model, much as a conception of common Hellenic civilization briefly enabled Greece's feuding city-states to ally against the Persians. In China, too, culture and language, rather than geography or territory, often defined political space. In consequence, according to Gerrit W. Gong: "Tradition dictated that China deal with the Europeans not in accordance with the developing European philosophy that states represented by respected plenipotentiaries interact as sovereign equals, but rather in accordance with the Confucian patterns and principles which demanded that all from near and far acknowledge China's standard of 'civilization'."[49]

China continues to adapt its Confucian traditions to contemporary conditions and attempts to reconcile divisions between empire and regions – and various ethnicities – that are as old as the civilization itself. The memory of China's durable civilization even today unites disparate communities: "China today is an amalgam of aspects of Chinese tradition, Stalinism, and the East Asian economic model as found in places like Taiwan and Singapore. This amalgam, created by revolution, is being tested by the forces unleashed by reform . . . China, after all, is not the regime created by Mao and partly dismantled by Deng. *It is a civilization, even a world.*"[50]

The dominance of territorial states in Europe that, as Rousseau phrased it, touched "each other at so many points that not one of them can move without giving a jar to all the rest"[51] and the absence of supranational ideology or institutions fostered the perception of an interstate security dilemma. This perceived dilemma fanned a technological arms race that provided Europeans with weapons unavailable to non-Europeans and encouraged Europeans to make use of innovations such as gunpowder that had actually been invented elsewhere.[52] In addition,

---

[49] Gerrit W. Gong, "China's Entry Into International Society," in Hedley Bull and Adam Watson, eds., *The Expansion of International Society* (Oxford: Clarendon Press, 1984), p. 174.
[50] Arthur Waldron, "After Deng the Deluge: China's Next Leap Forward," *Foreign Affairs* 74:5 (September/October 1995), p. 153. Emphasis in original.
[51] Jean-Jacques Rousseau, "Abstract of the Abbé de Saint-Pierre's Project for Perpetual Peace," in M. G. Forsyth, H. M. A. Keens-Soper, and P. Savigear, eds., *The Theory of International Relations* (New York: Atherton Press, 1970), p. 136.
[52] William H. McNeill, *The Pursuit of Power: Technology, Armed Force, and Society since A.D.1000* (Chicago: University of Chicago Press, 1982), p. 118.

the invention of sovereignty combined with suitable applications of coercion afforded Europe's rulers access to most of the resources of the territory over which they ruled. Secular and specialized bureaucracies provided the organizational skills to collect the taxes and other resources essential to state power.[53] In this way, Europe's states could build larger and better-equipped armies and navies than could the tribal or personalist polities with which they collided, first in the Americas and later in Asia and Africa. Thereafter, a territorial conception of political space was extended beyond Europe and, in the process, was imposed upon older competing conceptions of political space.

From territoriality to postterritoriality

The past three centuries (more or less) constitute the territorial epoch in global politics. That epoch is ending. A postinternational epoch is, in many crucial respects, a postterritorial epoch.

Let us not over-do this argument. Sometimes states find themselves disadvantaged by being chained to a particular territory. Although the relationship between influence and physical distance has diminished, Haiti, Mexico, and Cuba still feel the proximity of their neighbor, the United States. Of course, citizens in many states still depend upon their national governments for physical protection and a minimum standard of welfare, and some citizens are victims of state repression. As for TNCs, corporate physical plant facilities are less "footloose" than investment capital, and a firm's being situated in a particular country's legal jurisdiction does pose constraints (assuming the influence flows from government to firm rather than the other way around). Conversely, TNCs may find state regulations useful to help curb market abuses and uncertainty.

However, as observed earlier, respect for territorial frontiers, to the extent it continues to exist, paradoxically, is substantially a consequence of the declining importance of territory and of the boundaries that delineate it. More territory no longer (if it ever did) necessarily translates into more power[54] or wealth, nor less territory into less power or wealth, witness Singapore and Hong Kong. In many respects, territory counts (and accounts) for less and less.

---

[53] Charles Tilly, *The Formation of Nation-States in Western Europe* (Princeton: Princeton University Press, 1975). p. 29.

[54] See John Agnew, "Political Power and Geographical Scale," in Ferguson and Jones, eds., *Political Space*, pp. 115–129.

Today, occupation of territory is often a source of weakness rather than strength in the face of politically conscious and mobilized masses. Where it took few Europeans to conquer the likes of India, Algeria, and Indochina in earlier centuries, no number of highly armed European soldiers would have sufficed to retain imperial control by the late twentieth century. Russia's experience in Afghanistan and Chechnya is a metaphor for the fate of unwanted occupiers everywhere, as is America's in Vietnam and, as argued by opponents, America's efforts in Afghanistan and Iraq. Moreover, as we have noted, other boundaries diverge from those demarcating sovereign territory – economic, cultural, and ethnic among others. And in those cases where territory still matters – for example, along the frontiers of Russia, Kuwait, Israel/Palestine, Kashmir, Tibet – it has hardly been left uncontested.

Nor does territoriality apply to many of the most critical issues in global politics. No one who experienced economic collapse in Asia or Argentina doubts the reality of the global capital market even though it does not appear on a map. And cyberspace has its own rules (see Chapter 8). After all: "Traders do not need to come to market any more because computer networks can take markets to traders, wherever they are . . . Younger American exchanges, such as Nasdaq, cannot be said to be based anywhere in particular. Nor can its new online brokers, such as E*Trade, whose services are directly available through any computer hooked up to the Internet."[55]

Terrorists, religions, and nongovernmental organizations like Greenpeace have their own nonterritorial conceptions of space. Indeed, many flows of ideas, persons, and things – as well as the TNCs and mafias that Strange labeled "counter-authority"[56] to the state – do not appear on standard maps. Instead, all exist in political spaces that do not conform to familiar nation-state boundaries.

This fact has produced some imaginative spatial analogies, including that of Moisés Naím. Naím argues that the 1994 economic crisis in Mexico, the controversial bankruptcy of Orange County in California, and the collapse of Barings Bank had "some common characteristics":

> In all three cases, mismanagement and speculation played important roles. More important, however, is that all three entities fell victim to an international financial system that offers sweeping new opportunities but also inflicts immediate, lethal punishments on those who make the

[55] "Capitals of Capital," *The Economist*, special report, May 9–11, 1998, pp. 3, 5.
[56] Strange, *The Retreat of the State*, p. 93. Also pp. 110–121.

wrong calls ... In the past, the main international actors in the unfolding of a country's economic collapse were international commercial banks, the IMF, and the World Bank. Now, the priority of the finance minister of any troubled country is to persuade money managers and other private institutional actors not to take their money out ... Today, the magnitude of funds controlled by private investment managers makes the volumes typically supplied by the IMF and the World Bank almost irrelevant.

Naím highlights what he terms the growing "neighborhood effect":

In the aftermath of the latest Mexican crisis, financial markets moved to attack currencies in Thailand, Spain, Hong Kong, Sweden, Italy, and Russia, substantially weakening them. The Canadian dollar hit an eight-year low against the US dollar, and financial markets in Poland, South Korea, Turkey, Nigeria, Bulgaria, India, Malaysia, Hungary, Pakistan, and the Philippines all experienced sharp drops ... The Mexican crises of 1982 and 1994 show that increasingly financial markets tend to cluster those countries perceived to be in the same "neighborhood" and to treat them roughly along the same lines. This time, however, the neighborhood is no longer defined solely in terms of geography. The main defining criterion is the potential volatility of the countries; the contagion spread inside risk-clusters, or volatility neighborhoods.[57]

In trying to describe the changing nature of political space in Europe, Christer Jönsson, Sven Tägil, and Gunnar Törnquist come up with another depiction of a complex reality that is a far cry from an inter-state model. They conclude that the world "is not held together in the manner it used to be. The image that emerges is one of a fragmented territory, an archipelago of self-reliant regions linked together through different types of networks."[58]

Territorial polities seem old-fashioned and stodgy next to actors that are increasingly transterritorial and even nonterritorial. For their part, states are seeking new ways to overcome territorial limitations. They create or collaborate with international institutions that pursue collective goals and that offer or manage some extension of state political capacity and authority. States form tacit alliances with transnational corporations and banks, as well as with various nongovernmental organizations. Bureaucrats and other networks in different countries increasingly

[57] Moíses Naím, "Mexico's Larger Story," *Foreign Policy* 99 (Summer 1995), pp. 121–23, 125.
[58] Christer Jönsson, Sven Tägil, and Gunnar Törnquist, *Organizing European Space* (London: Sage, 2000), p. 152.

exchange information and coordinate policies and actions quietly, especially in technical areas. A few countries, not least the superpower or hegemon, the United States, send their military or police beyond their frontiers (sometimes in violation of international law, which is, after all, the law of states) to capture terrorists and drug kingpins, or they assert extraterritorial authority in an attempt to prevent foreign firms and foreign subsidiaries of indigenous corporations from dealing with adversaries such as Iran and Cuba.

A number of long-term interstate conflicts, especially in areas of the developing world that resist postinternational change, such as those involving Palestine and Kashmir, continue to reflect the critical role of territory. Nevertheless, as territoriality becomes less important and as the wall between "foreign" and "domestic" crumbles, the essential bases of sovereignty, as we shall see in the following chapters, are coming under siege. Territorial control, the main prerogative of state sovereignty, no longer affords control of ideas and information. Nor does it assure the loyalty or support of politically active citizens. Complex networks of communication, existing largely but not exclusively in cyberspace, undermine the capacity of states to impose hierarchy upon interest groups or individuals and afford nonterritorial polities both wealth and influence.[59]

The false distinctions between domestic, foreign, and comparative politics

The postinternational world belies the contention in much of international-relations theory that one can differentiate and contrast an orderly and pacific domestic realm and an anarchic and bellicose interstate realm. Theoretical progress will be difficult until theorists escape the blinders imposed by a model of separate domestic and foreign realms in favor of a conception of political space that reunites these two aspects of political life, takes account of overlapping[60] and shared authority, and emphasizes dynamic processes of fission and fusion. This means,

---

[59] See, for example, Wolfgang H. Reinecke, "The Other World Wide Web: Global Public Policy Networks," *Foreign Policy* 117 (Winter 1999–2000), pp. 44–57.

[60] Some years ago, Stephen D. Krasner sought to substitute the metaphor of "tectonic plates" for the realist metaphor of global structure as a game of billiards. "Regimes and the Limits of Realism: Regimes as Autonomous Variables," *International Organization* 36:2 (Spring 1982), pp. 497–500. Krasner thought the metaphor could describe international regimes, but it is even more useful for connoting the nesting and potential friction among polities that overlap one another.

as Robert Putnam expresses it, moving "beyond the mere observation that domestic factors influence international affairs and vice versa, and beyond simple catalogs of instances of such influence, to seek theories that integrate both spheres, accounting for the areas of entanglement between them."[61] Modest reform will not do the trick, and, even in his departure from the traditional separation, Putnam maintains it in positing only "two-level games," when, in fact, the generic subject is politics with any number of levels depending on one's theoretical framework and the issues at stake.

In the main, realists and neorealists envision a political world consisting exclusively of states, and they "black box" those states, arguing that the realms of foreign and domestic affairs are autonomous. In their eyes, the national interests of each state depend largely on the distribution of power and nature of threats. Despite persuasive efforts that began as early as the 1950s to show the links between the "domestic" and "international" realms, and to open the black box, and the more recent work on the changing state and the emergence of "new" actors, a good deal of scholarship and teaching still proceeds from the false premise that there is a clear boundary between an anarchic interstate system and a pacific domestic one. Thus, Mearsheimer argues that "states and other political entities behaved according to realist dictates" between 1300 and 1989.[62] Like other structural realists, he speaks of states (whether in 1300 or 1989) as timeless "billiard balls of varying size."[63] Mearsheimer applauds the staying power of realism in light of "the tremendous political and economic changes that have taken place across the world during that lengthy period."[64] Since neither structure nor process has, by his account, changed, it is difficult to decipher what "tremendous" changes he has in mind.

Sovereign states claim to enjoy exclusive control over the space enclosed by their frontiers, but, as we have seen, they actually share authority with a variety of other authorities, some transnational or effectively deterritorialized. This is a key reason why the distinction between interstate and intrastate politics is so tenuous. Like the space defined by a Westphalian State's territorial sovereignty, all polities occupy a discernible *space*, even if in our age of electronic networks, it is

---

[61] Robert D. Putnam, "Diplomacy and Domestic Politics: The Logic of Two-level Games," *International Organization* 42:3 (Summer 1988), p. 433.
[62] John J. Mearsheimer, "The False Promise of International Institutions," *International Security* 19:3 (Winter 1994/95), p. 44.
[63] *Ibid.*, p. 48.   [64] *Ibid.*, pp. 44–45.

"cyberspace."[65] And, like the authority the state enjoys over its citizens and their resources, all polities have an analogous "reach" of sorts, but it is rarely exclusive in the sense connoted by traditional descriptions of sovereign states. Unlike the state system that defined the international world, the postinternational world, as we continue to stress, consists of innumerable polities that layer, overlap, and interact.

Like states, other polities survive and prosper because human beings identify with them, parcel out their loyalties among them, and sometimes feel passionate about them. Those persons who identify with a polity regard it as having authority – although not necessarily exclusive authority – over its domain. All polities, including those that can scarcely be located in a territorial sense, have such a domain that includes those who identify with it, the space they occupy, and the issue(s) over which the polity exercises influence. Like physical space, a capacity to exercise authority or governance is often shared. In terms of authority, polities may be hierarchically layered, partially overlapping, nested, or (rarely) isolated.

European integration has produced particular conceptual difficulties for scholars like Krasner because regional, state, and other authorities occupy the same space as does the European Union. Indeed, the European Union is a hybrid polity that is simultaneously growing in four directions: upwards as greater authority is ceded to Brussels, downward as more decisions are given to and greater interaction takes place at the regional level, across as in the ERASMUS/SOCRATES Program that supports educational improvement and cooperation, beyond as in the Mediterranean program with its efforts to promote a special relationship with the Maghreb.[66] Ruggie uses the example of the European Community and its "transnational microeconomic links" to illustrate the inadequacy of equating territorial control with political authority:

> Consider the global system of transnationalized microeconomic links. Perhaps the best way to describe it . . . is that these links have created a nonterritorial "region" in the world economy – a decentered yet integrated space-of-flows, operating in real time, which exists alongside the space-of-places that we call national economies. These conventional spaces-of-places continue to engage in external economic relations with

---

[65] See, for example, John Agnew, "The Territorial Trap: The Geographical Assumptions of International Relations Theory," *Review of International Political Economy* 1 (Spring 1994), pp. 53–80.
[66] We owe this observation to an anonymous external reviewer.

one another, which we continue to call trade, foreign investment, and the like, and which are more or less effectively mediated by the state. In the nonterritorial global region, however, the conventional distinctions between internal and external . . . are exceedingly problematic, and any given state is but one constraint in corporate global strategic calculations. This is the world in which IBM is Japan's largest computer exporter, and Sony is the largest exporter of television sets from the United States.[67]

"This nonterritorial global economic region," concludes Ruggie, "is a world, in short, that is premised on what Lattimore described as the 'sovereign importance of movement,' not of place."[68]

Michael Keating's and Liesbet Hooghe's description of how overlapping authorities within the same territorial "regions" in the European Union enjoy relatively autonomous political space is an even more complex conceptualization of political space than is Ruggie's. They emphasize that no "homogeneous regional tier of government in the EU" has emerged: "There remain a variety of levels of territorial mobilization: historic nations; large provincial regions; units in federal or quasi-federal states; cities and city regions . . . In some cases, the regions can be identified with a structure of government. In others, civil society or private groups are more important in defining and carrying forward a regional interest." Neither is there a "new regional hierarchy," nor can policymaking "be explained simply by inter-state bargaining." Instead, "national politics are penetrated by European influences through law, bureaucratic contacts, political exchange, and the role of the commission in agenda-setting. Similarly, national politics are penetrated . . . by regional influences." In sum, what seems to be happening is "a Europeanization and a regionalization of national policymaking" coupled with "a Europeanization of the regions and a regionalization of Europe."[69]

Although Europe is a special case, shared political space is a worldwide condition. In the Near East, as elsewhere, such sharing, though relatively informal, is largely a consequence of the widespread historical nesting of polities. Michael Barnett's apt description of the overlapping identities and loyalties among Arabs is applicable in other contexts as well:

[67] John Gerard Ruggie, "Territoriality and Beyond," p. 172.   [68] *Ibid.*
[69] Michael Keating and Liesbet Hooghe, "By-Passing the Nation State? Regions and the EU Policy Process," in Jeremy J. Richardson, ed., *Policy Making in the European Union* (London: Routledge, 1996). For another view of European relationships, discussed in Chapter 4, see Jönsson, Tägil, and Törnqvist, *Organizing European Space.*

Until the late nineteenth century, inhabitants of the Fertile Crescent existed within a variety of overlapping authorities and political structures. The Ottoman Empire, Islam, and local tribal and village structures all contested for and held sway over various features of peoples' lives. While the Ottoman Empire's decline, imperialism, and new ideas of nationalism combined to challenge local political structures and identities, great power intrusions primarily were responsible for setting into motion statist and transnational forces that created a disjuncture between where political authority was to reside and the political loyalties of the inhabitants of the region. Specifically, while the great powers established a new geopolitical map, the political loyalties of the inhabitants enveloped these boundaries and challenged the very legitimacy of that map.[70]

In this case, however, "A map anticipated reality, not vice versa. A map was a model for, rather than a model of, what it purported to represent."[71]

In its most distorting form, the traditional distinction between the foreign and domestic realms contrasts domestic "tranquillity" with international "anarchy." In some respects, the reverse is closer to the truth, as urban centers from Bogotá and Karachi to Moscow and Jerusalem are variously afflicted by organized crime, ethnic conflict, and random terrorism. By contrast, interstate wars thankfully are becoming infrequent if not rare. Notwithstanding Mearsheimer, fewer and fewer theorists any longer claim that *intra*national politics is peaceful and predictable or that the *inter*state realm is invariably violent and unpredictable. Even fewer any longer assert that outcomes in the interstate arena are comprehensible in isolation from intrastate events or vice versa. Indeed, it is difficult to identify a major issue that is not located in both arenas at the same time.

In the grip of habit

Nevertheless, the wall between the two arenas continues to stand (however much in danger of collapse) because theorists, in Wendt's words, treat "the identities and interests of agents as exogenously given."[72] Change notwithstanding, many theorists still subscribe to neorealist Waltz's "ordering principles":

[70] Michael N. Barnett, "Sovereignty, Nationalism, and Regional Order in the Arab States System," *International Organization* 49:3 (Summer 1995), p. 492.
[71] Benedict Anderson, *Imagined Communities*, 2nd ed. (New York: Verso Press, 1991), p. 73.
[72] Alexander Wendt, "Anarchy Is What States Make of it: The Social Construction of Power Politics," *International Organization* 46:2 (Spring 1992), p. 391.

> Domestic systems are centralized and hierarchic. The parts of international-political systems stand in relations of coordination. Formally, each is the equal of all the others. None is entitled to command; none is required to obey. International systems are decentralized and anarchic. The ordering principles of the two structures are distinctly different, indeed, contrary to each other.[73]

Waltz's claim is empirically very misleading. In most contexts there is an abyss between the formal status of governments and their real capacity and influence. Waltz's claim rests on his use of the word "formally" and reflects an ideal type expressed in the legal and logical fiction of sovereignty. It is ironic that such a prominent neorealist should rely so heavily on a "legalistic" premise. Whether one looks at sixteenth-century relations between the Valois kings in France, French Huguenots, and the Catholic League, or between party and government in the twentieth-century Soviet Union, the gap between formal structure and political reality can be striking.

The differences that exist between political arenas are not rooted in the sovereign status of polities or the lack thereof, or in the absence or presence of central government. States vary enormously in terms of capacity and autonomy. Few governments have kept pace with the growing demands of citizens, and in many cases the gap between the demands of citizens and the capacity of governments to satisfy them has become almost impossibly wide.[74] Relations between states range from very violent to entirely peaceful. Internally, states such as Somalia and Liberia have often been violent and chaotic, while others tend to be reasonably ordered. Some states like Belarus are highly penetrated from without, while others are relatively free from external influence. Some are fractured along ethnic, tribal, or religious lines (for example, Sudan, Cyprus, Sri Lanka, Rwanda, or Afghanistan), while others are reasonably homogeneous. These continua are applicable to both inter- and intrastate politics and do not provide criteria for differentiating between the arenas.

However theoretically indefensible is the distinction between inter- and intrastate politics, it does serve mundane interests such as organizing bureaucracies and writing academic job descriptions that, in turn,

---

[73] Waltz, *Theory of International Politics*, p. 88.
[74] Rosenau refers to this phenomenon as the "declining effectiveness" of governments that are unable "to provide their clients . . . with the conditions and services that reflect the goals they have set for themselves and that their clients expect." Rosenau, "A Pre-Theory Revisited," p. 278.

help perpetuate the dichotomy.[75] Other than top political appointees and a congressional liaison, the State Department has few employees who can inform policymakers about the "domestic" effects of foreign policies, and the Intelligence Community is forbidden from taking account of American politics when conducting estimates of developments "out there." Despite the globalization of trade, business, and finance, agencies like the Treasury, Commerce, Agriculture, and Labor still respond to constituents whose focus is primarily domestic. And, of course, members of Congress continually worry about facing the folks back home in the next election. The practical problems posed by domestic–foreign assumptions have been forcefully brought to light in the intelligence failures that preceded the 9/11 attacks, especially FBI–CIA turf battles and failure to communicate vital information.

Accordingly, by the time the effort is made to look at both faces of an issue, it is already subject to the pulling and hauling of bureaucratic and local electoral politics, in which "domestic" and "international" interests are pitted against one another. Resulting policies usually reflect the relative clout of participants rather than "rational" integration of the issue's two faces. Since most issues have consequences for both the intra- and international arenas, it would be preferable if policy formulation took account of both early on, but any effort to reorganize the foreign-policy establishment to achieve this would encounter insurmountable opposition from entrenched interests.

Since some scholars write for practitioners or harbor aspirations to formulate policy in Washington and since practitioners find it convenient to divide the world as did their instructors, it is not surprising that scholarship mirrors practice. However, there are additional, largely nonintellectual, reasons why theorists accept a wall between the interstate and intrastate arenas. From the outset of their careers, graduate students are indoctrinated – by the structure of graduate programs and qualifying examinations, and by the research of instructors and peers – to accept as valid the reality of traditional subfields like international politics (interstate politics), comparative politics (intrastate politics in several societies), and American politics (intrastate politics in a single society). Violating the frontiers among subfields invites difficulty in forming dissertation committees, qualifying for teaching and research

---

[75] The division of the world into two arenas illustrates what Marion J. Levy called "the fallacy of misplaced dichotomies." Levy, "'Does it Matter if He's Naked?' Bawled the Child," in Knorr and Rosenau, *Contending Approaches to International Politics*, p. 95.

assistantships, and "fitting" job descriptions. Even the advertising of teaching positions by academic associations mirrors the standard sub-fields, as do the titles and content of scholarly journals. This is intellectually absurd when almost all important contemporary questions not only require addressing across subfields but across disciplines as well.

Breaching the wall

Practitioners of global politics have arguably been more prepared than theorists to recognize that interstate and intrastate politics cannot be isolated from each other. Even the Peace of Westphalia of 1648, regarded by some to have "legislated into existence" the "system of states,"[76] explicitly sought to defuse the religious controversies that had triggered ferocious communal strife *within* as well as *among* polities during the Thirty Years War. Statesmen in 1815 established the Concert of Europe in part to suppress the sort of *domestic* revolutionary activity that they believed to have been responsible for the wars that ravaged Europe for more than two decades. And in the 1919 Versailles Treaty, world leaders tried to establish the rights of national minorities *within* the countries of Central Europe even as Wilsonian ideology equated democracy at home with global peace worldwide.

For its part, the United Nations has not shied away from intruding into members' internal politics, notwithstanding the Charter's avowal of the sovereign equality of states and its prohibition against intervention "in matters which are essentially within the domestic jurisdiction of any state." When a majority in the General Assembly or Security Council wishes to ignore Article 2, paragraph 7 of the Charter, it does so simply by declaring issues to be threats to "international peace and security." Thus, the organization regularly intervenes in the domestic affairs of member states for humanitarian, peacekeeping, and even human-rights purposes,[77] and claims of exclusive control over territory and freedom from external interference have been greatly compromised in recent years (see Chapter 9).

In the scholarly community, over four decades have passed since real-ist John Herz declared that "some of the factors which underlay the 'modern state system' as it emerged about three hundred years ago and

---

[76] Clive Parry, "The Function of Law in the International Community," in Max Sorensen, ed., *Manual of Public International Law* (New York: St. Martin's Press, 1968), p. 14.
[77] Jarat Chopra and Thomas G. Weiss, "Sovereignty Is No Longer Sacrosanct: Codifying Humanitarian Intervention," in Steven L. Spiegel and David J. Pervin, eds., *At Issue: Politics in the World Arena*, 7th ed. (New York: St. Martin's Press, 1994), p. 408.

which determined rather stably its structure and relationships have now undergone such fundamental changes that the structure of international relations itself is different, or in the process of becoming different, and can no longer be interpreted exclusively in traditional terms."[78] Herz recognized that military technology had developed to the point where the frontiers ("territoriality" or "hard shell") of states – originally developed to provide physical protection for subjects – no longer served this end. Herz appears prescient in light of what has transpired since 1959,[79] yet many contemporary theorists still seem reluctant to embrace his conclusions or their implications. For example, even though Krasner argues that centuries earlier the "driving forces behind the gradual elimination of universal institutions and the predominance of the sovereign state were material" and "states benefited from . . . new military technologies that advantaged larger units,"[80] he is not prepared to acknowledge that similar forces might be eroding the capacity of states today.

The wall separating the domestic and foreign realms was greatly shaken by the introduction of transnational insights in the 1970s. The idea of transnationalism grew from recognition that the frontiers of Westphalian States did not prevent significant interactions among societies without the mediation of governments. While Herz had emphasized military technology, the transnationalists were inspired by economic change. Especially influential were functionalists and neofunctionalists who in the 1950s and 1960s had focused attention on the growth of interstate institutions and on the experiments in economic integration in Europe and elsewhere. There were also other currents. As early as 1966, Raymond Aron spoke of a "transnational society" that "reveals itself by commercial exchange, migration of persons, common beliefs, organizations that cross frontiers and, lastly, ceremonies or competitions open to the members of all these units."[81]

---

[78] John H. Herz, *International Politics in the Atomic Age* (New York: Columbia University Press, 1959), p. 11.

[79] Herz later came to doubt his own conclusions: "The theory of 'classical' territoriality and of the factors threatening its survival stands. But I am no longer sure that something very different is about to take its place." John H. Herz, "The Territorial State Revisited: Reflections on the Future of the Nation-State," in Herz, *The Nation-State and the Crisis of World Politics: Essays on International Politics in the Twentieth Century* (New York: David McKay, 1976), p. 227.

[80] Krasner, "Westphalia and All That," p. 261.

[81] Raymond Aron, *Peace and War: A Theory of International Relations*, trans. Richard Howard Fox and Annette Baker Fox (New York: Praeger, 1968), p. 105. See also Robert O. Keohane and Joseph S. Nye, Jr., eds., *Transnational Relations and World Politics* (Cambridge, MA: Harvard University Press, 1971).

By the mid-1970s, Robert O. Keohane and Joseph Nye, Jr. were writing of a world "in transition" characterized by devalued sovereignty in which the choices of statesmen were constrained by the conditions of complex interdependence and the proliferation of international regimes.[82] At the same time, the present authors and John Burton were characterizing global politics as a "web" of relationships, with "nonstate" actors engaged in many issues.[83] Raymond Hopkins explained how "bureaucracies whose mandate is primarily 'domestic' . . . are responsible for the promotion, monitoring, and regulation of a wide variety of activities whose scope is international" and how this required broadening "the concept of international organization."[84] Peter Gourevitch described the reverse process, arguing: "The international system is not only a consequence of domestic politics and structures but a cause of them . . . International relations and domestic politics are . . . so interrelated that they should be analyzed simultaneously, as wholes."[85] More recently as we have seen, Putnam, after observing that "our theories have not yet sorted out the puzzling tangle" of domestic politics and international relations, introduced the metaphor of "two-level games" to describe how "central decision-makers strive to reconcile domestic and international imperatives simultaneously."[86] All of these were efforts to modify the foreign–domestic dichotomy without abandoning it altogether.

More sustained efforts to overcome the dichotomy have informed the work of Ruggie and Rosenau. Both are impressed by the ways in which modern technology has rendered obsolete territorial frontiers, altering the essential nature of space and time in global politics. Ruggie denounces the "impoverished mind-set . . . that is able to visualize long-term challenges to the system of states only in terms of entities that are institutionally substitutable for the state." Nevertheless, in the end he

---

[82] Robert O. Keohane and Joseph S. Nye, Jr., *Power and Interdependence: World Politics in Transition* (Boston: Little, Brown, 1977). See also Stephen D. Krasner, ed., *International Regimes*, special issue of *International Organization* 36:2 (Spring 1982), and Robert O. Keohane, *After Hegemony: Cooperation and Discord in the World Political Economy* (Princeton: Princeton University Press, 1984).

[83] Richard W. Mansbach, Yale H. Ferguson, Donald E. Lampert, *The Web of World Politics: Nonstate Actors in the Global System* (Englewood Cliffs, NJ: Prentice-Hall, 1976), and John W. Burton, *World Society* (Cambridge: Cambridge University Press, 1972).

[84] Raymond F. Hopkins, "The International Role of 'Domestic' Bureaucracy," *International Organization* 30:3 (Summer 1976), pp. 405–406.

[85] Peter Gourevitch, "The Second Image Reversed: The International Sources of Domestic Politics," *International Organization* 32:4 (Autumn 1978), p. 911.

[86] Putnam, "Diplomacy and Domestic Politics," pp. 427 and 460.

resists any suggestion that Westphalian actors might become irrelevant, affirming that the "central attribute of modernity in international politics has been a peculiar and historically unique configuration of territorial space."[87]

Rosenau's seminal theorizing about the comparative study of foreign policy[88] evolved from a research agenda that would subject "national-international linkages" to "systematic, sustained, and comparative inquiry."[89] He viewed this topic as part of a larger effort "to develop theoretical constructs for explaining the relations between the units [political science] investigates and their environments."[90] Like Ruggie, however, he retained the foreign–domestic distinction while recognizing that the barrier between them was less a solid wall than a link fence.[91] Instead, as we have noted, he posited two political worlds, one labeled "state-centric" that consists of "sovereignty-bound" states, and the other "multi-centric," with "hundreds of thousands" of "sovereignty-free" actors.[92] As we saw in Chapter 1, by the early 1980s, Rosenau was struck by the inadequate attention he had paid to change in general and in particular to changes in the distribution of global authority. He blamed the interstate model for the failure to predict the revolutionary changes in global politics that were becoming visible at the time.[93] "Macro changes" in global politics, in his view, had evolved out of changes at the "micro level," mainly the greater knowledge and skills of individuals and their growing sense of efficacy.[94] New authority structures were emerging, and competition for identities and loyalties was growing between these structures and governments.

Ruggie, Rosenau, and others have loosened the grip of models that divide the world into two realms. Their work has poked holes in the intra–interstate wall, but, unlike Joshua, has stopped short of tearing

---

[87] Ruggie, "Territoriality and Beyond," pp. 143 and 144.

[88] James N. Rosenau, "Pre-theories and Theories of Foreign Policy," in R. Barry Farrell, ed., *Approaches to Comparative and International Politics* (Evanston, IL: Northwestern University Press, 1966), pp. 27–93.

[89] James N. Rosenau, "Introduction: Political Science in a Shrinking World," in Rosenau, ed., *Linkage Politics* (New York: Free Press, 1969), p. 2. Rosenau's analysis of linkages anticipated the growing interest in the 1970s in "transnational politics" and "international regimes."

[90] *Ibid.*, p. 4. See also James N. Rosenau, "The External Environment as a Variable in Foreign Policy Analysis," in Rosenau, Vincent Davis, and Maurice A. East, eds., *The Analysis of International Politics* (New York: Free Press, 1972), pp. 145–165.

[91] See by Rosenau: *Linkage Politics*; and *The Scientific Study of Foreign Policy* (New York: Free Press, 1971).

[92] Rosenau, *Turbulence in World Politics*, pp. 249–253.

[93] Rosenau, "A Pre-Theory Revisited," p. 251.   [94] *Ibid.*, pp. 253–255.

down the wall completely and uniting those realms.[95] How far we yet have to go to achieve "a thoroughgoing jailbreak" is apparent in the neorealist–neoliberal debate,[96] the related agency/structure literature, and additional contributions from political/historical sociology. The neorealist/neoliberal debate does not get us very far. Robert Powell, for example, identifies three "issues at the center of the neorealist-neoliberal debate": "the meaning and implications of anarchy, the problem of absolute and relative gains, and the tensions between cooperation and distribution."[97] Charles Kegley sees the "neoliberal challenge" as being more about the institutional and normative implications of interdependence and transnationalism, including a sort of reformed Wilsonian idealism (neoidealism).[98]

Thus, the dialogue among self-proclaimed institutionalists, constructivists, neoliberals and others has so far been disappointing, dwelling mostly on the extent to which (and why) interstate institutions, less formal regimes, and norms have theoretical significance apart from states. Do institutions, regimes, and norms merely constitute the interplay of state interests, or do they reciprocally shape state behavior? Do states "learn" in collective company? To what degree do institutions and norms proceed directly or indirectly from structural interdependence, thus owing more to structure than to agents? Once established, to what extent should we see institutions and regimes as autonomous actors? And so on. Institutionalists have embraced Putnam's conception of "two-level games" without exploring its full implications. As they interpret it, we must now look within the state "black box" to see how state interests are affected by "domestic" politics, but we still have to keep the state firmly in place as gatekeeper between foreign and domestic politics.

The agency/structure debate might have provided the needed wrecking ball. Asking what the agents and structures actually *are* is a healthy

---

[95] Walker is an exception, declaring: "What is at stake in contemporary debates about the possibility of moving on . . . is less the perverse humour of some imaginary premodernity than claims about the character and location of political life prescribed by distinctly modern accounts of the sovereignty of states." *Inside/Outside*, p. 6.

[96] See especially Keohane, ed., *Neorealism and its Critics*; and David A. Baldwin, ed., *Neorealism and Neoliberalism: The Contemporary Debate* (New York: Columbia University Press, 1993).

[97] Robert Powell, "Anarchy in International Relations Theory: The Neorealist-Neoliberal Debate," *International Organization* 48:2 (Spring 1994), p. 329.

[98] Charles W. Kegley, Jr., "The Neoliberal Challenge to Realist Theories of World Politics: An Introduction," in Kegley, ed., *Controversies in International Relations Theory and the Neoliberal Challenge* (New York: St. Martin's, 1995), pp. 10–14.

subversive question, potentially opening up consideration of a wide variety of polities and domains. Unfortunately, the answer has been limited largely to the familiar question of the relationship of domestic agents and states. We repeat: Describing the world as "anarchic" fails to capture, not only the cooperative choices of states, but also the routine "governance" exercised by a galaxy of polities, some inside states' sovereign frontiers, some outside, and still others transcending lines on a territorial map.

The agency/structure literature has roots in political sociology where theorists are also caught in a state-centered trap. Theda Skocpol – whose pioneering work centered on social revolutions – characterizes "the state" as a "set of administrative, policing, and military organizations headed, and more or less coordinated by, an executive authority."[99] Although coordination is rather "less" than "more" in many states, Skocpol does recognize that each state is unique, not least because of its particular "Janus-faced" history. States, in her view, are Janus-faced because they are linked on one side with "class-divided socioeconomic structures" and on the other with a complex and dynamic international system.[100] Once again, the foreign–domestic wall is porous but remains.

Closer to the mark is Michael Mann when he observes that: "Social relationships have rarely aggregated into unitary societies," however much states may have had "unitary pretensions." Societies are "organized," "confederal, overlapping, intersecting networks" rather than "simple totalities"; and social institutions draw to varying degrees (in a "promiscuous" fashion) upon his four "sources of social power." Society in this case is clearly distinguished from state, which, for Mann, is only one power center among many.[101] So far so good. However, Mann,[102] along with historical sociologists like John A. Hall,[103] Wallerstein,[104]

---

[99] Theda Skocpol, *States and Revolutions; A Comparative Analysis of France, Russia and China* (Cambridge: Cambridge University Press, 1979), p. 29.

[100] *Ibid.*, p. 32.

[101] Mann, *The Sources of Social Power*, vol. I, ch. 1. Mann applies his analysis of the four sources of power to the evolution of the post-Westphalian state in Europe in *The Sources of Social Power: The Rise of Classes and Nation-States, 1760–1914*, vol. II (Cambridge: Cambridge University Press, 1993).

[102] Michael Mann, "The Autonomous Power of the State: Its Origins, Mechanisms and Results," in John A. Hall, ed., *States in History* (Oxford: Basil Blackwell, 1986), pp. 109–136. See also *States, War and Capitalism* (Oxford: Basil Blackwell, 1988).

[103] John A. Hall, *Powers and Liberties: The Causes and Consequences of the Rise of the West* (New York: Basil Blackwell, 1985).

[104] Wallerstein argues that the interstate system accompanied the emergence of "the capitalist world economy." "The Inter-state Structure of the Modern World-system," p. 89.

and Tilly,[105] overemphasize the central (albeit not exclusive) and supposedly "autonomous" role of states, gained in part from the historical primacy of central governments in war, capitalism, and constitutional invention.[106] At least Mann, as we have seen, in his extraordinary analysis of social power reaching back to ancient Mesopotamia, dealt with a wide range of social actors.[107] As for the state, Mann concludes that only "through the long nineteenth century [did] civil society bec[o]me more substantially . . . the province of the nation-state."[108] Unfortunately, when he strays beyond the water's edge of states' territorial boundaries, he is at sea. He acknowledges some sort of "geopolitical organization" that "is not reducible to the 'internal' power configuration of its component states"[109] – and there the fog rolls in. Only in his later work does he more clearly attempt to distinguish the state's role in the contemporary period from that of other transnational actors.[110]

Whether in fog or sunlight, the foreign–domestic dichotomy remains at the center of most versions of international politics. Much of the intellectual incrementalism we have described moves us away from the realist black box, while still anchoring this dichotomy at the center of our mental maps. Why, one might ask, does this matter as long as states serve the practical ends of diplomats and teachers? The answer requires us to recall what theory is all about, especially the limited virtue of parsimony. The fundamental role of theory is to highlight matters that are important to our understanding.

The most basic habits of discourse inhibit efforts to transcend the barrier between foreign and domestic that accompanied the hardening of the Westphalian State in Europe. Despite the changed nature of global politics in our day, the same language and the conceptual baggage persist. Efforts to acquire a postinternational vocabulary founder in timid distinctions (we ourselves employ) like that between "state" and "nonstate" actors.[111] As Ruggie puts it, "no shared vocabulary exists in the literature to depict change and continuity" in contemporary global politics. Indeed, he believes it is impossible to explore "the

---

[105] Tilly, *The Formation of Nation-States in Western Europe*.
[106] See, for example, Mann, *States, War and Capitalism*, esp. ch. 1.
[107] Mann, *The Sources of Social Power*, vol. I.
[108] *Ibid.*, vol. II, p. 23.   [109] *Ibid.*, vol. I, p. 27.
[110] See especially Michael Mann, "States and Other Rule Makers in the Modern World," pp. 24–20.
[111] Perceptive critics of *The Web of World Politics* observed that we were retaining some of the linguistic baggage of the very model we were rejecting.

possibility of fundamental institutional discontinuity in the system of states" because "prevailing modes of discourse simply lack the requisite vocabulary."[112]

Comparative politics: Quo vadis?

If our logic to this point is persuasive, then the future autonomy of the study of comparative politics, as traditionally conceived, is endangered. As long as the state-as-primary-actor was accepted as axiomatic, we were trapped in a box that led Martin Wight to explain the paucity of international-relations theory as a consequence of thinking of international politics "as the untidy fringe of domestic politics."[113] The field, as Wight implied, was invented to account for relations *among* sovereign states at a time when the big guns in political philosophy were aimed at explaining the origins of states, the extent and limits of state authority, and the relationship between states, society, and citizens.

As we have seen, for several centuries most scholarship in the area of global politics was conducted on the assumption that the interstate realm could be described and explained with little or no reference to the intrastate realm. Indeed, some theorists and practitioners believed that involvement in domestic politics only muddied their conceptions of state interest and the dispassionate conduct of foreign affairs. Thus, separate groups of scholars and statesmen evolved to allow those on each side of the wall to develop their own institutions, norms, and practices. In academia, this created a positive climate for the evolution of a subfield called comparative politics that focused *inside* states and then applied the comparative method to their institutions and behavior.[114]

If, however, the wall between foreign and domestic is demolished and if there is nothing theoretically special to justify differentiating the two arenas, then it becomes unnecessary to encourage specialists in each. Instead, it suggests that the fields should be merged. The comparative method is, after all, hardly available only to those looking at states. More importantly, the processes of most interest to us are applicable to political life generally rather than to any single branch of any discipline.

---

[112] Ruggie, "Territoriality and Beyond," pp. 140, 143.
[113] Martin Wight, "Why Is There No International Theory?" in Herbert Butterfield and Martin Wight, eds., *Diplomatic Investigations: Essays in the Theory of International Politics* (Cambridge, MA: Harvard University Press, 1968), p. 21.
[114] To this day, it remains unclear where foreign-policy studies should be placed.

The fission and fusion of polities

Political space is constantly shifting. The engines of political change are processes involving the elaboration of larger networks of interaction and interdependence along with the fission of collectivities sometimes into vulnerable and tiny units of self-identification. As Rosenau argues, "dynamics . . . conduce to systemic integration on the one hand and systemic disintegration on the other," and "centripetal forces. . . . today are making groups and nations more and more interdependent even as centrifugal forces are increasingly fragmenting them into subgroups and subnations."[115] It almost appears that the "planet is falling precipitately apart and coming reluctantly together at the very same moment."[116] In our language, polities are always "becoming" something other than they are at present.

Over time, the speed of "becoming" varies dramatically. Sometimes change is so slow as to be almost imperceptible, and, at other times, the pace of change is startlingly fast. Processes of change were gradual and lengthy during the emergence of European states with the waning of the Middle Ages when "the international system went through a dramatic transformation in which the crosscutting jurisdictions of feudal lords, emperors, kings, and popes started to give way to territorially defined authorities."[117] Change was far more rapid after World War II, including the disintegration of Europe's' colonial empires, the development of regional integration in Europe, the demise of the Soviet Union, and the virtual collapse of states in extensive areas of Africa – all in just under four decades.[118]

Whatever the pace, in every historical epoch, some individual polities or types of polities grow, either at the expense of others or at moments when existing polities merge. Other polities contract, overlap, nest, or (rarely) disappear without a trace. These simultaneous processes tend to speed up when it appears that existing institutions are unresponsive to the needs of adherents. In such cases, old polities may reappear or be reconstructed in some fashion to meet those needs or new ones may

---

[115] Rosenau, "A Pre-Theory Revisited," pp. 256–257.

[116] Benjamin Barber, *Jihad vs. McWorld*, (New York: Times Books, 1995), p. 53.

[117] Spruyt, *The Sovereign States and its Competitors*, p. 3. Also Krasner, "Westphalia and All That."

[118] See Richard W. Mansbach and John A. Vasquez, *In Search of Theory: A New Paradigm for Global Politics* (New York: Columbia University Press, 1981), p. 166, for the points along the continuum of coalescence and fragmentation – unitary actor, coalition, faction, and competing actors – and the characteristics of these several points.

emerge,[119] like the Westphalian State during Europe's Middle Ages. In some cases fusion simply produces larger versions of existing political forms, as in the merger of the thirteen states to form the United States. In other cases, it produces qualitatively different political forms, as did the Ch'in unification of China's city polities, the union of cities in northern Europe to form the Hanseatic League, or the agreement of Europe's Westphalian States to form the European Union.

The path that political evolution takes – whether toward centralization of authority and larger polities or the dispersion of authority and the proliferation of small polities – depends on contextual factors. The Westphalian State was the product of the fission and fusion of earlier polities, and it never stood alone as a focus of loyalties. From the outset it drew sustenance from various ideals in the Roman and medieval traditions and from older loyalties to church, lord, guild, and even city. The Westphalian State prospered, both as an idea and as a fact, to the extent that it incorporated other identities, some of which have remained actual and potential challengers to the existing order. And events from Sarajevo to Brussels remind us that the fission and fusion of polities have not ceased even in Europe, the cradle of Westphalian interstate theory.

At any moment, we can identify three generic tendencies among polities – status quo, expansive, or contractive. Status quo polities are often (though not always) those that are, in a given context, the principal authoritative foci of loyalties. In Europe, at least, some states have enjoyed this status for several centuries. Other polities, from churches to cities, continued to exist, and ideologies other than state nationalism continued to appeal to citizens, but states were at the top of the regional pecking order. Loyalties to other ethnic "nations" (for example, Scottish and Catalonian ethno-regions), localities, and even clans were always potential contractive polities that might undermine the authority of the center. Simultaneously, Westphalian States were challenged by potentially expansive polities based on economic, class, religious, and even imperial ideas and ideologies.

Expansive polities, by contrast, challenge the primacy of status quo polities, whereas contractive polities are in the midst of decline as foci of people's loyalties. In recent decades, the European Union has played the role of an expansive polity. The pressure on states in Europe both

---

[119] This was a key premise in functionalist theory. See David Mitrany, *A Working Peace System* (London: Royal Institute of International Affairs, 1943).

to expand and to fracture is apparent in the contradiction between the growing functions and logic of the EU and the centrifugal pressures of ethno-regional loyalists like Basque and Corsican separatists.

The contradiction, however, is more apparent than real; in fact, fusion and fragmentation can be mutually generative. Modern Europe, as well as other regions and even global politics as a whole, is witnessing the elaboration of polities that can efficiently "specialize" in meeting particular human needs. Such specialized polities, whether the IMF or the Scottish Parliament, are simultaneously expansive and contractive in relation to the Westphalian State. Their domain is more inclusive than that of many states, while the scope of their authority is usually more issue-specific. As a result, citizens in Europe and elsewhere divide their loyalties among expansive polities that promise them a brighter future in certain respects, but otherwise seem remote from their daily lives, and more parochial polities that provide them with the psychological satisfaction of "belonging" to something close and familiar.

Competition among status quo, expansive, and contractive polities can be relatively subdued – managed at the negotiating table as it has been in Europe since World War II – but this is not always the case. The wars in the former Yugoslavia reminded us that fragmentation can concentrate ethnic tensions in smaller units; the close and familiar may include "other" historical enemies who do not "belong." Issues arise, like the future of Macedonia, which can provoke serious conflict among polities. An example, on a larger scale, was the 1992 ERM crisis in Europe, which was a setback for one expansive polity – the EU – and reflected the growing clout of transnational financial firms.[120]

Currently, Europe may confront a broader and more long-term crisis. Recent years have witnessed the dramatic expansion of the EU to the East and the effort to extend EU authority further and further into the "high politics" of foreign and defense policy. However, tensions within Europe during the run-up and aftermath of the 2003 invasion of Iraq may reflect pressures toward fission. Thus, the idea of "old" and "new" Europe, featured in a derisory remark by US Secretary of Defense Donald Rumsfeld has some foundation, although it hardly fits even all of the "coalition of the willing" like Italy.

---

[120] As Susan Strange argued, we must pay greater attention to diplomacy between governments and firms, and among firms themselves. Strange, "An Eclectic Approach," in Craig N. Murphy and Roger Tooze, eds., *The New International Political Economy* (Boulder, CO.: Lynne Rienner, 1991).

The threat posed by one expansive polity, "Fortress Europe" – as well as emerging market giants in Asia – provided incentives for another expansive polity, NAFTA. Debt crisis adjustments of developing states in the 1980s and their loss of bargaining power after the end of the Cold War helped convince Mexican leaders that the time had come to dilute nationalistic trade barriers. The challenge of contractive nationalism is even more complex in the case of Canada's relationship to NAFTA. NAFTA may increase general prosperity, thereby enhancing the rewards of being Canadian, but Quebec or other separatists may counter that an expansive polity like NAFTA makes a united Canadian economy less important.[121]

Paradoxically, fission has accompanied political and economic integration. Civil wars, ethnic conflicts, and tribal violence have broken out with growing frequency. Violence generates floods of refugees in backwater areas of Africa and elsewhere in the developing world that exacerbate the terrible effects of poverty, famine, and other natural disasters. These strains conspire to overload state capacity. The fact of regional and global institutional integration occurring alongside widespread disintegration is no mere coincidence. The processes are linked. The local and the weak have limited capacity, while the global and the strong have limited sentimental appeal. Thus, small entities like the Baltic republics believe that the military threat to their security has greatly diminished and, in any event, that they can now rely on the umbrella provided by the Western alliance. They are also confident they will have new associations with globalized business and regional markets to replace whatever economic relationships they choose to sever with the former dominant power. NATO and the EU provide some of the additional capacities that these republics lack on their own.

At the same time, smallness and the rediscovery of ethnicity and religion provide a psychological refuge for individuals and groups who are bewildered by the pace of change or who fear cultural homogenization. Arab fundamentalism, for example, has been at least partly a reaction against Westernization of their societies. Such examples reflect

---

[121] Robert A. Pastor cites a study based on surveys that indicate a convergence of value systems from the early to late 1980s in all three NAFTA countries. Pastor concludes that the "narrow nationalism that had been dominant since the 19th century is gradually giving way to a more cosmopolitan sense of identity." Pastor, "NAFTA as the Center of an Integration Process: The Nontrade Issues," in Nora Lustig, Barry P. Bosworth, and Robert Z. Lawrence, eds., *North American Free Trade Agreement: Assessing the Impact* (Washington, DC: Brookings, 1992), p. 195.

Thomas Friedman's idea of the individual need for an "olive tree" – "everything that roots us, anchors us, identifies us and locates us in this world."[122] Friedman contrasts the "olive tree" with the "Lexus," a robotics-generated car that to him symbolizes the generic advanced technology of a globalized world. For Benjamin Barber, it is "the numbing and neutering uniformities of industrial modernization and the colonizing culture of McWorld."[123]

There is a dialectical quality to these apparent contradictions. On the one hand, the growth of large polities creates problems of control that can be solved by fission that, in turn, reduces capacity that in turn makes greater size more and more attractive. The forces of fission, as manifested in ethnic and religious "subgroupism," react to the forces of globalization that threaten to limit local autonomy and undermine traditional norms and cultures; cultural contestation becomes political contestation, and the two reinforce each other.[124] It is this connection that Rosenau grasps when he argues: "Both the Danish government's aspiration to European unity and their public's original rejection of the idea . . . are part and parcel of the same underlying global processes."[125] As the source of governance becomes less sharply defined and more remote from its consequences, there is a backlash in which individuals seek psychological refuge in smaller, more proximate polities, trying (and usually failing) to isolate themselves from forces they only dimly understand. The growing impact of alien cultures and the threat of cultural homogenization produce localizing hostility to "cultural outsiders." Refuge is sought and identity recast and reaffirmed in local government, religion, ethnicity, profession, and even urban street gangs. Such gangs are analogous to "tribes" whose members reveal their identity through dress and lifestyle.[126] Small polities can slake the thirst for intimacy, tradition, and localism in the midst of the globalizing of individuals who have a "fragmented sense of self" in which past, present, and future remain disunited.[127] The process comes full circle when the large polity eventually fragments and its successors prove too small to meet the demands of their constituents. Pressures build for selective or full-scale reunification

---

[122] Friedman, *The Lexus and the Olive Tree*, p. 27.   [123] Barber, *Jihad vs. MacWorld*, p. 12.
[124] See Rosenau, *Along the Domestic-Foreign Frontier*, pp. 99–143.   [125] *Ibid.*, p. 115.
[126] Michel Maffesoli calls such groups "tribus." *The Time of the Tribes: The Decline of Individualism in Mass Society* (London: Sage, 1996), p. 140.
[127] David Harvey, *The Condition of Postmodernity* (Oxford: Blackwell, 1990), p. 53.

or invite various forms of involvement by polities outside the original boundaries.

Technological change also fosters the redesign of political space. As new authorities utilize changing technology to expand (whether stirrups "about the turn of the fifth–sixth centuries A.D."[128] or the microelectronics revolution in recent years), such change may overwhelm old local political structures and cultures and the accompanying norms that had anchored identities and previously provided clear and powerful prescriptive guidance. Instead of an international world of distinctive cultures, the postinternational world features a global culture that places a premium on individual choice and market forces.

Owing to fission and fusion, then, the new postinternational world is, at once, new and old. Francis Fukuyama could not have got it more wrong: "history" has not "ended," and the liberal democratic state has hardly triumphed.[129] However rapid or protracted the processes in different contexts, they are ceaseless and universal. Today history is being resurrected and reconstructed, albeit in a somewhat new and rapidly changing context. History is having its revenge on the Westphalian State, and there are also shocks from a future that is as yet only partially perceived.

As non-sovereign polities successfully institutionalize themselves and anchor the loyalties of adherents, existing states may be submerged into larger political communities, subdivided into smaller ones, witness a contraction in the scope of their authority, or perhaps even expand their functions in some respects. Economic interdependence pushes states into larger regional or global regimes and institutions, which (not even considering a largely autonomous private sector) reduce the authority and capacity of governments to make their own economic policies. Where frontiers were imposed by colonial authorities, complex ethnic and tribal cleavages erode loyalties to governments and push states toward collapse.[130] Inhabitants there and in other areas of the world have never been comfortable with what Mann aptly calls "caged societies."[131]

---

[128] McNeill, *The Pursuit of Power*, p. 20.

[129] Fukuyama, *The End of History and the Last Man*.

[130] Krasner observes that in the Third World: "The state is often treated as but one more compartmentalized unit." Stephen D. Krasner, *Structural Conflict: The Third World Against Global Liberalism* (Berkeley, CA: University of California Press, 1985), pp. 40, 41.

[131] Mann, *The Sources of Social Power*, vol. I, p. 40.

Conclusion: postinternational space and time

The postinternational world hosts an array of political forms, both old and new, that are undergoing dramatic shifts in authority. State authority is already less consequential in regions where an alien Westphalian framework was imposed by Europeans and embraced by privileged indigenous elites. The sovereign territorial boundaries of states like these – as well as others where the nesting of tribal or clan polities is widespread – mean little to inhabitants. Real political space is divided very differently.

The end of the Cold War, like the end of the Thirty Years War, made it easier for expansive and contractive polities to reawaken old identities and create new patterns of authority. In addition to contests over religion, conflicts that bill themselves as tribal or ethnic simmer on every continent, and demands for self-determination even threaten the spread of democracy that followed the end of the Cold War. Indeed, simple secession may no longer suffice to satisfy the proliferation of nonterritorial nations demanding territorial statehood.[132] Such conflicts also threaten to spread owing to intervention, especially by neighbors with claims of kinship. At the very least, there will need to be new forms of autonomy invented (or old forms resurrected) for politically mobilized identity groups. Then, additional arrangements will need to be sought to knit the pieces together into larger and more functional polities.

Recognizing that territoriality provides an insufficient basis for describing what goes on in global politics today, the search is on for conceptions of political space that emphasize variability and plasticity. Such conceptualizations gainsay the premise that history somehow culminated and ceased with the Westphalian State. Although Westphalia is often thought to have ratified a Platonic political form, in fact, the Westphalian form has itself changed dramatically in the intervening centuries owing to its post-Napoleonic adaptation to democracy and popular sovereignty, industrialization and expansion of welfare, and the Wilsonian link to self-determination and its wedding in this century to precolonial forms in the developing world.

In Chapter 4 we will focus in more detail on the evolution of the Westphalian State itself because, in the postinternational world,

---

[132] See, for example, Lee C. Buchheit, *Secession: The Legitimacy of Self-Determination* (New Haven: Yale University Press, 1978).

as Jessica Mathews declares: "The absolutes of the Westphalian system – territorially fixed states where everything of value lies within some state's borders; a single secular authority governing each territory and representing it outside its borders; and no authority above states – are all dissolving."[133] It is critical to understand from where we have come before we can begin to discern where we are going.

[133] Jessica Mathews, "Power Shift," *Foreign Affairs* 76:1 (January/February 1997), p. 50.

4   States and other polities

Myriad polities have emerged, declined, and substantially vanished throughout history, and the theme of continual change among political communities has been a perennial one in political philosophy. Aristotle described the growth and contraction of political associations; Machiavelli was preoccupied by the expansion and decline of princely realms; and Hobbes and Rousseau employed the imaginary but provocative metaphors "state of nature" and "contract" in order to explain the conditions of political birth. More recently, Samuel Huntington wrote of civilizations that they "are dynamic; they rise and fall; they merge and divide; and as any student of history knows, they also disappear and are buried in the sands of time."[1]

All polities are evolving ("becoming" in our terminology) and, while some endure, none lasts anything like "forever." Yet both individual polities and polity types rarely disappear completely; rather, they remain as a part of the world's "living museum," sometimes as an historical oddity or an exhibit that sooner or later may go back on show or be reconstructed in one fashion or another. At any given time, individual polities of a particular (ideal) type differ substantially in their characteristics and capacities, and exercise influence or control only within limited domains. And, as we have seen, domains often overlap in whole or in part, and polities thus regularly share some political space.

In this respect postinternational thinking is antithetical to much of the theorizing about global politics, especially realism and neorealism. Thus, although Kenneth Waltz concedes that: "States are not and never have been the only international actors," he does not describe either a

---

[1] Samuel P. Huntington, *The Clash of Civilizations: Remaking of World Order* (New York: Simon & Schuster, 1996), p. 44.

"prestate" or "poststate" era.[2] He insists that, although "[s]tates vary widely in size, wealth, power, and form," they "perform . . . tasks, most of which are common to all of them."[3] According to Waltz, functional differentiation is only possible in systems that are not anarchic. States differ but, because they are multifunctional entities, not so much as to matter. Like other neorealists, Waltz infers the idea of anarchy from a system of independent states lacking supranational authority and, from this, reasons that interstate conflict is inevitable.

In fact, states have *never* enjoyed a monopoly of political behavior. Kinship groups and various local entities like cities have exercised both authority and effective influence or control over their respective domains since the dawn of political association. Much of global history has featured empires or, in some respects as Huntington insists, "civilizations" rather than states. In cases like those of Germany or Turkey, state-formation postdated and was dependent upon empire. We might well ask in those cases: where, in terms of ideology and institutions, did empire shade off into state and vice versa?

The Westphalian system, even at its height, was never the only game in town, and its relative importance is ebbing. The state is only one of many collective actors – such as interstate bureaucratic alliances, transnational organizations, alliances and networks of firms, world cities,[4] and social movements, to name a few. The European Union, a host of functional regimes, and "global cities" were well advanced before the Cold War ended. Today, intergovernmental organizations (IGOs) continue to proliferate, as do nongovernmental organizations (NGOs) and international nongovernmental organizations (INGOs), and many have established complex webs of cross-border relationships and alliances that resemble those pioneered by transnational corporations and banks. Peter Willetts estimated that as of 1997 there were 10,000 single-country NGOs, 300 IGOs, and 4,700 INGOs. "Using people as the measure, many NGOs, particularly trade unions and campaigning groups in the fields of human rights, women's rights, and the environment, have their membership measured in millions, whereas 37 countries in the UN have populations of less than one million."[5] Until recently, most NGOs functioned

---

[2] Waltz, *Theory of International Politics*, p. 93.   [3] *Ibid.*, p. 96.
[4] For a recent symposium on this subject, see the contributions of Peter J. Taylor *et al.* in *Political Geography*, 19:1 (January 2000), pp. 5–53.
[5] Peter Willetts, "Transnational Actors and International Organizations in Global Politics," in John Baylis and Steve Smith, eds., *The Globalization of World Politics: An Introduction to International Relations* (New York: Oxford University Press, 1997), p. 290.

to place issues on the global agenda by bringing them to the attention of states. Increasingly, however, they have become authoritative actors in their own right, with legitimacy derived from expertise, information, and innovative political techniques, especially direct action. Thus, Kobrin observes that "there is no question that Greenpeace played a major role in international politics by mobilizing public and governmental opinion against the deep sea disposal of Shell's Brent Spar platform. Whether it performed that role as a public or private actor may no longer be a relevant question."[6]

Even as many European Union member governments continue to implement their common Euro currency, the EU must also continually re-fashion relationships with its various regions and – like NATO – consider the full implications of an expansion in membership. At stake are formidable issues of the redistribution of formal and effective political and economic authority not only in Europe but also elsewhere as well. Governments have transformed a largely powerless GATT into the more authoritative WTO; the NAFTA market has substantially united North America's economies; and further trade cooperation is envisaged for the Western Hemisphere and for the Asia Pacific region. Despite such institutional innovations – and, paradoxically, partly because of them – governments are less and less in charge of the world economy or capable even of managing their own national economies. The advance of capitalism, the current free-market ethos (however tarnished by corporate scandals), and the increasingly global character of business and finance emphasize, as never before, that "private sector" resources far exceed those of governments. Whatever their financial weaknesses and ethical foibles, corporations also seem much more able than governments to formulate and pursue coherent "interests," to "think globally," and to respond rapidly and flexibly to events.

One again, however, there is more than one possible story. Alternatively, we can view institutions beyond the state as extensions of the authority of member states. States may use international institutions and regimes to accomplish tasks they cannot do alone, and some arrangements like the Euro may, paradoxically, offer individual states greater protection from external pressures. Additionally, some states have much to gain from globalizing institutions that have a stabilizing effect and/or provide an excuse for unpopular austerity and open market policies at home. If states are still in the driver's seat, some may also have the

---

[6] Kobrin, "Back to the Future," p. 380.

capacity to reverse various aspects of globalization, witness the recent turn in United States policy toward militant unilateralism and increased selective protectionism.

It is no wonder that the changing nature and role of the territorial state is a central preoccupation of postinternational thinking. As Stanley Hoffmann argues, "world politics, and therefore world order, are no longer monopolized by states. . . . On the other hand, the various peoples of the world, as opposed to governments, are more turbulent than ever before."[7] We are seeing the emergence of new authority structures and the growing importance of new forms of "governance" as well as an extensive cast of violent and destabilizing "sovereignty-free actors," as in earlier epochs.

The state and social science

We have frequently observed how political science and its subfields evolved, at least in the West, as a state-centric discipline. The only (unlikely) alternatives to unitary states students were offered were world government or world empire; and realism's sway, especially among American scholars, resulted in "a concentration on questions of war and peace" and "a security fetish that reinforced a billiard ball model of a world of states." To be sure, the subfield of international political economy gradually emerged, but it took the form, initially, of a new emphasis on the "interdependence" of states and then on "regimes" supposedly tailored by member states to serve their own state interests.[8]

Many political scientists retain an emotional attachment to "the state" because they associate it with public goods as opposed to "venal" private interests. In fact, even in the United States, where the free market is an ideological given, "private" business interests have influenced public policy since the Republic was founded, and government, in turn, routinely makes use of the knowledge and resources of the private sphere for public purposes. Elsewhere too, the "public" good and the "national interest" are often indistinguishable from the good of influential "private" interests.[9] This connection is evident in the cases of "Japan Inc."

---

[7] Stanley Hoffmann, "Delusions of World Order," *New York Review of Books*, April 9, 1992, p. 37.
[8] Peter J. Taylor, "Embedded Statism and the Social Sciences: Opening Up to New Spaces," *Environment and Planning* 28 (1996), pp. 1924–1925.
[9] See Bob Jessop, "Bringing the State Back in (Yet Again): Reviews, Revisions, Rejections, and Redirections," *International Review of Sociology* 11:2 (2001), pp. 149–173.

and "Singapore Inc."[10] and, more generally, the "crony capitalism" that characterizes much of Asia. There has been also deep suspicion about cronyism in the George W. Bush administration's energy policy and the awarding of postwar contracts in Iraq.

Not surprisingly, the extensive privatization that has been taking place in many of the world's economies also makes political scientists profoundly uneasy. The very focus of their studies – that is, government – appears to be withering away. Moreover, the worldwide resurgence of "ethnicity" is a phenomenon they prefer to regard as a return to "tribalism" – a barbaric remnant that the modern state was supposed to have eradicated or tamed into citizenship – rather than as a cultural phenomenon that is as perennial as it is fundamentally fictive and dangerous.

Political scientists are not alone. Social scientists more generally reflect what political geographer Peter J. Taylor calls "embedded statism."[11] Taylor argues that modern social science was indelibly shaped by "the social world that existed around 1900":

> Beginning with the traditional function of war-making, modern states had added economic policies to their portfolio in the mercantilist era before the French Revolution. In the period after the revolution, states became associated with cultural continuities termed nations, and with sovereignty deemed to lie with the "people as nation", states gradually took on more and more social responsibilities in looking after the welfare of their people. The result was what Giddens has famously called the power container: the state became supreme not just in politics but in economic, cultural, and social policy as well.

Taylor continues: "But this does not explain why this should not have been problematized rather than taken for granted. The key process here is the linking of the political with the cultural. The state became 'nation-state' overseeing 'national economy' for the benefit of 'national society'."[12]

Taylor's view is compatible with that of Agnew and Corbridge who insightfully point to "three contextual factors" that they regard as responsible for the preoccupation of social scientists with states. The first is a "preference for abstract and 'closed-system' thinking among

[10] See Usha C. V. Haley, Linda Low, and Mun-Heng Toh, "Singapore Incorporated: Reinterpreting Singapore's Business Environments Through a Corporate Metaphor," *Management Decision* 34:9 (1996), pp. 17–28.
[11] Taylor, "Embedded Statism and the Social Sciences," pp. 1917–1928.
[12] *Ibid.*, pp. 1919–1920.

advocates of a scientific (positivistic) approach to international relations." States make for parsimony and "can be written about without reference to the concrete conditions in which they exist." A second factor is the "muddling" of "state" and "nation." A third is "the intellectual division of labour in political science that emerged in the aftermath of the First World War," in which "'international' (meaning inter-state) was theorized as separate and distinct from the national/domestic" and thus "required a more homogenous and uniform conception of the state as an actor than that adopted by students of 'domestic' political life (the image of family coziness is shared!)." Underlying these three contextual factors, according to Agnew and Corbridge, were "three key geographical assumptions." "First, state territories have been reified as set or fixed units of sovereign space." "Second, the use of domestic/foreign and national/international polarities has served to obscure the interaction between processes operating at different scales, for example, the link between the contemporary globalization of certain manufacturing industries and the localization of economic development policies." Third, as Taylor also observes, "the territorial state has been viewed as existing prior to and as a container of society."[13]

In Taylor's view, sociology has actually been "the weakest of the mainstream disciplines in terms of international studies." Even more than political scientists, sociologists have tended to see the realm of interstate relations as anarchic, that is, "beyond society and therefore of no interest."[14] "The sociologist's 'society', or social system, or social formation, depending on the theory, has been found, or rather assumed, to coincide in space with political boundaries. Hence 'British society', the 'American social system', or the 'French social formation' each have the taken-for granted property of existing within the same named sovereign territories."[15]

Historians, too, have tended to organize scholarship around the Westphalian State,[16] especially in the nineteenth-century heyday of nationalism when they were busily constructing the historical narratives and myths of their homelands. Some contemporary historians like William H. McNeill have also written about civilizations and empires, but many,

---

[13] Agnew and Corbridge, *Mastering Space*, pp. 83–84.   [14] *Ibid.*, p. 1924.
[15] Taylor, "Embedded Statism and the Social Sciences," p. 1919.
[16] For a typical definition of this version of the state based on recognized territory, see Gianfranco Poggi, *The Development of the Modern State: A Sociological Introduction* (Stanford: Stanford University Press, 1978), p. 1.

like McNeill himself, retain a strong realist bias, emphasizing state power and military technology.[17] "So far," he insists, "no promising alternative to the territorial organization of armed force has even begun to emerge."[18]

Economists, too, developed their discipline with a focus on states as complete economic units. Writes Taylor: "Similarly, macroeconomic theories all equate economy with economic transactions contained within the territorial boundaries of states. Whether we call it the US economy or the American economic system, we all know where it begins and ends. Of course, from its earliest days economics allowed such theories as that of comparative advantage, but textbooks normally discussed trade and currencies" "as a small add-on feature after the 'real' economics dealing with national economies had been extensively treated." "Hence the discipline of economics remained locked in a world of 'trading nations' that has not changed since Adam Smith and David Ricardo."[19] The Keynesian revolution stressed the extent to which state policies might not only manage national economies but also minimize the harm done by pernicious foreign influences.

More than other disciplines, however, international relations made the state and relations among states the alpha and omega of analysis. Except for a brief era in the nineteenth century during which the British and American liberal tradition achieved ascendancy, continental power theory was dominant and regarded as almost paradigmatic. States were conceived as unitary actors pursuing their "national interest defined in terms of power." In an anarchic world of state billiard balls, the security dilemma was acute, national security the primary foreign-policy goal, military might the most important capability, and sovereignty the most important attribute of actors. Claims that sovereignty should assure a state's freedom from external intervention and sustain a wall between the domestic and foreign arenas also encouraged the illusion that states could be treated as unitary actors despite the fact that all states are rent by political faction and are subject to bureaucratic infighting and interest-group politics, today often transnational in nature.

---

[17] See, for example, McNeill, *The Pursuit of Power*. McNeill pays relatively little attention to the economic and ideological factors that shaped state consolidation in the past and undermine it in the present.

[18] William H. McNeill, "Territorial States Buried Too Soon," *Mershon International Studies Review* 41, Supplement 2 (November 1997), pp. 273–274.

[19] Taylor, "Embedded Statism and the Social Sciences," p. 1925.

Sovereignty

Many international-relations scholars still regard state sovereignty as "the normative basis" of their field. Sovereignty, Ian Hurd declares, "is arguably the foundational principle on which the rest of international relations is constructed" and "exhibits the stability it does because it is widely accepted among states as a legitimate institution."[20] "World order as we know it," declares Franke Wilmer, "arose in connection with European experience. It is therefore characterized by a high degree of normative consensus among international power elites in European societies and states created and now politically controlled by descendants of European colonizers."[21]

Alternative political forms challenge that order. In contrast to traditional accounts of sovereignty, postinternational thinking approaches the concept, as do Biersteker and Weber, as a "social construct."[22] To be sure, states' "claims to sovereignty construct a social environment in which they can interact as an international society of states, while at the same time the mutual recognition of claims to sovereignty is an important element in the construction of states themselves."[23] However, in practice, the meaning of sovereignty has been "negotiated" continuously since Europe's Middle Ages, and it is still being negotiated.

Intellectually, part of the problem in the field of international relations – built on the constitutive quality of sovereignty[24] and emerging from a tradition of the "law of nations" – is that it was conceived to focus on relations among peer polities, that is, Westphalian States. That focus initially had at least some grounding in historical reality. As Rodney Bruce Hall details, the aristocratic "state" (and state system)

---

[20] Ian Hurd, "Legitimacy and Authority in International Politics," *International Organization* 53:2 (Spring 1999), pp. 393, 397. Ruggie observes that the state emerged in the course of "a 'legitimation crisis' of staggering proportions" and that sovereignty "in its proper modern usage . . . signifies a form of *legitimation* that pertains to a *system* of relations." "Continuity and Transformation in the World Polity," p. 276. Emphasis in original.
[21] Franke Wilmer, *The Indigenous Voice in World Politics* (Newbury Park, CA: Sage Publications, 1993), p. 42.
[22] Thomas J. Biersteker and Cynthia Weber, "The Social Construction of State Sovereignty," in Biersteker and Weber, eds., *State Sovereignty as a Social Construct* (Cambridge: Cambridge University Press, 1996), p. 11.
[23] *Ibid.*, pp. 1–2.
[24] Of the four definitions of sovereignty provided by Krasner in *Sovereignty*, our usage incorporates elements of both what he calls "Westphalian sovereignty" – "political organization based on the exclusion of external actors from authority structures within a given territory," and "interdependence sovereignty" – "the ability of public authorities to regulate the flow of information, ideas, goods, people, pollutants, or capital across the borders of their state" (pp. 3, 4).

of the *ancien régime* was far different from the later models associated with nationalism and popular sovereignty.[25] Even Krasner (as we have seen) argues that Westphalia was only one step in the evolution of the sovereign state, though he believes nothing much has really changed as regards sovereignty.

A variety of myths surround the understanding of sovereignty. One is that states established a monopoly of violence in and total control over their territory; a second that states created impermeable boundaries; and a third that sovereign states enjoy a condition of equality. In reality, from the outset, sovereignty has always been more of an aspiration than a reality.[26] According to historian Joseph Strayer, state sovereignty was only legitimated when the "should" of aspiration was replaced by a widespread recognition that sovereignty was "needed" to manage violence and strengthen state capacity. Only this recognition permitted the state to share the identities and loyalties of subjects with other polities such as church, local community, and family.[27] Only then did the state have a claim to being a genuine moral community, and only as a moral community could the state demand a monopoly of the legitimate use of force on its territory.

Sovereignty proclaimed the state to be the final arbiter of legitimate violence because the threat of anarchic violence was real enough, and remained so. Nevertheless – and this is a theme running throughout this book – sovereignty, as Onuf declares, "is not a condition"; rather, it is "an ideal that is never reached, in a world where each step toward the ideal takes effort and costs resources, possibly in increasing increments, to prevent even smaller amounts of unwanted behavior." "[T]he ideal of a self-encapsulated set of rules, ordered by principle, abstractly rendered and exhaustively explicated is, again, the more difficult to achieve as it is approached. Practically speaking, officers of legal orders must be satisfied with something less than sovereignty."[28]

Sometimes sovereignty is equated with authority or competence and capacity, rather than seen as a vehicle for legitimating state authority.[29] In fact, sovereignty is a legal status that an actor either does or does not have, while *actual* authority, autonomy, and capacity are always variable attributes. The fact that legal scholars in Europe, especially legal

[25] Hall, *National Collective Identity*, pp. 133–213.
[26] J. L. Brierly makes this point in his description of Jean Bodin's view of sovereignty. Brierly, *The Law of Nations*, 5th ed. (New York: Oxford University Press, 1963), p. 8.
[27] Strayer, *On the Medieval Origins of the Modern State*, p. 9.
[28] Onuf, *World of Our Making*, p. 142.
[29] F. H. Hinsley, *Sovereignty*, 2nd ed. (Cambridge: Cambridge University Press, 1986), p. 1.

positivists, refused to think of sovereignty as divisible[30] – accurate enough in a strictly legal sense – enabled practitioners to leave other polities off their maps of the world. States bestow sovereignty (and therefore whatever legitimacy derives from that status) on one another, while they withhold it from entities different from themselves or from groups located within or across their sovereign boundaries. This is one reason why states have historically found it difficult to achieve consensus on the legal status of indigenous peoples.

Because indigenous peoples such as American Indian tribes were not regarded as sovereign in the sense that states were, Europeans had few qualms about renouncing treaties that had been concluded with them. Nonetheless, what treaties remained and defined autonomous arrangements like reservation lands and tribal councils have not proved inconsequential; indeed, they came into their own in the late twentieth century as the status of tribal reservations again emerged as a political and normative issue. As in Quebec, the Pacific Northwest, upstate New York, and elsewhere, Indians have dusted off old treaties and begun to interpret them to include the widest possible land claims and legal autonomy. Discoveries of oil and other valuable mineral reserves on some reservations have caused repeated wrangling among tribal councils, multinational firms, and the US Bureau of Indian Affairs. Various tribes have also taken advantage of their peculiar legal status to establish booming tax-free shopping malls and fabulously successful gambling casinos, thereby undercutting potential government revenues from and authority over similar enterprises. Meanwhile, the current climate of political correctness, combined with the New Age nonsense that indigenous peoples are morally superior because they have always lived in harmony with their environment, makes it more difficult for politicians to alter the terms of the relationship as it has evolved.

Still, tribes as nomadic groups in which individuals were connected by claimed common ancestry and blood were different than states, whereas for centuries it was regarded as axiomatic that if all states were sovereign, they must also be homologous units. This logical assumption disguises the empirical fact that real states have little in common with one another *except* legal sovereignty. Today's list of nearly 200 states includes one superpower and a host of "mini-states," including tiny islands of the Caribbean and South Pacific, that are scarcely viable and in some instances may disappear beneath the waves as global warming

---

[30] Onuf, *World of Our Making*, p. 141.

accelerates: 87 states have fewer than 5 million inhabitants, 58 have less than 2.5 million, and 35 fewer than 500,000.[31] Tuvalu is a Pacific atoll with a population of 10,000, and an area of 9.5 square miles, which sold the rights to the web address "tv," a $50 million deal worth more than the half its annual GDP earned from subsistence agriculture and fishing. Nauru is another atoll of 8 square miles, with 8,000 inhabitants, many of whom became rich from the sale of phosphates, the supply of which is now exhausted. By contrast, the American state of California with over 31 million inhabitants and the world's fifth largest economy is not sovereign and, despite having a budget deficit in 2003 that is greater than the deficits of all other US states combined (excluding New York's) is not entitled to aid from the International Monetary Fund or the World Bank.

Consider the contrast between the prosperous and well-ordered city-state of Singapore and the state-like remains of Sierra Leone which features more than a dozen self-conscious ethnic groups, and has been victimized by repeated coups, brigands, and "sobels" (former soldiers), along with the misnamed Revolutionary United Front that engages in looting and diamond smuggling. In Sierra Leone, as well as elsewhere in Africa, argues William Reno, illicit commercial networks help compensate for the loss of traditional patronage systems that were reinforced by aid from former colonial powers and Cold War rivals.[32] In many of these countries, the idea of sovereignty is turned on its head; instead of providing citizens with security from foreign aggression by guarding the country's borders, the army is *the* source of insecurity for citizens who are desperate to flee the army by crossing those very borders. "Private" mercenaries are often employed to substitute for a national military or protect a government from its own army.[33]

The model of global politics that was constructed out of the logic of sovereignty embodied a variety of additional false assumptions. Commonly, the legal independence derived from sovereignty – itself merely recognition by other sovereign states that a new territorial polity should be admitted to the club[34] – is confused with genuine authority and autonomy.[35] After all, sovereignty *asserts* that outsiders *should* not

---

[31] Statistics from *The Economist* 1998, an article based on the work of Harvard economist Alberto Alesina.
[32] William Reno, "Privatizing War in Sierra Leone," *Current History* 96 (1997), pp. 227–230.
[33] Some ninety private armies operate in Africa.
[34] See Oyvind Osterud, "The Narrow Gate: Entry to the Club of Sovereign States," *Review of International Studies* 23:2 (April 1997), pp. 167–184.
[35] On this point see Alan James, *Sovereign Statehood: The Basis of International Society* (London: Allen and Unwin, 1986).

intervene in a state's internal affairs and that citizens *should* respect its legitimacy and obey its laws, but there is no guarantee that they will. Thus, Jorge Domínguez writes of "a persistent fear" that haunts Latin America, "what the economist Albert Hirschman once called *fracaso-manía* or an obsession with failure." "Many still believe that economic success is ephemeral and that democracy's worst enemies are the politicians who claim to speak in its name. There is also a sense that levels of official corruption are intolerably high, [that reformers] are crooks waiting in the opposition."[36] About the only thing that can be said for sovereign independence since World War II is that it has offered modest protection against military predation and boundary changes.[37] In some cases, this amounted to what Robert Jackson calls "negative sovereignty," that is, little more than protection for corrupt regimes.[38]

Regrettably, there is still a tendency to anthropomorphize states, when almost inevitably the real "actors" or "agents" are either governmental and/or social subgroups or effectively transnational. Indeed, the distinction between "public" and "private," so important in political philosophy and international law, is itself a false premise derived from sovereignty's dichotomy of "states" and "others." The public–private distinction has always been difficult to sustain. At the beginning of the Westphalian era, many European flesh-and-blood sovereigns found themselves deeply indebted to Italian banking houses for the money to make war and keep their courts afloat. In general, the literature underestimates the crucial role played by "private" capital and those who generated and controlled it through market activities both local and long distance: individual merchants, associations, fairs, firms, and banks – and also nobles and peasants.

Except in fully socialized economies, which have been relatively rare in history, the resources (albeit unconsolidated) of individuals, firms, and other "private" groups such as religious organizations have vastly outstripped anything available to kings or most governments even of contemporary states. Now, especially with the deregulation of capital

---

[36] Jorge I. Domínguez, "Latin America's Crisis of Representation," *Foreign Affairs* 76:1 (January/February 1997), p. 101.
[37] See Robert H. Jackson and Mark W. Zacher, "The Territorial Covenant: International Society and the Stabilization of Boundaries," Institute of International Relations, The University of British Columbia, Working Paper No. 15 (July 1997).
[38] See Robert H. Jackson, *Quasi-States: Sovereignty, International Relations and the Third World* (Cambridge: Cambridge University Press, 1990). Jackson goes on to argue that, even if there is an abyss between reality and aspiration, sovereignty *does* provide states with a degree of legitimacy denied other actors.

markets, it is evident that the resources controlled by large firms and banks, and of certain super-rich individuals, outstrip dramatically the resources of the governments of most states. Around the world, countries like Argentina, buffeted by private market forces, are in a condition of economic and political near collapse that makes mockery of their sovereign status.

Whatever the "organized hypocrisy" inherent in sovereignty as a concept, European political philosophers nonetheless found it a useful logical device. In the absence of a higher legal authority, interstate relations were "necessarily" different from, and independent of, relations among individuals and groups *within* states. The notion of "international" as it emerged in the late eighteenth century also reflected Europe's debt to Rome and Roman law and the reality of the decline of feudalism in Europe, while the doctrine of sovereignty served as a legitimating ideology for the claims of states more generally.[39] As Krasner observes: "The idea of sovereignty was used to legitimate the right of the sovereign to collect taxes, and thereby strengthen the position of the state, and to deny such rights to the church, and thereby weaken the position of the papacy."[40] Thereafter, sovereignty acquired a status independent of its original purpose and became responsible for the maps that scholars and practitioners relied on to make sense of global politics.[41]

Beyond the myths and ambiguities associated with sovereignty is a growing recognition that numbers of contemporary states have been enfeebled or have ceased completely to meet the demands of citizens. In these instances, the gap between sovereignty and authority has become enormous. British intervention in Sierra Leone, French intervention in the Ivory Coast, and American involvement in Liberia all attest to renewed interest in trusteeship arrangements that fly in the face of sovereign equality. Perhaps, the ultimate symbols of a "failed state" are the remains of Liberia's Senate, House of Representatives, and Supreme Court that were looted and gutted "by the private army" of President Charles Taylor as he was leaving the country. "When people here say that democracy is in ruins, that is no metaphor."[42] Still, as Walker

---

[39] Ruggie, "Continuity and Transformation in the World Polity, p. 276.
[40] Krasner, "Westphalia and All That," p. 238.
[41] For a discussion of the interaction of ideas and institutions, see Judith Goldstein, *Ideas, Interests, and American Trade Policy* (Ithaca, NY: Cornell University Press, 1993), pp. 1–22.
[42] Tim Weiner, "Liberian House and Senate Left in Tatters. Is Peace Next?" *New York Times*, August 19, 2003 (www.nytimes.com/2003/08/19/international/africa/19CND-LIBE.html).

contends, sovereignty continues to have a role to play in global politics because of the absence of an effective substitute:

> Whatever avenues are now being opened up in the exploration of contemporary political identities, whether in the name of nations, humanities, classes, races, cultures, genders or movements, they remain largely constrained by ontological and discursive options expressed most elegantly, and to the modern imagination most persuasively, by claims about the formal sovereignty of states. The Cartesian coordinates may be cracked, identities may be leaking, and the rituals of inclusion and exclusion sanctified by the dense textures of sovereign virtu(e) may have become more transparent. But if not state sovereignty . . . what then?[43]

What, indeed? If sovereignty counts for less and less or its hold on popular imagination is declining, that trend casts a long shadow on the future of states.

The Westphalian State: a contingent outcome of place and time

How then did the mythology of the sovereign state acquire such a hold over political imagination? Most of the world did not consist of states, even during the Westphalian era. And in Europe, most of those states that did consolidate to a substantial degree did so (sooner or later) in the context of their transformation into empires. Others, Romanov Russia and Habsburg Austria-Hungary, were dynastic empires almost from the outset. Still others, Germany and Italy, consolidated historically late and, in some respects, did so in a highly unstable fashion. Eventually, the dissolution of the empires in the wakes of World Wars I and II and the Cold War spawned numerous "new states," nearly all of which bore little resemblance to their European progenitors even while espousing the rhetoric of national self-determination. Meanwhile, many of Europe's states have surrendered significant political and economic powers to the European Union, and allowed substantial autonomy, even in the "high politics" realm of military security, to NATO, the WEU, and other institutions.

There was nothing inevitable about the rise of the state in Europe, and, as Krasner argues, it was a process that took hundreds of years rather

---

[43] R. B. J. Walker, *Inside/Outside: International Relations as Political Theory* (Cambridge: Cambridge University Press, 1993), pp. 161–162.

than a literal "Westphalian moment." And historically, as in the present, the birth and evolution of states was uneven. The European state had serious rivals, and its triumph was gradual, tentative, and contingent. As Charles Tilly argues, "as seen from 1600 or so, the development of the state was very contingent; many aspiring states crumpled and fell along the way."[44] A few princes wrested exclusive control of dynastic domains, which they then expanded at the expense of neighbors, and in doing so seduced the loyalties of and joined forces with an emerging urban commercial class. People did not immediately surrender their local or transnational identities as villagers, Christians, or subjects of the Holy Roman Empire, but those identities became relatively less central to their lives as the state increased its extractive and regulatory capacities. Rulers, of course, employed various incentives to discourage subjects from showing more loyalty, for example, to Church than state, as Henry VIII did when he seized Church properties in England and required subjects to declare publicly their loyalty to him. The state-construction process in Europe was largely, though not yet entirely, completed by Napoleon's official abolition of the Holy Roman Empire in 1806 and the 1814–15 Congress of Vienna that followed his final defeat at Waterloo. All told, the sovereign state was Europe's most momentous political invention (at least prior to the EU), and it is not a little ironic that it was European imperial expansion that exported such a limiting concept to other regions of the world, imposing it on top of older political and social forms – and shaping as well all the social science disciplines and the Eurocentric field of international relations.

Although the process of consolidation was somewhat different in each country and remained incomplete nearly everywhere – especially in Germany and Italy – the personal realms of monarchs eventually evolved into territorial states endowed with sovereignty. International law codified this situation, detailing the practice, rights, and obligations of these young leviathans that were regarded as legal equals and subject to no higher authority than the Creator. The Westphalian State prospered because it was better able at the time than any other institution to reduce violence within its boundaries, manage and channel violence externally, and mobilize the abilities and resources of subjects. This capacity gradually attracted subjects' loyalties, and these were intensified by the explosion of nationalism that accompanied and followed the French Revolution. The identification of state and individual interests

---

[44] Tilly, *The Formation of Nation-States in Western Europe*, p. 7.

deepened with the wedding of nation and state, the political mobilization of inhabitants during industrialization and urbanization, and the transformation of subjects into citizens who were now partners in sovereignty and enjoyed the additional right of national self-determination.[45] The "nation" was a powerful non-territorial identity; it "resembled God even more closely than its deified predecessor."[46] And so, as Taylor suggests, the modern political map was born: "[B]y becoming nation-states, states were 'naturalized'. Their historical social constructions were interpreted as an inevitable outcome of political progress and the familiar boundaries on the world political map came to be viewed like 'other' natural features such as rivers, mountain ranges, and coastlines. Being 'natural', states precluded all other social worlds."[47]

By enthroning the people and enshrining them as the source of sovereignty, nationalism dramatically reinforced the idea of states as more than utilitarian, rather genuine moral communities. Thus, as Taylor explains, the sovereign states with familiar boundaries on the world political map that have "obvious political significance," nevertheless, "have been treated as much more than mere polities." "Nearly all social science has assumed that these political boundaries fix the limits of other key interactions." Other polities presumably lacked the same degree of legitimacy or practical clout.

Later, the principle of self-determination returned to haunt Europe, first when its colonial subjects demanded their own sovereign independence and then during the explosive resurgence of ethnic consciousness in recent decades. Since state and nation were still blissfully wedded, that principle was interpreted as the right of self-proclaimed nations to have their own territorial states, rather than the more limited guarantees for minorities intended by Woodrow Wilson at Versailles. The new states were, however, very different from their European parents, and the efforts of a generation of leaders such as Jomo Kenyatta and Julius Nyerere, many of whom had been educated in Europe, to build states on the European model were largely frustrated. The boundaries of many new states were not the product of centuries of extension and consolidation but of lines arbitrarily drawn by colonial authorities – lines that

---

[45] For the origins and evolution of national self-determination, see Derek Heater, *National Self-Determination: Woodrow Wilson and his Legacy* (New York: St. Martin's Press, 1994).
[46] See Liah Greenfeld, *Nationalism: Five Roads to Modernity* (Cambridge, MA: Harvard University Press, 1992), p. 167.
[47] Taylor, "Embedded Statism and the Social Sciences," p. 1920.

often caged hostile tribes or ethnic groups in a single state or divided those with shared identities into different states. For several additional decades, during the Cold War, those lines were essentially frozen.

The interstate map was the only one permitted by foreign offices and departments of political science, which gave the map some genuine substance but did not guarantee a fit with social or political reality. More important, the map seemed to universalize a particular sort of political community that was actually the product of a particular place and time, and idealized it as more secure and unified than it ever really was. In the words of Agnew and Corbridge, Eurocentric theorists, especially, "idealized fixed representations of territorial or structural space as appropriate irrespective of historical context."[48]

Turning to the historical context of the emergence of interstate Europe in somewhat richer detail, it is crucial to understand that that process involved difficult and continuing negotiations among elites with different resources and, as we have reiterated, was in no way predestined to succeed. Any such survey reveals that "failed state" is not just a recent phenomenon. As Herman Schwartz observes of Europe's past: "States that evolved ever better, ever cleverer, and ever more efficient means for extracting revenue, deploying armies and winning internal consent through submission rather than coercion were more likely to survive" – and from the fifteenth through the nineteenth century "over 300 potential states did not."[49] Those in Europe that did succeed relatively early on or later sometimes "captured" nested ethno-regional groups whose territories and loyalties were never wholly assimilated, such as Great Britain (English, Scots, Welsh, Irish), Spain (Catalans, Basques), and Belgium (Flemish and Walloons). Ironically (or perhaps there is a lesson here), one of the most successful was the unique Swiss confederation of French, Italian, and Swiss-German cantons, which declared its neutrality in big-power twentieth-century wars and pioneered in global banking. Even the "Model State" of France suffered a revolutionary bloodbath and effectively incorporated its southern provinces only late in the nineteenth century.

For all the hype about hard-shell territoriality, European territorial boundaries continued to shift and were regularly marched across by armies in serial wars. Neither Louis XIV nor Napoleon was respectful of state sovereignty or boundaries abroad, however much they glorified

[48] Agnew and Corbridge, *Mastering Space*, p. 80.
[49] Herman M. Schwartz, *States Versus Markets*, 2nd ed. (New York: St. Martin's, 2000), p. 22.

the state at home. It is instructive to recall the fact that the only European country that did not have its boundaries altered after the 1648 Peace of Westphalia was Portugal – and Portugal lost its empire and, from time to time, its independence. Indeed, what little peace and stability prevailed in Europe initially came through countervailing interstate alliances. The nineteenth-century fledgling international institution of the Concert of Europe, over time, came to have as much to do with umpiring the game of rival empires as with anything else.

The state-building story requires us also to consider Germany and Italy, which (as we have noted) consolidated late and, in different ways, without complete success. Not long after the many tiny German principalities finally coalesced around the *Zollverein* and Prussian military might in the late nineteenth century, the Kaiser led the new state into a disastrous world war. Hitler's subsequent plans for a Third Reich played on the lack of congruity between Germany's borders and German-speaking *Volk* in other countries. With the Axis defeat, Germany itself was divided into East and West, with the further divided city of Berlin stranded in the East. Upon the collapse of the Soviet empire, already federal West Germany was "united" with the East and has been suffering serious social and economic digestion pains ever since reunification. Long a strong supporter of the European Union, in which multilateral company it could exercise European leadership, Germany under the Schröder government emerged as an advocate of a strong two-house EU Parliament that would essentially create a federal Europe.

Italy's political history in the last century and a half, like Germany's, has been tumultuous. The flowering of Italian nationalism in the *Risorgimento* resulted in unification of peninsular Italy by 1870, but national identity and loyalty have remained elusive to the present day. As the late G. Federico Mancini commented: "Italy's experience with nationhood was far from happy: 60 years of goading and pushing by a nominally liberal but basically authoritarian ruling class, followed by 20 years of tyranny and bravado, and at the end a disgraceful implosion."[50] "On September 8, 1943, the Italian state collapsed – or rather dissolved – in a wink."[51] In fact, Italians have never felt entirely comfortable with the state as their only political community. The main point, according to Mancini, is that "the Italians have always liked and still like littleness." "The social unit where they feel snug and devote energy to the general

---

[50] G. Federico Mancini, "The Italians in Europe," *Foreign Affairs*, 79:2 (March/April 2000), p. 131.
[51] *Ibid.*, pp. 125–126.

welfare is their city – and sometimes even their quarter. . . . Indeed, was not Italy at its most glorious during the Middle Ages and the Renaissance, when it had not one capital city but ten, all of which were usually at war with one another? Today, intercity warring is largely confined to soccer stadiums."[52]

Partly as a result of lingering local and regional identities, the Italian center remains weak. Post-World War II governments rose and fell with dizzying speed, and political corruption became a way of official life. There have been successive internal wars with leftist terrorists and the Mafia, and the Milan-based Northern League has actively advocated secession. Perhaps most serious – and recalling our earlier discussion of the private sector – much of Italy's economy remains undocumented and untaxed. Where does the size of Italy's economy or its productivity exactly rank among others in Europe? No one actually knows. At least until the advent of the conservative Berlusconi government, which expressed greater skepticism, Italy was one of the strongest supporters of the EU. Writing in 2000, Mancini observed: "Apart from the damage caused by frequent infringements of EU rules – a product of hopeless inefficiency of its lawmaking and administrative bodies – Italy is the only large member state that has never triggered a major crisis or impasse in European integration."[53] Disillusioned by their own state, "Italians do not long for a new *patria* – and are keen on Europe because it does not aim to become one."[54] That orientation may well outlast Berlusconi.

Not all European polities were states or were ever intended to be. The Habsburgs presided over a multinational empire. Robin Okey writes:

> In 1982, when B. F. Hermann published his *Sketch of the Physical Constitution of the Austrian States*, most of the lands he discussed had been under a common ruler for two and a half centuries. Yet as his title showed they still had not acquired an official collective name, [pointing up] the problem, which was henceforth to dog the empire increasingly to the end of its days: its origin as a dynastic rather than ethnic union in a continent of emerging nationalisms. Even in the eighteenth century, when none expected ethnic and political boundaries to coincide, the Habsburg lands stood out for the number of self-conscious national traditions they encompassed.

Under the circumstances, what is remarkable is that "elements of identity became as strong as they did." Okey attributes this partial success to the "later Monarchy's bureaucratic traditions – cumbersome but

[52] *Ibid.*, p. 131.   [53] *Ibid.*, p. 133.   [54] *Ibid.*, p. 131.

125

relatively fair and efficient; the German cultural orientation of its educated classes; the conjunction of manufacturing and agrarian zones and
of a semi-official Catholic Church and tolerated religious minorities."[55]

The assassination of Archduke Francis Ferdinand dashed the hopes
for Habsburg succession and further reform, and the Empire collapsed
at the end of World War I. None of the states that the victors carved out
of the empire had an easy time creating secure borders or an identity of
their own, and Czechoslovakia and Hungary disappeared behind the
Iron Curtain after 1945. In Hungary, a 1956 revolt against the Soviet-
dominated government failed, and the "Prague Spring" was nipped in
the bud in 1968. Shortly after Soviet domination ended, Czechoslovakia
in 1993 split into the Czech Republic and Slovakia. Marshal Tito managed to wrest control of Yugoslavia from Stalin early on, but with his
death and the end of the Cold War, that country fragmented into several
competing polities with attendant ethnic cleansing. For its part, Austria
struggled to reconcile strong regional identities and ideological contests
with an Austrian identity (separate as well from German). Annexed by
Hitler following the *Anschluss*, after World War II Austria was divided
into sectors administered by the victorious Allies, became sovereign
again only in 1955, and joined the EU in 1993.

If the collapse of the "Union of the South Slavs" (Yugoslavia) into
bickering ethnicities (as had its parent empire decades earlier) had dire
consequences for the Balkans, the potential fracture of a post-Soviet
state poses far more frightening possibilities. The Russian Tsars established their empire over centuries, including a particularly bloody campaign in the North Caucasus that killed thousands and displaced more
than a million. As Rajan Menon and Graham T. Fuller note, the Russian
Federation's current problems in that polyglot region – Dagestan alone
has over thirty-four ethnic groups – should not come as a surprise.
The Bolsheviks subdued the North Caucasus once again with brutal
measures, culminating in the 1943–44 deportation of 618,000 Balkars,
Chechens, Ingush, and others to Central Asia. Menon and Fuller recount
that: "Using the classic divide-and-rule strategy, Joseph Stalin built artificial multiethnic republics that divided nations – and ultimately sowed
separatist and irredentist seeds." After the collapse of the Soviet Union,
only some regions were given quasi-independence "to the exclusion
of other, equally deserving ethnic regions. As a result, Russia today
remains a mini-empire, not a voluntary federation. Its republics are now

---

[55] Robin Okey, *The Habsburg Monarchy* (New York: St. Martin's, 2001), p. 3.

coming apart under the pressures of old grievances, a newly resurgent national consciousness, and dissatisfaction with the quality of life."[56] In the successor states to the south especially, such as Tajikistan, Uzbekistan, and Turkmenistan, oil and militant Islam create further turbulent prospects.

Although optimistic that "the center can hold," Sam Nunn and Adam N. Stulberg acknowledge that the Russian Federation today is a loose (and further loosening) conglomeration that has "many faces." There is a "new pragmatic regionalism" spreading across Russia's 89 components of 21 ethnic republics and 68 administrative regions. "In today's Russia power and authority are steadily devolving from the center to rest increasingly with regional leaders who are neither politically beholden to nor strategically oriented toward Moscow. Provincial players and interests now intrude into the making of foreign and security policy, once Moscow's sacrosanct domain." Local leaders are carving out horizontal ties between regions and with foreign states that exclude Moscow. Russia itself, "as a weak federal state," is hard pressed "to balance national and regional interests and to make credible foreign commitments" when it is being "increasingly undercut from below."[57]

Even as many observers believe that the entry of the USSR's former bloc in the EU will bring stability to a traditionally unstable region, Europeans are struggling with the question of what political and military shape the European Union should assume. Even Krasner sees a tension between the EU and the autonomy of Europe's sovereign states: "The European Union offers another example of an alternative bundle of characteristics: it has territory, recognition, control, national authority, extranational authority, and supranational authority. There is no commonly accepted term for the European Union. Is it a state, a commonwealth, a dominion, a confederation of states, a federation of states?"[58] And scholars and practitioners will continue to have difficulty capturing the nature of the ever-changing European project.

Putting aside labels, the basic question is: To what extent is the EU more than the sum of its parts? The currently fashionable liberal intergovernmental perspective suggests that over time European governments have surrendered bits and pieces of their sovereign prerogatives

---

[56] Rajan Menon and Graham E. Fuller, "Russia's Ruinous Chechen War," *Foreign Affairs* 79:2 (March/April 2000), pp. 33–34.
[57] Sam Nunn and Adam N. Stulberg, "The Many Faces of Modern Russia," *Foreign Affairs* 79:2 (March/April 2000), pp. 46–47.
[58] Krasner, *Sovereignty*, p. 235.

to the EU, which taken together have altered states' sovereignty.[59] Roger Morgan maintains, along the same general line, that an observer of Europe "focusing on the capacity of states to inflict grievous damage on one another, and on the nature of the states-system that makes this easier or harder, more or less likely, must have difficulty in accepting the Milward thesis that the nation-state has been 'rescued,' if that is taken to mean restored to the external autonomy which was historically one of its strongest characteristics."[60] He continues,

> [W]e have to be very skeptical of A. J. P. Taylor's dictum that 'states will be states.' To be sure, states are still a central feature of the life of Europe . . . their functions have even increased in some respects, and their peoples' sense of national identity may owe more to perceptions of their past history than of the complexities of the present situation. But in reality they have become something very different.[61]

Since Europe invented the sovereign state, it is perhaps surprising that European integration has progressed as far as it has. One reason might be that getting the state first offered Europeans some advantages in understanding and transcending the limits of sovereignty. Krasner evades the issue by claiming that the EU is unique, and "is not a model other parts of the world can imitate." He attributes EU success to the support of the United States and the special need to find a way of reconstructing Germany after World War II. In his view, the EU is unlikely to become anything like a "United States of Europe" "because the interests, cultures, economies, and domestic institutional arrangements of its members are too diverse."[62] Similarly, Morgan argues that if we wish to explain why the EU has not gone farther, "we need to explore and take into account less tangible factors, such as subjective perceptions of national identity, the ideas people hold about their 'national character' (and the characters of other nations), and 'collective memory' in the sense of peoples' mental pictures of their own national histories and the history of others."[63]

This raises the additional question of whether Europe's states – precisely because of their long histories – are more entrenched than other

---

[59] One might insist that the member states are still just as sovereign as they always were, rather they are simply less autonomous – but we will not pursue that discussion here.
[60] Roger Morgan, "A European 'Society of States' – But Only States of Mind," *International Affairs* 76:3 (July 2000), p. 570. His reference is to Alan S. Milward, *The European Rescue of the Nation-State* (Berkeley: University of California Press, 1992).
[61] Morgan, "A European 'Society of States'," p. 574.
[62] Krasner, "Sovereignty," pp. 2–29.
[63] Morgan, "A European 'Society of States'," p. 572.

states elsewhere in the world where statehood is "newer." Or is the drive for national autonomy more powerful where independent statehood is a relatively new experience? In seeking an answer, it is important to note that the threat to statehood in Europe takes the form of fusion, whereas in the less developed world states are faced with fission. The former may imply a popular sense of security that the state will be there when it is needed, whereas the latter suggests a willingness to see the state disappear completely. Looking at both fission and fusion, Jönsson, Tägil, and Törnquist focus on process.

> One school of thought [they declare], claims that the governments of member countries are the key negotiators. . . . In this view, the national interests and relative power of member states determine negotiation outcomes, which typically have the character of "the lowest common denominator." . . . Another school points to the informality and accessibility of EU negotiations and emphasizes the multitude of actors rather than the predominance of states. Government representatives get involved in coalition building with lobbyists, experts and NGOs [and] there is room for supranational leadership by the Commission and the European Parliament.

Jönsson and his colleagues conclude that both schools depict different aspects of the same reality. "For instance, major 'history-making' decisions, such as the Maastricht Treaty, are preceded by intergovernmental negotiations, whereas the many specific decisions in specialized issue areas, which are made continuously in Brussels, involve informal negotiations to a much larger extent. It is the combination of grand bargains and day-to-day negotiations that constitute governance in the EU."[64]

If Jönsson and his colleagues had stopped there, their work would still have constituted an important contribution to understanding the complexity of the EU "negotiated order." But they did *not* stop there. The volume urges readers to consider the nature of "European space" in many different respects – all of them illuminating various aspects of European "reality," and some going beyond the EU as an institution. The authors pay particular attention to cities and various kinds of regions within and across state borders, and to the role of networks and epistemic communities. Furthermore, in their assessment, trends

---

[64] Jönsson, Tägil, and Törnquist, *Organizing European Space*, pp. 127–128. For a more explicitly neorealist approach, see Matthias Kaelberer, *Money and Power in Europe: The Political Economy of European Monetary Cooperation* (Albany, NY: SUNY Press, 2001). Kaelberer's view is summarized in his conclusion that: "Asymmetries in the distribution of power shape the patterns of monetary cooperation" (p. 201).

that are "particularly graphic" in Europe, in fact, are increasingly global in the sense that "the state is losing power 'upwards,' to supranational entities, as well as 'downwards,' to regional entities and transnational networks. It has been argued that the state has become too big for the little things and too small for the big things."[65]

Moral communities in historical perspective

The Westphalian polity was constituted internally as a moral community in Europe at the same time as relations among "civilized" states in a "Christian commonwealth" created an even larger European moral community governed by international law. Underlying both the process of norm articulation and the changing nature of global violence is the relationship between identity and borders or boundaries. The construction of moral communities presumes a normative consensus among individuals *at least on some key issues* which is expressed explicitly or implicitly as a politically relevant identity.

The state system began as an emerging moral community among European states, a community among sovereign equals subscribing to the basic norm of reciprocity. Violence by the state *within* its boundaries was relatively unregulated and was (the metaphor or analogy with a construction of the private/public distinction should be noted) a matter of "domestic jurisdiction."[66] The "moral community of [European] states" agreed on the norm of nonintervention in one another's internal affairs. Both nonintervention and domestic jurisdiction are protected by the United Nations Charter that implicitly reflects the assumption that states constitute boundaries of moral community internally, where citizens "contracted" as equals to construct legally binding rules of behavior on the basis of an internal norm of reciprocity. The state's use of violence in relations with other states, however, has been the main subject of founding documents for the League of Nations and the United Nations, as well as both customary and positive laws of warfare like the overly ambitious Kellogg–Briand Pact or Pact of Paris (1928). In the regulation of violence by states, a distinction has been made between aggression and self-defense, and all exercise of external violence is subject to the laws of war. Article 51 of the UN Charter recognizes the inherent right to individual or collective self-defense only in the event

---

[65] Jönsson, Tägil, and Törnquist, *Organizing European Space*, p. 173.
[66] This began to change with the Congress of Vienna and the subsequent but short-lived Concert of Europe.

of armed attack and then only until the UN has taken "appropriate action." The George W. Bush administration's assertion of a right to pre-emptive military strikes in self-defense remains highly controversial and indeed was carefully avoided by the Kennedy administration in the 1962 Cuban Missile Crisis, precisely because of fear of allowing other states a similar loophole. Kennedy's policymakers relied on the Organization of American States and the UN Charter's allowance for matters appropriate for regional organizations to resolve.

Between the French Revolution and the era of Wilsonian self-determination, nationalism became closely associated with citizenship and loyalty; and "civilization" with European or Western identity. The two identities reinforced each other much of the time, but, of course, identities can be manipulated to alter the boundaries of moral communities in both positive and negative ways. In a path-breaking study of the North Atlantic community, Karl Deutsch and his colleagues pondered multiple boundaries and the ways in which they could shift.[67] They developed the idea of a "security community" whose members will resolve disputes peacefully. As a consequence of high levels of positive transactions over time and a recent history of friendly relations, members become responsive to one another's concerns and problems, and they develop trust, compatible norms, and feelings of mutual identification. Deutsch's group identified two types of security community. The first they called "amalgamated," by which they meant territorial states like Germany that had been born by unifying smaller polities and the parts of which have surrendered legal independence. The second type, "pluralistic," consisted of actors that retain formal independence but cannot imagine fighting with one another. In such a community, widespread and frequent communication and interaction facilitate the exchange of information and expand the pool of common tastes, memories, and perceptions. Elites empathize with each other and are sensitive to one another's needs, thereby minimizing misperception and conflict. The European Union and the North Atlantic Treaty Organization are pluralistic security communities. Some pluralist communities such as Canada and the United States or the United States and Great Britain[68] are less formal.

---

[67] Karl W. Deutsch *et al.*, *Political Community and the North Atlantic Area: International Organization in the Light of Historical Experience* (Princeton: Princeton University Press, 1957).

[68] See, for example, Bruce M. Russett, *Community and Contention: Britain and America in the Twentieth Century* (Cambridge, MA: MIT Press, 1963).

Specifically, the articulation and application of norms pertaining to violence follows from actors' agreement about how to distinguish "bad" from "good" violence[69] or enforcement, as well as actors' willingness to submit to what Hans Kelsen called the *Grundnorm*, which can be thought of as a norm of reciprocity or moral equality.[70] Such reciprocity does not connote specific agreement about the content of a moral or ethical code, but rather the belief by members *within* a moral community that they are obligated to treat one another fairly and equitably on the basis of a reciprocity of obligation. Legal philosophers often wrangle with the norm of reciprocity as the basis for legal obligation,[71] and theorists like Robert Axelrod and Robert Keohane[72] see it as the basis for cooperation.

As we have seen, the state itself was intended as a solution to the unregulated violence that swept across Europe during the Thirty Years War in which civilians were as much the targets of war-making as soldiers. "The horrors of an ungoverned soldiery," writes R. R. Palmer, "were remembered, especially in Germany after the Thirty Years War,"[73] when war and attendant disease killed perhaps one-third of Germany's population. Consequently: "Princes were supposed to wage war in such a way as to minimize the harm done both to their own soldiers, who deserved humane treatment if they happened to be captured or wounded, and to the civilian population."[74] In this way, war was rationalized to try to prevent the destructive savagery that characterized the religious strife of the sixteenth and seventeenth centuries, and armies

---

[69] We do not deny that "good" violence may also be violence that serves the interests of dominant actors, and "bad" violence that which obstructs their interests, but when these are translated into normative terms, and particularly when norms are codified as regulation or law, they are constructed qualitatively.

[70] Taking into account the problem of "anthropomorphizing" the state, what we are really suggesting is that those acting on behalf of the state do so within a normative framework constructed historically through diplomatic and international discourses. Thus the statement "the articulation and application of norms among actors follow from their normative agreement" refers to individuals acting on behalf of the state within a dynamic and ongoing normative discourse.

[71] We agree with those like Niklas Luhmann who see reciprocity as an antecedent to legal obligations in a liberal society. Luhmann, *A Sociological Theory of Law*, trans. Elizabeth King and Martin Albrow (Boston: Routledge and Kegan Paul, 1972).

[72] See Robert M. Axelrod, *The Evolution of Cooperation* (New York: Basic Books, 1984), and Robert M. Axelrod, and Robert O. Keohane (1993). "Achieving Cooperation under Anarchy: Strategies and Institutions," in David A. Baldwin, ed., *Neorealism and Neo-liberalism: The Contemporary Debate* (New York: Columbia University Press, 1993), pp. 85–115.

[73] R. R. Palmer, "Frederick the Great, Guibert, Bülow: From Dynastic to National War," in Peter Paret, eds., *Makers of Modern Strategy: From Machiavelli to the Nuclear Age* (Princeton: Princeton University Press, 1986), p. 93.

[74] Martin van Creveld, *The Transformation of War* (New York: Free Press, 1991), p. 37.

were designed in part to avoid the sort of random butchery that had characterized that period.

The evolution of norms such as the balance of power, as articulated by observers such as Emmerich de Vattel, David Hume, Rousseau, and Lord Brougham, and those aimed at "civilizing" war, as articulated in the Geneva and Hague conventions, were further intended to shield states, their rulers, their agents, and productive civilians from the consequences of unrestrained violence. Balance-of-power rhetoric made clear the obligations that sovereign states were believed to owe one another. The Prussian civil servant Friedrich von Gentz spoke of balance of power as "that constitution subsisting among neighbouring states more or less connected with one another."[75] Rousseau saw the balance as the result of Europeans' "identity of religion, of moral standard, of international law."[76] Others echoed the same theme. "Institutions like neutrality and the balance of power," argues Janice E. Thomson, "constrained states to behave in particular ways toward other states but they also empowered them to expand their authority and control over even such powerful actors as the mercantile companies."[77]

In effect, the Westphalian polity reached a tacit arrangement with its male subjects/citizens. On the one hand, they would provide the state with resources necessary to fight wars, give the state their allegiance, and let the state and its armies get on with things without civilian interference. On the other, the state would demand little of its civilian subjects/ citizens in wartime and protect them from the ravages of war. Thus, rulers preferred strategies "which in wartime interfered as little as possible with civilian life."[78] If civilians took up arms, as they did in Spain against Napoleon, they were viewed as criminals or, even worse, as rebels and could expect no mercy. Since armies fought one another according to rules that supposedly limited violence and protected civilians, the line between war and banditry was clearly demarcated.

As we argued earlier, an international order based on a system of Westphalian polities was a product of European sociohistorical processes, and then extended globally through European colonization and twentieth-century decolonization. What presently undermines that

---

[75] Cited in M. G. Forsyth, H. M. A. Keens-Soper, P. Savigear (eds.), *The Theory of International Relations: Selected Texts from Gentili to Treitschke* (New York: Atherton Press, 1970), p. 281.

[76] Cited in *ibid.*, p. 133.

[77] Janice E. Thomson, *Mercenaries, Pirates, and Sovereigns* (Princeton: Princeton University Press, 1994), p. 150.

[78] Palmer, "Frederick the Great, Guibert, Bülow," p. 92.

traditional global order and current efforts to regulate violence are contestations and transformations of identities, and consequently the intersubjective agreement necessary to constitute a stable moral community. These contestations and transformations are among, within, and across core European states, non-Western states, and in relations between the two. One obvious manifestation of these struggles is the tension between globalized and localized identities.

The Westphalian State: no longer center stage

Global politics was never as simple as the model of interstate anarchy portrayed it. Nevertheless, a state-centric way of viewing the political universe has made it difficult to appreciate either the anomalies that have always existed or the dramatic changes of recent decades.

Loyalty flows only to polities in exchange for psychological and material benefits. The state (or any polity) is generally respected and obeyed if it is not too big for the little things or too small for the big things, but, when it fails to deliver, citizens become disillusioned at least with the politicians currently in power. When changes of leaders repeatedly fail to generate improvement, which is the case in many contemporary states, an extended crisis of legitimacy is likely to result, not just for leaders but as regards the political order itself. That sense of crisis is further intensified by general anxiety about an unknown future. As Strange observes, with the possible exception of a few cases where security or even survival is immediately at risk and the state is seen as an indispensable protector: "Today it is much more doubtful that the state – or at least the majority of states – can still claim a degree of loyalty from the citizen greater than the loyalty given to family, to the firm, to the political party or even in some cases to the local football team."[79] Where is a citizen to turn? Most social scientists were very late in addressing such issues, and many have yet to do so.

One reason for tardiness was the degree to which the Cold War for so long froze both global politics and thinking about it. The Cold War, and especially the role of the United States, as Little observes, made it difficult "to deny that the state possessed an important, powerful and autonomous role" and encouraged "what Easton refers to as the 'double life' of the state, with political scientists exploring its internal features and specialists in international relations examining its external

---

[79] Strange, *The Retreat of the State*, p. 72.

features."[80] Under these conditions, postinternational perspectives remained "roads not taken" until the real world of the post-Cold War period forcefully intruded on theory.

Today, recognition grows that, although states will doubtless continue to exist, a world map divided into exclusive territorial boxes is only slightly more useful than the maps of America available to Columbus. The states that remain are different than their precursors both in form and function; they are "less sovereign," less autonomous, and less able either to protect or inspire citizens. "The sovereign state of old," declares Jan Aart Scholte, "almost exclusively represented and promoted so-called 'domestic' or 'national' – read *territorial* – interests." In contrast, states today are "less a medium for holding a territorial line of defence of its 'inside' against its 'outside'" and are more "an arena of collaboration and competition between territorial and supraterritorial interests" such as "global capital."[81]

Recalling the importance of uneven development, we must be cautious about taking this line of argument too far. The erosion of state institutions and frontiers is furthest along in postcolonial areas, whereas the capacity of states to carry out multiple roles and to cooperate in forming successful regional and transnational institutions remains greatest among the richer and older states. There are states and there are states; they are not, as noted earlier, homologous; and, again as noted earlier, they reflect their paternity and genealogy.

Thus, much of the Arabic world retains the tribal and clan-based identities and nomadic practices of its origins. Saudi Arabia, for example, retains Wahabi Muslim and tribal roots. Mongolia may even be thought of as "preterritorial" because Mongolians still follow nomadic traditions in which notions of land as private and bounded remain largely alien. For years, several Latin American states with traditional agricultural economies were essentially extended family concerns, which existed largely to protect the property rights of wealthy elites and the privileges of military establishments from any challenge by the masses. Colombian elites have been locked in a decades-old deadly struggle with leftist guerrillas and druglords, in which social categories have regularly overlapped.

---

[80] Richard Little, "The Growing Relevance of Pluralism?" in Smith, Booth, and Zalewski, eds., *International Theory*, pp. 73, 74.
[81] Jan Aart Scholte, "Global Capitalism and the State," *International Affairs* 73:3 (1997), p. 45. Emphasis in original.

In Africa, the existence of governments that are extensions of tribal power, along with the failure of authorities to cope with explosive socioeconomic problems, weaken loyalties to the state while intensifying and deepening older tribal identities that colonial and postcolonial leaders had sought to dampen. The Nigerian government and armed forces are largely instruments to perpetuate Hausa political power. "National" politics in Kenya is mainly a reflection of relations among the Luo, the Kikuyu, and other tribal groups. A number of African states like Congo/Brazzaville currently express their sovereignty chiefly through the diplomatic protocols of the United Nations. Rwanda and Burundi exist largely in atlases; in reality, the organizing labels are Hutu and Tutsi, Bakongo and Ovimbundu, and so forth. The Liberian state is dead; the country is little more than an arena for conflict among the Krahn, Mende, and Gbandi. Some states, like Sierra Leone and Somalia, have been sustained (barely) by humanitarian organizations[82] and international institutions.

Similar trends are visible in Asia as well. Afghanistan is once more reliving ancient intra-Islamic and intertribal feuds, pitting Pashtun against Hazara, Tajik, and on and on. Pakistan reflects similar divisions but is even more complex. Indeed, large areas in both countries are beyond the control of their governments.

In sum, the interstate model of global politics has always been misleading, but today it hopelessly distorts global politics. Today, all states share authority with other polities; all confront transnational and subnational challenges; and in some extreme cases state institutions have collapsed. Even in Europe, the birthplace of the Westphalian State, autonomy is challenged from above by the European Union, NATO, and other organizations, and from below by regional and ethnic forces.[83] The sheer pace of change bewilders governments, which intensifies factionalism and bureaucratic competition and often leads to gridlock and inertia.

Counter-arguments

The state is *not* vanishing, and the habit of patriotism is slow to erode in those countries where it was engendered in the first instance. But

[82] See P. J. Simmons, "Learning to Live with NGOs," *Foreign Policy* No. 112 (Fall 1998), pp. 82–95.
[83] See, for example, John Newhouse, "Europe's Rising Regionalism," *Foreign Affairs* 76:1 (January/February 1997), pp. 67–84.

patriotism should not be confused with faith in government or politicians, and except for the burden of paying national taxes (if one does not evade them) patriotism tends to be a "cheap" sentiment, limited to flag waving and road signs demanding that we "support our troops."

One response to claims of state erosion might be that citizens are prepared to die for their country, but not for their corporation. Strange acknowledges that "the global company does not call on its employees to face death for the good of the firm." "But then," she adds, "in today's world [in stable political societies], the state does not ask citizens to die for it either." "Loyalty of the kind that is ready to die for a cause is more often found among ethnic or religious minorities . . . than it is among the ordinary citizens in an average state."[84] Surely the behavior of Islamist militants reaffirms her claim. Yet, it is hard to imagine citizens of modern states lining up as they did between 1914 and 1918 to join armies in battles that will cost thousands of lives.

State erosion is not universally recognized in part because of three paradoxes that Strange describes.[85] The first is that, while overall state power and capacity have declined and privatization initiatives are widespread, many governments retain a key role in public education, policing, and health and welfare. Moreover, the intervention of government agencies in certain aspects of citizens' lives has continued to increase. Government regulations outlaw certain chemicals, create affirmative action quotas, establish high-occupancy traffic lanes, force automobile passengers to wear seat belts, and so on. Still, virtually all governments persistently get low marks for their performance in public opinion polls. None are able to protect citizens from globalization shocks. The advance of education and skills has made ordinary citizens harder to persuade and satisfy, and, in the developing world, has helped to create a veritable explosion of expectations and demands with which governments find it virtually impossible to cope.

As the United States' own experience illustrates, the relative authority and capacity of polities vary over time. When more and more authority was transferred to Washington in the United States federal system in the 1930s and 1940s, bureaucracies at the state level continued to grow as well. This was partly because government at all levels was taking on more functions *vis-à-vis* civil society, partly because agencies like the FBI and the Social Security Administration needed local offices, and partly because states themselves had to administer numerous federally

---

[84] Strange, *The Retreat of the State*, p. 72.   [85] *Ibid.*, pp. 4–7.

sponsored programs. In recent years, with Republican conservatives dominating Washington and a conservative Supreme Court, more and more functions from welfare to speed limits on highways are being transferred back to state authority. Like so many nested polities in human history, the states of the United States are making a comeback of sorts.

For its part, the US Supreme Court has had to wrestle with constitutional issues of major importance affecting the very nature of federalism. In one case, the Court (narrowly) decided against the capacity of states to set term limits for those persons elected to Congress; in another, against Washington's extending its power to regulate "interstate commerce" so far as to make it a Federal crime to possess a gun near a school. Yale Law School Professor Paul Gewirtz observed that Justice Clarence Thomas's dissent in the term-limits case actually embodied "the first principles of those who opposed ratification of the Constitution." Gewirtz recalled that American patriot ("Give me liberty or give me death!") Patrick Henry had declared in 1788, "I am not really an American, I am a Virginian," and complained that the authors of the Constitution had no authority "to speak the language of 'we the people' instead of 'we the states'." Justice John Paul Stevens, for the majority in the term-limits case, pointed out that the Preamble to the Constitution mentions the Founders' intention to create "a more perfect union." However, Justice Thomas countered that the original formulation of the Preamble was "We the people of the states of New Hampshire, Massachusetts," and so on, and that the phrase "the United States" is used consistently throughout the Constitution "as a plural noun."[86]

Strange's second paradox is that, notwithstanding the state's "retreat," there is a growing "queue" of groups that want to have their own state. As former US Secretary of State Warren Christopher put it, if matters continue as they have, "[w]e'll have 5,000 countries rather than the hundred plus we now have."[87] Die-hard interstate theorists like to seize on this apparent paradox to insist that, surface appearances to the contrary, nothing has really changed – the state is doing fine, thank you, since everyone seems to want one. In doublethink fashion, defenders of the theoretical status quo transform a problem for their map of the world – the fact states may be disintegrating and boundaries therefore might be altered from the inside – into a virtue. Is this the final triumph

---

[86] Quoted in *New York Times*, May 29, 1995, p. A19.
[87] Quoted in *New York Times*, February 2, 1993, p. 1.

of the nation-state ideal? In fact, where statehood is the goal, the likelihood of actually achieving sovereign independence is small, but such campaigns are likely to go on causing big trouble for established states nonetheless. Where they do succeed, the result may often be a mere "façade of statehood" as in Bosnia or East Timor.

Defenders of the state like to have their cake and eat it too. When they are not arguing that violent national self-determination movements actually show the attraction of the state ideal, they point to the fact that – notwithstanding the Iran–Iraq war, Iraq's invasion of Kuwait, the Somali–Ethiopian War, or transborder "civil wars" elsewhere in Africa – interstate attempts to alter state boundaries have been remarkably few in recent decades. Indeed, the 1991 Gulf War suggests that sovereign boundaries may still count for something when someone marshals an army and crosses them as a naked aggressor. Thomson and Krasner refer to the "low annihilation rate of states since World War II" that is "enhanced by the growing significance of juridical sovereignty."[88] "In the twentieth century, and especially since 1945," declare Jackson and Zacher, "states have not only come to a judgment that they should not murder each other, they have adopted the position that they should not maim each other – that is to say, they should not cut off pieces. Today states are more respectful of each other's independence and territory than they have ever been, or in a different terminology, they are more normatively committed to the territorial covenant."[89] The apparent decline in territorial ambitions leads Zacher to conclude that "the underlying premise of the territorial integrity norm is not a commitment to separateness but a commitment to a global political order in which people have excised a major source of international violence."[90]

The Cold War rivalry did restrain boundary changes, but it is significant that there were few challenges to existing boundaries when the Cold War ended. Of course, one key reason for the decline in interstate aggression is that legal boundaries now matter less and less in practice – except to ethnic groups fixated on a "homeland" – because they can so

---

[88] Janice E. Thomson and Stephen D. Krasner, "Global Transactions and the Consolidation of Sovereignty," in Ernst-Otto Czempiel and James N. Rosenau, eds., *Global Changes and Theoretical Challenges: Approaches to World Politics for the 1990s* (Lexington, MA: Lexington Book, 1989), pp. 206, 207.

[89] Jackson and Zacher, "The Territorial Covenant," p. 26.

[90] Mark W. Zacher, "The Territorial Integrity Norm: International Boundaries and the Use of Force," *International Organization* 55:2 (Spring 2001), p. 246. Zacher cites John A. Vasquez, *The War Puzzle* (Cambridge: Cambridge University Press, 1993) to show the role of territory in the outbreak of war.

easily be transcended. Also, the cost of war has continued to increase. Yet another reason is the alternative offered to states by new forms of political association. For instance, a small state like Estonia that never previously stood a chance alone on the playing field of global politics now finds its security protected by NATO and its economy enhanced by ties with transnational capitalism, as well as membership in the European Union.

The third paradox that Strange cites is the apparent success of the Asian state model. Are not detractors of "the state" themselves being Eurocentric by not paying more attention to successes in Asia? To the contrary, Strange believed Asian "exceptionalism" to have been the product of special conditions that are now being eroded and will not be repeated, mainly post-World War II development aid and technology from the West, coupled with a dispensation to pursue closed-market policies. One difficulty with advancing the Asian model as evidence is that some Asian states are hard to differentiate from their private sector. A strategic alliance existed between government and the private sphere, especially in economic planning and managed development.[91] Singapore's government started out by identifying sectoral opportunities within the global economy for national and transnational firms, but somewhere along the line the private-sector tail started wagging the dog. Moreover, Japan's persistent economic difficulties and the financial crisis that struck Southeast and East Asia in 1997 and 1998 have revealed grave strains in the alliance between government and the private sphere.

As Asian governments face greater pressures to adopt nondiscriminatory trade and investment policies, Strange argued, things are going to unravel: "[T]here will be contests for control over the institutions and agencies of governments in most of the Asian countries. There will be contests between factions of political parties, between vested interests both in the private sectors and in the public sector. There will be power struggles between branches of the state bureaucracy. Both the unity and authority of governments is bound to suffer."[92] Indonesia and, to a lesser extent, Japan and Malaysia already reflect these contests. And, even in China, the regime succeeded in maintaining a strong central state partly by allowing the private sector and prosperous regions significantly increased autonomy. It remains to be seen whether strong central control in China can survive privatization of state-owned enterprises

---

[91] See, for example, Eun Mee Kim, *Big Business, Strong State: Collusion and Conflict in South Korean Development, 1960–1990* (Albany, NY: State University of New York Press, 1997).
[92] Strange, *The Retreat of the State*, p. 7.

and resulting unemployment, the growing pluralization of society that is accompanying market reforms, and boom and bust cycles in the world economy.

An additional counter-argument is that states can recover some of their lost capacity by cooperating with one another through international organizations and regimes and by using humanitarian and other nongovernmental organizations – entities that have a capacity to operate across sovereign boundaries. In other words, by "outsourcing" (rather like firms) to other polities, states may be able to salvage their authority partly by creating and making use of transnational institutions that they still control. This is likely to prove effective for some; but the results are likely to differ from issue to issue; and the ultimate effect on citizen identities and loyalties remains to be seen.

Conclusion: fragmented authority

Today's postinternational world exhibits boundaries among authorities and networks of authorities that overlap with and transcend the sovereign boundaries of states. That world, in the midst of background globalization trends, is also one of highly specialized spheres of authority or polities that often are only loosely connected with territorial space, that is, "out of place." In recent decades, fission and fusion have taken a steep toll on sovereign states. In Europe, the historical heartland of nation-states, states face strong centralizing challenges from the European Union and localist pressures from resurgent regions such as Northern Italy, the Rhône-Alpes, and Catalonia (not to mention Basques and Corsicans, ambitious cities, the Italian Mafia, and German *Länder*).[93] Elsewhere, even where democratic reforms have been gaining force as in much of Latin America and the former Soviet bloc, there remains a profound sense of malaise based on the conviction that government can no longer deliver the goods and may even be hopelessly corrupt.

The postinternational world is one in which authority is fragmented among polities with little hierarchical arrangement among them. They, in turn, allocate values locally and, some of them, transnationally and globally. In focusing on the role of a rich tapestry of individuals and groups in shaping outcomes, this chapter returned us to the relationship among parts and wholes, as well as multiple and shifting identities and loyalties.

[93] See Newhouse, "Europe's Rising Regionalism."

Since sovereignty is essentially a legal claim, all the speculation in the regime literature about it somehow being increasingly "divided" is rather misleading. Effective control over or influence in specific sociopolitical issue areas has always been divided. Even when states' formal scope of authority is substantial, some governments may be so paralyzed by disunity that they are incapable of acting, except on the rarest occasions, in anything like a coherent fashion – and in this sense, "the state" hardly seems like a "real" actor at all. When policies finally emerge, the result often seems like the triumph of parochial bureaucratic interests or a reflection of powerful private interest groups, rather than the admirable expression of the public interest that some political scientists still hope will somehow triumph.

Finally, as we have repeatedly emphasized, the question is not whether sovereign states continue to exist and "matter" in some respects, for, of course, they do. The contention that states are no longer relevant and may soon disappear is routinely cited and lampooned by present-day defenders of the state as a sort of straw person. It makes an easy target: state-centric theorists can show that there is some life in the old state yet, and thereby avoid addressing the *relative* decline of and changes in states in late twentieth- and early twenty-first-century global politics. Georg Sørensen is correct in suggesting that a more productive way of looking at some of the same matters is simply to ask – not whether states are "winning" or "losing" relative to other polities – rather how states are changing or adapting to new conditions.[94] This is a useful question. However, considering that question by no means excludes the other, which is not only fair but also important. By contrast with the nonissue (whether states are likely to become extinct), we still can ask to what extent states are ill-equipped to cope with the demands imposed upon them from above and below? How are they faring relative to other polities – and why?

---

[94] See especially by Georg Sørensen: *Changes in Statehood: The Transformation of International Relations* (London: Palgrave, 2001); and *The Transformation of the State* (London: Palgrave, 2004).

5 Identities in a postinternational world

In denouncing the use of military tribunals to try enemy prisoners seized by American troops in Afghanistan, an *Economist* editorial declared that British ministers "have asked for British citizens caught in Afghanistan to be sent home for trial in British courts."[1] The editorial involves the confusion of identities to alter the nature of an argument. The individuals in question are *British citizens*, but surely it is *not* correct (as the editorial implies) that their Britishness is central in this case. Nowhere in the editorial is any reference at all made to ethnicity or religion, which were the *real* identities that drove these individuals to fight for the Taliban. Were the United States to regard British citizenship as the key identity, then it would have had reason to take its closest ally to task for harboring terrorists or giving them passports to travel abroad. The editorial reflects a narrowly international view of a postinternational universe and helps to illustrate why identities merit our attention.

"The years after the Cold War," wrote Samuel Huntington, "witnessed the beginnings of dramatic changes in peoples' identities and symbols of those identities. Global politics began to be reconfigured along cultural lines."[2] Phenomena involving dramatic shifts in identities and identity hierarchies, ranging from the collapse of communism to a proliferation of Islamic terrorism, are having a significant impact on global life. A dramatic resurgence in identity theory, in earlier decades largely confined to the study of nationalism, is apparent in scholarship as diverse as Fukuyama's *The End of History and the Last Man* and Huntington's *The Clash of Civilizations and the Remaking of World Order* to the various strands of constructivist thought.

---

[1] "Unjust, Unwise, Un-American," *The Economist*, July 12–18, 2003, p. 9.
[2] Huntington, *The Clash of Civilizations and the Remaking of World Order*, p. 19.

The subjective dimension of global politics is reviving after decades in the shadow of a realist/neorealist focus on states and power distribution and the scientific demand for data and measurement. In fact, theorizing about the subjective dimension is hardly unprecedented, and many of today's "innovations" owe much to pioneers such as Karl Deutsch, Harold Lasswell, Gabriel Almond, Robert Jervis, and others who contributed to theorizing about communication, integration, political culture, nationalism, and perception. It is indeed "remarkable," as Yosef Lapid suggests, "that in the subtle struggle of the prefixes, the 're-' ... has lately been scoring some impressive victories over the 'post-'."[3]

The collapse of communism brought an end to an epoch that seemed as though it might go on forever and triggered a new epoch of rapid and dramatic change. Rosenau comments: "Many observers ... did not allow for the possibility that the Cold War and the Soviet Union could come to abrupt ends. In retrospect, such failures border on the inexcusable."[4] Unfortunately, theory, especially perceptions of continuity and normative preferences for political and social stability (hallmarks of the Cold War era) masked what was happening. It is, as Friedrich Kratochwil observes, "no accident that the question of 'culture' and identity most clearly comes to the fore when we focus on problems of change."[5] And Lapid's 1996 prediction is coming to pass:

> Embracing the idea that cultures and identities are emergent and constructed (rather than fixed and natural), contested and polymorphic (rather than unitary and singular), and interactive and process-like (rather than static and essence-like) can lead to pathbreaking theoretical advances. Such insights raise the possibility that our intuitive notion of fully formed, stable actors, producing and reproducing a predictably stable and invariant world may be seriously misleading.[6]

Nations, states, and nation-states

For over three centuries, peoples' identities and loyalties were anchored in complex ways in the territorial state, as "subjects" and later

[3] Yosef Lapid, "Culture's Ship: Returns and Departures in International Relations Theory," in Yosef Lapid and Friedrich Kratochwil, eds., *The Return of Culture and Identity in IR Theory* (Boulder, CO: Lynne Rienner, 1996), p. 5.
[4] Rosenau, *Distant Proximities*, 21.
[5] Friedrich Kratochwil, "Is the Ship of Culture at Sea or Returning?" in Lapid and Kratochwil, p. 213.
[6] Lapid, "Culture's Ship," p. 8.

"citizens."[7] With legally recognized boundaries and sovereign recognition, and with sufficient coercive capability to regulate most of what crossed those boundaries, European states provided a reliable territorial basis to fix and enforce boundaries of identity. "The modern territorial state," as Agnew and Corbridge declare, "steadily replaced the plurality of hierarchical bonds with an exclusive identity based upon membership in the common juridical space defined by the writ of the state. . . . Identification of citizenship with residence in a particular territorial space became the central fact of political identity."[8]

Before the nineteenth century, however, the identities of "rulers" and "ruled" in European states were largely incompatible, and the "interests" of the latter rarely reflected the "interests" of the former. This connection was not accomplished until the merging in the late eighteenth and nineteenth centuries of *state* and *nation* and growing popular participation in politics. Although the idea of "nation" grew in popularity, its meaning remained controversial. A key reason why is that it is typically a second-order trait constructed from one or several more specific traits like language, ethnicity, or religion.[9] In this respect, either "melting pot" or multicultural images of United States ("American") nationality is a prominent exception to the rule. There are others, of course, like Canada, Switzerland, or Malayasia. Nationalism's only consensual attribute is that "nationals" have some sense of ownership of the nation as a whole. As Walker Connor observes, "the essence of a nation is intangible. The essence is a psychological bond that joins a people and differentiates it,"[10] though what constitutes a "people" also remains undefined.

However ill-defined, many nation-states succeeded in convincing citizens that putting their lives on the line for their "fatherland" or "motherland" – *Dulce et decorum est pro patria mori* – was somehow a noble expression of self and a means of defending home and loved ones as well. Propaganda and close-order drill instilled the message in impressionable young males. Those whom the nation-state could not convince, it tried with varying success to suppress.

---

[7] Rodney Bruce Hall has reviewed the evolution of the identity and sources of legitimacy of European states from their birth to the end of the Cold War. See Hall, *National Collective Identity*.

[8] Agnew and Corbridge, *Mastering Space*, p. 85.

[9] See John Hutchinson and Anthony D. Smith, eds., *Nationalism* (New York: Oxford University Press, 1994).

[10] Walker Connor, "A Nation Is a Nation, Is an Ethnic Group, Is a . . ." in Hutchinson and Smith, eds., *Nationalism*, p. 361.

Outside of Western Europe, the nation-state concept was to prove more problematical, for example, where the territorial polities imposed by colonial masters did not coincide with the frontiers of precolonial polities or where empires and territorial states housed multiple self-conscious nationalities. The danger obviously increased with the rise of the principle of national self-determination.

Where democratic institutions flourished, nation-states enhanced their legitimacy by promoting tolerance and allowing a diversity of identity groups substantial autonomy. In the West especially, citizens enjoyed considerable latitude in defining themselves and scripting their identities. As long as citizens paid taxes and performed military service – and did not deface public monuments – the state left them alone. One could have a family, practice a profession, worship god, drink at a social club, and so on without any particular concern for the state.

Yet, during the second half of the nineteenth century, even as national historians were busy constructing it, the idea of *nation* came under strain. Social and political issues divided classes (the urban proletariat grew with industrialization), genders (especially where the question of enfranchisement mattered), and races (when a new wave of European imperialism accelerated). In nondemocratic societies such as Prussia, Austria, and Russia, nationalism assumed an intolerant and exclusivist face as it was ruthlessly exploited and manipulated by authoritarian leaders to increase their popularity and to promote militarization. Germans murdered German Jews even though most were loyal Germans.

Now, in the early twenty-first century, there appears to be a marked decline in patriotism if not state identity. Again the United States is an exception, although a crisis of legitimacy continues to bedevil Washington politicians. More and more citizens in the West are convinced of a diminished need for military protection (except against terrorism), impatient with high tax burdens, cognizant of official incompetence and corruption, and generally dubious as to whether government is any longer capable of delivering on its promises. There is a growing sense that problems have become too complex for public policy, and that welfare beyond an uncertain minimum can only be a function of individual initiative and transnational economic cycles. States are confronted with the economic and social challenges of globalization, and many face fissiparous tendencies at home. In Thomas Franck's words: "At the beginning of the third millennium one senses the coming of a new identity crisis. Increasingly, our psychic and even our material rewards seem to rest on fragmented and compounded self-identification."[11] The identity of Westphalian citizen faces growing challenges from other identities, ideologies, and authorities – some old, some reconstructed, and some new.

As we have observed, the end of the Cold War did not bring "the end of history,"[12] rather the reverse, as superpower contest restraints were removed. There was an almost immediate upsurge in civil conflicts and tribal violence. Even on the fringes of Europe and Canada there still reside "ethno-national" groups that claim that their culture has been submerged or swallowed up by majorities within nation-states – Spanish Basques, French Bretons and Corsicans, Canadian Québécois, Canadians Inuits and native Americans, Northern Irish Catholics, Celtic Scots and Welsh, and others. Fortunately, as Michael Keating stresses in his examination of Quebec, Catalonia, and Scotland, "minority nationalism" need not be "tribal" and may be willing to settle for some form of autonomy rather than full-fledged independence.[13]

Quebec is an instructive case of how complex overlapping identity questions can be. Former Parti Québécois premier Jacques Parizeau blamed his secession forces' loss of a 1995 referendum on "money and the ethnic vote," highlighting the presence of a large number of non-Francophone English and other minorities ("allophones") in his province. To complicate matters further, Cree and other indigenous Indian groups who claim half the territory of Quebec were so alarmed by the referendum that they threatened to secede on the basis of the same right to national self-determination that the Québécois were claiming. And, were Canada eventually to fall apart, Quebec might well not be the only departure, because there are regional/provincial identities as well as ethnic ones.

In sum, the familiar ideas of nation and nationalism have taken on a distinctly subversive, anti-state connotation across much of the globe. Some theorists are sufficiently concerned by the growing tension between nation and state that they are abandoning the nation-state

---

[11] Thomas M. Franck, "Tribe, Nation, World: Self-Identification in the Evolving International System," *Ethics and International Affairs* 11 (1997), p. 151.
[12] Francis Fukuyama, "The End of History?" *National Interest* (Summer 1989), pp. 3–18.
[13] Michael Keating, "Must Minority Nationalism Be Tribal? A Study of Quebec, Catalonia and Scotland," in Kenneth Christie, ed., *Ethnic Conflict, Tribal Politics: A Global Perspective* (Richmond, UK: Curzon Press, 1999). By contrast with Quebec, Keating notes: "In Catalonia, nationalism has always had a strong civic dimension and since the 1960s this has been dominant. Nationalists repeatedly stress that anyone who lives in Catalonia and wishes to belong is Catalan."

label altogether,[14] about which trend one can only say – it is high time.

A world of multiple identities

Each of us is many persons. Identities are essentially part of who we and others think we are at any moment in time. They help us give ourselves meaning and are necessary for others to "fit" us into their perceptions. Any definition of self is multidimensional and fluid. Our personalities are built from different bundles of traits – our descent, physical features, place of birth, religious affiliation, profession, gender, language, and so forth. Some identities generate immense passion; whereas others are more functional and routine in nature.

In theorizing about the social construction of identities, we are also describing the changing criteria for defining *us* and *them* as bases for political action. As this suggests, self-identities are rarely primordial, although bits and pieces of the stuff with which they are constructed may have a long history. Indeed, the debate between primordial and modern nationalists is largely irrelevant, reflecting little more than a misunderstanding of how history works *with* novelty to produce identities. In the course of their lives, people are likely to recognize only relatively few of their traits as worthy of self-definition, and the behavior of other communities toward them may even promote new traits or the rediscovery or reconstruction of old ones. Which common features will animate individuals is by no means predetermined, since identities are more a state of mind or social construction – identity adopted and/or imposed – than anything else. Political actors seeking additional power or legitimacy may produce new categories of *others* to provide mirror images for new or revived identity groups they wish to lead. Sometimes the course of events, particularly cataclysms, sharpen identities and the distinction between *us* and *them*.

Historically, French revolutionaries played a key role in producing a shift in identification from subject of the dynastic *état* to citizen (*citoyen*) of *la patrie*. Individualization, a consequence of education, prosperity, and secularism, was a necessary prerequisite for this shift, but an additional push from middle-class intellectuals seeking an end to feudal anomalies and Bourbon incompetence was also needed. Later, *Liberté!*

---

[14] See, for example, E. J. Hobsbawm, *Nations and Nationalism Since 1780* (New York: Cambridge University Press, 1990), pp. 46–79.

Egalité! Fraternité! were highjacked by Napoleon to sever the ties of subjects to dynastic rulers elsewhere in Europe. The Jacobins and Bonapartists in turn found it necessary to inflame nationalism in order to defend themselves. Over a century later, Lenin recognized that revolution had to be given a push by the ideology of a "vanguard of the proletariat" whether or not structural conditions were promising.

The French Revolution, like the fate of nationalism more generally, illiustrates how elites can manipulate the same identity for dramatically different ends. According to James Mayall, "liberal" nationalists regarded self-determination as "a liberal principle" and "objected to the idea that the cause of freedom and self-determination could be served by the deliberate use of force."[15] Liberals like Mazzini believed that national identities were crucial to bring about a new republican order in Europe and so eliminate the reasons for war. This version of nationalism triumphed in Europe with the revolutions of 1848 but later their failure became contaminated by racial myths and worship of violence.

By contrast, "historicist nationalists" took a different view of force. "[T]he line can be traced from Hegel's insistence that the conquests of the historical nations contribute to human progress through the frenzied enthusiasm of the belligerents during the early stages of the First World War, to the contemporary scene of freedom fighters engaged in real and imaginary wars of national liberation."[16] Gradually after 1848, nationalism became synonymous with exclusion and otherness.[17] No longer were the boundaries between nation-states softened by the cohesion of governing elites from a common class.

A recent example of manipulation of national passions for personal political reasons led to the collapse of Yugoslavia. Slobodan Milošević evoked old tales of Turkish predation to revive Serbian nationalism, ended the autonomy of Kosovo, and advanced claims against the other regions of his country, especially Croatia. Until civil war erupted in the former Yugoslavia, Bosnian Muslims had rarely identified themselves in religious terms. "We never, until the war, thought of ourselves as Muslims," declared a school teacher. "We were Yugoslavs. But when we began to be murdered, because we were Muslims, things changed. The

---

[15] James Mayall, *Nationalism and International Society* (Cambridge: Cambridge University Press, 1990), p. 30. See also Michael Lind, "In Defense of Liberal Nationalism," *Foreign Affairs* 73:3 (May/June 1994), pp. 87–99.
[16] Mayall, *Nationalism and International Society*, p. 31.
[17] See Andrew Linklater, *Men and Citizens in the Theory of International Relations* (London: Macmillan, 1982).

definition of who we are today has been determined by our killers."[18] Chechens had a similar experience after Russia's invasion. Prior to that event: "Nobody talked about religion. But these days it seems that nobody can stop talking about it. Nearly every Chechen soldier swears allegiance to Allah, taking *gazavat*, the holy oath to die fighting the invaders."[19] Likewise, for black Christians and animists in the Sudan, the war waged against them by the Arab Islamic regime in Khartoum "is a war of identity."[20] In some ways the American experience at the time of its Revolution was similar. According to Rodney Hall: "both Hans Kohn and, in a similar account, Liah Greenfeld, suggest that this treatment undermined the self-identification of the British colonials with the British state, and fostered the creation of a uniquely American collective identity."[21]

In other words, no trait *necessarily* becomes a category of identification without some manipulation, but any trait can. Any two individuals who happen to share skin color probably have more attributes in common with others who may or may not have the same or similar skin color. Undeniably, skin color provides a visible and potent basis for *racial* discrimination in societies, especially when it serves the objectives of ruling elites to play the race card, yet skin color has often been ignored. Much the same is true of *gender* and *class* as well. Although there have always been men and women, gender has only recently "arrived" as a potent identity.[22] By contrast, "class" has served as a potent political identity for many centuries, but its meaning has changed extensively to make it fit the issues of the day. With Marxism in eclipse since the end of the

---

[18] Cited in Chris Hedges, "Wars Turns Sarajevo Away from Europe," *New York Times*, July 28, 1995, p. A4. See also Roger Thurow, "Muslims From Bosnia Find Refuge in Islam While Adrift in Europe," *Wall Street Journal*, September 6, 1994, pp. A1, A5.

[19] Cited in Michael Specter, "Faith Reinforces Hate in the Caucasus," *New York Times*, January 15, 1995, sec. 4, p. 5. See also "Chaos in the Caucasus," *The Economist*, October 9–15, 1999, pp. 23–26.

[20] Donatella Lorch, "Sudan's Long Civil War Threatening to Spread," *New York Times*, November 22, 1994, p. A3.

[21] Hall, *National Collective Identity*, p. 113.

[22] In J. Ann Tickner's words: "Including previously hidden gender inequalities in the analysis of global insecurity allows us to see how so many of the insecurities affecting us all . . . are gendered in their historical origins, their conventional definitions, and their contemporary manifestations." J. Ann Tickner, *Gender in International Relations* (New York: Columbia University Press, 1992), p. 129. The present authors have been described (with some justice) as advocating "studying authority patterns 'out there' while not recognizing the gender-eclipsing authority 'in here'." Christine Sylvester, *Feminist Theory and International Relations in a Postmodern Era* (New York: Cambridge University Press, 1994), p. 218.

Cold War, class at least temporarily seems to have faded as a leading identity category.

At this point, we must clearly distinguish between identity itself and identity hierarchy. At *any moment*, a political issue is likely to evoke only one or a few of an individual's multiple identities. Individuals are aware of a variety of existing identities of different degrees of importance to them. In state-centric models, the state was always at the top of such rankings or hierarchies. In reality, however, the ranking of identities will vary significantly depending on context, and that hierarchy varies and evolves issue by issue. Thus, virtually every issue elicits a different cast of players and different sets of allies and adversaries. Hierarchy also shifts as the significance attached to political relationships with others is altered, especially in the context of new or redefined issues. When confronting abortion questions, for example, religion and gender are likely to play a greater role in determining an individual's political perspective than in most other issues. Similarly, wage and labor issues will evoke identities based on class or economic status. In neither of these cases is national origin or citizenship usually an important identity, and individuals may find themselves supporting or opposing the position taken by their state.

History is instructive here as well. In practice, identities based on states have always shared pride of place with other identities, including at the height of the Westphalia era, but the rivalry among alternate identities has intensified in recent decades. The numerous identities characterizing individuals can and often do evolve into loyalties to nonsovereign polities. Today, new technologies facilitate the spread of modernity and of the secular culture associated with it. Three consequences are the politicization of larger segments within societies, especially segments that were previously politically inert; the erosion of norms that previously had encouraged passivity and obedience and on which traditional elites had built their authority; and the growing capacity of individuals and groups to communicate over vast distances. To the extent that the masses are loosed from traditional moorings, they become available for mobilization and manipulation by a wider range of elites for political and economic ends. Under the banner of religion or ethnicity, some traditional elites (with only limited success – see Chapter 8) try to prevent or at least stem this process by managing and taming the stream of ideas that flow across national frontiers in the form of TV images conveyed by satellites, videos, electronic mail, and the Internet. A capitalist, consumerist, and secular culture associated with globalization is advancing, at different rates, almost everywhere. The result is a remarkable cultural "soup" or what Peter Berger and Huntington term "many globalizations."[23]

The central role of culture

In the process of cultural homogenization,[24] new elites are created, and the authority of old ones is eroded. Instead of a world of distinctive local cultures and traditional values reinforced by religion and custom, there is developing around the world a wealthy and upwardly mobile sector, which places a premium on individual choice and market forces. These values are widely associated with the West, especially (but not exclusively) with the United States. It is less important that urban elites dress much the same, eat some of the same foods, and listen to some of the same music than that people substitute the mainly secular norms of the West, particularly possessive individualism, for stabilizing customs and norms on which traditional authority structures rest. As new local elites are empowered and integrated into the global culture, leaders of traditional social groups, fearful of losing authority, mobilize to resist the "strange," "secular," or "sensual" flows from outside.

Lapid and Kratochwil observe that "culture" is currently experiencing a revival in theories of global politics.[25] However, as Lapid correctly suggests (quoting Jepperson and Swindler), the "cargo" carried on "culture's ship" is in serious need of "inventory,"[26] owing to the lack of clarity inherent in the concept of "culture." At one end of the analytic spectrum, the concept of culture is almost impossible to distinguish from the supposed "civilizations" that Huntington has lately been predicting will "clash" in the next stage of global politics.[27]

Huntington's clash-of-civilizations thesis has enjoyed something of a revival since the apocalyptic attacks on the World Trade Center and the

---

[23] Peter L. Berger and Samuel P. Huntington, eds., *Many Globalisations: Cultural Diversity in the Contemporary World* (Oxford: Oxford University Press, 2002).
[24] Bryan Turner sees the growth of tourism, trade, and global television as central to the process. Bryan S. Turner, "Contemporary Problems in the Theory of Citizenship," in Turner, ed., *Citizenship and Social Theory* (London: Sage, 1993), pp. 1–18.
[25] Lapid and Kratochwil, eds., *The Return of Culture and Identity in IR Theory*.
[26] Lapid, "Culture's Ship, p. 3.
[27] Samuel P. Huntington, "The Clash of Civilizations?" *Foreign Affairs* 72:3 (Summer 1993), pp. 22–49. Huntington's stress on the role of religion in defining cultures received growing attention after 9/11.

Pentagon, but it is riddled with contradictions and more than a little pernicious as well. Each of the "civilizations" he identifies (for example, Islam) has any number of faultlines. Even Huntington seems to ignore his own civilizational divisions by highlighting tensions between "the West and the Rest." What he misses is a central fact of history since day one: multiple identities tend to persist yet may shift with the march of events and specific issues. With regard to particular issues and contexts, the West and the Rest may be salient; with regard to others, not so – Egyptian leaders may regard Islamic fundamentalists as dangerous extremists, and so on. At the end of the day, less rigid categories like Berger's and Huntington's "many globalizations" seem much closer to the mark; not to mention the micro level, since individuals themselves have very different orientations and attitudes toward specific issues. Rosenau, for example, posits twelve different "worlds" or positions regarding globalization and individuals who regularly shift among these worlds as they focus on one issue or another.[28]

"Culture" is another vague concept. R. B. J. Walker comments:

> [T]he significance of the concept of culture in the analysis of international relations is not that it offers a convenient category of socio-scientific explanation, or a convincing account of human nature, or a helpful classification of the different kinds of human practices there have been. Rather it hints at all the uncertainties of modernity, and at a multitude of struggles – on the grounds of tradition or postmodernity, of gender, race, religion and ethnicity, or socialism or capitalism, of the Other, of the future, of the local community, of the state and of the planet – to reconstitute the conditions of human existence in the face of tremendous structural transformations.[29]

In this book, we do little better in defining culture quite simply as socially collective ways of viewing the world. Without doubt, even as there are multiple and overlapping identities, so there are multiple and overlapping cultures.

The corrosive effect of homogenization-by-globalization on local cultures and norms is increasingly triggering backlashes such as that which in the late 1970s brought down the Shah of Iran or thereafter brought the Taliban to power in Afghanistan. No aspect of the emerging postinternational world is more controversial than the clash between yesterday's and today's cultural values. "A global MTV generation" is

[28] Rosenau, *Distant Proximities*, chs. 4–6.
[29] R. B. J. Walker, "The Concept of Culture in the Theory of International Relations," in Jongsuk Chay, ed., *Culture and International Relations* (New York: Praeger, 1990), pp. 12–13.

emerging, declares one economist, in which young people both in developing and developed countries "prefer Coke to tea, Nikes to sandals, Chicken McNuggets to rice."[30] Religious fundamentalism (whether that of Islamists in Algeria, Orthodox Jews in Israel, Hindu militants in India, or the Christian Coalition in the United States), gender conflict, interethnic or intertribal rivalries, and national revivals all involve cultural backlash.

What is far less clear is how identities are formed, and why certain of them and associated political forms come to the fore at particular times and not at others.

Collective identities and new boundaries?[31]

Whatever one's principal identity – militant Islamist, capitalist entrepreneur, Nigerian Yoruba, Hindu "untouchable" – identity helps to predict political position on relevant issues and who will be one's "friends" and "enemies." Rodney Hall is probably correct when he argues that "our individual identity – our ideas about who we regard ourselves to be – are derived in a social context" so that both individual and collective identity "are co-constituted."[32] Individuals are drawn to others who share a common fate and are repelled by those who threaten fate-companions. Thus, the establishment of refugee camps in Jordan, Lebanon, and Gaza after Israel's war of independence and the later Six-Day War, and the collective treatment of these refugees by the United Nations played a role in producing a Palestinian identity distinct from the Arab states.

Communication has to foster not only a sense of common identity but also of political efficacy, a belief on the part of individuals that they can improve their lot or at least protect what they have if they associate with one another. As this suggests, then, although individual identities initially arise within the self, they must be "ratified" by the perceptions and behavior of others. "Common knowledge," as Wendt argues, "requires 'interlocking' beliefs, not just everyone having the same beliefs. This interlocking quality gives common knowledge, and the cultural forms it constitutes, an at once subjective and intersubjective character."[33] Such

---

[30] Cited in Bernard Wysocki Jr., "In Developing Nations Many Youths Splurge, Mainly on US Goods," *The Wall Street Journal*, June 26, 1997, p. A1.
[31] Some of the following appeared in Ferguson and Mansbach, "Global Politics at the Turn of the Millennium," pp. 77–107.
[32] Hall, *National Collective Identity*, p. 36.
[33] Wendt, *Social Theory of International Politics*, p. 160.

intersubjective perception logically demands at least one comparison group that is seen as "different" in some key respect. Identity groups tend to become moral communities in which members are obliged to treat one another according to shared norms, rules, and standards that need not be applied to "outsiders." Sameness provides the legitimacy for moral communities, which in turn legitimates the regulation of behavior by members of the community. This does not mean that there need be conflict among different identity groups but that the potential for conflict exists if an issue arises that is linked to the differences in their identities.

In traditional rural societies, information about shared fates will remain relatively limited and local. Urbanization and industrialization dramatically extend the interaction of individuals and their knowledge of one another and create potential for expansion of community boundaries. Modern communications and transportation technologies have revolutionized the availability of greater information about others at limitless distances and have made possible the rapid extension of existing or new identities, making state boundaries more and more porous and tenuous. Individuals no longer have to be concentrated in settings like refugee camps to communicate with others, perceive common traits, or act conjointly upon that perception. We must nonetheless be aware of the "digital divide" that still separates those who do and those who do not have these technologies.

Boundaries demarcate who is "inside" and who is "outside" the boundaries of civic and moral obligation, and that issue is regaining an importance for political theory and global politics not seen since the triumph of the Westphalian State. This is complicated because identities, and therefore boundaries, may frequently change depending on revisions in identity hierarchies. Moreover, although there are a finite number of states, there is no fixed limit to the number of identities one might have and the number of polities with which one might associate.

As polities proliferate, sovereign boundaries succeed less and less in demarcating spaces or in "nationalizing" people's activities, perceptions, and beliefs, and "citizenship" becomes only one of numerous attributes. People periodically have to make painful choices among identities and related moral communities. When the American Civil War erupted, for instance, Robert E. Lee had to decide whether he was a Virginian or an American first, and the early Hanoverian kings of Great Britain repeatedly appeared to be Hanoverian rather than British.

The processes of centralizing and decentralizing authority, with the consequent struggle over and shifts in identities and loyalties, produce a dialectical and continuous cycle of political institutionalization and demystification that allows individuals literally to remake themselves in an extremely fluid fashion. In moving among moral communities, individuals may activate different identities every day. This may even entail experiencing different cultures in the manner of younger people in traditional societies who spend their days with "globalized" friends and return at night to "traditional" homes. Both poor and rich are aware of this cultural tidal wave: "They can see and hear it in their media, taste it in their food, and sense it in the products they buy."[34]

Understanding contemporary resistance to new identities requires exploring the historical sources of state authority and the conditions for its recent decline. This, in turn, demands careful consideration of how *power* becomes *authoritative* and legitimacy is eroded. For its part, the Westphalian State was a product of social and political forces arising from Europe's particular experience. It was the young state's ability to make demands on homogenizing national identities in the sixteenth and seventeenth centuries that provided legitimacy for the state's claim to monopolize coercion, initially the sovereign's claim to the loyalty of his (as a father) children-subjects. Religion and divine right were major sources of legitimacy for European sovereigns in the run-up to Augsburg and Westphalia. The legitimacy principle and dynastic ownership of territory served that role until the American and French Revolutions. Especially after the emergence of the nation-state, the boundaries of states marked sharp discontinuities of identity and loyalty.

Today, new or remade identities are institutionalized in a rich universe of polities, each with a capacity to mobilize adherents for political ends. For a variety of reasons, especially the explosive advances in information and communication technologies, individuals are invoking other identities with greater and greater frequency. Many alternative identities, especially in the developing world, have never been anchored in territory. Partly for this reason, they are not easily amenable to the conventional diplomatic and military practices used by states, but they are available for manipulation by political leaders. Such identities regularly collide with state interests or policies. Just as the congruence of the frontiers of territorial states with the identities and interests of elites

---

[34] David Rothkopf, "In Praise of Cultural Imperialism?" *Foreign Policy* 107 (Summer 1997), p. 38.

reinforced the legitimacy of the state system during recent centuries, so its absence is undermining that legitimacy today.

Increasingly, identity boundaries, whether based on cultures, markets, ethnic groups, and religions generally cut across and often stretch beyond sovereign boundaries. Consider the crazy-quilt pattern of politically relevant boundaries in the contemporary Middle East. To appreciate the complexity of regional politics, start with a standard political map showing the boundaries of states. Then superimpose additional boundaries that represent identities such as Kurdishness, Sunnism and Shi'ism, Muslim and Christian, tribalism, Arab and Persian, and various sects, clans, or groupings of the foregoing, family, and so on and so on. This only begins to paint a more realistic picture of identities, but it shows that the potential alignments and cleavages in the region dramatically exceed anything that could be imagined in an interstate world – or in Huntington's civilizations, for that matter.

Changing identities and loyalties

Since a wide variety of features might serve as a basis for self-identity, all individuals are to some extent both the same and different from one another. However, most identities are insufficiently stable or salient to provide clear political cues or durable boundaries between political communities.

State polities, as we have seen, are pulled in two directions. On the one hand, state fragmentation and "neo-tribalism" have accompanied the reemergence of old identities and loyalties that were repressed by colonial authorities and by commissars. In this sense, ethnic conflict is partly a problem of shifting identity boundaries in a state system constructed by Europeans in non-European settings. By contrast, developed regions have become a "pluralistic security community" in which war is inconceivable.[35] Here, states are more and more enmeshed in larger political and economic systems that limit their capacity to behave autonomously or to protect citizens from spillover from those systems. Under such conditions, it is not surprising that local, national, and regional identities challenge citizenship in importance.[36]

---

[35] Deutsch, *Political Community and the North Atlantic Area.*
[36] Michael Keating and Liesbet Hooghe make this point in regard to Europe. "By-Passing the Nation State? Regions and the EU Policy Process," in Jeremy J. Richardson, ed., *Policy Making in the European Union* (London: Routledge, 1996).

But fission and fusion are largely descriptive processes, and a persuasive and coherent theory of identity change remains to be elaborated. After all, as Peter Dombrowski observes:

> Before individuals can act as rational value maximizers in the Douglass North mode, before they can offer or withhold "loyalties" as in the Ferguson and Mansbach explanation, and even before they can self-actualize their personal skills and capacities as suggested by Rosenau, they must be sufficiently free from the bonds of tradition to "act" . . . to become agents of historical change, not simply passive vessels or blindly reactive forces.[37]

Dombrowski goes on to argue that the process of "individualization" associated with Europe's Renaissance and Reformation, the rise of market capitalism, and, in the end, the Westphalian State explain how passive subjects became active consumers of rival identities and their ideologies and acquired a capacity to make a self-interested choice among them. Dombrowski's own argument is also an historical description of a single process rather than a serious theoretical generalization.

Despite the role of history, coercion, utility, and manipulation in creating the conditions in which identities are recognized, identities are ultimately assumed by those who have them and who, along with like-minded others, arrive at an intersubjective consensus. Consequently, the identities and loyalties that help to create and sustain territorial states or any polity are neither necessary nor permanent conditions of political life. Increasingly, scholars (though rarely political scientists) are investigating "the role of memory and rhetorics of collective identity in constructing and maintaining the nation-state,"[38] as well as other "imagined" communities. To argue that people have multiple and sometimes conflicting loyalties and, as a result, are responsive to different authorities in various walks of life is hardly new. What is new is a growing awareness that, in recent decades, global politics is in the midst of a period of rapid and highly consequential revision of identities.

Although people are indeed susceptible to new or revived forms of political and social association, we must take care lest we fall into a "temptation" that Charles Tilly calls "the siren call of individualism,

---

[37] Peter Dombrowski, "Fragmenting Identities, Shifting Loyalties: The Influence of Individualisation on Global Transformations," *Global Society* 12: 3 (September 1998), p. 377.
[38] Jonathan Boyarin, "Introduction," in Jonathan Boyarin, ed., *Remapping Memory: The Politics of TimeSpace* (Minneapolis: University of Minnesota Press, 1994), p. viii.

with its invention of autonomous, decision making actors."[39] What orig-inates as a "constructed" meaning or interest in time may become a "given." As a result, it turns out again that we cannot entirely ignore either the influence of primordialist conceptions of identity-shaping choices or of constructivist arguments describing how communities are invented and how individual "choices" about belonging are shaped by myth, symbol, and propaganda. Hence, Tilly sees "citizenship and public identities as social relations that remain incessantly open to interpretation and negotiation."[40]

Identity hierarchies and loyalties are subject to change. Sometimes change is slow and continuous, and other times, it is rapid and tumul-tuous. But such change always legitimizes some forms of governance and delegitimizes others. Certain historical epochs are transitional, fea-turing unusually dramatic shifts in identities, loyalties, and attendant political forms. Some of these epochs were the sixth century AD in the Near East, when an existing clan system and an aspiring universal reli-gious community competed for loyalties; the sixteenth and seventeenth centuries in Europe and Latin America, when the Westphalian State was ratified by the global community and when Spain and Portugal imposed European political forms on top of tribal ones in the New World; the late eighteenth and nineteenth centuries, when nationalism and industrial-ism added newly explosive elements to global politics and European empires consolidated their control over much of Africa and Asia; and World Wars I and II and their aftermath, which saw the emergence of two superpowers and the start of European integration. The end of the Cold War, the globalization of economic markets, and fears of apocalyp-tic terrorism appear to be ushering in yet another transitional epoch.

During transitional epochs, incompatible identities, loyalties, and political forms fiercely compete. This was the case between Westphalian polities and the larger conception of Christendom that confronted Euro-pean rulers in the seventeenth century. Andrew Linklater describes the tension at that time:

> The modern European state emerged within the confines of a single civilization united by the normative and religious power of Christen-dom. During its rise the state sought to free itself from the moral and religious shackles of the medieval world. But while it pursued this

---

[39] Charles Tilly, "Citizenship, Identity and Social History," in Charles Tilly, ed., *Citizenship, Identity, and Social History* (Cambridge: Cambridge University Press, 1996), p. 12.
[40] *Ibid.*

aim the state was aware of the dangers of totally undermining earlier notions of an international society. . . . Quite clearly, the state set out to employ the notion of a wider society of states for the explicit purpose of maintaining international order. Its aim was to enjoy the benefits of preserving an international society without incurring the risk that individual citizens would challenge the state's legitimacy by proclaiming their allegiance to a higher cosmopolitan ethic.[41]

Authority crises, local and global, commonly take place during such transitional epochs. During those periods, global life is unpredictable and dangerous and norms and customs are in flux.

When different identities clash, as in the case Linklater describes, individuals and collectivities may experience paralyzing dissonance as they try to decide which of their loyalties should prevail. Religion, for example, may force people into making difficult personal choices regarding reproduction, diet, dress, and customs. Bolsheviks in the years following the October Revolution were at once the servants of the Soviet Union and the vanguard of a worldwide movement. In 1939, communists around the world were shocked by Moscow's ideological and political reversal represented by the non-aggression treaty with Germany, and many faced disabling dissonance.

New identities often emerge when individuals come to believe that association will bring benefits and when conditions permit them to act upon that belief. Recognition, invention, and/or imposition of common identity is only a first step in the formation and institutionalization of a polity.[42] Also required are leadership, institutions, ideology, and a capacity to mobilize persons for political purposes (value satisfaction or relief from value deprivation). Every polity has its own domain, consisting of individuals and other resources upon which it can draw and specific issues in which it is engaged. Each is authoritative within its domain to the extent that adherents willingly recognize its authority in appropriate contexts. Effective control need not be enshrined in law or even be considered legitimate, although polities that enjoy legal status and broad approval are all that more secure. Identity may be imposed, but loyalty must be earned by producing satisfaction.

---

[41] Andrew Linklater, cited in Michael N. Barnett, "Sovereignty, Nationalism, and Regional Order in the Arab States System," *International Organization* 49:3 (Summer 1995), p. 496.
[42] Rosenau defines such a group as a "movement" – "a loosely knit aggregate of like-minded individuals and organizations who seek to have influence on one or more aspects of human affairs," *Turbulence in World Politics*, pp. 125–126. Rosenau's concept of movement shades into what we call "polities" when he suggests that movements "may have informally recognized leaders or spokespersons." *Ibid.*, p. 126.

Those in authority in most polities are usually active in only a relatively narrow range of issues. Different polities routinely engage in the same issues, whether as allies or adversaries. Since individuals have multiple identities, issues arise that force polities to compete in attracting and mobilizing their loyalties and the resources (for example, votes, taxes, contributions, and skills) that they command. Competition may be minimized if polities address different issues or stake out identical or compatible political positions on the same issue(s). By contrast, conflict will be greater, and efforts to achieve compromise far more elusive if cleavages involve identities that reinforce one another. Where identities and resulting boundaries do so, as do race and class in the United States, conflict potential is great; when identities crosscut, conflict potential is reduced. The fact that the Israeli–Palestinian and Indian–Pakistani conflicts are among the most durable and complex in global politics owes much to the involvement of identities associated with both religion and territory. And as identity hierarchies evolve, some boundaries harden and others soften, even as still others emerge, grow, shrink, or vanish.[43]

Manipulating myths and maps

The importance of élite manipulation of identities in competing for loyalties places a premium on the control of ancient myths and symbols or on their "invention." Even revolutionary elites recognize the legitimating power of foundation myths that imply that they are part of a continuous historical stream, not least if mythical origins include some type of divine sanction. Indeed, manufacturing old myths and refurbishing them for contemporary political purposes is an ancient and (sometimes) honorable practice.[44]

Mythmaking entails a struggle over how history is written, the memories it evokes and, therefore, competition for control of political meaning; and it raises the question of how using history confronts the problem of assigning meaning to facts.[45] Few political issues are more compelling than what Jonathan Boyarin calls "the question of who controls the archives."[46] After all, the past itself has limited objective content

[43] Mansbach and Vasquez, *In Search of Theory*, pp. 143–185.
[44] See, for example, William H. McNeill, *Mythohistory and Other Essays* (Chicago: University of Chicago Press, 1986), p. 23.
[45] See, for example, Joanne Rappaport, *The Politics of Memory* (New York: Cambridge University Press, 1990).
[46] Boyarin, "Space, Time, and the Politics of Memory," in Boyarin, ed., *Remapping Memory*. p. 15.

apart from the interpretation placed upon it by those who record and analyze it. Determining its meaning affords serious political authority and power to legitimize and delegitimize. Did Christopher Columbus's "discovery" of the New World mark the first step in Europe's "civilizing" mission; was it the beginning of Europe's extermination of vibrant indigenous cultures; or was it a morally neutral "clash" or "encounter" of "civilizations"? Was Israel's occupation of the West Bank in 1967 a fulfillment of a biblical promise, or was it a Zionist variation of Europe's penetration of the developing world? The triumph of state-centric premises in Western history and social science reflects Europe's centuries-old control over historical meaning and the related forgetting of rival forms of identity both in the context of the contest among political forms in Europe after the Middle Ages and in Europe's conquest over rival forms in non-European regions.

As Boyarin suggests, "identity and memory are virtually the same concept."[47] For Anthony Smith, "there can be no identity without memory (albeit selective), no collective purpose without myth,"[48] and "the constituents of these identities and cultures – the myths, memories, symbols and values – can often be adapted to new circumstances by being accorded new meanings and new functions."[49] For such reasons, it is difficult to overestimate the importance of the act of remembering. Such rituals reinforce and renew collective myth and memory. Whether memorializing an idealized Battle of the Boyne by Irish Protestants or the Battle of Kosovo by Serb nationalists, almost any (even fictionalized) historical event can be resurrected to mount a challenge to authority or to establish a usurper's claim to govern.

Acts of remembering, such as national pageants, recollections of ancient wrongs, tribal ceremonies, religious convocations and pageants, ethnic parades or rituals, and even monuments, are all part of the contest over the meaning of history. Historical memories and myths sustain old identities and loyalties so that they may flicker for generations, even centuries, awaiting the emergence of issues and leaders that activate adherents and enfeeble dominant polities. Religion, literature, dialect, poetry, painting, music, and ritual are only a few of the ways in which ancient identities are nourished. Any or all may be factors in

---

[47] *Ibid.*, p. 23.
[48] Anthony D. Smith, *The Ethnic Origins of Nations* (New York: Basil Blackwell, 1986), p. 2. Smith is writing of nation and is a strong proponent of the nation-state idea, but his claim has far wider applicability.
[49] *Ibid.*, p. 3.

the "rediscovery" of "nation" and demands for autonomy or "national self-determination."

Policy cooperation and coordination

Kosovo and Macedonia unite Albanians who are citizens of neither country, and mention of them may trigger religious identity in the minds of many Muslims regardless of whether or not they are Albanian. Although both Albanians and Muslims may support the goal of uniting Kosovo and Macedonia in a "Greater Albania," the two groups also differ in a variety of ways. For Albanians, Serbs may be the adversaries; for Muslims, the adversaries may be Slavs, Christians, or even Russian Orthodox. Each identity group has different boundaries and focuses on a different "other." We see here, too, how identities can reinforce one another and can imagine some of the cleavages that might arise. "[W]hat better way," as Anthony Smith asks, "of suggesting and inducing that sense of belonging than by 'rediscovering' submerged or lost ethnic roots in the mists of immemorial time?"[50]

Historically, too, mythmaking has repeatedly legitimated authority by establishing distinctive traditions for a political community that can be used to delineate boundaries between it and others. Even revolutionary elites recognize the legitimating power of foundational myths that imply that they are part of a continuous historical stream of rulership, especially if mythical origins include some type of divine sanction. Chinese dynasties routinely depicted themselves as heirs to China's mythical sage kings of antiquity who were divinely mandated by Heaven to create and sustain the empire. Fictitious blood links to past dynasties provided legitimacy to reinforce the "Mandate of Heaven." Shinto, which proclaimed Japanese emperors to be divine, depicted an unbroken dynastic line of over two millennia from the founding sun goddess. A foundation myth of literary importance was that of Augustan Rome. The Emperor Augustus commissioned Virgil to write the *Aeneid* both to legitimize imperial Rome (and Augustus as emperor) and, by claiming Trojan ancestry, to emphasize Rome's continuity and to differentiate Romans from Greeks.[51]

Manipulating myths and symbols continues to play a prominent legitimating and mobilizing role, but success is chancy. Thus, newly acquired

---

[50] *Ibid.*, p. 2.
[51] J. P. V. D. Balsdon, *Romans and Aliens* (Chapel Hill, NC: University of North Carolina Press, 1979), p. 30.

identities in post-Soviet republics in Central Asia are at best very shallow. States such as Tajikistan and Uzbekistan had *not* existed prior to their inhabitants being absorbed by the Soviet Union. Stalin invented "national" roots for the Soviet Union's nomadic Muslim communities in order to dilute the more threatening Turkic and Islamic identities. "The Soviets sought to prevent that by establishing five Central Asian republics, forcing on each a distinct 'national' language and culture," and "Soviet policy firmly established the 'nationalities' into which Central Asia is now divided. In pre-Soviet Turkistan, people had defined themselves primarily as Turkic or Tajik Muslims, identities that could have permitted the evolution of a unified polity across the region."[52]

Since "national" roots are not deep in the steppelands of Central Asia, the post-Soviet states of the region have rummaged in their mythic pasts to find nation-building (really, state-building) symbols. In the case of Kirghizistan, this has led to a revival of an epic poem about a hero called Manas who is said to have resisted the Chinese. In Kazakhstan, the government has revived interest in the nineteenth-century poet and novelist Abai Kunanbaev, and in neighboring Uzbekistan, the fourteenth-century conqueror Tamerlane has been trundled out as a symbol of Uzbek nationalism.[53] Despite these efforts, Islamists propagating a historic religious identity threaten to undermine the regimes in the region.[54]

Like Central Asia, the Middle East also has experienced the "'rediscovering' of submerged or lost roots." The founding of Israel in 1948 drew upon collective memory carried through centuries of Diaspora. "Jews," writes Smith, "trace their ancestry to Abraham, their liberation to the Exodus, their founding charter to Mount Sinai, and their golden age to (variously) the Davidic and Solomonic kingdom or the era of the sages in the late Second Temple period or after. These are all myths . . . and they retain their religious potency today." But, Smith continues, Zionism's potency was intensified because Judaism was more than a religious identity alone. Jewish myths "remain, even for secular Jews, charters of their ethnic identity. Here, too, as with the Greeks and Armenians, the Irish and Ethiopians, there is a *felt* affiliation, as well as a cultural affinity, with a remote past in which a community was formed,

---

[52] James Rupert, "Dateline Tashkent: Post-Soviet Central Asia," *Foreign Policy* 87 (Summer 1992), p. 178.

[53] "A Time of Heroes," *The Economist*, September 23–29, 1995, p. 28.

[54] See, for example, Stephen Kinzer, "Zealots' Latest Targets Are Poor, Remote and Vulnerable," *New York Times*, October 31, 1999, sec. 4, p. 3; "The Militants Take Aim," *The Economist*, August 26–September 1, 2000, pp. 32–33; "Islamic Nerves," *The Economist*, October 14–20, 2000, p. 51.

a community that despite all the changes it has undergone, is still in some sense recognized as the 'same' community."[55]

Writing of the region's Arabs, Michael Barnett argues that: "Manufacturing consent through the reconstruction of political identity can prove to be a cost-effective method of creating support," and "even Mu'ammar al-Kaddafi . . . attempted to create a 'Libyan Arab' national identity through historical texts, holidays, and monuments. In Iraq the Ba'athist party, which stresses pan-Arabism and the singularity of the Arab people, established an ongoing project to demonstrate the existence of an Iraqi identity that had roots in Mesopotamia."[56] While he remained in power, Saddam Hussein sought to foster his links to this ancient identity; since his overthrow, a concerted effort has been made to do the same in order to prevent the breakup of the country.

The Middle East in general reflects the grave tension between state and transnational Islam. Barnett argues that advocates of national independence of separate states in the region triumphed over advocates of pan-Arabism, insofar as interaction among Arab states created new "state identities, roles, and interests" that produced "stable expectations and shared norms"[57] associated with sovereignty. These included the principle of noninterference, "in which state elites had a vested interest." However:

> Despite the construction of the League of Arab States with sovereignty at its core, Arab states continued to occupy two social roles that conferred contradictory behavioral expectations: sovereignty demanded that they recognize each other's legitimacy, borders, and the principle of noninterference; while pan-Arabism held that Arab states were to defend the Arab nation, to uphold regional standards of legitimacy, and indeed to deny the very distinction between the international and the domestic.[58]

But "sovereignty is not permanently anchored," and "Arab leaders must continually work to reproduce the state's sovereignty, its domestic and

---

[55] Anthony D. Smith, *National Identity* (Reno: University of Nevada Press, 1991), p. 33. Emphasis in original.

[56] Barnett, "Sovereignty, Nationalism, and Regional Order in the Arab States System," p. 498. For a discussion of how archeology is used in the Middle East to forge a national identity, see Asher Silberman, *Between Past and Present: Archeology, Ideology, and Nationalism in the Modern Middle East* (New York: Henry Holt, 1989); also Samir al-Khalil, *The Monument: Art, Vulgarity, and Responsibility in Iraq* (Berkeley: University of California Press, 1991).

[57] Barnett, "Sovereignty, Nationalism, and Regional Order in the Arab States System," pp. 480, 481.

[58] *Ibid.*, pp. 494–495.

international authority, and the distinction between domestic and international space. The failure of statist ideologies has resurrected primordial, ethnic, and, most famously, religious identities,"[59] which in turn threaten state sovereignty. "While Islamic movements may or may not be compatible with juridical sovereignty," declares Barnett, "they do challenge the internal sovereignty of many Arab states."[60]

Currently, Arab societies are in the midst of a collision between the European-imposed model of sovereign states and competing memories of Arab tribes and clans and a greater Islamic community that ignores state frontiers. In a few cases, such as those of the Kurds or the Druse, religion and ethnicity reinforce one another and foster transnational communities. One of the earliest political movements that emerged to promote transnational Islamic identities was the Muslim Brotherhood, which was founded in Egypt in 1928. In sum, as Bassam Tibi declares, "neither internal sovereignty, with its conception of citizenship and national identity and loyalty, nor external sovereignty, with its idea of mutual recognition of boundaries and authority over that territory, has a real counterpart in Arab-Islamic history."[61]

Militant Islamists, including Osama bin Laden's *Al Qaeda* organization, believe they are acting on behalf of a universal Islamic community. That cause gained global attention with the earlier overthrow of Iran's monarchy by Shia supporters of Ayatollah Khomeini. Khomeini claimed to act not as an official of the Iranian state but as a spiritual leader of Shia Muslims everywhere. For Islamic militants the enemy is variously the United States, Israel, Christianity, globalization, or the secular West in general. Militants argue that, in Judith Miller's words, "rule is a prerogative not of the people, but of God, who appointed the prophet, who, in turn, prescribed the general precepts of governance in God's own words, the Koran."[62]

In sum, events from Afghanistan, Indonesia, Nigeria, and Tajikistan to Bosnia, Chechnya, Algeria, and the Philippines have deepened Islamic identities, encouraged militant transnational Islamic loyalties, and

---

[59] *Ibid.*, p. 509.

[60] *Ibid.*, p. 509n108, p. 509. For an analysis of the compatibility between Islam and judicial sovereignty, see James Piscatori, *Islam in a World of Nation-States* (New York: Cambridge University Press, 1986).

[61] Bassam Tibi, "The Simultaneity of the Unsimultaneous: Old Tribes and Imposed Nation-States in the Modern Middle East," in Philip Khoury and Joseph Kostiner, eds., *Tribes and State Formation in the Middle East* (Berkeley: University of California Press, 1990), p. 127.

[62] Judith Miller, "Faces of Fundamentalism," *Foreign Affairs* 73:6 (November/December 1994), p. 137.

incited some to fight in foreign lands. Muslim veterans of the war against the Soviet Union in Afghanistan, calling themselves the Harkat-ul Ansar, have infiltrated Indian-occupied Kashmir, fought Indian troops and police, and kidnapped and murdered Western hostages.

Whether fairly or unfairly, strident Islam appears to Western observers in "images of car bombs, murder, and young, bearded holy warriors bent on historic revenge,"[63] and as a major challenge to the ideology of modernity. "Around the 1980s," writes Miller, "an eruption of militant Islamic passion sent tremors through the Middle East."[64] "Islam," concluded Huntington, "has bloody borders,"[65] and some Western officials speak of a "green menace" in terms once reserved for "red" communists.

When states cannot co-opt, modify, or successfully compete with alternate identities, they may seek to suppress them, as does France when its authorities ban the wearing of Muslim headscarves in school or when Saddam Hussein imprisoned Kurdish and Shi'ite leaders. Unfortunately, states currently confront ever more serious challenges to their primacy as objects of inhabitants' identities and loyalties at a time when their repertoire of potential responses is being limited by future-shock trends. The Westphalian State is still sovereign, but being so seems to guarantee less and less in terms of effective control, self-sufficiency, or autonomy. The state is increasingly unable to insulate citizens from the actions of others. Their lives are touched not only by wars, terrorists, and microbes traveling on jetliners but also by the decisions of investors, consumers, and voters who go about their daily business unconscious of the full consequences of their actions. In a real sense, the promise (or threat) of a substantially global system is finally being realized, with profound implications for governance and both individual and group participation.

Religion and the state

As the discussion of Islamic fundamentalism implies, religion is the most widely discussed nonterritorial identity in contemporary global politics. Religious identity was especially important in Europe before 1648 and is today again growing in significance. God and the state were enshrined together, and sometimes religious and citizen identities

---

[63] *Ibid.*, p. 126.   [64] *Ibid.*, p. 123.

[65] Huntington, "The Clash of Civilizations?" Huntington admitted later that this was perhaps the most memorable phrase in his 1993 article.

closely reinforced one another. Historical theocracies like John Knox's Scotland and John Calvin's Geneva find echoes in contemporary cases as varied as Shia Islam and Iran, Sunni Afghanistan, Judaism and Israel, Catholicism and Ireland, India and Hinduism, and Burma and Buddhism. Buddhist identities keep alive memories of independent statehood in Mongolia and Tibet, and even transnational churches can give birth to highly nationalist variations as in Poland (where, paradoxically, it helped undermine a national regime based on another transnational identity, communism). Historically, the great schisms between Holy Roman Empire and Catholic Church, between Roman and Avignon popes, and between Catholics and Protestants dominated European politics in the centuries before the emergence of independent states and, to some extent, accelerated the emergence of states. Today, as in centuries past, Islam threatens the West.

Often, however, religious sentiment and identity challenge a citizen's state identity for primacy, at least on issues with religious content. Before Westphalian States could achieve primacy, European sovereigns had to throw off papal pretensions, gain the loyalties of national clergy, and take over church resources within their realm (though in cases such as Spain and Ireland church and state continued to reinforce each other). Thereafter, the Catholic Church provided legitimacy for monarchs – variously titled "Catholic Sovereigns," "Most Catholic" and "Most Christian" – who were prepared to accept the superiority of the cross over the scepter. The investiture controversy, the Reformation, the Thirty Years War, and the Counter-Reformation were all part of the struggle between church and state in Europe; and the flight of persecuted believers to North America and the separation of church and state laid down in the Constitution bear witness to the importance of the issue in United States history.

Rulers as varied as ancient Romans and modern Spanish fascists recognized that religion, when harnessed to secular authority, is a powerful asset. The secular Machiavelli in Chapter XI of *The Prince* declared that "ecclesiastical principalities" can survive without ability or fortune because "they are sustained by ancient religious customs, which are so powerful and are of such quality, that they keep their princes in power in whatever manner they proceed and live."[66] And, in Chapter XI of *The Discourses*, he praises Rome's official religion and describes religion

---

[66] Niccolò Machiavelli, *The Prince and The Discourses*, Modern Library College Editions (New York: Random House, 1950), p. 41.

as "the most necessary and assured support of any civil society . . . for where religion exists it is easy to introduce armies and discipline."[67] That same Rome, however, when confronted by those who refused to bow the knee to Roman gods, had recourse to coercion. Many Jews chose death at Masada rather than accept Roman rule; and, in time, Christianity first penetrated, then conquered, and finally inherited Rome's empire.

Contemporary states, too, routinely seek to harness religion to promote legitimacy or at least to co-opt religious identities that might undermine the loyalty of citizens. Russia's postcommunist leaders are reinventing themselves as defenders of Eastern Orthodoxy like the Tsars of old. And the extensive ruling family of Saudi Arabia, as well as Nigeria's northern regions, have made *sharia* the law of their countries. Whether in Calvin's Geneva or the mullahs' Iran, state authority becomes indistinguishable from a religious movement, and, in still others, religious values and beliefs pose a serious challenge to secular territorial rule.

However, it is in the spread of Islamic fundamentalism that the transnational challenge posed by religious identities to citizenship loyalties is most evident. Events in Islamic history, some dating back fourteen centuries, have been revived to undermine existing state practices. Throughout the Muslim world secular leaders are the targets of Islamists, willing to use the ballot where possible and the bullet where necessary, in order to make the Koran the law of the land. In the case of Europe, separation of church and state was secured by the spilling of oceans of blood and confirmed by the Treaties of Augsburg and Westphalia before the role of religion in Europe diminished. Only then was it possible for nationalism to spread, and in time to allow the state to achieve its full potential as a political institution. Islam has not yet experienced a similar historical process or resolution to the problem of how religion and rulership are related.

In fact, Muslims are not alone in professing fundamentalist principles – governance in accordance with religious dogma. Similar principles also inform some Christian movements in the United States, as well as Orthodox Judaism in Israel, and Hindu nationalism in India. Extreme Hindu nationalists have for some time enjoyed great influence in various heavily populated Indian states – Maharashtra (including the city of Bombay), Gujarat, and Rajasthan. The Hindu nationalist party, Bharatiya Janata, became the leader in a coalition that assumed power in New Delhi after elections in spring 1996, and extremists in Shiv

[67] *Ibid.*, pp. 146, 147.

Sena were instrumental in the 1992 destruction of an ancient mosque at Ayodhya in Uttar Pradesh and the ensuing violence that swept Bombay. Shiv Sena means the "army of Shiva," who was a seventeenth-century Hindu warrior king, and the party seeks to transform India into a Hindu state in which Muslims would be relegated to second-class status (unrelated to the existing caste system).[68] The Kashmir controversy is among the most dangerous in global politics owing to the intermingling of religious and territorial conflicts, as it pits the Hindu nuclear bomb against the Muslim bomb.

Nesting and the challenge of new polities

But what is the process by which memories and myths are enshrined and old identities handed down, making them available for revival or refurbishing? We refer to that process as *nesting,* by which we mean the ingestion of one polity by another without the disappearance of either. Nesting has always complicated political maps because some identities are territorially organized and are separated from one another by vertical boundaries; whereas others are organized on a nonterritorial basis, thereby producing horizontal boundaries that can separate people within the same physical location.

During nesting, new identities, loyalties, and accompanying symbols are forged; and old ones are redefined or diluted. In its course, some polities are partly[69] or completely embedded within others. Old loyalties, identities, and political forms rarely disappear completely. Some find a comfortable niche in more inclusive polities and continue operating quite peaceably in their limited domain. Those that are outlawed and suppressed tend to become dormant or merge with other loyalties and identities in the manner that Christianity and Christian myths incorporated prior pagan[70] and Jewish symbols and stories. Old loyalties, identities, and forms may then reappear with considerable vitality at a later (sometimes much later) date, usually when dominant authorities are unusually vulnerable.

---

[68] See Stuart Corbridge, "Cartographies of Loathing and Desire: The Bharatiya Janata Party, the Bomb, and the Political Spaces of Hindu Nationalism," in Ferguson and Jones, eds., *Political Space*, pp. 151–169.

[69] Partial nesting refers to the fact that the boundaries of newer polities may "cut" existing polities apart; some adherents live within the newer polity, separated from their brethren by new frontiers. Kurdish, Islamic, Korean, and Palestinian are prominent identities that today are separated by state frontiers.

[70] Such as the Isis myth.

In the course of enlargement, a polity tends to create, in a sense, its own nemesis – the conditions for later fragmentation – as older identities nest, only to cause indigestion sooner or later. The extension of central authority to additional territory or persons entails the growth of bureaucracies that are not only harder to manage efficiently as they grow but may also develop interests different from the center and even encourage breakaway ambitions. Bureaucrats near and far are tempted to govern as autonomously as they can and, as a polity grows, are likely to have greater opportunity to do so. Also, expansion or consolidation of a major polity often precipitates important economic and social changes that make society more complex and hence more difficult to govern. Lastly, expansion or consolidation may whet appetites for further expansion, with risks of disastrous reversals or at least administrative overreach.

An expansive polity may take over or share the functions of the newly nested or embedded polity and the loyalties of individuals to it. In the process, the nested polity may lose much of its autonomy even while some of its features are assumed by the host polity. Because new identity groups may arise alongside older identities, a nested polity is either the remnant of an earlier form or the embryo of one that is emerging.[71] The process involved may be imposition or emulation, or it may involve outright subversion of one polity type by another.

Nesting continues today. Consider Europe: none of Europe's Westphalian States is fully responsible for its own defense. Many economic functions have been taken over by the European Union, or have been ceded to transnational enterprises and global financial markets. Demanding environmental, consumer, and refugee groups add to the strains upon individual member states and the EU as a whole. In actuality, there has been such a mixing and layering of political forms in Europe that no historical model does justice to the enormously complex patterns of authority that are taking shape there. Now the EU is again expanding, with major – though as yet unpredictable – implications for its essential nature, organization, and capacity. Will an expanded EU cement European identity or dilute it? Will the result be greater

---

[71] Polities may acquire one another's characteristics not only by nesting, subordination, and conquest, but also by contact at the periphery. In ancient Mesopotamia, for example: "Urartu – the major rival of Assyria – was the creation of Assyria itself. . . . The constant Assyrian incursions into the Taurus and beyond . . . familiarized the people of Urartu with much of the culture and infrastructure of a major kingdom." H. W. F. Saggs, *The Might that Was Assyria* (London: Sidgwick & Jackson, 1984), p. 90.

centralization or decentralization of authority and administration? Nobody knows, which speaks volumes – not least because Europe is the place where the Westphalian State as a model first appeared – about the volatility of polity formation, shifts in authority and influence, and evolving identities and loyalties in today's world. Whether the EU's constituent sovereign states will ever become fully nested remains in doubt. But there is no doubt that continued expansion of European integration means dramatic shifts in the authority domains of those states.

In sum, the historical processes whereby some polities grow and others are nested helps explain why there are so many variations among institutions, ideas, and behavior within each class of polity, including states. Each reflects the unique impact of its own history and other polity types that are nested within it. Some of the worst consequences of nesting are visible in the passionate nationalisms and separatist yearnings that grip Serbian Muslims, Croatians, Albanians, Armenians, Tibetans, and others. These reminded Daniel Patrick Moynihan of John Milton's "Pandaemonium," that "was inhabited by creatures quite convinced that the great Satan had their best interests at heart."[72] On virtually every continent: "National movements are regaining popularity, and nations that had once assimilated and 'vanished' have now reappeared."[73] These movements reflect the unleashing and manipulation of old (or forged) identities and memories. But nesting not only threatens existing polities, it can also legitimate them, when old identities are manipulated and wedded to later political forms to reinforce and intensify loyalties. Thus, the EU is partly legitimized by the longstanding symbol of "Europe" with its shared history and culture, along with more recent icons such as democracy and free markets.

Once we take account of the nesting of some polities within others, it becomes evident that the frontiers of Westphalian polities never demarcated political life as theorists imagined. Even in its European cradle, the state succeeded mainly by serving identities often unrelated to the state itself and arguably never became the primary loyalty, at least over family, religion, and self, for many individuals under many circumstances. Westphalian frontiers regularly enclosed potentially rival authorities, divided others, and were themselves enclosed within the frontiers of

---

[72] Daniel Patrick Moynihan, *Pandaemonium: Ethnicity in International Politics*. (New York: Oxford University Press, 1993), p. 174.
[73] Yael Tamir, *Liberal Nationalism* (Princeton: Princeton University Press, 1993), p. 3.

still larger polities. Indeed, because political structures are superimposed upon one another, we need the skills of an archeologist in order to dig with care from level to level, assessing the impact each has had on the others.

Identities and changing moral communities

Within the past decade or so, however, theorizing about identity has increasingly assumed a social constructionist perspective. Whether there are objective categories of identity or not is less important than how the subjective process of identity construction and maintenance figures in the process of political legitimation. The presumption is that some degree of normative agreement flows from common identity.

Any category of difference presumes a category (or hegemonic identity in Gramscian terms) of sameness against which difference is measured. This is why it is hard to imagine the triumph of any liberal identity with "humanity" as a whole. Race, ethnicity, and even gender are categories of identity that are significant, not because of some intrinsic objective content, but because of the *significance attached to their difference in contrast with another or others and often an allegedly privileged identity category*. Theorizing about identity, therefore, reveals the cognitive underpinning of *us* and *them* as bases for political action and legal regulation. Such theorizing is complicated by the fact that, as we recall, identities demarcate psychological rather than territorial space. Consequently, they can be overlapping and intersecting, as well as exclusive. While attention has been paid to the construction of "otherness" and the consequences of exclusivity for "others," there has been far less interest in exploring the significance of "sameness" as a social and political construction with moral consequences.[74] This is unfortunate, because it is only the significance attached to socially constructed sameness that provides the foundation for moral boundaries. These encompass communities of obligation based on reciprocity and fairness and, therefore, genuine political community.

For our purposes, moral communities may be formal (legal) or informal (normative) or both. In an informal sense, a moral community is a *community of caring* where members feel a special obligation to care for

---

[74] Susan Opotow, "Moral Exclusion and Injustice," *Journal of Social Issues* 46:1 (1990), pp. 1–20.

one another's well-being and view harm that comes to any members as harm to all members. Traditional kinship is an example of an informal moral community. Although the term community of caring may suggest a more conscious emotional attachment, this aspect of moral community can also be characterized in terms more commonly associated with the idea of citizenship and the state on matters of "common defense." The idea of collective security in international relations has a similar connotation, presuming that when acts of aggression take place, the global community's security (a component of well-being) should be understood as indivisible. Whether the solidarity that forms the basis for moral community is constructed in terms of kinship, class, ethnicity, gender, nationhood, citizenship, the "family of states," or "international society," all forms of reciprocal obligation rest on a perceived bond of *sameness*. It is for this reason that moral communities also inevitably function to define "others" and provide justification for treating others differently from those within the group.

By demarcating inclusion and exclusion on the basis of sameness and difference, moral communities draw boundaries of "inside and outside" according to which justice presumably is distributed. This has obvious application to the distribution of international justice through foreign policies, but such boundaries also serve to structure the distribution of justice internally, among members of the community. Consider the internal allocation of rights and responsibilities on the basis of age or maturity – the full range of rights and responsibilities of citizenship do not attach to members of a society until they reach an age of "majority" or moral competence.

While the case of the adult–child relationship may seem uncontroversial in the context of a simple model of a society of individuals who in every other way understand themselves as equals, it also underlies the construction of moral boundaries and the distribution of justice in other relationships both within and across the societies of states. For instance, the social, political, and economic marginalization of women in structurally patriarchal societies is predicated on the assumption of women's moral inferiority to men, reflected in language that characterizes women in relation to men as *children to adults*. The same problem extends to the status of women as an issue of human rights in highly conservative Muslim societies like Iran and Saudi Arabia. A similar structuring of relations is evident in policies relating to indigenous peoples and the supposedly morally superior "modernizing" majority or dominant group, as well as, until recently, the relegation of Africans/Blacks to "second-class citizenship" in South Africa and the United States.[75] On a global level, colonialism was based on an ideology of a "civilizing mission" or "white man's burden." Decolonization through the League of Nations system of mandates and the Trusteeship Council of the United Nations similarly reflected a ward–guardianship relationship between Western and non-Western peoples based on patriarchal premises.

Moral boundaries are also articulated authoritatively as central to a system of obligations and duties attaching to community membership. In this capacity, they serve to legitimate the use of sanctions, including coercion, by agents of the community against members who violate the terms of obligations attaching to membership. This provides the rationale for a structural "monopoly" of legitimate uses of coercive power. Through the structure of law, the community articulates obligations and consequences for violating them. So long as the obligations of citizenship are fulfilled, order is maintained and individuals are (in theory) secured against official uses of coercion against them. Violation of one's obligation, however, may invoke the legitimate use of coercion to preserve "law and order," and an individual convicted of violation becomes a legitimate target for collective coercion.

The emergence of the sovereign state was accompanied by the articulation of moral boundaries both within the state as civil society in which "internal" violence was regulated by the state, and interstate violence through the "laws of war." The "laws of war" were part of the "law of civilized nations," which was, as Emmerich de Vattel declared, "the law of sovereigns."[76]

Thus, even as the Westphalian polity emerged, "European," as a geopolitical and cultural identity, also came to serve as a basis for another level of moral community, the community of "civilized nations," in the language of seventeenth-century international law. Just as violence by European Christians against Islam (and vice versa) was regarded as legitimate in the Middle Ages, so few of the limitations on violence imposed by European states on one another were extended to indigenous "pagan" peoples such as North America's Indians, Australia's Aborigines, or New Zealand's Maoris. Since indigenous peoples, as Van Creveld observes, "did not know the state and its sharply-drawn division between government, army, and people," they "were automatically

---

[75] Wilmer, *The Indigenous Voice in World Politics*.
[76] Emmerich de Vattel, "Preface" to "The Law of Nations," in M. G. Forsyth, H. M. A. Keens-Soper, P. Savigear, eds., *The Theory of International Relations: Selected Texts from Gentili to Treitschke* (New York: Atherton Press, 1970), p. 100.

declared to be bandits."[77] In fact, the debate among lawyers and theologians eventually came to rest on the notion that a war conducted in order to Christianize a pagan people constituted a just war.[78] Only when missionaries and theologians, like the Dominican Francisco de Vitoria, backed eventually by the Spanish monarchy, declared that the indigenous people of the Americas had rights, did their situation improve.[79] Although the Westphalian State has been our focus here, similar boundaries between "inside" and "outside" occur in all cultural-historical contexts. The culturally based boundary between Europeans and non-Europeans, for example, was similar to the cultural divide envisaged by the Chinese when they described those beyond the reach of the Middle Kingdom as barbarians. The basic idea is also captured by the aggressive definition radical Muslims give to "jihad."

Even within Europe, when identities such as "Catholic" or "Hussite" counted for more than common citizenship, they produced boundaries among people that had little to do with the frontiers of states, and limits on violence were largely ignored. Religious dissidents such as France's Albigensians and Cathars, or of substate "rebels" such as the Scottish clans that came out for Charles Stuart in 1745, were accorded few of the rights that soldiers in national armies accorded one another.

So the Westphalian polity evolved within the historical context of shifting identities and boundaries that redefined the moral community. In sum, the legitimacy of emerging European states rested in great part on their capacity to manage violence by demarcating the boundaries of legitimate/illegitimate violence and on their ability to provide subjects/citizens with security, internal and external, where security is defined as the management of threats to civil order. Specialized bureaucracies enabled Europe's states to mobilize large populations for interstate war while pacifying the intrastate arena, and citizenship provided the main signpost for differentiating between "inside" and "outside."

---

[77] Van Creveld, *The Rise and Decline of the State*, p. 41. In many respects, the state regarded women as it did indigenous peoples. The state characterized both as "children" or "wards" whose domination was necessary to their "moral development." The founding of the Westphalian State maintained patriarchy as an authoritative structure for both public and private social order. For these reasons, we should not be surprised that violence against women and children was not the subject of institutional regulation until recently, and even now these restraints are erratically enforced.

[78] See James S. Anaya, *Indigenous Peoples in International Law* (New York: Oxford University Press, 1996).

[79] Vitoria argued that under natural law the Indians were free people and had owned their land before the Spaniards arrived. Gerhard von Glahn, *Law Among Nations*, 7th ed. (Boston: Allyn and Bacon, 1996), pp. 25–26.

This leads to an important observation. It is widely believed today that sovereignty is the main obstacle to assuring human rights and fair treatment of civilians in wartime. An obstacle it is, but the retreat of the sovereign state also has some highly unfortunate implications with respect to individual security. *To the extent that sovereignty outlawed violence within states and international law limited violence among states and against civilians, there was an established normative framework protecting individuals against unrestrained violence.* Where nationalism and sovereignty enjoyed the same identity boundaries, they reinforced one another, but where the cry of national self-determination arose in the nineteenth and twentieth centuries, it was accompanied by unregulated violence. Thus, Amitai Etzioni argues that self-determination and democracy are competitors: "While they long served to destroy empires and force governments to be more responsive to the governed, with rare exceptions self-determination movements now undermine the potential for democratic development in nondemocratic countries and threaten the foundations of democracy in the democratic ones."[80] Today, the erosion of state sovereignty is as responsible for abuses against civilians as for bringing an end to them. We are confronted with a Hobson's choice.

The amorphous nature of sovereign frontiers in recent decades makes it difficult to distinguish between interstate, transstate, and civil war, for example, in Afghanistan, Bosnia, Georgia, or Congo. Many postinternational wars are akin to those in Europe prior to the institutionalization of the territorial state, when "political, social, economic, and religious motives were hopelessly entangled," and "civilians suffered terrible atrocities."[81] As we have observed, the trend in the twentieth century has been in the direction of increasing proportions of civilian to military war deaths,[82] from 5 percent in World War I, and 50 percent in World War II, to 95 percent, for instance, in the 1980s Lebanese Civil War.

But, as usual, there is more than one story, which we explore more fully in Chapter 7. For all its protective restraint on violence within its territorial bounds, the modern state built the most formidable war machine in human history and used it repeatedly with devastating effect against enemy military and many civilians alike. The state's provision

---

[80] Amitai Etzioni, "The Evils of Self-Determination," *Foreign Policy* 89 (Summer 1992–93), p. 21.
[81] Van Creveld, *The Transformation of War*, p. 50.
[82] Frank Barnaby, *The Gaia Peace Atlas: Survival into the Third Millennium* (New York: Doubleday, 1988).

of "security" came at an awful human price, which somewhat blurs the moral boundary between international and postinternational wars.

Conclusion: identity politics

It is not yet clear what the mainstream of international politics – renamed global politics – will look like in the coming decades, but we can hazard a good guess. It will revolve around identity politics, with variable boundaries and loyalties that reflect an ever-changing meaning of us and them. The shift to identity politics, however advantageous in some ways, poses its own problems. Defining common identities in a way that finds universal agreement is a nightmare. For every common history, there are aspects of history that are not shared; for every language, dialects; for every religion, different versions of the one true faith. R. Brian Ferguson, for example, decries the "widespread tendency to identify ethnicity as a simple and primordial basis of conflict." In his view, we "must seek causes in the situations [of social stress] that give ethnicity salience," prompting "politicians to channel needs and anxieties into violent pathways, and thereby to profit from the results." "Mytho-histories are constructed, claiming timeless grudges, and placing blame on a demonized other." "These 'ethnic entrepreneurs' may tap into profound emotions, but the roots of the conflict lie elsewhere, in the life circumstances that make potential followers receptive to their appeals."[83]

Postinternational thinking will focus in substantial part on the polity implications of how leaders construct and manipulate identities to attract and anchor loyalties, rewrite history, harness literature and art, adapt ancient myths and create new ones. Whether Lenin trying to make proletarians of nationalist workers in 1914, Stalin appealing to "mother Russia" and Russian patriotism and jettisoning Marxism in 1941,[84] or Elizabeth I encouraging Shakespeare to glorify England, the English language, and its (Welsh) Tudor rulers – leaders manipulate identities to secure loyalties and acquire legitimacy (and therefore the authority) necessary for polities to be regarded as moral communities. Building a moral community is thus often a cynical job.

---

[83] R. Brian Ferguson, "(Mis)understanding Resource Scarcity and Cultural Difference," *Anthropology Newsletter* (November 1995), p. 37.

[84] On this point, recall Sergei Eisenstein's films "Alexander Nevsky" and "Ivan the Terrible." By the late 1930s Stalin had begun to recognize the need for nationalist appeals to mobilize Russians against Hitler.

Identity politics necessarily focuses on change and adaptation. As identities change, so do the relative strength and importance of different authorities. As the territorial state triumphed over rival polities, it provided "the link between identity and self-rule" and "laid claim to the allegiance of its citizens on the ground that its exercise of sovereignty expressed their collective identity." For hundreds of years, it answered "a yearning for political arrangements that can situate people in a world increasingly governed by vast and distant forces."[85] It can no longer do so, and citizenship must share its political influence with other identities.

It is uncertain what future identity hierarchies will resemble. Each of us is enmeshed in old identities and loyalties. Each time we look in the mirror the images will be changing. Two essential aspects of citizenship are being challenged: "belonging" and "status (understood as a bundle of rights)."[86] First, there is increasing evidence that the nature of belonging is shifting. Many states are using legal and political means to limit formal membership and thus the concomitant rights and responsibilities of those living within its borders.

Second, although citizenship in a particular state remains a major source of self-identity, it has never been sufficient to describe the rights and responsibilities needed and desired by individuals. Just as citizenship confers a "bundle" of rights on members, it is likely that the postinternational environment will increasingly involve a much wider bundle of associations and memberships.[87] Functioning multiple identities then become the rule rather than the exception. But when the obligations of membership in different groups come into conflict, it becomes critical to determine the hierarchical ordering of the multiple identities in question. Although it is premature to predict the toppling of citizenship from high on the identity hierarchy, other polities are competing with sovereign states, with important consequences for citizens' willingness to fight and die for their country.

But is it entirely accurate to suggest that identities are shifting away from the territorial state? Is the fear that citizenship is unraveling under the pressure of globalization exaggerated? Thomas Friedman thinks so:

---

[85] Michael J. Sandel, "America's Search for a New Public Philosophy," *The Atlantic Monthly* 227:3 (March 1996), 74.
[86] Friedrich Kratochwil, "Citizenship: On the Border of Order," in Kratochwil and Lapid, eds., *The Return of Culture and Identity in IR Theory* (Boulder, CO: Lynne Reinner, 1996), pp. 183–185 and 186–198.
[87] David L. Elkins, *Beyond Sovereignty: Territory and Political Economy in the Twenty-first Century* (Toronto, Canada: University of Toronto Press, 1995), p. 29.

"The struggle for power, the pursuit of material and strategic interests and the ever-present emotional tug of one's own olive tree continue even in a world of microchips, satellite phones and the Internet. . . . Despite globalization, people are still attached to their culture, their language and a place called home. And they will sing for home, cry for home, fight for home and die for home."[88] However, especially under current conditions of fission and fusion and multiple authorities, we do need to reassess continually what or where "home" is. The nation-state has *not* been the primary symbol of identification and loyalty for most individuals throughout most of history. Home has always been where the heart is, and the beauty of the globalizing present (for all its difficulties and uncertainty) is that humanity is beginning to have a lot more options – and is likely to exercise them.

[88] Friedman, *The Lexus and the Olive Tree*, p. 250.

6   A postinternational world economy

One consequence of the rapid transformation of global society at millennium's end has been to alter dramatically the relationship between territorial states and economic markets. As in other spheres of global life, the interstate system of exclusive territorial control is being buffeted by the deterritorialized logic of regional and global markets.[1] More and more states, regardless of history or culture, are privatizing government functions, deregulating major sectors of their economies, scaling down or reneging on welfare commitments, willingly and unwillingly tailoring their policies to the demands of intergovernmental and private financial institutions, and experiencing both bewilderment and policymaking gridlock in framing new rules for a highly unpredictable future. Meanwhile, globe-spanning transnational corporations (TNCs), like other restive polities with few territorial restraints, are challenging states for resources and legitimacy. Simply put: "Territoriality and production are no longer bound together."[2] Yet contemporary global political and economic worlds are not entirely old or new. Like all previous worlds, they are worlds in transition – the main difference, whatever the benchmarks, is the sheer pace of change.

Changes both in what Charles Tilly calls "big structures" and "large processes" have profound consequences for scholars as well as for

---

[1] It is important not to conflate the market with related economic concepts. Among the many recent works that grapple with contemporary economic changes are Ash Amin, ed., *Post-Fordism: A Reader* (Oxford: Basil Blackwell, 1994); Fred Block, *Postindustrial Possibilities: A Critique of Economic Discourse* (Berkeley: University of California Press, 1990); and Robert Heilbroner, *21st Century Capitalism* (New York: W.W. Norton, 1993).

[2] William I. Robinson, "Beyond Nation-State Paradigms: Globalization, Sociology, and the Challenge of Transnational Studies," *Sociological Forum* 13:4 (1998), p. 568.

practitioners and individuals.[3] For scholars, standard concepts and methodologies are less and less useful for explaining major events like the end of the Cold War, much less short-term phenomena like the current or likely future price of the dollar or the yuan. Just as new economic structures are playing a role today in pushing the world into a postinternational era, so economic structures were critical in creating the Westphalian State and the international system centuries earlier. In Europe, argues Spruyt, "the king's power grew as a result of support from the burghers for royal policy. Because of the expanding market, townspeople were in search of alternative political institutions more conducive to commerce and their way of life,"[4] and Western individualism flourished along with "the rediscovery of the concept of absolute and exclusive private property."[5] The emergence of the sovereign state in Europe was accompanied by the growth of national markets in which individual buyers and sellers could influence the terms of exchange, aided by standardized weights and measures.

The international economic system

We have seen how states emerged at different rates in Europe. France, Spain, and England are usually regarded as the earliest of Europe's territorial states, yet all retained feudal legal and economic features until after the French Revolution. And that epoch of interdependent yet autonomous sovereign states featured stronger bonds between elites in different countries than between those elites and fellow citizens. No "absolute" monarch, including Louis XIV, ever enjoyed anything approaching truly absolute power, but mercantilism was the early state's effort to do so and reflected the widespread conviction that economics should serve politics rather than vice versa.

States continued to evolve at different rates, and mercantilism did *not* disappear when Adam Smith and David Ricardo launched their two-stage attack on the doctrine and convincingly demonstrated the overwhelming material benefits of markets. Today, many countries,

---

[3] Charles Tilly, *Big Structures, Large Processes and Huge Comparisons* (New York: Russell Sage Foundation, 1984).
[4] Spruyt, *The Sovereign State and its Competitors*, pp. 105–106. See also Charles Tilly, *Coercion, Capital and European States: AD 900–1990* (Oxford: Basil Blackwell, 1990).
[5] Ruggie, "Territoriality and Beyond," p. 157.

developed and developing alike, practice various forms of neomercantilism, even while paying lip service to the free market. Regional markets have to some extent come to substitute for the system of imperial preference imposed by Europe's colonial powers in an earlier age, but whether they serve to open or hinder global markets remains unclear.

Mercantilism was pursued by Westphalian States in order to augment their military and political clout by following policies that impeded "natural" markets. In some cases where sovereign frontiers coincided with a market-based logic, as in the Austro-Hungarian Empire, political and national strains ultimately produced disintegration that ignored economic logic. The resulting nation-states, based on ethnicity, were economically crippled and became economic dependencies of Germany during the 1930s. In Germany, unification combined Prussian military might with a *Zollverein* to undermine hundreds of local Germanic principalities. In Italy, during the run-up to the Renaissance, cities incorporated various smaller jurisdictions in their *contados*; and in time some of these cities, such as Venice, Florence, and Milan, became regional polities (and Venice, a trading empire).

A key asset of the Westphalian State was its ability to mobilize the resources of subjects and utilize them for purposes of security and conquest, both of which increased the splendor of individual monarchs before the French Revolution. During the mercantilist era, the state began to assume more economic functions, and, in many respects, the modern state achieved its status as authoritative allocator of values by penetrating deeper and deeper into the economic and social life of citizens. Industrialization and the socioeconomic woes that accompanied it, plus the need to assuage increasing numbers of politically active citizens, led statesmen like Bismarck to propose novel forms of economic and social protection and welfare. However, industrialization began a process of fostering transnational ties that today, paradoxically, is *weakening* the state. "[T]he process of industrialization, with its inexorable dynamic," as Andreas Osiander argues, "is now destroying the very autonomy that it at first gave the nineteenth-century state."

> Industrialization is about division of labor, which it brings about on an ever greater scale. In the nineteenth century, this process raised the level of the most important economic circuits from the local to the "national" (that is, state) level; this evolution made the state more integrated and strong and gave us the sovereign state . . . as, intellectually, we know

it. Very quickly, however, industrialization went on to produce ever more division of labor and thus ever greater economic interdependence across state frontiers.[6]

In the United States, the federal power to regulate interstate commerce was a major step in the shift from a confederal to federal system. Public authorities taxed and regulated corporations but could not do so beyond the bounds allowed by traditional safeguards for private property and a political process heavily influenced by large campaign contributions and lobbyists. And, as deregulation of some industries has shown, much former "regulation" was little more than government protection of private sector price-fixing. From the outset, government was expected to provide the private sector with infrastructure and services. Then as now, complex political coalitions arose that deflect conceptions of a "national interest" into parochial channels. For instance, levels of American defense spending reflect – as much or more than "objective" readings of threats to security – the reluctance of the military establishment, defense industries, and local communities with affected bases or factories to endure substantial cuts. And trade reflects even greater parochialism. For example, corporations eagerly supported the NAFTA agreement in order to take advantage of open markets,[7] and Big Steel pressed President George W. Bush to reduce less expensive foreign steel imports despite his free-trade rhetoric and the anger of some of America's closest allies.[8]

As we shall emphasize shortly, global and regional patterns of trade, investment, and financial speculation largely transcend sovereign boundaries in the postinternational world. Historically, too, political boundaries have, to their disadvantage, often failed to coincide with economic zones. For thousands of years, merchant traders were important economic actors who often enjoyed special privileges in both home and host societies. As early as the ninth century, Baghdad banks had branches with checking accounts in key cities throughout the Islamic community. Until about the end of the thirteenth century, what R. H. C. Davis calls "the central clearing-house of European trade and finance"

---

[6] Osiander, "Sovereignty, International Relations, and the Westphalian Myth." See also *International Studies Review*, special issue, *Continuity and Change in the Westphalian Order* 2:2 (Summer 2000).
[7] There were other arguments, too, including the need to enhance political stability in neighboring Mexico and stem the tide of illegal immigration from Mexico into the United States.
[8] The World Trade Organization (WTO) ruled in 2003 that this action violates international trade law.

were the six annual transnational Fairs of Champagne. "Italian bankers sent agents who issued letters of credit which could be cashed in almost any stated currency and in any part of Europe." Davis speaks of an "essential unity of the European economy before 1250: there were no national customs-systems, no 'tariff walls,' and no restriction on the movement of merchants, ecclesiastics, scholars, or labourers from one country to another."[9] Trading companies and banks like those of the Bardi and Peruzzi became powerful. Some Italian traders settled in foreign trading centers, where they formed local associations or "nations" for mutual advancement and protection. Firms even created the equivalent of "permanent diplomatic missions" antedating those established by the Venetian state. Large banks established such a symbiotic relationship with local and foreign governments, as well as with the popes, that it was difficult to tell who was more dependent upon whom.

Where state and market frontiers were incompatible, political leaders sought to make them less so. As part of the effort to institutionalize state boundaries, authorities imposed "territorial currencies," especially in the nineteenth century, in order to strengthen "economic territoriality, the direct link between state and society, and the sense of collective identity that binds its inhabitants."[10] Extension of political frontiers by conquest to incorporate markets and sources of raw materials in the manner of ancient Rome or Japan in the 1930s was one expedient, and the creation of "closed" overseas empires in the manner of eighteenth and nineteenth-century Europeans was another. To some extent, as we have observed, the modern-day creation of regional free-trade areas is a successor to empires and imperial preference. More recently, the replacement of territorial currencies in Europe by the euro entails recognition of an EU-wide economic system and portends additional new currencies in the future to cope with increasingly globalized markets.

Territorial states also developed institutional expedients to extend their economic reach. Italian communes and German trading leagues like the Hanseatic League were imaginative institutional experiments on the part of small city polities to reduce the interference of feudal rulers in economic and political transactions and to replicate the benefits of scale associated with the internal markets of large territorial states such as France and England. The League provided physical protection to

---

[9] R. H. C. Davis, *A History of Medieval Europe: From Constantine to Saint Louis,* 2nd ed. (New York: Longman, 1988), pp. 377–379.
[10] Eric Helleiner, "Historicizing Territorial Currencies: Monetary Space and the Nation-State in North America," *Political Geography* 18 (1999), p. 332.

traders, extracted economic concessions from trading partners, afforded some standardization of weights and measures, and shielded its members from external economic competitors.[11]

Contemporary transnational corporations had their antecedents as well. Trading and plantation companies accompanied and played a role in the growth of Europe's empires around the world. The Dutch East India, the English East India, and the Hudson Bay companies among others extended the economic reach of states and merchants well beyond state frontiers. Dutch companies tended to be private while French companies were state enterprises.[12] Such companies, argues Janice Thomson, "were, as a rule, granted full sovereign powers. In addition to their economic privileges of a monopoly on trade with a given region or in a particular commodity and the right to export bullion, they could raise an army or a navy, build forts, make treaties, make war, govern their fellow nationals, and coin their own money."[13]

Politics and markets in the postinternational era

Encouraged by major polities such as the United States and European Union, the globalization of trade and financial markets has been made possible by the information revolution. Modern telecommunications permit the instantaneous movement of enormous amounts of money and financial data around the world, provide corporate executives with a means of communicating instructions to underlings wherever they may be, and allow producers and service providers to generate advertising tailored to meet local tastes. "[B]y the 1990s," declared Strange, "communication by fax and telephone was . . . becoming obsolete as electronic mail and the Internet became the preferred and habitual systems by which markets, financial and other, were integrated into a single system."[14] In this way, financial institutions and markets have been revolutionized and globalized by computers, microchips, and earth-orbiting satellites to the point where "[c]ross-border economic integration and national political sovereignty have increasingly come into conflict, leading to a growing mismatch between the economic and political structures of the world. The effective domains of economic markets have come to coincide less and less with national governmental

---

[11] Spruyt, *The Sovereign States and its Competitors*, pp. 109–129.
[12] Thomson, *Mercenaries, Pirates, and Sovereigns*, p. 33.
[13] *Ibid.*, p. 35.   [14] Strange, *Mad Money*, p. 25.

jurisdictions."[15] Financial markets grew up in the aftermath of the collapse of the international monetary system in the 1970s and the liberalization of national controls on transnational currency transactions. Now globalized finance has become something of a Frankenstein's monster – arguably the single most formidable obstacle to the reconstruction of an international monetary system and to further regional currency standardization. Real stabilization or the continued advance of a single currency would put too many speculators out of work.

Recent decades have witnessed an explosion in foreign exchange trading that has grown to well over a trillion dollars *per day*. By contrast, the total foreign-currency reserves of the major industrial countries is only a small percentage of that figure. "The foreign-exchange market," argues Jeffrey Frankel, "is a 1,000-pound gorilla and intervention is a flimsy leash. When the gorilla has a good idea where it wants to go, there is no point in trying to restrain him. But sometimes the gorilla is willing to be led."[16] In the 1980s, the bond market also was globalized. Between 1983 and 1993 alone, transnational sales of US Treasury bonds grew from $30 billion to $500 billion; and, between 1982 and 1994, the volume of international bonds soared from $259 billion to over $2 trillion.[17]

As Strange observed, "the relation of market authority to political authority has never been stable for long, and, at different times and in different places the pendulum has swung away from one and toward the other and back again, often in ways unforeseen by contemporaries."[18] Although the boundaries of markets and states have never been entirely congruent, they were certainly more so during the eighteenth century than at any time thereafter. The process by which a global market emerged began after World War II under United States leadership or "hegemony" and was largely completed when the former communist states and China "opted in." Although the globalization of markets has led to the erosion of state autonomy, the "shift from state authority to market authority" and the growing power of transnational corporations were at least indirect consequences of intentional state policy.[19] In fact, the "advanced industrial states have played an important role in the globalization process since the late 1950s."[20] This is, of course, the

---

[15] Miles Kahler, *International Institutions and the Political Economy of Integration* (Washington, DC: The Brookings Institution, 1995), p. xv.
[16] Cited in "Who's in the Driving Seat?" special report, *The Economist*, October 7–13, 1995, p. 30.
[17] *Ibid.*, pp. 9–10.   [18] Strange, *The Retreat of the State*, p. 45.   [19] *Ibid.*, p. 44.
[20] Eric Helleiner, *States and the Reemergence of Global Finance: From Bretton Woods to the 1990s* (Ithaca, NY: Cornell University Press, 1994), p. 21, cited in David M. Andrews and Thomas

starting point for arguments that, far from competing with state authority, economic globalization benefits selected market-oriented states by extending their reach in a subtle and apparently benevolent manner. That said, one does not have to be either a Marxist or a cynic to emphasize that private-sector elites have often effectively made "intentional state policy" their own. Indeed, Strange's longtime interest in Gramscian ideas is entirely consistent with a conclusion that "state" policy is frequently and perhaps usually a reflection of "private authority" in thin disguise.

Today, the frontiers of markets and states are more incompatible than at any time since Westphalia. Markets are substantially deterritorialized, even though some huge internal markets such as that of the United States still account for more actual transactions than external transactions from the same state. The regionalization and globalization of markets are characteristic features of economic integration, and, to extreme advocates of economic neoliberalism, efforts by states to impede or regulate the flow of goods, people, or ideas is, at best, undesirable and, at worst, dysfunctional. The greater mobility and autonomy of sellers, purchasers, and the global markets they produce contribute to undermining the authority of states and their capacity to control their own economic fortunes.[21]

Some commentators conclude that we are witnessing what Strange called a "retreat of the state" in which states have "surrendered" to the very markets that "they" (recall our earlier observation) originally created. Rosenau contends that: "The shrinking economic . . . distances that have transnationalized global affairs have greatly increased the vulnerability of domestic economies to external influences, so that domestic market forces are decreasingly capable of sustaining stability and progress."[22] For Strange, "the reality of state authority is not the same as it once was,"[23] and she points to ten areas of traditional state responsibility in which state authority is being reduced – (1) defense of national territory; (2) maintaining the value of the currency; (3) choosing the

D. Willett, "Financial Interdependence and the State: International Monetary Relations at Century's End," *International Organization* 51:3 (Summer 1997), p. 481.
[21] Two sets of essays with divergent conclusions about the impact of globalization on states are Robert O. Keohane and Helen V. Milner, eds., *Internationalization and Domestic Politics* (Cambridge: Cambridge University Press, 1996) and *National Diversity and Global Capitalism*, ed., Suzanne Berger and Ronald Dore (Ithaca, NY: Cornell University Press, 1996). The articles in the Keohane and Milner volume suggest that globalization will result in greater convergence of policies and politics among states, while those in Berger and Dore generally argue that national idiosyncrasies are more resilient.
[22] Rosenau, *Turbulence*, p. 131.   [23] Strange, *Retreat of the State*, p. 84.

type of capitalism to be followed; (4) correcting the cycle of booms and slumps; (5) provision of a social safety-net; (6) taxation; (7) control of foreign trade; (8) provision of economic infrastructure; (9) protecting "national champions" and monopoly privileges; and (10) monopoly of violence against citizens.[24]

Globalized capital flows, currency speculation, investment decisions, and markets dramatically complicate (and sometimes even dissolve) state capacity to set macroeconomic policies for its citizens. National trade policies are routinely undermined by massive intra- and interfirm trade, monetary policy by investment flows, corporate investment decisions, offshore and joint ventures, and the like. Others argue that even if the state has not retreated, at a minimum, its fundamental *raison d'être* has been altered. States now formulate policy on the basis of competitive strategies that seek to encourage markets and delegate responsibility for key decisions to private actors.[25] Indeed, the growing authority of private firms has further muddied the traditional distinction, albeit always tenuous, between "public" and "private" economic actors and issues. The editors of a recent volume on this subject argue that "firms may draw more heavily on the capacities of the state in constructing private authority, or the state may delegate or confer authority . . . Relatedly, the emergence of private authority where none existed previously may involve the displacement of arm's length impersonal market relations among firms or it may involve a displacement of public authority and public institutions by private authority and private institutions."[26]

The globalization of markets and the erosion of state capabilities are both causes and results of the increased authority of economic institutions that either are less tied to territory or that states themselves have created or supported to augment the scope and domain of interstate cooperation and extend their own economic reach. Many of these institutions are what Rosenau calls "sovereignty-free actors" that take advantage of the ways in which economic space is being altered, as Saskia Sassen notes in highlighting the growing concentrations of capital and skilled persons in a few cities such as New York, Tokyo, and London. Such cities are global centers linked to one another through a

---

[24] *Ibid.*, pp. 73–82.

[25] Peter Dombrowski, *Policy Responses to the Globalization of American Banks* (Pittsburgh: University of Pittsburgh Press, 1996).

[26] A. Claire Cutler, Virginia Haufler, and Tony Porter, "The Contours and Significance of Private Authority in International Affairs," in A. Claire Cutler, Virginia Haufler, and Tony Porter, eds., *Private Authority and International Affairs* (Albany, NY: State University of New York Press, 1999), p. 335.

financial "chain of production" yet largely disconnected from their own hinterlands,[27] and the operations they host represent an "embedding" of the "global" in the "national."[28]

Transnational corporations and other economic institutions

Of "sovereignty-free" economic actors, none are more adaptable than the transnational corporations that dominate global markets. TNCs have gained a capacity to exercise a wide range of political and economic functions, and have had authority thrust upon them by governments seeking the market's miracles without bearing ultimate responsibility for what follows. Markets, often more or less corresponding to neoclassical ideas of competition and openness, are forced to bear more and more of that responsibility. Whereas part of the impetus for the creation of territorial states was removal of local impediments to long-distance trading, in today's globalized world, economic enterprises often regard the state *itself* as an impediment to the rapid and free movement of goods and services.

State influence on TNCs varies. Although states continue to control most overt means of coercion, those assets avail little when capital takes flight, currencies fluctuate, or habitual trade deficits produce unemployment. By contrast, the flexibility of TNCs helps them compensate for the absence of coercive instruments by moving investment capital quickly from place to place or converting currencies in order to take advantage of local market and labor conditions. The actual degree of flexibility can be exaggerated, for companies do have physical installations that they are loath to abandon, and, in any event, they need to have a presence in centers of economic activity. But, by any measure, companies are much more "footloose" than states. Their flexibility allows TNCs to move offshore, establishing alliances and networks with one another, and to take advantage of ever-accelerating technological changes. In the words of Caroline Thomas:

> It is . . . evident that, in manufacturing – and indeed in mining and agriculture – the nature of innovatory technology is such that both

[27] Saskia Sassen, *Cities in a Global Economy* (Thousand Oaks, CA: Pine Forge Press, 1994), pp. 42–57.
[28] Saskia Sassen, "Embedding the Global in the National: Implications for the Role of the State," in David A. Smith, Dorothy J. Solinger, and Stephen C. Topik, eds., *States and Sovereignty in the Global Economy* (London: Routledge, 1999), pp. 158–171.

the products and the processes of their production are becoming more capital intensive and less labour intensive than those they replace. The combination of added costs of investment and diminished time for the realisation of profits from the product or process has effectively pushed firms into seeking larger markets from which to extract the income necessary to amortise the debts incurred for capital investment in time to be ready for the next wave of technological innovation.[29]

Some TNCs have enormous resources that make those available to most governments seem paltry by comparison, and TNC resources are being wielded across state frontiers with increasing impunity and almost unimaginable rapidity. The 50 largest transnational companies have annual sales revenue greater than the GNP of 131 members of the United Nations,[30] and one-quarter of the entire workforce of the industrialized countries are employed in some aspect of international business. TNCs are the world's major sources of investment capital. To obtain private investment, states are pressured to reduce official corruption and increase their economies' transparency, making public formerly privileged information.[31] For these as well as other reasons, TNCs are often able to play off states against each other in order to cope with an unfriendly local political climate or to avoid taxes or trade impediments. Writes one commentator:

> While multinational companies can invest or disinvest, merge with others or go it alone, rise from nothing or disappear in bankruptcy, the state seems stodgy and stuck in comparison. The state is glued more or less to one piece of territory, fighting off entropy and budget crises, the national community usually assessing the latest foreign attacks upon a condition of declining competitiveness and the vulnerability in its domestic markets.[32]

Initially, most business expansion beyond national boundaries involved establishing production facilities abroad to take advantage of local cheap labor and raw materials – or to sneak in under tariff

---

[29] Caroline Thomas, *In Search of Security: The Third World* (Boulder, CO: Lynne Rienner, 1987), p. 27.

[30] The smallest of the fifty had sales of $32.5 billion in 1994. Statistics from Peter Willetts, "The Role of 'Non-State Actors': Transnational Actors and International Organizations in Global Politics," in John Bayliss and Steve Smith, eds., *The Globalization of World Politics: An Introduction to International Relations* (New York: Oxford University Press, 1996).

[31] Robert O. Keohane and Joseph S. Nye, Jr., "Power and Interdependence in the Information Age," *Foreign Affairs* 77:5 (September/October 1998), p. 93.

[32] Robert A. Isaak, *Managing World Economic Change*, 2nd ed. (Englewood Cliffs, NJ: Prentice-Hall, 1995), p. 264.

walls. Since the 1980s, however, direct investment abroad has grown explosively, but – for all that and full mergers – much of the action has been shifting to alliances and networks such as joint ventures, partnerships, knowledge agreements, and outsourcing arrangements. Some of these arrangements involve substantial investment in one another's businesses; more often, mutually supporting production, development, or knowledge-sharing. When there is mutual investment, it is often only a minority share, merely a symbolic bonding of the allied parties.

All of this vastly complicates the question of who is in charge. One result of corporate alliances is the growing difficulty in determining the country of origin of products, which (along with other factors) challenges traditional conceptions of trade policy. Intergovernmental efforts to liberalize tariff and nontariff barriers to trade, now, in fact, seem rather to be opening the door after most of the horses have already left the stable. Governments concentrate their efforts on a few remaining troublesome sectors and highly publicized disputes. Meanwhile, in the developing world and former Soviet countries, attention has shifted to IMF and World Bank preferences for austerity and free-market policies.

IMF conditionality produces a sense of powerlessness among recipients.[33] Such a reaction is typical in cases where a country is driven to go hat in hand to the IMF for assistance that is provided at a high price in terms of the loss of national control over the economy. The IMF was one of three pillars of the Bretton Woods system and its role then, as today, was to assist states that confront a persistent balance-of-trade deficit. In recent decades, however, it has become an "enforcer" of economic neoliberalism,[34] especially of open and unfettered markets. Its advocacy of separating economics and politics, government nonintervention, and free trade more generally reflect the economic liberal tradition in Great Britain and the United States. In regards to the tension between the need for market stability versus state autonomy, the IMF supports the former, its main focus being, in the words of one critic, "system-maintenance."[35]

---

[33] For an analysis of individual and group powerlessness in the face of globalization, see Giddens, *The Consequences of Modernity*, p. 150. For a vociferous denunciation of IMF and Western policies during the Asian crisis, see Rodney Bruce Hall, "The Discursive Demolition of the Asian Development Model," *International Studies Quarterly* 47:1 (March 2003), pp. 71–99.

[34] See M. D. Steger, *Globalism: The New Market Ideology* (Lanham, MD: Rowman & Littlefield, 2002), p. 9.

[35] Thomas, *In Search of Security*, p. 42. The IMF is dominated by a few developed states, especially the United States, owing to the system of national quotas and its role in determining voting power and consequent dominance of the IMF Executive Board.

IMF assistance is usually requested only when other private sources of funds are no longer available.

The IMF's economic philosophy is reflected in the conditions it generally attaches to its loans that exceed the first 50 percent of a nation's quota. IMF personnel visit the country requesting the loan, analyze the situation, and offer guidelines that the country must accept in the form of a letter of intent. Not surprisingly, the neoliberal orthodoxy of the IMF clashes with the ideological preferences of many of the recipients of IMF assistance. Proffered conditions often are in line with the IMF's monetarist leanings, especially "hard-currency spending targets to limit imports, and devaluation to stimulate exports, dampen domestic consumption and to check the expansion of bureaucracy."[36]

The result may be significant social costs, including high unemployment, rising cost of staples, reduced public services and spending, and a general economic slowdown. "A sudden negative swing in investors' perceptions," declares Ricardo Hausmann, "can have a far-reaching impact on the daily lives of individuals . . . People lose jobs and families cannot afford to keep children in school."[37] These conditions undermine government popularity and strain existing social and political institutions. Under these conditions: "The political stability of a country can be put at risk."[38] Accepting IMF conditionality, then, can entail a humiliating surrender of national control that may trigger serious domestic discontent like that which engulfed Indonesia in the spring of 1998. There are few alternatives for such countries other than default when a country is running out of adequate hard currency[39] to pay off international debts.

One may interpret TNC and IMF influence as reflecting the growth of autonomous global economic institutions that are eroding state sovereignty in general. However, a persuasive case can be made that such institutions are really agents or allies of a group of market-oriented states that seek to reduce the economic autonomy of nonmarket-oriented states in order to serve the interests of their own elites much as did the expansion of the law of the sea in the case of Great Britain in the nineteenth

---

[36] *Ibid.*, p. 51.
[37] Ricardo Hausmann, "Will Volatility Kill Market Democracy?" *Foreign Policy* 108 (Fall 1997), p. 54.
[38] Thomas, *In Search of Security*, p. 53.
[39] Currency that is acceptable around the world much as gold was in earlier centuries. The US dollar, European euro, and Japanese yen are the most popular hard currencies.

century. Certainly, the economic benefits of globalization flow dispro-portionately to those who are most deeply involved in service industries, especially the production of ideas and innovations.

Without doubt, overall, fewer and fewer governments can control their economy's own private sector. Fewer today have a reasonable grasp of what is happening in their own national economies, who is producing what, and what taxes are owed – let alone the capacity to col-lect them and keep the national Treasury from being deposited by cor-rupt officials in numbered accounts abroad. As we have mentioned, in Italy, the most dynamic part of the private sector (apart from the Mafia) – composed of smaller enterprises – is largely undocumented and virtu-ally untaxed. And one of the results is that it is almost impossible to rank accurately the productivity of leading European economies.

In addition to transnational corporations and international financial institutions, other globe-girdling economic polities include criminal car-tels that routinely pose a major challenge to many states. Authorities have been battling the likes of freebooters, pirates, smugglers, and illicit arms dealers since ancient times. Some governments have "combated" crime by establishing their own market shares. Indeed, one may con-ceive of the problem of large-scale crime as a market phenomenon, that is, another form of alliance – between criminal enterprises and their employees, consumers, and corrupt officials. For example, former Dominican dictator President Rafael Trujillo, his family, and immediate cronies controlled about two-thirds of the entire economy of the Domini-can Republic, and the national military in many developing countries have been involved in a host of unsavory activities. In Colombia and Italy, drug cartels and the Mafia, respectively, have made such inroads that "the state" itself has in recent years sometimes seemed almost con-gruent with criminal networks. Although the situation is not quite that bad in countries like Japan and Mexico, official corruption has been so pervasive that it has contributed to serious political instability. The Rus-sian Mafia, for its part, has set up what has been effectively a parallel economy to that of the state, which has been slow to privatize and adjust to changing conditions.

Institutions like drug cartels may rightly be seen as "macro" phe-nomena in global politics, but organized crime is also an integral part of social life at every level. Not only in Colombia but also in Peru, Bolivia, Mexico, and drug-trade countries elsewhere in the world, peasants have little alternative but to depend on drug lords for a livelihood and parts of the national territory are literally "off limits" to public authority. The developed world, too, is hardly immune. In the New York metropolitan area, for example, police corruption has been a perennial issue, and locals were long aware of the criminal control of New York's Fulton Fish Market, the Javits Convention Center, and garbage collection in New Jersey. The Russian Mafia is making inroads in various US neighborhoods and smaller cities, and Chinese gangs control many businesses in Chinatown and are deeply involved in illegal immigration from the Far East.

Efforts to insulate citizens from the corrosive effects of globalization cannot be made, as Strobe Talbott reminds us, "without also cutting [citizens] off from its opportunities and benefits." Yet for many people globalization "has brought economic disadvantage and social disruption."[40]

The implications of contemporary economic turbulence

Contemporary turbulence in global politics calls into question standard formulations about the relationship between politics and economics, the role of states, and the nature of markets. In the prestate era, it was not necessary or even possible to differentiate clearly between political and economic phenomena. The publication of Adam Smith's *Wealth of Nations* in 1776, however, posited the growing autonomy of the two spheres and provided a basis for evaluating their relationship to each other. Paradoxically, it was not theorists in the liberal Anglo-Saxon tradition but the "realist" successors to the continent's state-centric and power-politics tradition who asserted most vigorously the autonomy of politics. The field of international relations was built upon a model that focused solely on the history and behavior of Westphalian States. Especially after World War II, partly as a denial of Marxism and partly as a rejection of the liberal faith in economic progress as a way of ending war, realists proclaimed the separation of the political and economic arenas. "Power" was declared to be true political currency, analogous to money in economics, and Hans Morgenthau declared that "the concept of interest defined in terms of power . . . sets politics as an autonomous sphere of action and understanding apart from

---

[40] Strobe Talbott, "Globalization and Diplomacy: A Practitioner's Perspective," *Foreign Policy* 108 (Fall 1997), pp. 71, 70.

other spheres, *such as economics (understood in terms of interest defined as wealth)."*[41]

By the 1970s and 1980s recognition had grown that the parsimonious depiction of an autonomous global politics had failed to capture some of the most prominent features of the modern world, including the intermingling of political and economic factors. Assuming the autonomy of the political and economic realms ignores a world in which some states have lost control of their economic destiny and are fracturing politically or simply are becoming unable to allocate values authoritatively, and in which other states are becoming embedded in regional and global economic structures. The changing relationship between territorial states and deterritorialized markets is at once a cause and consequence of the erosion of state authority and the legitimizing of new transnational and even supranational networks of authority. While separation of the economic and political spheres was never justified – after all, the birth of the Westphalian State involved the emergence of competitive markets at the state level and, over time, on a global scale[42] – it is even less so today. Today, as in the past, changes in the relationship between states and markets are linked to dramatic shifts in authority patterns.

As with economics, the links between global politics and other social sciences such as sociology, psychology, and geography were also neglected, especially by North American scholars. The specialization of many international relations journals, and other professional incentives and disincentives diminished the opportunity for disciplinary cross-fertilization. However, just as economics and politics were reunited because of the conceptual demands of interdependence and globalization, international relations scholarship has benefited in recent years from interactions with other fields. At the metatheoretical level, constructivists owe debts to the sociology of Anthony Giddens and the historical scholarship of Benedict Anderson. In another example, scholars of global finance have increasingly adopted the insights of economic geographers and psychologists (witness the widespread use of terms such as "financial euphoria," "herd mentality," and "disaster myopia")

---

[41] Hans J. Morgenthau, *Politics Among Nations*, 6th ed., rev. Kenneth W. Thompson (New York: Alfred A. Knopf, 1985), p. 5. Emphasis added. See also Karl Polanyi, *Great Transformation: The Political and Economic Origins of our Time* (Boston, MA: Beacon Press, 1944).

[42] Tilly, *Coercion, Capital and European States*, pp. 11–20. See also Giovanni Arrighi, *The Long Twentieth Century: Money, Power, and the Origins of Our Times* (London: Verso, 1994), pp. 7–47.

to understand the significance of global financial centers and the origins of global financial crises, respectively.[43]

In reconsidering the relationship between politics and economics and moving beyond realist parsimony, some theorists have rediscovered the charms of traditional liberalism (denounced earlier by realists as "idealism").[44] Like the liberals of the late nineteenth and early twentieth centuries such as Richard Cobden, John Bright, and Norman Angell, the new liberals foresee economic interdependence as inexorably leading to peace and prosperity. The best representative of this view is Richard Rosecrance who confidently asserts that, "despite retrogressions that capture our attention, the world is making steady progress toward peace and economic security" and "that as factors of labor, capital, and information triumph over the old factor of land, nations no longer need and in time will not covet additional territory."[45]

Rosecrance initially contrasted the power-maximizing state with the "trading state"[46] but, shortly thereafter, conceptualized what he calls the "virtual state." The latter, built on information processing and service production, is almost unrecognizable as the heir of the territorial leviathans celebrated by realists. Rosecrance identifies a new global division of labor "between 'head' countries, which design products, and 'body' nations, which manufacture them."[47] The former specialize in "research and development, product design, financing, marketing, transport, insurance, and legal services,"[48] while the latter produce the physical product. Head (for example, Singapore) and body (for example China) states, therefore, enjoy a symbiotic relationship, helping to create a secure world based on open trade, uninterrupted production, and instantaneous communication among corporate subsidiaries. The growing importance of knowledge industries, Rosecrance believes, makes war obsolete because of the decreasing importance of territory.[49] Echoing Angell's pre-World War I classic, *The*

---

[43] Peter Dombrowski, "Haute Finance and High Theory: Recent Scholarship on Global Financial Relations," *Mershon International Studies Review* 42:1 (May 1998), pp. 5, 23.

[44] See Andrew Moravcsik, "Taking Preferences Seriously: A Liberal Theory of International Politics," *International Organization* 51:4 (Autumn 1997), pp. 513–553.

[45] Richard Rosecrance, *The Rise of the Virtual State: Wealth and Power in the Coming Century* (New York: Basic Books, 1999), p. xi, and Rosecrance, "The Rise of the Virtual State," *Foreign Affairs* 75: 4 (July/August 1996), pp. 45–61.

[46] Richard N. Rosecrance, *The Rise of the Trading State: Conquest in the Modern World* (New York: Basic Books, 1986).

[47] Rosecrance, *The Rise of the Virtual State*, p. xi.   [48] *Ibid.*, p. xii.

[49] Rosecrance, *The Rise of the Virtual State*, pp. 16–17. Rosecrance does *not* assume that the virtual state will enhance global democracy (pp. 18–19). See also Friedman, *The Lexus and*

Grand Illusion, he concludes: "The rise of the virtual state . . . inaugurates a new epoch of peaceful competition among nations."[50] Others agree with Rosecrance. Philip Cerny has argued that what exists today is a "competition state"[51] or a "residual state" composed of "a potentially unstable mix of civil association and enterprise association – of constitutional state, pressure groups, and firm – with state actors, no longer so autonomous, feeling their way uneasily in an unfamiliar world."[52]

The revitalization of liberalism and the decline in state socialism remind us that the vertical divisions that separate people occupying one physical space from those occupying another, much as walls or fences separate neighbors, do not do justice to the manner in which the world's poor and rich are spatially related to one other. The "poor" and "rich" and "developed" and "less developed" are not neatly separated into different states; they are also divided by horizontal identity boundaries that separate people within the same geographic space, as in the case of class or caste. Wealthy populations and the poor, far from being segregated geographically into different states and regions, can be found within the *same* states, implying "developed and undeveloped *populations* with no nationally defined geographic identity."[53] As a result, characterizations such as "first world" or "third world" mean less and less. The postinternational world, then, is increasingly characterized by horizontal identities that distinguish economic and technical elites from other citizens. Thus, the responsibility for defining and ranking the expectations, loyalties, and values of people and for allocating those values are shifting from sovereign states to other authorities, especially transnational economic enterprises, that operate within the demanding confines of large-scale market exchange processes and that have little respect for static political boundaries or alternative forms of social control.

---

the *Olive Tree*; and Daniel Yergin and J. Stanislaw, *The Commanding Heights* (New York: Simon and Schuster, 1998).

[50] Rosecrance, *The Rise of the Virtual State*, p. xv.

[51] Philip G. Cerny, *The Changing Architecture of Politics: Structure, Agency, and the Future of the State* (London: Sage Publications, 1990), p. 236; Cerny, "The Dynamics of Financial Globalization: Technology, Market Structure, and Policy Response," *Policy Sciences* 27 (1994), pp. 241–24; Cerny, "The Infrastructure of the Infrastructure: Toward 'Embedded Financial Orthodoxy' in the International Political Economy," in Ronen P. Palan and Barry Gills, eds., *Transcending the State–Global Divide: A Neostructuralist Agenda in International Relations* (Boulder, CO: Lynne Reinner, 1994), p. 3.

[52] Philip G. Cerny, "Globalization and the Changing Logic of Collective Action," *International Organization* 49:4 (Autumn 1995), p. 619.

[53] Robinson, "Beyond Nation-State Paradigms," p. 578. Emphasis in original.

From the perspective of global stability, the most important implication of the above is that the attributes of wealth and poverty tend to reinforce particular identities, increasing the prospect of conflict, often within states. Thus, economic differences between Shi'ites and Sunnis in Lebanon and Iraq add to the hostility produced by differences in dogma. In China, as we have seen, the growing wealth gap between the country's peasant masses and its modernizing coastal sector is viewed as a growing threat to political stability. Similar cases have produced potentially dangerous fissures in many other countries as well.

Historical patterns

The whole question of shifting boundaries is, as noted earlier, linked to the changing role of physical distance. In past centuries, time lags inherent in long-distance communication and travel limited the scope of economic exchange. During much of history, rudimentary technologies of communication and transportation helped diminish economic authority at a distance. Exchange was necessarily local, and dependence on horse and sail limited the type and amount of goods that could be traded over great distances. Schwartz emphasizes the persistence of microeconomies centered on market towns surrounded by an agricultural hinterland of about 20 miles. With the exception of microeconomies that had access to water and ships, he writes: *"Until the era of canals and railroads, and indeed well into that era, no such thing as a 'national economy' existed*. The global economy – that is, a complex division of labor linking economic areas located in different political units – existed long before transportation improvements brought all microeconomies into close economic contact within most political units."[54] Although we might object that Schwartz's definition of a "global economy" could still be a regional one, his argument is really about the role of expanded, ultimately often imperial, markets and mercantilism in state-building.

Improvements in transportation and communication were slow to arrive; it was only in the nineteenth century that the speed of travel and transmission of messages could exceed the speed of horses. Distance also helped to limit the capacity of some societies to benefit from trade and specialization and thus impeded their ability to accumulate capital and achieve economic take-off.

---

[54] Schwartz, *States Versus Markets*, p. 14. Emphasis in original.

For Schwartz the expansion of economic space was closely connected to the success of the Westphalian State. He describes a complicated three-way relationship between kings, nobles, and merchants. "Kings could increase their internal authority only to the extent that they could, first, replace nobles' local monopoly of violence with police forces [professional armies] controlled from the center, and second, shift control over law and taxation from the nobility to their own hired hands, that is, bureaucrats with no independent source of power."[55] Nobles controlled local lands and wind and water mills, and lived with their peasants "in a delicate balance of terror." For nobles, the problem was to determine how much they could "extract" before the peasants would rise in rebellion,[56] and political leaders "had a common interest in keeping the peasants under control and fending off other predatory states. During the sixteenth and seventeenth centuries, the nobility faced nearly constant internal and external threats, forcing them to calculate finely how much of the surplus they needed to relinquish to their king in order to get collective protection."[57] Kings also sought to establish and retain the right to confirm the inheritance of fiefs, which, in turn, required the nobility to give loyal military service.[58] Here and elsewhere the war-making story beloved by realists intersects with economics.

The introduction of money tied the economic and political realms still closer together. "Kings and would-be kings," notes Schwartz, "sought to monetarize the microeconomies in order to shift part of the peasants' surplus away from nobles and toward themselves."[59] Monetarization also allowed them to charge tolls on roads to market towns. However, the "real money" (gold, silver, or copper) needed for monetarization was largely in merchants' hands.[60] Kings could seize merchant's funds, but this usually proved counterproductive, since merchants would only pick up and leave the area.

> Erratic ripoffs yielded to regular borrowing from merchants. Merchants liked this since it provided an outlet for surplus funds. And since kings in effect used this money to monetarize microeconomies, they increased the markets available to merchants by integrating them into the network of waterborne trade and removing the internal tolls nobles threw up along trade routes. Finally, merchants benefited from the kings' ability to deploy violence on their behalf against competing merchants and predatory nobles and kings.[61]

[55] *Ibid.*, p. 17. [56] *Ibid.*, p. 15. [57] *Ibid.*, p. 16.
[58] *Ibid.*, p. 17. [59] *Ibid.*, p. 16. [60] *Ibid.*, p. 17. [61] *Ibid.*, p. 19.

Kings encouraged long-distance trade, and over time this blossomed into far-flung empires guided by a policy of mercantilism. The idea was to boost exports of finished goods and limit imports of anything but raw materials from within the empire itself. As Schwartz notes, although mercantilism might not seem to make much sense in terms of neoclassical economic theories, it did in fact have a "compelling and rational political logic"; profits from trade and precious metals "were the most practical way for kings to monetarize their realms. Because of limits on overland grain transport, a unified global market emerged much sooner than 'national' markets almost anywhere. The waterborne economy contained more moveable resources than did any given king's collection of microeconomies."[62]

As in the growth of dynastic states, the diminishing impact of territory and distance are at the heart of globalization. Today, production can be global in scope, and commodity exchange and capital flows take place in highly integrated global markets.[63] Many economists, political economists, and sociologists have sought to identify the broad parameters and consequences of economic change in recent decades. Unlike realists who see states and markets evolving independently of each other, neo-Marxists like Immanuel Wallerstein see a close connection between the two. Wallerstein argues that the state system "is . . . the only kind of structure that can guarantee the persistence of the partially free market which is the key requirement of a system based on the ceaseless accumulation of capital." He continues: "Capitalism and the modern state-system were not two separate historical inventions (or conceptions) that had to be fitted together or articulated with each other. They were obverse sides of a single coin . . . Neither is imaginable without the other. They were simultaneously developed, and neither could continue to exist without the other."[64]

At the highest level of abstraction globalization simply refers to the triumph of the market form at a global level. Markets have widened and deepened to encompass more economic relations within and among societies. In many areas of the world, traditional sectors are giving way to modernizing sectors – for example, from subsistence agriculture and pastoralism to the production of agricultural commodities. In advanced industrial and postindustrial societies, long-term trends seem to favor

---

[62] *Ibid.*, pp. 21–22, see also pp. 31–41.
[63] For a critical perspective on globalization see Hirst and Thompson, *Globalization in Question*.
[64] Wallerstein, "The Inter-State Structure of the Modern World-System," p. 89.

less state intervention in economic affairs and less regulation of markets. Moreover, the last significant regions not included in the global marketplace – including the independent states of the former Soviet Union, the former Soviet allies in Central and Eastern Europe, and the People's Republic of China – are now being "marketized."

What holds it together? Peter F. Drucker writes that "[corporate] alliances, formal and informal, are becoming the dominant form of integration in the world economy."

> Some major companies, such as Toshiba, the Japanese electronic giant, and Corning Glass, the world's leading maker of high-engineered glass, may each have more than 100 alliances all over the world. Integration in the [EU] is proceeding far more through alliances than through mergers and acquisitions, especially among the middle-sized companies that dominate European economies . . . Businesses make little distinction between domestic and foreign partners in their alliances. An alliance creates a relationship in which it does not matter whether one partner speaks Japanese, another English, and a third German or Finnish.[65]

Alliances are only part of the picture of economic globalization. The composition of transactions occurring within global markets has undergone considerable change as well. In US accounts, contrary to classical theory based on national comparative advantage, on the order of half of all trade in goods and services is intraindustry and intrafirm (for example, sales by Ford Europe to Ford USA). And in some economic sectors TNCs enjoy oligopolistic positions that enhance their bargaining positions relative to states and other polities. Perhaps the most widely noted phenomenon is the shifting balance between trade in "real" goods – commodities and manufactured goods – and trade in services – from transportation to data processing – and financial products. Economists readily acknowledge that services are so hard to track that they may well be underestimating their actual flow by as much as 50 percent. The United States has the largest share of services trade among the developed countries, followed by the United Kingdom. Japan is at the bottom of the list. Hence the much-ballyhooed trade deficit between the United States and Japan may not be much of a real deficit at all because measures

---

[65] Peter F. Drucker, "Trade Lessons from the World Economy," *Foreign Affairs* 73:1 (January/February 1994), pp. 103–104.

of trade such as current account balances and national trade deficits are largely obsolete.[66]

In terms of production (especially, in export sectors), observers have noted the rise of post-Fordism.[67] Taylorist and Fordist approaches to mass production and consumption based on standardization are giving way to flexible production based on continuous technological innovation and the use of skilled workers capable of adapting to rapid technical change. Post-Fordist practices have emerged, at least in part, in response to the fickle nature of consumer preferences in a multimedia world. Global telecommunications systems simultaneously and instantaneously allow sellers to bombard huge swathes of the world's population with advertising and permit sellers to identify and reach marketing niches based on geography, cultural preferences, social status and shared vocations.[68] No longer need one size fit all.

Such developments may contribute to the pressures producing a redefinition of citizenship in the postinternational world. More capable and informed workers make more capable and informed citizens; alternately, the ability to communicate with, and satisfy, many marketing niches may contribute to more parochial and noninclusive conceptions of belonging and rights. Under such conditions, the ideological battle over the proper mix of markets and other means of organizing economic relations has shifted in favor of markets. Cerny has analyzed the triumph of "embedded financial orthodoxy" where deregulation and liberalization guide policymakers and regulators alike.[69] Biersteker has documented how repeated global debt crises, and pressure from aid donors and international financial institutions have encouraged developing countries to abandon state-based approaches to modernization and instead adopt market-oriented policies of liberalization and openness.[70] In general, governance through democratic and bureaucratic institutions is giving way to market-oriented decisionmaking.

[66] Robert Gilpin, *The Political Economy of International Relations* (Princeton: Princeton University Press, 1987), p. 254.
[67] Amin edits a helpful selection of readings introducing the central ideas of post-Fordism in *Post-Fordism*.
[68] Some refer to this process as one of "glocalization." See Roland Robertson, "Glocalization: Time-space and Homogeneity-heterogeneity," in Mike Featherstone, Scott Lash, and Roland Robertson, eds., *Global Modernities* (London: Sage, 1995), p. 28.
[69] Cerny, "The Infrastructure of the Infrastructure," p. 226.
[70] Thomas J. Biersteker, "The 'Triumph' of Neoclassical Economics in the Developing World: Policy Convergence and Bases of Governance in the International Economic Order," in Rosenau and Czempiel, *Governance without Government*, pp. 102–131.

In sum, the globalization of markets has put enormous pressure on states. In terms of ability to provide political and economic protections and services for their populations, territorial states are playing catch-up to innovative private firms and rapidly evolving financial and services markets. Ours is a world in which the ability of states or other institutions to set limits or assert control over markets is limited, at least at socially acceptable costs. Surely, few need reminding of the horrible privations suffered by those living in countries such as North Korea, Belarus, and Myanmar that pursue national autarky. Officials and ordinary citizens alike must take the reaction and operations of markets into account in making political and economic choices. If globalized markets are not exactly sovereign, they have come to represent a "structural characteristic, similar to anarchy" in the global system that states cannot ignore.[71] Market demands, as Robert Keohane and Helen Milner declare, are "a fact that individual states confront and can only ignore or seek to change by paying such high costs."[72] For most countries, these are not realistic options. In the long and short run, markets do not respect even the most rigid of sovereign boundaries, a fact brought home to Asia in 1997 and to countries like Argentina and Brazil in 2002.

Globalization, nationalism, and the Korea case

Under conditions of globalization, states and peoples everywhere are economically interdependent, and when problems occur they are likely to spread rapidly from place to place. Although capital movements may discipline states' economic behavior, the resulting turmoil may be contagious as speculators seek to take advantage of currency fluctuations and withdraw funds not only from the country at risk but also from others that are seen to have similar problems. Indeed, the absence of capital controls may increase the speed at which investment can flow in and out of a country, thereby seriously exacerbating a currency crisis. This contagion effect was apparent during the Mexican crisis of 1994 – what was called the "Tequila Effect"[73] – and it reappeared as Asia's financial woes spread from Southeast Asia northward to currency and stock markets in Korea and Hong Kong in 1998.

In Mexico, President Salinas took office in 1988 and proceeded to renegotiate his country's foreign debt in order to undertake market

---

[71] Keohane and Milner, eds., *Internationalization and Domestic Politics*, p. 257.
[72] *Ibid.*   [73] Hausmann, "Will Volatility Kill Market Democracy?" p. 54.

reform and privatization that would boost foreign investor confidence and make it possible for Mexico to join NAFTA (the North American Free Trade Agreement). Between 1990 and 1994 Mexico received more foreign investment than any other country except China. The government hoped that the country's continuing attractiveness to foreign investment would keep Mexican money invested at home, and that dependence on foreign capital would lessen as the large gap between imports and exports gradually closed.

Salinas not illogically believed that Mexican exports would soar once NAFTA reduced trade barriers. Unfortunately, foreign investment helped keep the peso greatly overvalued, led to a surge of imports, and encouraged Mexicans to use their overvalued money to invest in the United States and elsewhere outside the country. The Federal Reserve raised interest rates in the United States, a revolt flared among Mayans in Mexico's Chiapas region, and the Mexican bubble burst. There was the equivalent of a run on the Mexican bank, which threatened to spread to other countries, when the Clinton administration moved to plug the dike with highly controversial loan guarantees.

The global economic system as a whole may be at risk, when a "volatility neighborhood" is extensive, as it was in the 1994 Mexican case and then again in the 1997–98 Asian crisis. The collision between the forces of economic globalization and nationalism was nowhere more evident than in the economic free fall that began in Southeast Asia, spread northward, then leapfrogged to Russia, and finally subsided in Brazil. Governments under economic siege are likely to seek political cover by placing the onus on outsiders. Rather than placing the blame on themselves for an inferior economic performance, they are likely to blame others, as did Malaysia's Prime Minister Mohamad Mahathir during the "Asian Contagion."[74] Confronted by economic crisis, Mahathir and other Asian leaders reacted with anger and frustration, equating globalization with Western influence. Mahathir sought to explain Southeast Asia's economic woes as a plot by international (read Western) speculators:

> Presently we see a well-planned effort to undermine the economies of all the ASEAN countries by destabilizing their currencies. Our economic fundamentals are good yet anyone with a few billion dollars can destroy all the progress we have made. We are told we must open up,

[74] Mohamad Mahathir, *A New Deal for Asia* (Subang Jaya, Malaysia: Pelanduk Publications, 1999). Mahathir was not the only national leader to adopt this line at the time, but he was the most vociferous and acted by limiting currency movements, contrary to IMF orthodoxy.

> that trade and commerce must be totally free. Free for whom? For rogue speculators. For anarchists wanting to destroy weak countries . . . to force us to submit to the dictatorship of international manipulators.[75]

The collision between states and markets reflects the tension between the overall system's need for stability and the demand for autonomy on the part of states within that system. "On the one hand," declares Gilpin, "the state is based on the concepts of territoriality, loyalty, and exclusivity."

> On the other hand, the market is based on the concepts of functional integration, contractual relationships, and expanding interdependence of buyers and sellers . . . For the state, territorial boundaries are a necessary basis of national autonomy and political unity. For the market, the elimination of all political and other obstacles to the operation of the price mechanism is imperative. The tension between these two fundamentally different ways of ordering human relationships has profoundly shaped the course of modern history and constitutes the crucial problem in the study of political economy.[76]

Owing to the "mismatch" between "economic and political structures," when financial instability shakes one country, it is likely to spread outward like a ripple in a pond with tidalwave potential. Indeed, from the perspective of investors, countries are regarded less as autonomous political entities than what one observer calls an "investment jurisdiction."[77]

In the Asian context, however, the meltdown represented something else as well, something perhaps more fundamental, that is, two cultural traditions, one of which threatens to swallow the other and homogenize values in a global mix. In the Korean context, the tension between globalization and nationalism reflected a clash between two very different paths to social, political, and economic harmony and returns us to our earlier emphasis on culture. On the one hand, much of what is called globalization involves Western traditions of unfettered capitalism, individual self-realization, limited government, and political democracy. Indeed, Western observers were quick to reassert the claim that there is a link between democracy and economic development when much of Asia was reeling from the economic crisis. By contrast, Koreans, like other Asians, have vigorously articulated an alternate path featuring a

---

[75] Cited in Hausmann, "Will Volatility Kill Market Democracy?" p. 56.
[76] Gilpin, *The Political Economy of International Relations*, pp. 10–11.
[77] Robinson, "Beyond Nation-State Paradigms," p. 575.

higher degree of state involvement in economic planning. Korea's economic crisis prompted Western observers to ask whether the "Asian model" had "gone wrong."[78]

That model had evolved, as first Japan and then Asia's newly industrializing countries (NICs), especially Korea and Taiwan, and finally the little "tigers" of Southeast Asia clawed their way from poverty to prosperity. "Asian values" or the "Asian path," as articulated by regional leaders such as Singapore's Lee Kwan Yu and Malaysia's Mohamad Mahathir,[79] combine benign authoritarianism, forced savings, and public construction with a form of "managed" or state capitalism involving an intimate alliance among political and economic elites in which governments helped guide and facilitate export-led growth, while erecting barriers to foreign competition in local markets. This path also holds great attraction for the last and most important of Asia's "tigers," China, where leaders struggle to reconcile an authoritarian political system with an increasingly open and vibrant market and where the state continues to play a central role in promoting exports, attracting foreign investment, and protecting home industries.[80]

The contagion strikes Korea

On September 30, 1996, South Korea celebrated its entry into the elite "rich man's club," the Organization for Economic Cooperation and Development (OECD), waving a proud farewell to the developing world. Only a year later, the country turned to the International Monetary Fund for help, and the IMF quickly responded with a $57 billion rescue package. In previous years, the remarkable economic growth of South Korea had been based upon a close working relationship between the government and Korea's business sector. The government nurtured gigantic business conglomerates (*chaebols*) through preferential credit, tax cuts, and subsidies, protecting them from foreign competition in both the domestic and foreign markets. That alliance initially was very successful.[81]

---

[78] "Asia and the Abyss," *The Economist*, December 20, 1997–January 2, 1998, p. 15.
[79] This should not obscure the enormous variation in development within different Asian countries. See, for example, Ahn Choong Yong, "Models of Industrial Development in East Asian Economies: Uniqueness and Mutual Emulation," paper delivered to the Japan Society of International Economics, Seinan-gakuin University, October 10, 1997.
[80] See Kim Dae Jung, "Is Culture Destiny? The Myth of Asia's Anti-Democratic Values," *Foreign Affairs* 73:6 (November/December 1994), pp. 189–194.
[81] See especially Kim Eun Mee, *Big Business, Strong State: Collusion and Conflict in South Korean Development, 1960–1990* (Albany: State University of New York Press, 1997).

In the early 1990s, South Korea's economic fortunes began to wane. Three factors contributed. First, the business conglomerates had failed to invest sufficiently in research and development (R&D) to produce high-value-added commodities and develop more sophisticated production technologies. Instead, they took quick and easy routes to profits – real estate and stock market speculation. In the 1980s, *chaebols* spent more than $16.5 billion in buying land for speculation, luxury hotels, and golf courses, accounting for 25 percent of their total investment during that time. Second, *chaebol* overinvestment resulted in deficits in the country's balance of payments, which increased dramatically from $4 billion in 1993 to $4.5 billion in 1995, and again to $23.7 billion in 1996. Similarly, Korea's balance of trade with its neighbors worsened dramatically. Third, competition from other East Asian countries using less expensive labor eroded Korea's competitive edge. The myth of the Korean miracle ended suddenly when Vice Prime Minister Chang Yol Lim called the IMF for help.

As is its practice, the IMF set conditions affecting several macroeconomic policy areas.[82] Korea's high level of external debt and the depletion of its foreign-currency reserves made foreign banks wary of greater exposure than they already had, thereby precluding further private loans. According to the IMF–Korea agreement, the objective of the rescue program was to "narrow the external current account deficit to below 1 percent of GDP in 1998 and 1999, contain inflation at or below 5 percent, and – hoping for an early return of confidence – limit the deceleration in real GDP growth to about 3 percent in 1998, followed by a recovery toward potential in 1999."[83] For South Korea, the program's key monetary and exchange rate requirements were:

- tightening monetary policy to restore and sustain calm in financial markets.
- raising interest rates from 12.5 to 21 percent to reduce liquidity and limit money supply in order to contain inflation at or below 5 percent per year.[84]

---

[82] It has been argued that IMF-mandated economic reforms were inappropriate for what was really a "banking crisis." For a description of how a banking crisis unfolds, see Hausmann, "Will Volatility Kill Market Democracy?" pp. 57–58. When financial flows outstrip conventional trade in goods as a component of global trade, banking crises become more critical.

[83] Republic of Korea–IMF Arrangement, December 5, 1997, http://www.imf.org/external/np/oth/korea.htm.

[84] Interest rates rose to 32 percent by December 1997.

- Floating the exchange rate with minimal official intervention.
- Achieving a balanced budget or a modest budget surplus.
- Increasing the value added tax (VAT) and increasing corporate and income tax bases in order to reduce inflation.[85]

Among the most politically important IMF conditions were a lengthy list of institutional and structural reforms. These included freeing the Bank of Korea from the country's central bank in order to separate the government from the *chaebols*, shutting down troubled merchant banks, introducing debt/equity ratios as recommended by the Bank for International Settlements (BIS), and allowing foreign investors into the domestic financial sector. Additional reforms included trade and capital account liberalization, a review of *chaebol* governance practices and structure, and, most controversially, labor market reform that would force unemployment to grow.

Many of these proposed reform measures met with strong opposition. Koreans have a long historical memory and a mythology of victimization by foreign invasions which have promoted a version of nationalism that sees the country as beleaguered and beset by powerful outsiders bent on ending what is distinctively Korean. This attitude is captured by the term *uri* (us), which expresses the core of Korean self-identity. "The key to understanding the notion of *uri*," writes one observer, "is a shared experience of hardship and tribulations that is credited with helping to preserve the Korean identity. In modern-day South Korea, *uri* has come to mean 'our country first' and 'foreigners have no business meddling in our business.'" He continues: "The same concept has been pushed to its logical extreme in North Korea in its state ideology of *juche*, or self-reliance."[86]

Viewing the financial crisis through the lens of the country's earlier experiences, the "interference" of the IMF was regarded by many Koreans as the first foreign intervention since Japanese colonial rule had ended in 1945. Korea's first international treaty, signed with Japan under intense pressure in 1876, had eventually led to Japanese colonization in 1910. The colonial power forced Koreans to sell their land, and, by 1908, Japanese nationals owned about 40 percent of the Korean peninsula. Following independence, Korean xenophobia was reflected in a law that banned ethnic Chinese-Koreans from owning farmland

---

[85] Republic of Korea–IMF Arrangement.
[86] Shim Jae Hoon and Charles S. Lee, "Unlocking the Citadel," *Far Eastern Economic Review* (March 26, 1998). Website (http://www.feer.com), p. 2.

or properties. And at the time the financial crisis erupted, Korean law still only permitted foreign ownership of land for business purposes. As a result, less than one-half of 1 percent of Korea's land belonged to foreigners. Historical reasons alone, then, were enough to account for Koreans' resistance to IMF conditions.

Many Koreans also remained unhappy with the IMF requirement for tight fiscal and low economic growth policies that increased prices and unemployment, and some Koreans were suspicious that the United States and Japan were using the IMF to take advantage of the crisis to squeeze concessions from the Seoul government. Provision for opening domestic markets to foreign automobiles and other key Japanese industrial goods by mid-1999 and for allowing layoffs by businesses were regarded, at least by some, as irrelevant to the principal objectives of the reform package.

Not surprisingly, Koreans tended to blame the IMF for the very real and difficult economic conditions in the aftermath of the crisis. Previously, once hired, workers expected to retain their jobs for life in return for which they remained loyal "children" of their employer. Thus, Korean society was accustomed to full employment. In a matter of a few months, with the new system of layoffs Korea's unemployment rate skyrocketed. Almost every family was touched by the layoffs, the impact of which was captured by *Newsweek* in its description of a shipyard worker:

> Incense burns in the hallway at the Korean Federation of Trade Unions, wafting over a black-and-white photo of a young shipyard worker, draped in black ribbon. Choi Dae Rim, 41, was angry at the government's recent decision to legalize layoffs, abolishing with a stroke the guarantee of lifetime employment in South Korea. He became angrier when his union backed away from a nationwide strike this month to protest the change. Following a long line of Korean union martyrs, Choi recently climbed the hull of a ship in the construction yard, doused his clothes with paint thinner and set himself on fire. Then he jumped to his death. "As the economy gets worse, the rich get richer," he wrote in an emotional will and farewell note, "while the lives of poor workers get worse."[87]

The Korean case, like others such as Argentina, suggests that the IMF might do better if it tried working more closely with states rather than imposing general principles and practices upon them. Currency stabilization has serious social and economic costs, and, if it is to

---

[87] Dorinda Elliott. "A Long, Hot Springtime," *Newsweek*, March 2, 1998, p. 34.

work, governments should be encouraged to eliminate corruption, provide additional social services, and pursue policies aimed at reducing poverty. In some cases, for example, where corrupt dictatorships hold power, the IMF should probably avoid making loans at all, whereas it might ease its conditions where reformist democracies are at risk.

The financial crisis was a profound challenge to Asian values in general and Korean values in particular. Western observers, smarting under a decade of Asian criticism of Western values, were quick to point this out. Typical was a British editorial that announced that "political development in East Asia has not kept pace with its breakneck economic growth, and that this is not just part of the problem but one of its principal causes."

> Lack of democracy in many of the Asian "tigers" has led to loans and contracts being awarded to political cronies rather than on economic criteria . . . It is up to the West to point out that much of Asia's prosperity has been built on fragile political foundations, and that this defect just might bring the whole edifice down . . . [W]e must not allow ourselves to be fobbed off with talk of "Asian values" or deterred by claims that attempts to strengthen democracy constitute unacceptable interference.[88]

The conditions imposed on Korea in return for foreign funding amounted to nothing less than a demand that the country abandon practices that had brought it prosperity in the first place.

Anglo-American values

The Korean crisis illustrates the way in which local practices may be altered under the pressure of globalization. This is not only the case with economic philosophy but with other sovereign features as well. As globalization exerts greater influence in national contexts, a range of local customs and norms are likely to erode and be replaced by amorphous and homogenized global norms, often with roots in the West.

Since the 1980s, United States' values with respect to the political and economic order of society have reflected an increasingly extreme brand of neoliberalism, in contrast to earlier Keynesian assumptions. Proclaiming "the rolling back" of the state, neoliberalism during the

---

[88] "No More Talk of Asian Values," *The Independent* (London) as reproduced in *The Korea Herald*, January 19, 1998, p. 9. The classic work on the relationship between economic and political development is Samuel P. Huntington, *Political Order in Changing Societies* (New Haven: Yale University Press, 1968).

Reagan and Thatcher era embraced policies that involved, as expressed by David Held, "the extension of the market to more and more areas of life; creation of a state stripped of excessive involvement both in the economy and in the provision of opportunities; the curtailment of the power of certain groups (for instance, trade unions) to press their aims and goals; and the construction of a strong government to enforce law and order."[89] Held further summarizes essential neoliberal ideology:

> A free-market system is the basis for a genuinely liberal democracy. In particular, the market can ensure the coordination of decisions of producers and consumers without the direction of a central authority; pursuit by everybody of their own ends with the resources at their disposal; and the development of a complex economy without an elite which claims to know how it all works. Politics, as a governmental decision-making system, will always be a radically imperfect system of choice when compared to the market. Thus, "politics" or "state action" should be kept to a minimum, to the sphere of operation of an "ultra-liberal" state . . . An "oppressive bureaucratic government" is the almost inevitable result of deviation from this prescription – from the model of "legal democracy."[90]

With this orientation, the Thatcher and Reagan governments attacked the bases of state intervention and control, and their successors – in the Clinton administration's case, from an "opposition" political party – did little to reverse prevailing priorities. Most recently, the George W. Bush administration has zealously extended the neoliberal agenda at home while adopting a militant "neoconservative" posture in foreign policy.

Placing individual liberty atop their value hierarchy, neoliberals, however, limit the idea of equality to *equality of opportunity*. This version of equality emphasizes *differences* among individuals, not similarities, and accords with the views of University of Chicago economist Milton Friedman:

> Equality before God – personal equality – is important precisely because people are not identical. Their different values, their different tastes, their different capacities will lead them to want to lead very different lives. Personal equality requires respect for their right to do so, not the imposition on them of someone else's values or judgment, Jefferson had no doubt that some men were superior to others, that there was an elite. But that did not give them the right to rule others.[91]

---

[89] David Held, *Models of Democracy* (Stanford, CA: Stanford University Press, 1987), p. 243.
[90] *Ibid.*, pp. 250–251.
[91] Milton Friedman and Rose Friedman, *Free To Choose* (New York: Avon Books, 1979), p. 120.

In his restatement of liberalism from Locke to J. S. Mill, political philosopher Robert Nozick rejects the superiority of any social or political collective over individuals – "there are only individual people with their own individual lives."[92] Only individuals know what they want, and only they can be the ultimate judges of their own needs and ends and the final judges of government action. Therefore, the less the state interferes in people's lives, the greater their opportunities for freedom. The only way to order or organize human and material resources is through voluntary exchange among individuals. Accordingly, the only justifiable political institutions are those that guarantee individual autonomy, freedom, or rights.

Korean values

South Korea's rapid economic growth and development in the 1970s and 1980s provided a setting in which "Asian values" arising in a Confucian tradition were rediscovered. During the decades of rapid economic expansion, Asian leaders had praised the export-driven model of "crony capitalism" in which economic and public elites were closely linked and local markets were closely protected. Asia's "crony capitalism," it seemed, had overtaken and was even surpassing Western "casino capitalism" of unregulated competition, open markets, and limited government intervention.

Korean political culture and Confucianism are inseparable. "Confucianism," declares Gregory Henderson "was, first of all, a universalistic system." "It provided for a comprehensive explanation and rule of life. It penetrated, during its long dominance, every portion of the peninsula and, with differing depth, every level of society. Its terms were resorted to not only for state organization and conduct but for that of family, guild, and clan."[93] In a Confucian order, property is only contingently private, and there is no genuine theory of private property. In addition, individual privacy is regarded with suspicion, even as possibly subversive, and political status determines economic status. Thus, in Korea the monarch and his officials had first claim on all land and could, in theory, distribute and redistribute it as they saw fit.[94] Although it has begun to change, Korea remains Confucian.

---

[92] Robert Nozick, *Anarchy, State and Utopia* (Oxford: Basil Blackwell, 1974), p. 33.
[93] Gregory Henderson, *Korea: The Politics of the Vortex* (Cambridge, MA: Harvard University Press, 1968), pp. 23–24.
[94] Byung Nak Song, *Korean Economy*, 3rd ed. (Seoul: Park Young Publishing Co., 1998) (in Korean), pp. 32–33.

While most Americans are primarily concerned with maximizing individual freedom and prosperity, the majority of Koreans remain loyal to social values such as equality of outcome, while treating liberal norms of individual liberty and the free market as alien. Korean values strongly reflect the continuous impact of Confucianism, and the norms that underlie contemporary Korea's economic growth are collectively called New Confucianism or Confucian capitalism. As in China, Confucianism in Korea is based upon the "Five Relationships": father and son, husband and wife, king and minister, elder and younger brother, and friend and friend. The essential characteristic of all these relationships except the last is *in*equality. The obedience of son to father is the core of the relationship, and enforcing this obedience and this relationship is a paternal obligation.

While it may seem contradictory to argue that an authoritarian society like Korea is also egalitarian. the apparent contradiction lessens when we distinguish between state and society. Koreans do emphasize hierarchy in social order, as in family. Those at the top have privileges denied to those at the bottom. Egalitarianism exists only among those at the *same level* in the hierarchy. In the family elders have the same rights, and children have the same rights. But elders and children have very different rights and privileges. Thus, following the analogy, those who enjoy high political status are entitled to economic rewards and privileges denied to those of lower rank.

With this in mind, among the most important premises of the New Confucianism is that individuals are not regarded as isolated and self-sufficient entities but as links in a complex system of human relations. Interpersonal and social harmony and cooperation are more important than individual success, and obligation to the community is more highly esteemed than individual rights. Second, in New Confucianism the family is viewed as the essential building block in social relations. The role of family is so important that social relations cannot easily be separated from family relations. The family is the primary unit for consumption, production, income, and welfare, and serves as a metaphor for social relations more generally. Korea's social stability, political order, and economic order are based on the family, and institutions are expected to function like extended families and reflect collective values. The Korean language itself reflects this; concepts like *kookga* (state) and *daega* (great achiever) also connote family.

Third, according to the New Confucianism, the state should serve as a role model in every aspect of social life and must play a leading role in economic development and public welfare. The state is regarded as analogous to the father of a family who controls every aspect of family life. But while acknowledging the authority of the state, Koreans do not accept inequality among citizens. This egalitarianism is expressed in the slogan: "No man above man, no man below man," and it implies that no artificial barrier – social, political, and economic – should be erected against individual self-actualization.[95] Korean society is egalitarian not only in terms of equal opportunity but also in terms of the outcome of socioeconomic distribution.

The 1997–98 financial crisis, combined with the dramatic upturn in the American economy in the 1990s, seemed to deny the superiority of Asian values and placed its advocates on the defensive. Many Koreans believed that the financial crisis forced Korea to adopt the American model as an exemplary competitiveness strategy for surviving in the global economy. Yet the norms of this model permit deregulation, weak unions, and a minimalist welfare state, practices that are incompatible with traditional Korean social values. Many Koreans would sympathize with Huntington's provocative conclusion that:

> In recent years Westerners have reassured themselves and irritated others by expounding the notion that the culture of the West is and ought to be the culture of the world. This conceit takes two forms. One is the Coca-colonization thesis. Its proponents claim that Western, and more specifically American, popular culture is enveloping the world: American food, clothing, pop music, movies, and consumer goods are more and more enthusiastically embraced by people on every continent. The other has to do with modernization. It claims not only that the West has led the world to modern society, but that as people in other civilizations modernize they also westernize, abandoning their traditional values, institutions, and customs and adopting those that prevail in the West. Both of these project the image of an emerging homogeneous, universally Western world – and both are to varying degrees misguided, arrogant, false, and dangerous.[96]

Although fear of foreign cultural hegemony is hardly new in Asia, the explosive surge in overall foreign investment and the growing impact of new technologies that ignore sovereign frontiers add urgency to such fears. Like Korea, other Asian governments are being pressed to ignore

---

[95] Bae Ho Han and Soo Young Uh, *Korean Political Culture* (Seoul: Bupmon Publishing Co., 1987), p. 119.
[96] Samuel P. Huntington, "The West: Unique, Not Universal," *Foreign Affairs* 75:6 (November/December 1996), pp. 28–46.

the customary practices of powerful domestic interests and to institute "reforms" that run counter to deeply embedded political, economic, and cultural norms. As each national economy is pried open, it is forced to become what Cerny calls a "competition state."[97] When faced with hard choices, as Caroline Thomas argues, "authoritarian governments are far more capable of implementing IMF policies than democratically elected ones."[98] Is it possible to encourage authoritarian governments to be responsive to democratic norms if TNCs, regional bureaucracies, and other nonstate institutions are making decisions that matter? Thus, economic neoliberalism is as infused by politics as is direct state control, thereby persuading economist Benjamin Cohen to decry the political dimension of "economic" issues:

> On the one hand, we have our theory . . . On the other hand, we have the real world . . . Rarely in the economics profession do we encounter greater dissonance between what we are taught in principle and what we observe in practice. And try as we might to find logical reasons for all this in the tenets of our own discipline, ultimately we are tempted simply to throw up our hands and proclaim "It's all politics!"[99]

The growing potency of markets relative to states is described by Strange as "the biggest change in the international political economy to take place in the last half of the twentieth century,"[100] The state's surrender of authority to markets in many aspects of economic life and its retreat from welfare obligations have produced a global reordering of social values. The Korean case illustrates how markets exert greater and greater authority over countries and demand ever more economic discipline from politicians. These conditions invite neoliberal prescriptions. However, the human suffering, whatever the potential longer-range benefits, will be considerable, and states that either resist globalization or do relatively worse than others may become aggressive and nationalistic in order to place blame for economic woes on "others." In the end, even neoliberals may have to wonder sometimes what sort of angel the untamed market is.

---

[97] Cerny, *The Changing Architecture of Politics*, pp. 236, 241–244, and Cerny, "The Dynamics of Financial Globalization, p. 321.

[98] Thomas, *In Search of Security*, p. 61.

[99] Benjamin J. Cohen, "The Political Economy of International Trade," *International Organization* 44: 2 (Spring 1990), pp. 261–262.

[100] Strange, *Retreat of the State*, p. 43. Strange argues that "technological advance" has been put in at the service, "and at the expense – quite literally – of small business and of the individual citizen" (*Ibid.*, p. 100).

The normative implications of changing economic boundaries

Variations in the scope and domain of political and economic institutions and their effective boundaries have been both the source and consequence of shifts in normative preoccupations. For example, nationalism and self-determination, especially during and after what Eric Hobsbawm calls the "Age of Revolution,"[101] imposed a new set of obligations and responsibilities on states. With the French Revolution, the ascribed content of *national interest* replaced *raison d'état* in that it entailed satisfying the demands of "citizens" rather than merely the expectations of a small ruling elite. The industrial revolution posed dramatic new normative dilemmas that pitted economic liberals against socialists and Marxists. Indeed, Friedrich Engels's *The Conditions of the Working Classes in England* (1844) is a memorable and passionate normative denunciation of some of the worst human consequences of that revolution that was published even as the Chartist movement grew more powerful in Great Britain.

In the liberal societies of Western Europe, notably Britain, sentiments favoring justice and freedom for individuals accompanied the growing popularity of *laissez-faire* economic policies. In much of the West, the specter of revolution and the extension of the suffrage, both companions of the nineteenth-century industrial revolution, encouraged concern for spreading the material benefits of economic and social progress to all citizens. In time, a new social contract took root in which sovereign states assumed responsibility for citizens' social and economic welfare in return for their obligation to pay taxes and defend their country.[102]

Growing state responsibilities generated a need for greater state capacity and, in consequence, greater state bureaucratization, administrative rationalization, and intrusion ever deeper into civil society. Statistics, taxes, mandatory education, regulatory policy, and welfare programs all served this end.[103] Under Bismarck, as we have noted, Prussia developed a rudimentary welfare state, at least in part, so that the regime could pursue other aspects of its conservative domestic agenda and aggressive foreign policies free from the distraction of social unrest. In Meiji Japan, the state sought to catch up with the West by nurturing

---

[101] Eric Hobsbawm, *The Age of Revolution, 1789–1848* (London: Weidenfeld & Nicolson, 1962).

[102] High rates of tax evasion and avoidance of military service such as seen in Russia today, as well as in other countries, are key indicators of declining state legitimacy.

[103] Van Creveld, *The Rise and Decline of the State*, p. 354. See also pp. 354–377.

selected industrial sectors and investing heavily in national infrastructure. By the beginning of the twentieth century, the United States, too, witnessed an expansion of state capacity with the creation of a more effective civil service, professional army, regulatory bureaucracies,[104] and an early attempt at modern social policies.[105]

Paradoxically, it was the erosion of the horizontal cleavage between aristocracy and commoners, itself an anomaly from a pre-Westphalian era, that helped harden interstate boundaries. As realists like Walter Lippmann, George Kennan, and Hans Morgenthau have observed, the triumph of nationalism and the participation explosion that accompanied it increased the potency of public opinion and reduced the flexibility of diplomats. No longer did the links among elites cross-cut the differences between citizens in different states. No longer could personal understandings, acute sensitivity to one another's needs, or devices such as a fat bribe or a wink and a nod grease the diplomatic wheels and soften interstate conflicts. In an odd way, the hardening of interstate boundaries reduced the autonomy of states and of those who acted as their surrogates.

State capacity and state responsibility for citizens reached a peak at the end of World War II with what Ruggie (we have noted) calls the "compromise of embedded liberalism."[106] At conferences in Bretton Woods and Havana, states agreed to promote free trade internationally while tolerating domestic intervention to cushion the impact on citizens of the harshest aspects of markets in order to promote domestic political stability. For four decades, this compromise survived, as the GATT promoted multilateral tariff reductions while tolerating or ignoring nontariff barriers protecting influential social groups. Reflecting embedded liberalism at least in part, public spending as a proportion of GNP increased dramatically in Western Europe and the United States after 1950. Social expenditure soared, leading to inflation and deficits in much of the West.[107]

But the consensus in favor of embedded liberalism was coming to an end. In 1973 President Richard M. Nixon abandoned much of the

---

[104] Steven Skrowonek, *Building a New American State: The Expansion of National Administrative Capacities, 1877–1920* (Cambridge: Cambridge University Press, 1982).
[105] Theda Skocpol, *Protecting Soldiers and Mothers: The Political Origins of Social Policy in the United States* (Cambridge, MA: Belknap Press of Harvard University Press, 1992).
[106] John Gerard Ruggie, "International Regimes, Transactions, and Change: Embedded Liberalism in the Postwar Economic Order," *International Organization* 32:2 (Spring 1982), p. 209.
[107] Van Creveld, *The Rise and Decline of the State*, p. 364.

Bretton Woods edifice; in his 1981 inaugural address, President Ronald Reagan vowed "to check and reverse the growth of government."[108] Margaret Thatcher pursued similar aims in the United Kingdom; and the Clinton administration further eroded America's welfare system.[109] With these changes, income gaps in the West once more began to widen,[110] a process that persisted during the subsequent Bush years. As described by van Creveld: "Toward the year 2000, economic policy in most countries . . . had made a complete about-turn. The trend toward greater state intervention in the economy which had started in the 1840s . . . was dead or dying; its place was taken by a renewed emphasis on private enterprise and competition."[111]

The conditions that had fostered embedded liberalism, especially two world wars and a great depression, have faded from public consciousness; and the expansion of markets, combined with the end of the Cold War and its narrow military definition of security, have eroded both the political will and technical capacity of even the largest states to manage global economics or politics in a way that successfully reconciles electability and responsibility. Neoliberal economics have fostered unfettered markets, which have been "disembedded" from underlying social structures. This has led Ruggie to call for "a new 'embedded liberalism' compromise, a radically new formula for combining the twin desires of international and domestic stability, one that is appropriate for an international context in which the organization of production and exchange has become globally integrated, and a domestic context in which past modalities of state intervention lack efficacy, and often legitimacy."[112]

The declining economic capacity of states has led to privatization in a variety of domains, some of which are quite surprising. Some have even surrendered their security function to mercenaries and private security agencies, and US politicians are considering doing the same with at least a proportion of social security. Private firms run prisons and schools, dispose of urban waste, and carry out other tasks that had defined the public responsibility of the state, at least in the West beginning with

---

[108] Cited in *ibid.*, p. 365.
[109] By contrast, continental European states such as Germany, France, and Italy resisted the Reagan–Thatcher policies, and governments have had a difficult time sustaining (while trying to reform) welfare policies.
[110] Van Creveld, *The Rise and Decline of the State*, pp. 366–367.   [111] *Ibid.*, pp. 376–377.
[112] John Gerard Ruggie, *Winning the Peace: America and World Order in the New Era* (New York: Columbia University Press, 1996), p. 173.

Bismarck. In some cases, privatization may also assist corporations and other economic actors to escape taxes or regulation at a cost to citizens.

The rise of modern democracy in the nineteenth and twentieth centuries and the popular legitimization of the state in the West are associated with protecting citizens against unrestrained market forces, cushioning them against economic bad times, reducing inequality, and providing public services, especially social security and welfare. As states surrender these tasks, either by choice or by enfeeblement, they force citizens to find alternatives – families, charitable organizations, businesses, and both public and private international institutions. These institutions, however well intentioned, are not even ostensibly democratically accountable to individual citizens. Thus, David Held, among others, recognizes a paradox in the spread of democracy at the Cold War's end because "while the idea of 'the rule of the people' is championed anew, the very efficacy of democracy as a national form of political organization is open to doubt" and "changes in the international order are compromising the viability of the independent democratic nation-state."[113]

Furthermore, growing service sectors, which are the driving force of the postinternational economy, are capital-, not labor-intensive. Thus, the division of the world between relatively small groups of knowledge elites and the burgeoning numbers of those outside the service sectors has created new horizontal, class-like we–they boundaries that cut across national boundaries. Among the main beneficiaries of information economies are managerial and technocratic elites, money launderers and drug smugglers, currency traders, fund managers, and others in the private sphere with few responsibilities to citizens. All of these, as Strange observed, "are hierarchies, not democracies." Comparing corporate elites to Renaissance princes, she continues: "they can usually divide and rule. No single elected institution holds them accountable. The cartels and oligopolists that practise private protectionism and manage markets for their own comfort and convenience are even less accountable. Neither are the insurance businesses or the big-time accountancy partnerships. And the mafias least of all."[114] Remarkably, this passage from Strange was written before the Enron and other recent corporate scandals.

---

[113] David Held, "Democracy, the Nation-State and the Global System," in Held, ed., *Political Theory Today* (Stanford: Stanford University Press, 1991), p. 197.
[114] Strange, *The Retreat of the State*, pp. 197–198.

The emergence of new horizontal cleavages in global society has split liberalism in two: some, epitomized by Rosecrance and Rosenau, view the growing service economy as highly beneficial for the world as a whole. Others argue that this problem pays insufficient attention to the growing stresses *within* national societies that accompany the proliferation of high-tech service industries. After all, hamburger cooks and janitors are also service workers, and, as noted, pressures for greater productivity have promoted a retreat from welfare and health care and the privatizing of previous state functions. Neoliberals are also forcing states to deregulate and open their markets and are imposing corporate values on their own citizens.

More radical opponents of unfettered markets conclude that global capitalism unchecked by democratic accountability is dangerous. They insist that the only values favored by postinternational economic actors like oligarchic or monopolistic TNCs are *efficiency* and *profit*, for which productivity (cost per unit of production) is vital. Efforts are focused on cutting costs, which leads to a so-called race to the bottom in limiting wages and ignoring environmental harm. TNCs regard anti-trust, health and safety issues, and other restrictions formerly imposed and policed by the state, as non-tariff forms of protectionism.

Such opponents focus especially on the conditions of workers in transnational corporations such as Nike in poor countries. The most publicized aspects of this are allegations of depressed wages and "sweat shop" conditions for workers in the developing world. Often, however, such conditions reflect traditional local practices, allow host states to keep costs sufficiently low to attract TNCs, are actually better than those enjoyed by other local workers, and provide employment to individuals and groups who would otherwise be unemployed.[115]

Those who are concerned about the environmental consequences of TNC activities have moved beyond criticism of exploitation of local resources and failure to observe Western environmental guidelines in non-Western settings. They now recognize that advancing technology and globalization in trade is an explosive combination. Routinely, they complain that alien animal and insect species and invasive plants move – usually unwittingly – across oceans. Even worse, in the view of some, is the export of genetically modified (GM) plants, especially American grains and foodstuffs. Some fear that health risks may grow; but, even if

---

[115] Although improvement in workers' conditions anywhere is to be welcomed, we should note that labor unions in wealthy countries often take the lead in criticizing poor working conditions in the developing world.

they do not, concern over biodiversity and, therefore, future food supplies, persist. By contrast, TNCs like Monsanto insist that GM foods are cheaper and safer than conventional foods because they eliminate the need to use large amounts of pesticides or herbicides. Whatever the facts, probably the strongest source of resentment against genetically modified products is that recipients appear to have little choice, especially since governments are in violation of international trade law if they try to bar their import. The autonomy of people and sovereignty of states seems to be pitted against the interests of TNCs.

According to some critics, TNCs manipulate and are assisted by institutions like the World Bank and IMF, which pursue policies to force client states to reduce inflation, stabilize currency rates, and free up global markets. Such policies, it is alleged, widen the gap between rich and poor and harm those at the bottom of the pecking order. A new global corporate aristocracy, concentrated in world-class cities like New York, London, and Tokyo,[116] are the chief beneficiaries of these policies.

Without the "compromise of embedded liberalism," states are too weak to resist market forces. This threatens what Jacques Attali, former president of the European Bank for Reconstruction and Development, calls "the rise of the market dictatorship" and the declining influence of citizen control of national economies.[117] Citizens have little voice in the working of the market, and there is no one to provide remedies in the case of market failure. Indeed, repeatedly, banks and other lending institutions have not been made to confront the moral hazard implicit in their loans. These claims have reawakened interest in features of Marxist analysis, and such analysis, with its normative baggage, underlies a substantial portion of contemporary postmodernist discourse. Although Marxism was a product of "modernism," its powerful emancipatory ethic made it a harbinger of postmodernist thinking. Oddly, postmodernists rarely acknowledge their debt to Marxism, leading Darryl Jarvis to ask, why "the progressive abandonment of Marx and Habermas for Derrida and Foucault?"[118] The provocative answer he gives is "old-style Marxism" which "could sustain a mass movement,

---

[116] See, for example, Saskia Sassen, *Globalization and its Discontents* (New York: The New Press, 1998). Another unusually well-balanced critique is Rorden Wilkinson and Steve Hughes, eds., *Global Governance: Critical Perspectives* (London: Routledge, 2002).

[117] Jacques Attali, "The Crash of Western Civilization: The Limits of the Market and Democracy," *Foreign Affairs* 107 (Summer 1997), p. 59.

[118] Jarvis, *International Relations and the Challenge of Postmodernism*, p. 136. Foucault is especially important in this context for his reconceptualization of power and its relationship to oppression.

incite revolution, provide solace for the oppressed and marginalized, or a critical metanarrative to explain history, purpose, and destiny" had died, and some Marxists sought to graft "Nietzsche's cultural politics onto Marx."[119] Jarvis concludes that critical postmodernism "has proved the life raft of Marxism, shedding Marxism of its teleological determinism, economism, and crude structuralism."[120]

As states yield authority to markets, the essential nature of citizenship is being irrevocably altered. It is important then to follow up on Rosenau's important question: "If world politics is presently marked by the emergence of new forms of governance without government, what does this imply for the world citizens who have long been accustomed to governance being sustained by governments?"[121] According to Tilly, theorists since the pioneering work of T. H. Marshall[122] have often "postulated a progression from civic to political to social citizenship, the latter presumably culminating in the full welfare state."[123] Yet, as Tilly has warned elsewhere, it is a "pernicious postulate" to assume that "[t]he main processes of large-scale social change take distinct societies through a succession of standard stages, each more advanced than the previous stage."[124] Specifically, scholars must avoid "the standard temptations in studies of citizenship and identity" such as "the snare of evolutionism with its supposition that because of its adaptive superiority thick citizenship triumphs inexorably and definitely over thin citizenship or none at all."[125]

Conclusion: the economic globalization juggernaut continues?

Growing incompatibility between the boundaries of states and markets and the growing influence of markets in relation to states are among the most salient features of a postinternational world. So matters stood when on September 11, 2001 the terrorist attacks on the World Trade Center and Pentagon occurred. To many observers, it seemed as though the movement of persons, things, and ideas across national boundaries

---

[119] *Ibid.*   [120] *Ibid.*, p. 191.

[121] James N. Rosenau, "Citizenship in Changing Global Order," in Rosenau and Czempiel, eds., *Governance without Government*, p. 272.

[122] T. H. Marshall, *Citizenship and Social Class* (Cambridge: Cambridge University Press, 1950).

[123] Tilly, "Citizenship, Identity and Social History," p. 3.

[124] Tilly, *Big Structures*, see n. 3, p. 11.

[125] Tilly, "Citizenship, Identity and Social History," p. 12.

was itself a source of the terrorist problem, and expensive efforts were initiated by governments to regain control of national frontiers. Airport and seaport security, immigration laws, tracing of illegal aliens, the employment of forms of "protective custody," and the status of foreign students were only some of the matters addressed by United States authorities and various other states.

Among other things, the attacks jeopardized recovery from what was already a sharp recession in the United States, which in turn deepened existing economic difficulties in Europe, Japan and elsewhere in Asia and much of Latin America. Businesses at the heart of globalization such as airlines, airplane manufacturers, and tourism were among the hardest hit. The American budget surplus turned into a large deficit because of lower revenues and increased military spending for the War on Terrorism, and a lengthy bull market ended in the collapse of stock values, massive corporate layoffs, scandals over widespread accounting irregularities, and bankruptcies of big-name TNCs like Enron, Global Crossing, and WorldCom. (Surely the scandals did as much or more damage to financial markets than Al-Qaeda.) Hype about a "new economy" ended abruptly with a sagging technology sector and the demise of fledgling dot.com enterprises.

Beyond the United States conditions were no better or even worse well into 2003. World trade slumped to growth rates not seen since the 1980s. The situation in Latin America came to resemble the desperation of the Great Depression of the 1930s. Argentina effectively went "belly-up," with grave effects on Brazil and the entire Mercosur region; civil war continued in Colombia; and increased political unrest swept Venezuela, Bolivia (where the runner-up in the presidential election was head of the cocaine-growers' association), Peru, and Ecuador. Meanwhile, the Afghanistan phase of the War on Terrorism dragged on without the capture of Osama bin Laden or many of his close associates and with little progress in creating genuine state institutions; the Israeli/Palestinian conflict escalated to bloody tit-for-tat violence; India and Pakistan for a time hovered on the brink of nuclear war; North Korea resumed its development (and probable acquisition) of nuclear weapons; and the Bush administration invaded Iraq and pledged to carry its campaign against terrorism to the farthest corners of the globe.

Against such a gloomy background, one might have suspected, the globalization juggernaut would have slowed. Quite the contrary, at least at the start, except insofar as the slump in the world economy was real and serious. The War on Terror stole the headlines from protestors and made their demonstrations seem almost unpatriotic, and worsening economic conditions created powerful – and ultimately successful – arguments for getting neoliberal economic growth literally back on a fast track.

The anti-globalization movement at least temporarily lost much of its steam, while stalled WTO negotiations at last bore some fruit, and in August 2002 the US Congress ended a longstanding partisan deadlock and gave President George W. Bush the "fast-track" authority to negotiate trade agreements, which had expired in 1994, that it had repeatedly denied his predecessor.[126] In November 2001, the WTO assembled 2,600 officials, 800 journalists, and some 400 business and NGO representatives under unprecedented security at Doha, Qatar. The result was remarkable apparent progress and symbolic agreement to continue substantive talks on such thorny issues as agricultural subsidies, barriers to developing-country textiles, debt relief, and generic drugs. Most importantly, the meeting seemed to revive the WTO by avoiding a Seattle-like stalemate and reaching broad agreement on an agenda for a near-future "extended work program" (the term new "round" of talks was avoided, to signal an intention to break constructively with the past). Active WTO preparations for the September 2003 Cancún meeting continued, surviving such strains as bitterness over Bush administration sanctions imposed against foreign steel, global concern over a new wave of US agricultural subsidies that critics alleged were blatant measures to buy Republican votes in the Midwest, and US–European friction over the Iraq war.[127] At the same time, both the IMF and the World Bank have reflected a hardened Bush administration policy of reluctance to bail out countries like Argentina without full-scale "reforms."

Economic globalization thus initially continued even in hard times, albeit with a widening gap between rich and poor that was increasingly a subject of discussion. However, that divide now appears seriously to threaten further advances. Despite an atmosphere of relative optimism at the outset of the Cancún meeting of the WTO, the meeting collapsed when a Group of 21 developing countries eventually walked out. Not long before the meeting, US and European negotiators signaled their

---

[126] Congress may still vote down such agreements, but cannot amend them, which eliminates one of the principal doorways for protecting special interests. However, it should be noted that Congress did effectively resist the efforts companies like Stanley Tools and Accenture made to shift their tax homes "offshore."

[127] A serious effort was begun to ease this friction at the economic summit held in Evian les Bains in spring 2003.

willingness to liberalize the sale of inexpensive drugs to countries facing medical emergencies and, indeed, to accept substantial cutbacks in the more than $300 billion in subsidies paid every year to their own farmers. The developing countries spurned the specific proposals regarding agriculture at Cancún, charging that they were completely inadequate, and also refused to agree to suggested new trade rules on investment and government procurement. Whether the Cancún failure is merely one stage of a longer-range negotiation that will ultimately bear significant fruits – or portends increased developed-country intransigence over the needs of the poor and even increased protectionism remains to be seen. Certainly the Doha goal of reaching a new general world trade agreement by January 2005 seems unlikely to be met.

7   War in a postinternational world

War, as we have observed, has been central to theorists and practitioners of global politics, and violence has been a feature of global life since history has been recorded. Whatever the methodology or theoretical assumptions employed, any effort to explain the causes, nature, and probable future of war has always been fraught with serious difficulties. Even defining it is problematic. Surveying the relevant literature in 1993, John Vasquez concluded that the scientific study of war had not advanced very far, in part because data gathering had often proceeded on the shaky theoretical foundation of realist theory.[1] There have been few subsequent breakthroughs, and they will become still more elusive as we move further into the postinternational epoch with its weakened states, proliferation of non-Westphalian polities, globalizing technologies, new identities, and fundamentalist ideologies. Certainly the recent literature on the so-called democratic peace is plagued with internal problems and is fatally state-centric.[2]

One perennial and central difficulty has been the definition of war itself: violent conflict now ranges from potential nuclear exchanges to interstate "conventional war," "civil war," "proxy war" (with state or nonstate proxies), "guerrilla war," "ethnic cleansing," "tribal" warfare, and "terrorism" perpetrated against innocent civilians by individuals (e.g., suicide bombers) and groups (e.g., Al-Qaeda or Hamas). Actual conflicts not only overlap some of these categories but also, importantly, vary enormously in their intensity and duration. Unfortunately, most notions of "war" (and therefore war-related data and the search for war's causes) have been mired in state-centric models drawn from the

---

[1] John A. Vasquez, *The War Puzzle* (Cambridge: Cambridge University Press, 1993).
[2] See Ferguson and Mansbach, "Remapping Political Space," pp. 93–94.

European experience and, more recently, the Cold War. Indeed, European practitioners and theorists were prone to ignore events outside their own continent as did pre-World War I military planners regarding the American Civil War and the Russo-Japanese War.

In addition to definitional issues, any comprehensive analysis of war must take account of a host of political, social, technological, economic, legal, and psychological factors that persist in some respects and are undergoing rapid change in others. Politicians typically try to prevent the last war, and military professionals, especially winners, typically prepare for the last war. Such tendencies are part of the living museum and often incur what they seek to prevent. By contrast, leaders can also be misled by future shock, fascinated by some promising new technology that seems to sweep away past impediments to victory. In dealing with war, some fundamentals, one senses, have hardly changed since Alexander the Great, while others almost certainly have – the challenge is to know which are which, and how those play out in specific current conflicts. The nature of the challenge is changing even as are the means to meet it that are at the disposal of modern militaries.

Although there have been few interstate wars in recent years other than the Persian Gulf, the Ethiopian–Eritrean, and Iraq conflicts, we do not live in a peaceful world. Civil wars and other forms of local conflict abound, afflicting somewhere between one-third to one-half of all the world's societies. The end of the Cold War actually increased the total amount of global violence, because Russia and the United States reduced their overseas commitments, remain preoccupied with domestic issues, and became less able or willing to manage the behavior of former "clients" such as Iraq and Israel. Ethnic, religious, economic, and political rivalries long suppressed by self-interested superpower interventions have resurfaced – some with vast amounts of small arms provided by the superpowers in earlier years – and old conflicts that had been defined in Cold War terms have continued under new labels. The potential for redrawing boundaries among identity groups inside countries has encouraged militants to pursue their ambitions and prompted others to adopt violence as a means of defense. In a growing number of cases, states have simply lacked the capacity to manage violence at home.

The threat of nuclear war between the former superpowers now seems to have vanished, but we still have to cope with the consequences of past and continuing proliferation. Nuclear, chemical, and biological weapons of mass destruction (WMD) in the hands of bitter traditional rivals like

India and Pakistan, "rogue states," especially North Korea and perhaps Iran, and apocalyptic terrorists top the list of contemporary security concerns. Some analysts like Kenneth Waltz, Martin van Creveld, and John Mearsheimer argue that nuclear weapons maintained peace during the Cold War and will continue to do so despite WMD proliferation. At one time, Mearsheimer hoped the Ukraine would retain the nuclear missiles it inherited from the old Soviet Union in order to deter future Russian aggression or blackmail.[3] In response to the testing of nuclear weapons by India and Pakistan, Mearsheimer declared: "Nuclear weapons are a superb deterrent for states that feel threatened by rival powers."[4] Such a position is probably wrong for a number of reasons; one is that new nuclear powers are at lower levels technologically than earlier nuclear powers and thereby lack second-strike capability. India and Pakistan are geographically so close to each other that neither would have sufficient warning time to consider their responses carefully; their leaders have little experience in dealing with nuclear crises; and, probabilistically, more fingers on more triggers entail the law of gambler's ruin. In addition, chemical and biological weapons, though posing delivery problems, are relatively inexpensive and accessible even to small countries or terrorist groups. The anthrax attacks on US citizens that began in the autumn of 2001 illustrate how even limited bio-attacks can sow near panic and bring complex bureaucratic institutions to a halt. In this respect at least, WMD – as terrorism has always been regarded – are becoming weapons for the weak against the strong. Richard Betts comments: "They no longer represent the technological frontier of warfare. Increasingly they will be weapons of the weak – states or groups that militarily are at best second-class."[5]

Violence in the postinternational world, then, persists and assumes substantially different forms than during the interstate epoch. Indeed, much of the data compiled to study war is obsolete because projects such as the Correlates of War (COW) at the University of Michigan were almost entirely based on the interstate variant of the phenomenon. It has little to contribute to understanding the intrastate and transborder violence that is one of the hallmarks of the postinternational world.

---

[3] John J. Mearsheimer, "The Case for Ukrainian Nuclear Deterrent," *Foreign Affairs* 72:3 (Summer 1993), pp. 50–66.
[4] Cited in Ronald E. Powaski, *Return to Armageddon: The United States and the Nuclear Arms Race, 1981–1999* (New York: Oxford University Press, 2000), p. 36.
[5] See, for example, Richard K. Betts, "The New Threat of Mass Destruction," *Foreign Affairs* 77:1 (January–February 1998), p. 27.

There are historically, not surprisingly, many similar cases. Thus, the hundreds of years of war between England and France that followed the Norman conquest of England in 1066 can also be conceived as a conflict among Frenchmen for control of ancestral lands. In other words, far from being interstate war of the post-Westphalian era, it was closer to the feudal wars between noble members of a military caste.

The system of sovereign states was at least partly the result of an effort to limit and regulate collective violence, both between and within states following the destructive pre-Westphalian religious wars, and to legitimize the use of violence by sovereigns against opponents. From a military perspective, the Westphalian State was superior to rival political forms such as city-states, fiefdoms, tribes, villages, confederations, and at least some empires in terms of social and political organization and economies of scale. Confronted by widespread internal and transborder violence, the emerging polities presumed to channel and manage both interstate and nonstate conflict in order to enhance their own stability and prosperity and increase the security of the sovereigns themselves.

Given the historical conditions under which states emerged in Europe, it may be more than coincidental that – as sovereign states surrender relative authority in the present era – management of global violence is also eroding and its use is in a sense being decentralized. Meanwhile, the pace of technological change – the implications of which are only dimly understood by theorists or practitioners – keeps accelerating. In the face of these trends, which are aspects of what we have labeled history's revenge and future shock, it is hardly surprising that the nature of warfare is changing in the postinternational world. Moreover, as we shall see, there is also a growing gap between norms based on state/state system efforts to regulate or manage violence and the sort of violence that plagues the new millennium – terrorism, proliferation of weapons of mass destruction, crimes against civilians, ethnic or communal conflict, and full-scale genocide.

War and the emergence of the sovereign state

The state system was conceived and born in warfare. "War," as Tilly declares, "made the state, and the state made war."[6] "Had it not been

---

[6] Charles Tilly, "Reflections on the History of European State-Making," in Tilly, ed., *The Formation of National States in Western Europe*, p. 42. See also Charles Tilly, "War Making and State Making as Organized Crime," in Peter Evans, Dietrich Rueschemeyer, and Theda Skocpol, eds., *Bringing the State Back in* (Cambridge: Cambridge University Press, 1985), pp. 169–191.

for the need to wage war," declares van Creveld, "then the development of bureaucracy, taxation, even welfare services such as education, health, etc. would probably have been much slower."[7] For Biersteker and Weber, the rise and decline of "geographically-contained structure(s) whose agents claim ultimate political authority within their domain"[8] are inextricably connected to the nature of warfare. Transformation in military technology and the capacity of monarchical bureaucracies to organize violence, against subjects as well as foreigners, was necessary for the evolution and triumph of the sovereign territorial state and, in turn, for Europe to establish its commanding role in global politics for more than three centuries.

The escalating costs of war, associated principally with firearms and fortress construction, and the growing size of armies increased "the minimum size necessary to make political units militarily viable."[9] Such changes in warfare indicated "to political elites and social groups which type of organization was most efficient, and they subsequently adopted the most competitive institutional form,"[10] that is, the territorial state. For these reasons, according to Alexander B. Murphy, the "principal political-geographic story of the seventeenth and early eighteenth centuries" was "the growing ability of state rulers in western and central Europe to exert control over their realms."[11] Most wars of the time were waged over territory. Territorial expansion provided the human and material resources necessary for waging war, and greater physical space provided protection from enemy attack. As long as territory provided security and resources, acquiring additional territory became a principal objective of statesmen and soldiers. Combined with the conservative philosophy that had gained ascendancy in Europe after 1648, this is one reason why the era was punctuated by a rapidly shifting balance of power and numerous short or "limited" wars over provinces and boundary areas.[12]

Political authority, like economic activity, in Europe during the Middle Ages had been essentially local in scope, concentrated partly in the

---

[7] Van Creveld, *The Rise and Decline of the State*, p. 336.
[8] Biersteker and Cynthia Weber, "The Social Construction of State Sovereignty," p. 2.
[9] Van Creveld, *Technology and War*, p. 108.
[10] Spruyt, *The Sovereign State and its Competitors*, p. 178.
[11] Alexander B. Murphy, "The Sovereign State System as Political-Territorial Ideal: Historical and Contemporary Considerations," in Biersteker and Weber, eds., *State Sovereignty as Social Construct*, p. 93.
[12] See Edward Vose Gulick, *Europe's Classical Balance of Power* (New York: W. W. Norton, 1955).

hands of a caste of warrior-gangster knights who could afford armor, war-horses, leisure to train, and the other trappings of their profession. Moreover, under the medieval system of overlapping property rights and obligations, it was virtually impossible to differentiate between internal and external wars; the very distinctions between "inside" and "outside" were obscure. For similar reasons, the boundary between war and crime was at best amorphous. Despite the efforts of the medieval Church to limit the consequences of violence in Europe by expedients such as the Peace of God and the Crusades (for which, of course, there were additional religious and ideological reasons), general insecurity limited progress in commerce and encouraged political fragmentation in Europe.

Over time, a combination of economic factors (growing markets, a prosperous urban commercial class, and the growing use of specie), and military innovations (crossbows, gunpowder and the *trace italienne*) gradually made Europe's medieval political order obsolete. Military technology and especially "fortress warfare," writes van Creveld, demanded "financial muscle, bureaucratic organization, and technical expertise" that "were to be found less in the feudal countryside than in the bourgeois-capitalist town economy."[13] Only kings could organize the specialized bureaucratic resources necessary to field large armies and to take advantage of increasingly complex economies, and only these monarchs had the resources to wage sustained interstate war, while at the same time pacifying their own domains. For these reasons among others, the territorial state enjoyed advantages over competing political forms.

The fiscal imperatives of states caused by the military revolution in early modern Europe also encouraged bureaucratic specialization and the gradual expansion of states' administrative apparatus. Among the most important features of the emerging paradigm of warfare were its centralizing and bureaucratizing effects.[14] Political leaders sought to centralize authority in order to mobilize the human and material resources necessary to fight. To be efficient and effective, the centralizing power structures required that the dynastic courts and family-based organizations of medieval Europe give way to rationalistic, merit-based bureaucracies capable of coping with the financial, logistical, and operational exigencies of large-scale war. Governments and government

---

[13] Van Creveld, *Technology and War*, pp. 107–108.
[14] Bruce D. Porter, *War and the Rise of the State: The Military Foundations of Modern Politics* (New York: Free Press, 1994), pp. 12–13.

revenues grew apace. In the long run, the state-enhancing dimension of war introduced a "ratchet effect" in which "the rapid growth of government and massive tax increases that occur during war usually level off at postwar levels much higher than were in effect before the conflict."[15]

The emergence of territorial polities embedded in "a competitive political order in which states were free to extend their territory in an endless series of border wars" was an example of European exceptionalism.[16] And, so long as territory remained the principal focus of political ambition and "territoriality . . . the functional equivalent of property rights,"[17] people were more likely to fight neighbors than others (a fact reinforced or countered by the relative state of technology at the time).[18]

Elsewhere, for example in China, periods of wide-scale conflict had led directly to imperial consolidation with the "successes by one of the warring states or by an outside polity taking advantage of the weaknesses produced by warfare."[19] In Europe, by contrast, and despite Louis XIV's ambitions, the system of competing territorial states did not evolve into a single empire, but rather into a "balance of power" in part because, until Napoleon Bonaparte, European armies had very limited military capabilities. Logistical problems imposed physical limits on states, and normative inhibitions remaining from earlier religious wars also had a dampening effect on conflict. Thus, a military stalemate of sorts prevailed within Europe proper, even as the continent's "peculiarly fragmented political geography" fostered a spirit of competitive entrepreneurship. The resulting growth of technology and bureaucratic organization laid a foundation for Europe's conquest of much of the world.[20]

Most discussions of the Westphalian State include some reference to its presumed monopoly of the legitimate exercise of coercion within its frontiers. Max Weber contributed this fiction, ignoring what should be

---

[15] *Ibid.*, p. 14.
[16] On the state as a "container" see, Peter J. Taylor, "The State as a Container: Territoriality in the Modern-World System," *Progress in Human Geography* 18: 2 (1994), p. 153.
[17] Gilpin, *War and Change in World Politics*, p. 37.
[18] See, for example, Kristian S. Gleditsch and J. David Singer, "Distance and International War, 1816–1965," in M. R. Khan, ed., *Proceedings of the International Peace Research Association, Fifth General Conference* (Oslo: International Peace Research Association, 1975), pp. 481–506, and J. David Singer, "Accounting for International War: The State of the Discipline," *Journal of Peace Research* 18:1 (1981), pp. 1–18. Probably the best summary of empirical analysis on the relationship among territoriality, contiguity, and war is to be found in Vasquez, *The War Puzzle*, pp. 123–152.
[19] Taylor, "The State as a Container," p. 153.   [20] McNeill, *The Pursuit of Power*, p. 114.

the obvious fact that the legitimacy of violence arises from the ends it is deemed to serve rather than its institutional source. Put another way, not all states are able to exercise coercion effectively, nor are all those that are able to do so regarded as legitimate. Various non-sovereign actors still today challenge particular states and enjoy far more legitimacy than the states among their followers. Weber, however, is not alone in confusing a particular set of circumstances that (arguably) prevailed for a relatively short period in European history with an ideal case or a universal condition. Legal positivists associate sovereignty with the capacity to command backed by the threat of force.[21] For political theorists, Thomas Hobbes's Leviathan, whatever other tasks it undertook, had to keep peace among its subjects and protect them from foreign threats. It was the putatively anarchic nature of seventeenth-century English political life, after all, that inspired Hobbes's metaphor of the uncivilized state of nature as a "war of all against all," just as civil war in France had inspired Jean Bodin to develop his idea of sovereignty a century earlier.

War in Europe's Middle Ages resembled banditry or "private" warfare – in contrast to warfare between Europeans and outsiders – with members of the military caste of knights raiding one another's lands, ravaging the land, and creating general insecurity. There emerged, as Adda Bozeman observes, a "localization of the concepts of war and peace" that incidentally "helped to reduce the total incidence of fighting that had disturbed the Western European world."[22] Later, centralization of authority and the normative demarcation between crime and war went hand in hand with a growing acceptance of a distinction between inside and outside the state and a burgeoning state capacity relative to other political forms to mobilize resources and, therefore, to wage war. Centralized authority in Europe – whether in England under the Tudors, in France under Louis XI, or in Spain under Ferdinand and Charles V – was reinforced by the construction of national identities, manifested in the spread of national languages, cultural practices, and bounded histories. Sovereign identities in turn provided the basis for legitimacy and, therefore, loyalty to the new states. Significantly, this was also an era of civil wars among nobles and religious factions with competing claims to authority. Thus, it was *through* violence that the state was founded, and critical to its establishment was acquiring a monopoly over what was

---

[21] Jeffrie Murphy and Jules Coleman, *The Philosophy of Law: An Introduction to Jurisprudence* (Totowa, NJ: Rowman and Allanheld, 1984), pp. 22–23.
[22] Bozeman, *Politics and Culture in International History*, p. 272.

asserted to be right and proper coercion.[23] Although the transformation in thinking was gradual, in time it came to be regarded as legitimate for the state to bash the heads of subjects and foreign enemies; individuals and other groups lacked this right.

A logical consequence of the state exerting centralized authority within its frontiers and directing violence against outsiders was its capacity to channel, limit, and, on occasion, routinize violence between itself and other sovereign states *beyond* its frontiers, thereby bringing an end to the sort of uncontrolled violence that swept Europe during the Thirty Years War. Of this violence Hugo Grotius had written in the introduction to his 1625 treatise, *The Law of War and Peace*: "Throughout the Christian world I observed a lack of restraint in relation to war, such as even barbarous races should be ashamed of; I observed that men rush to arms for slight causes, or no cause at all, and that when arms have once been taken up there is no longer any respect for law, divine or human; it is as if . . . frenzy had openly been let loose for the committing of all crimes."[24]

If sovereignty meant states could control affairs at home, it was also taken to imply that states had no legal superior, that is, that the international system was in a condition of anarchy. One legal authority notes "that curious metamorphosis which transformed the doctrine of sovereignty from a principle of internal order, as Bodin and even Hobbes had conceived it, into one of international anarchy."[25] But did Westphalian polities *ever* actually exercise such extensive control over the means of coercion? Although by the eighteenth century transborder violence *within* Europe was largely controlled by states, their reach beyond Europe was tenuous indeed. In fact, state control of violence outside of Europe was a process not completed until the following century. As recently as "little more than a century ago," according to Janice E. Thomson, "the state did not monopolize the exercise of coercion beyond its borders." She explains that the process of centralizing the means of coercion was slow, that it accompanied the strengthening of state institutions in the nineteenth century and that, in fact, states were "reluctant to exert authority and control over nonstate violence."[26] States ultimately

[23] Youssef Cohen, Brian R. Brown, and A. F. K. Organski, "The Paradoxical Nature of State Making: The Violent Creation of Order," *American Political Science Review* 75:4 (December 1981), pp. 901–910.
[24] Hugo Grotius, *Prolegomena to the Law of War and Peace* (New York: Bobbs-Merrill, 1957), p. 21.
[25] Brierly, *The Law of Nations*, p. 45.
[26] Thomson, *Mercenaries, Pirates, and Sovereigns*, p. 143.

did so when they found that it was necessary in order to overcome some very specific problems "involving fundamental issues of authority" that arose in the course of Europe's outward colonial expansion:

> If a sovereign ruler had the authority to commission privateers, then the corsairs raised the question of who was to be recognized as sovereign. . . . If nonstate violence emanated from the territory over which no recognized ruler claimed sovereignty, pirate commonwealths raised the question of who should be accountable for their actions. If the state could delegate its sovereign powers to nonstate actors, the mercantile companies raised the question of who was sovereign over the territories that the companies claimed as their private property. If individuals could join the foreign army of their choice, then mercenaries raised the question of who had the sovereign power to make war.[27]

European state-building entailed superimposing top-down processes and a sovereign "civic culture" upon local forms of identity and community. Sovereignty provided a normative basis for legitimating the state and attracting loyalty. The boundaries of Westphalian States, internalized in the form of identities tied to territory and citizenship, gradually took precedence over, and in some cases erased, local boundaries delineated by regional, religious, or ethnic affiliation. Civic identity was accompanied by the obligations of citizens/subjects to the state, as both Hobbes and Locke argued, and this identity reinforced the claim that transborder violence should be authorized and organized by the state and the state alone. As the product of agreements among states, it is hardly surprising that international law or "the law of nations" further legitimated the state's claim to a monopoly on coercion.[28]

War as an extension of politics

The exemplary military thinker of the Westphalian State was the Prussian general Karl Maria von Clausewitz. His incomplete masterpiece, *On War (Vom Krieg)*, written and revised between 1810 and 1830, has guided succeeding generations of military specialists, but, far from embodying a universal conception of war, the work reflects a relatively small slice

---

[27] *Ibid.*, pp. 67–68.
[28] The 1933 Montevideo Conference, as well as the Buenos Aires (1936) and Lima (1938) Conferences, laid out the rights and duties of states, including the principle of nonintervention. The treaties also reaffirmed a state's inherent right to self-defense, later qualified by the UN Charter's Article 51.

of time and place. In fact, Clausewitz's ideas are less relevant to contemporary warfare and were becoming out-dated even in his own time.[29]

Clausewitz, who had fought against Napoleon for his native Prussia and then, after its defeat, for the Russian Tsar, observed that the Napoleonic Wars, unlike wars in the eighteenth century, bore little relation to narrowly defined reasons of state. Rather, they portended limitless contests in which the political objectives – that is, the aims of states for which the wars had been initiated – were forgotten or subordinated to military necessity. Jacobin and Napoleonic warfare featured enormous armies of conscript soldiers, identification of the fate of "citizens" with that of *la patrie*, extinction of the independence of sovereign states, and removal of legitimate dynastic rulers. Retrospectively, what was probably most significant about these wars was that they reflected the wedding of two identities, state and nation. Frenchmen were now *citoyens*. The nationalist emotions that were unleashed, coupled with the demands of increasingly large and complex military machines, could lead to what Clausewitz regarded as excess and folly.

Although armies engage in organized violence, the true objective of war, taught Clausewitz, is to coerce an enemy to accede to political demands. "Force . . . is . . . the *means*; . . . to impose our will upon the enemy is the *object*."[30] The political reason for war "which called it into existence, naturally remains the first and highest consideration to be regarded in its conduct." For Clausewitz, war, like diplomacy or trade, was a political instrument, albeit a bloody one, "not merely a political act but a real political instrument."[31] War was only one of a variety of tools available to the state for rationally achieving its interests. "[T]he object of the attack" determined the intensity and extent of the conflict. For this reason, there could be wars of all sizes: "The object of the strategic attack is conceivable in an infinite number of gradations, from the conquest of the whole country down to that of the most insignificant spot."[32]

Clausewitz's views were the products of a particular era, the "halcyon era" of the sovereign state and balance of power.[33] The regimentally

---

[29] Some recent analysts have sought to bury Clausewitz, metaphorically if not literally. See, for example, Steven Metz, "A Wake for Clausewitz: Toward a Philosophy of 21st-Century Warfare," *Parameters* (1994–95). pp. 126–132.

[30] Karl von Clausewitz, *On War*, trans. O. J. Matthijs Jolles (New York: Random House, Modern Library, 1943), book I, ch. 1, p. 3. Emphasis in original.

[31] *Ibid.*, book I, ch. 1, p. 16.   [32] *Ibid.*, book VII, ch. 3, p. 511.

[33] Gulick, *Europe's Classical Balance of Power*. The belief that wars were "limited" at this time should not be taken to mean that they were not bloody. Indeed, military tactics of the period assured plenty of bloodshed.

organized European armies he favored were extensions of state power, designed to carry out the policies of sovereign leaders without threatening the stability of the political system that was the source of their status and prosperity. He represented a world in which, "before the French Revolution, the regiment was a device for restraining the violence of warriors and harnessing it to the purposes of kings."[34] Armies were highly disciplined and were stationed in remote regimental towns to keep them away from major urban centers where they might be dangerously politicized.[35] They were a distinct improvement over earlier mercenary bands but still were inherently unpredictable.

Although Clausewitz had personally witnessed violations of the norms of "civilized" warfare, especially in the Russian campaign, he thought a compromise could be reached between war as a means of furthering state interests and "absolute" war as a threat to the broader European state system. Preserving that state system was Clausewitz's core objective. "'War as the continuation of policy'," observes John Keegan, "was the form Clausewitz chose to express the compromise for which states he knew had settled. It accorded respect to their prevailing ethics – of absolute sovereignty, ordered diplomacy and legally binding treaties – while making allowance for the overriding principle of state interest."[36]

Unfortunately, just as Clausewitz feared, the idea of war as a cool and rational instrument of policy was steadily being undermined in the nineteenth century. In the Napoleonic era, conscription, close-order drill, and the advance of the concepts of the nation and nationalism were a recipe for slaughter on behalf of the state at least as destructive and irrational as the previous wars of religion and ethnicity. Industrialization increased the potential destructiveness and complexity of military machines, and national emotions grew even more strident and dangerous with the addition of racial and civilizational identities in the pseudo-Darwinian atmosphere late in the century. Clausewitz's universe continued to vanish with experiences in the first half of the twentieth century. A major factor in the onset of World War I was the "logic" of mobilization timetables, and the technology balance of the day created an early stalemate of opposing trench-lines. It was a war that spread in ways that few initially wanted and resulted in the appalling loss of a generation of young men. The Great War resisted any form of political settlement until the

---

[34] John Keegan, *A History of Warfare* (New York: Knopf, 1993), p. 27.
[35] See van Creveld, *The Rise and Decline of the State*, pp. 243–245.
[36] Keegan, *A History of Warfare*, p. 5.

United States came fresh into the fray, and the war caused the collapse of Tsarist Russia, Ottoman Turkey, and the Austro-Hungarian Empire. World War II, which in some respects was a continuation of the 1914–18 conflagration, not only was fought all over the world but also featured intentional victimization of civilians. From the bombings of Rotterdam and Dresden to the Holocaust – the world seemed to have embarked on an epoch of "absolute" or "total" war. Pacifists have to confront the fact that from the Allied side the issues in World War II still seem to have been worth fighting for, but, on the other hand, there is no escaping the conclusion that it lent very little credibility to the state system's capacity to manage violence.

After the World War II, developments at both ends of the technological spectrum accelerated trends unfavorable to the state. At the high end, nuclear weapons, their intercontinental delivery systems, and the fact that they were targeted at civilians, were evidence of the declining relevance of geographic factors generally and of the territorial state in particular. Already, by the late 1950s, Herz argued that developments in military technology (as well as economic interdependence and ideological competition) had made territorial states obsolete because they enabled penetration of the state's "hard shell" of "impenetrability."[37] His claim was well reasoned but premature in the military realm, as he acknowledged later, in part because the intentional first use of nuclear weapons seemed to have become almost what others later termed "unthinkable" or genuinely MAD (Mutual Assured Destruction). Nevertheless, as Herman Kahn maintained in his book, *Thinking About the Unthinkable*,[38] the actual situation was such that no one could absolutely rule out even the first use of the absolute weapon – nor, perhaps worse, his hypothetical "doomsday machine" that makes today's WMD seem pale by comparison.

At the lower end of violence during and after World War II, guerrilla war, as practiced by Marshal Tito, Mao Zedong (who, along with his admirer "Ché" Guevara, also theorized about such war), and Ho Chi Minh, placed little emphasis on controlling territory. They stressed the need to coerce and persuade civilians, while behaving like "fish"

---

[37] John H. Herz, *International Politics in the Atomic Age* (New York: Columbia University Press, 1959). As noted in our chapter 3, Herz later backed away from his original contention, claiming that he could see the rise of a "new territoriality." John H. Herz, "The Territorial State Revisited: Reflections on the Future of the Nation-State," in John H. Herz, ed., *The Nation-State and the Crisis of World Politics: Essays on International Politics in the Twentieth Century* (New York: David McKay, 1976), pp. 226–252.

[38] Herman Kahn, *Thinking About the Unthinkable* (New York: Horizon Press, 1962).

in a peasant sea. Their message was as fully ideological as anything emanating from Moscow's or Washington's Cold War propagandists and sometimes just as impractical – witness Mao's later disastrous Cultural Revolution and Ché's efforts to radicalize Bolivian peasants whose response was to betray him. Ho Chi Minh seems the wisest in retrospect, a clear-eyed strategist who knew what his objectives were and the conditions on the ground that favored their achievement. Taken together, the nuclear standoff between rival superpowers, brandishing ultimate weapons and transcendental ideologies – and guerrilla movements, with agendas beyond the narrowly "national" – had at least one apparent and common implication. Both reduced the traditional role of state territorial contiguity as a predictor of conflict.

It is noteworthy that Clausewitz's work, despite its time-capsule character, continued to influence strategists even during the Cold War. Perhaps that is not surprising, given its original reputation as a classic work. Yet it is decidedly ironic that Clausewitz was resurrected to help modern strategists, mostly civilians, make sense of nuclear weapons, perhaps the ultimate in indiscriminate weapons and the negation of war as a rational extension of politics. For many Cold War strategists, the idea was to replicate Clausewitz by using deterrence and coercive diplomacy in a coherent strategy that would not require early resort to nuclear weapons in warfare and would allow states to tailor their military effort to specific contingencies. Thus, economist and bargaining theorist Thomas Schelling proclaimed: "The power to hurt is bargaining power. To exploit it is diplomacy – vicious diplomacy, but diplomacy."[39] So influential was Schelling's work that the first prominent civilian nuclear strategist, Bernard Brodie, wrote of him: "Although no single author could be an adequate 'guide' to us in our present problems . . . the startling insights that leap up at us from so many pages of his great work are still often directly applicable to our own times. There has been no one to match him since."[40]

Nevertheless, too much water has flowed under too many bridges to retain some of Clausewitz's key premises and insights. Advancing technology, proliferation of WMD, the virtual abandonment of deterrence with the cancellation of the 1972 ABM treaty, growing mass politicization, changing identities, the resurgence of premodern conflict, and

---

[39] Thomas C. Schelling, *Arms and Influence* (New Haven: Yale University Press, 1966), p. 2. Despite the brilliant efforts of strategic theorists like Schelling, it remains difficult to imagine how nuclear war can be interpreted according to the precepts of Clausewitz.
[40] Bernard Brodie, *War and Politics* (New York: Macmillan, 1973), p. 446.

terrorism have all combined to make Clausewitz's conceptions of war largely obsolete. In the postinternational world, warfare is evolving in two very different directions: (1) toward high technology, cyber or networked forms, and (2) toward low-intensity, premodern forms. Both, however, are lineal descendents of earlier trends and the two classifications are by no means exclusive.

Postinternational warfare

The interstate wars of the Westphalian epoch are giving way to forms of violence that are increasingly intrastate or transstate (transnational). These include low-tech violence, especially in the developing world, which sometimes threatens the more economically advanced world at various technological levels through terrorism. Steven Metz divides the strictly low-tech category into "informal wars" where at least one combatant is "a nonstate entity" and "gray area wars" which "combine elements of traditional warfighting with those of organized crime."[41] At the other end of the spectrum is high-tech warfare in which conventional armies and political frontiers play a much less significant role than in the past. Let us turn first to the low-tech variant.

The irrelevance of Clausewitz's emphasis on interstate war is particularly evident in those growing regions where the threat of interstate conflict is being replaced by civil war, and by ethnic and tribal violence. Some of this violence involves a resurgence or reconstruction of premodern and even primordial warfare.[42] Some argue that low-intensity warfare has been a perennial feature of global politics. The armies of Britain's George III experienced it in various parts of the American colonies when ragtag colonials sometimes refused to stand and fight like "gentlemen," in proper uniforms and formation on an honorable field of battle. Napoleon confronted formidable grassroots resistance in Spain and Russia, which he dealt with summarily, as depicted in Goya's series of paintings on the horrors of irregular war in Spain.[43]

---

[41] Steven Metz, *Armed Conflict in the 21st Century: The Information Revolution and Post-Modern Warfare* (Carlisle, PA: Strategic Studies Institute, 2000), p. xii. US naval operations against the Barbary pirates at the beginning of the nineteenth century remind us that gray-area warfare has been with us a long time.

[42] Maoist "low intensity" or "people's" war was the predecessor of such warfare, However, Maoist strategy was more in the Clausewitzian tradition because it had clear political ends that shaped the form it took.

[43] Painting, along with other arts, has long portrayed vividly these aspects of warfare, including the Dutch artists in the seventeenth century and Picasso during the Spanish Civil War.

The United States found its war against Philippine irregulars at the turn of the twentieth century far more costly than defeating Spain to acquire the islands. The Nazis encountered guerrilla and partisan war throughout occupied Europe, not least in the Soviet Union and Yugoslavia. Following World War II, low-intensity wars were fought against European colonialism in Africa, Asia, and the Middle East, and the failure of the superpowers to defeat the guerrillas in Vietnam and Afghanistan respectively were major events in the Cold War.[44] Like the use of WMD by terrorists, the violation of diplomatic immunity, and the terrorizing of civilians, low-intensity warfare can be used effectively by the weak against the strong and by non-sovereign entities against sovereign states. Those that enjoy military superiority will always wish to outlaw or, at least, prevent the use of weapons and strategies that might endanger that superiority, as the British sought to outlaw the use of submarines after the 1914–18 conflict.

Much of today's low-level violence is in those regions where Europe planted its flags, disrupted existing patterns of authority, and left behind at least some political forms and practices. It is also related to the reemergence or reconstruction of older political identities and loyalties that lack territorial conceptions of space. Violence of this nature has proliferated since the end of the Cold War and – except where religion is involved – is less ideological than the guerrilla wars of the Cold War era. In many instances, it entails struggles for the remains of states, for personal power, and for the opportunity to pillage natural resources. The impact of shifting military technology, as Manuel Castells sums it up, is multifaceted. "Low-tech armies are not armies at all, but disguised police forces."[45] Such armies are often more effective in threatening their own governments and rival military factions than they are in containing domestic insurrection or defending state frontiers.

Conflict in much of the developing world does not pit states against each other but rather resembles conflict in the Great Lakes region of Central Africa (the region around Lakes Kivu and Victoria) with its "bewildering number of combatants, all with slightly different agendas participating in a group of interconnected wars set in motion by the long-standing enmity between members of the Hutu and Tutsi ethnic groups."[46] As in this example, many of today's wars are among uncontrolled and fragmented groups, or, in other cases, involve private

---

[44] Van Creveld, *The Rise and Decline of the State*, pp. 394–400.
[45] Manuel Castells, *The Power of Identity* (Oxford: Blackwell, 1997), pp. 263–264.
[46] James C. McKinley, Jr., "African Firestorm," *New York Times*, October 28, 1996, p. A6.

armies.[47] To the extent political objectives are involved, they are generic – struggles to alter peoples' relationship with one another or with the state regarding the distribution of and the terms by which authority is exercised.

Clausewitz does not shed much light on cases such as these. What Clausewitz's formulation "made no allowance for at all," continues Keegan, "was war without beginning or end, the endemic warfare of non-state, even pre-state peoples, in which there was no distinction between lawful and unlawful bearers of arms."[48] This prompts Keegan to conclude: "War is not the continuation of politics by other means." Clausewitz's interstate world bears little resemblance to one in which "armies and peoples become indistinguishable" and where "states are replaced by militias or other informal – often tribal – groupings whose ability to use sophisticated weaponry is very limited."[49] Armies are not organized, nor do they represent sovereign states. Instead, they are armed gangs led by "big men" or warlords like the Serbian "paramilitary" gangs used against civilians in Bosnia and later in Kosovo. In Liberia, for example, Charles Taylor was elected president of the country in 1997 because residents believed it was the only way to end the brutal civil war that Taylor had initiated. Until US intervention in 2003, his fighters were the "Liberian Army," and their job was to maintain "Charles Taylor, Inc." and his control of regional diamond mines.[50]

States themselves have hardly been paragons of virtue and peace; they were war-making machines from the outset. However, the more successful states did exercise some control over other potentially violent actors and states. They also developed some system-level rules for the conduct of war, treatment of captured soldiers, and the like. Postinternational war has witnessed an erosion of state-enforced restraints on violence and its continued decoupling from reason of state. The ruthlessness and brutality of Hitler's Holocaust shocked his contemporaries because it went so far beyond any rational motive. So did Pol Pot's "killing fields" in Cambodia. In recent years in Bosnia, Liberia, Sierra Leone, East Timor, or the Congo, which, in the words of a

---

[47] See Bernedette Muthien and Ian Taylor, "The Return of the Dogs of War? The Privatization of Security in Africa," in Hall and Biersteker, *The Emergence of Private Authority in Global Governance*, pp. 183–199.

[48] Keegan, *A History of Warfare*, p. 5.

[49] Roger Cohen, "In Sarajevo, Victims of a 'Postmodern' War," *New York Times*, May 4, 1995, sec. 1, pp. 1, 8.

[50] Norimitsu Onishi, "In Ruined Liberia, its Despoiler Sits Pretty," *New York Times*, December 7, 2000, p. A18.

European diplomat "doesn't really exist anymore as a state entity,"[51] it has been difficult to distinguish between organized war "as a real political instrument" and mindless savagery or crime. Thus, we have come full circle, with warfare that would have been more familiar to some ancients (many preinternational polities were highly organized) or to Hugo Grotius in the seventeenth century than to the leaders of states in the brief era that Clausewitz idealized.

Contemporary terrorism is even harder to pigeonhole, because it is at once anti-state and anti-state-system. Instead, it is increasingly transnational/civilizational (for want of better terms). Unlike pirates, terrorists today claim that they fight to achieve some version of justice – although some of these goals are justifications for unjustifiable atrocities. Like piracy and revolution during the nineteenth century, terrorism is viewed by many states as a threat to the security of all states. Of course, especially when the struggle has a transnational ideological dimension, one state's terrorist may be another state's martyr. Violence initiated by Islamic fundamentalists is both directed at specific states (for example, at Israel by Hamas) or more broadly at the United States and other western states (for example, by Al-Qaeda) – at the distribution of power in the global system and, more generally, at globalization's inequities and threat to traditional culture. Terrorism can be as low-tech as suicide bombers, not-very-high-tech like steering hijacked aircraft into the World Trade Center, or very high-tech like developing WMDs ranging from lunchbox nuclear devices to sophisticated chemical and biological agents.

High-technology warfare

The polar opposite of the low-tech variant of postinternational warfare is the kind of high-tech warfare previewed (with Cold War era weapons) in the 1993 Gulf War, actively utilized in Kosovo in 1999, and updated for the Afghanistan (2001–02) and Iraqi (2003) campaigns. Yet the two types of warfare were not so much separate as juxtaposed both in Kosovo and Afghanistan. Indeed, high-tech warfare has been developed in part to dominate conventional armies and to avoid casualties on both sides or bogging down in the "quagmires" associated with low-tech theaters like Vietnam or Somalia.

---

[51] Cited in Howard W. French, "Mobutu, Zaire's 'Guide,' Leads Nation into Chaos," *New York Times*, June 10, 1995, p. 6.

Whether these are its results remain to be seen. On the one hand, the American-led coalitions of 1991 and 2003, armed with the latest high-tech weaponry, easily defeated Iraq's conventional forces, yet neither accomplished many of their original goals. In 2003, US tanks and personnel carriers swept across the Iraqi desert, while much of the US arsenal consisted of precision weapons ranging from small armed drones to cruise missiles and laser-guided munitions dropped by giant bombers. Looking down the road, one frightening possibility would be for countries that cannot compete at the high-tech level to conclude that acquiring conventional weapons such as tanks or jet aircraft is futile and instead to intensify the development of WMD for reasons of deterrence or intimidation. The resulting proliferation of WMD would be the very antithesis of what countries armed with tech-weapons are seeking to accomplish.

The United States and a few of its allies are undergoing what some have called a "revolution in military affairs" (RMA) that is already altering the essential nature of communication, coordination, planning, and intelligence. There is no single definition of what constitutes an RMA in general or what characterizes the current RMA. According to one team of authors: "An RMA is a phenomenon that occurs when a significant discontinuous increase in military capability is created by the innovative interaction of new technologies, operational concepts, and organizational structures."[52] Another refers to it more simply as "major changes in technology and weapons with substantial implications for conducting war in the [twenty-first] century."[53] Technological innovation (for example, information processing, telecommunications, and remote sensing) and new weapons (for example, precision-guided munitions) may lead to a "radical increase in the effectiveness of military units" that will substantially shift the military balance between those countries that have experienced the RMA and those countries that have not.[54]

Some RMA analysts argue that a new "American Way of War" is emerging that depends heavily upon high-tech weaponry and that emphasizes speed, precision, and stealth.[55] At the heart of this way of

[52] Paul K. Van Riper. and F. G. Hoffman, "Pursuing the Real Revolution in Military Affairs: Exploiting Knowledge-Based Warfare," *National Security Studies Quarterly* 4:3 (Summer 1998), p. 2.
[53] Williamson Murray, "Thinking About Revolutions in Military Affairs," *Joint Forces Quarterly* (Summer 1997), p. 69.
[54] Steven Metz, "Racing Toward the Future: The Revolution in Military Affairs," *Current History* (April 1997), pp. 184–185.
[55] Metz, *Armed Conflict in the 21st Century*, pp. xv–xvi.

war "is a vast improvement in the quality and quantity of information made available to military commanders by improvements in computers and other devices for collecting, analyzing, storing, and transmitting data"[56] in order to manage and control the battlefield. The goal is to create a "system of systems" linking sensors in space, on the ground, in the air, and at sea in order to provide unprecedented information for purposes of command, control, coordination, and precision warfare. "Smart" weapons such as cruise missiles and devices like micro air vehicles – small pilotless drones – developed by the US Defense Research Projects Agency[57] and deployed in Kosovo and Saudi Arabia and even more extensively and effectively in Afghanistan and Iraq (where some were armed in order to enable immediate attack) make a mockery of the "hard shell" of impermeability. The near future may see technological innovations that will dwarf current innovations – robots for combat and intelligence, microelectromechanical systems (MEMS), and nanotechnology.[58]

Enthusiastic advocates of the new technologies argue that they will reduce the proverbial "friction" and "fog of war," as well as limit casualties and collateral damage. A reimagined and scaled-down "Star Wars" defense system is being built to protect against limited nuclear missile threats from "rogue states."[59] "Dominant battle space knowledge" will allow precision-guided munitions mounted on platforms remote from the battle zone to locate and destroy targets from vast distances. Soldiers will not have to slog it out in mud, jungle, or desert or fight it out house to house. There will be no more Stalingrads or Leningrads, and civilians will once more enjoy relative safety in warfare. According to British strategic thinker Lawrence Freedman, "the technologies of the information age . . . allow military power to be employed to its maximum efficiency with speed, precision, and minimum human cost. There is no need to target civilians intentionally, nor even to hit them inadvertently."[60]

---

[56] Metz, "Racing Toward the Future," p. 185.
[57] "A Personal Eye in the Sky," *The Economist*, January 9–15, 1999, pp. 73–74.
[58] Metz, *Armed Conflict in the 21st Century*, pp. 66–68.
[59] There are some doubts about the adequacy of existing technology to achieve this, and the US decision to proceed with the system resulted in bringing an end to the 1972 ABM agreement. More importantly, even if the system is aimed at achieving a missile defense against countries like North Korea and Iran, it is hard to see how China and perhaps (still) Russia will not view it as a potential threat to their second-strike nuclear capability. The danger of a new nuclear arms race cannot be fully discounted.
[60] Lawrence Freedman, "The Changing Forms of Military Conflict," *Survival* 40:4 (2000), p. 44.

One of the key elements of the "American Way of War" – the relative unwillingness to put soldiers at risk and concomitant emphasis on reducing casualties – has its roots in a perception that citizens are more selective in their willingness to die for the state than was the case in the American Civil War and World Wars I and II. In addition, Western norms are increasingly incompatible with large-scale collateral damage even against adversaries. Defending against – and then retaliating for – terrorist assaults on homeland targets is one thing; serving in the military and fighting in foreign wars without a powerfully convincing "national interest" at stake is quite another. The trend began in the stalemates of Korea and Vietnam and deepened with the end of the Cold War and America's disillusioning peacekeeping experience in Somalia. One policy watershed in the United States was the end of conscription and the creation of a paid all-volunteer military. President George Bush did manage to drum up public and foreign support for turning back Saddam Hussein's naked aggression against Kuwait, and his son George W. Bush persuaded American public opinion – though not opinion in many other countries – to overthrow Saddam over a decade later, but the endgames of both wars added to the growing list of bitter military disappointments.

High-tech war has its benefits but there are also growing pains, limitations, and drawbacks. How well does it, in fact, work? US technology pounded Saddam's army in Kuwait, Baghdad and other sites in Iraq, but some of his main military units survived. Concern about keeping the political coalition against Iraq intact was a major factor in stopping US-led forces at the Iraqi border, yet fears of mounting casualties and the challenge of subduing and subsequently reconstructing Iraq also figured importantly in the decision. No amount of high-tech capacity could force the dictator to allow weapons inspectors to stay in his country indefinitely. In the Kosovo case, no sooner had NATO halted its air campaign in Serbia, than the debate began about its effectiveness. Independent analysts questioned both the level of destruction claimed by NATO and the role played by such destruction in the decision of Slobodan Milošević to accede to NATO demands.[61] Only after weeks of bombing did NATO recognize how difficult it was to coerce Serbia to bring an end to the expulsion of ethnic Albanians without seizing and controlling the territory on which the Serbian–Albanian conflict

---

[61] See, for example, Nick Cook, "War of Extremes," *Jane's Defence Weekly* (July 7, 1999).

was being waged.[62] Despite the high level of popular support for intervention against Al-Qaeda in Afghanistan,[63] that opening theater in the War on Terrorism was in many respects even stranger than Kosovo. High-tech warfare encountered a bewildering conglomeration of rival ethnicities, religious factions, criminal networks, and warlord bands. The Taliban and Al-Qaeda were put to flight relatively easily, but the search for Osama Bin Laden and most of the Al-Qaeda leadership came up miserably short because of difficult terrain and its ultimate dependence on unreliable Afghan and Pakistani proxies.

The Afghan campaign left difficult problems in reconstruction and unification. Still, Afghan unity had never been very great, and the country had traditionally been divided into tribal areas. Iraq, by contrast, had enjoyed a strong central government and central institutions despite its ethnic and religious cleavages. The successful 2003 Anglo-American military campaign eliminated many of the country's central institutions, deepened existing cleavages, and posed massive difficulties for political, social, and physical reconstruction of the country.

There have been additional problems connected with high-tech warfare. In the former Yugoslavia and in Afghanistan serious coordination difficulties arose between the United States and its allies (NATO, UN, and local) in part because of the incompatibility of weapons technologies and command structures. These difficulties were one reason why the United States was willing to intervene in Iraq with almost only British military support. Also, the best and most effective high-tech weapons (for example, Tomahawk cruise missiles and B-2 stealth bombers) are hugely expensive and, to date, available only in relatively limited quantities. Moreover, high-tech systems are still vulnerable to human error, as witness, for example, the precision-guided missile that destroyed the Chinese Embassy in Belgrade and the almost daily reports of mistaken deaths of innocent civilians as collateral damage in Afghanistan and, later, Iraq.

High-tech systems themselves may be vulnerable to high-tech attack. Already, there are signs of a struggle over cyberspace to supplement the traditional struggle over territory. Additionally, high-tech computer-based systems tend to be highly centralized and, like other centralized

---

[62] "Are They Too Clever by Half?" *The Economist*, May 1–7, 1999, pp. 46–47.
[63] See Shoon Kathleen Murray and Christopher Spinosa, "The Post-9/11 Shift in Public Opinion: How Long Will it Last?" in Eugene R. Wittkopf and James M. McCormick, eds., *The Domestic Sources of American Foreign Policy*, 4th ed. (Lanham, MD: Rowman & Littlefield, 2004), pp. 97–115.

systems, create serious vulnerabilities that do not afflict decentralized systems. Concerns about the possible exposure of US computer systems to cyberattacks led the Clinton administration to prepare plans for a comprehensive computer monitoring system.[64] "Instead of using explosives to kill and destroy," declares Metz, "the warrior of the future" may be armed "with a laptop computer from a motel room," and "[h]acking, virus-writing, and crashing data information systems – as well as defending against enemy hackers and virus writers – may become core military skills, as important as the ability to shoot."[65] Future war "may see attacks via computer viruses, worms, logic bombs, and trojan horses rather than bullets, bombs, and missiles."[66]

There are further concerns about high-tech warfare to which we shall turn later in our discussions of technological change and normative concerns in Chapters 8 and 9. Suffice it to say here that high-tech warfare is less costly in human life, which of course is laudable, but that this very characteristic may lead it to be employed with less reluctance than other forms of warfare. Moreover, its complexity, sophistication, and cost mean that it is fully available only to technologically advanced and wealthy polities, while recent experience suggests that it will be employed primarily against developing-country targets.

Some consequences of the new forms of warfare

Will today's RMA have broad political and socioeconomic ramifications as did previous military revolutions? In the seventeenth century, the creation of the modern state "based on organized and disciplined military power"[67] was, in part, a product of a "military revolution" that took advantage of the longbow, gunpowder, and improvements in fortress architecture. "The 17th century revolution," Murray writes, "laid the basis for the modern state. Until that point, armies and navies were under only the loosest control of central governments. Their employers more often than not failed to pay the troops who in turn looted and pillaged."[68] By contrast, centralized state bureaucracies ensured that soldiers were paid on time and were disciplined in both peace and war. Thereafter, the nationalism roused by the French Revolution energized and reinforced state power, giving rise to a dramatic increase in the

---

[64] John Markoff, "US Drawing Plan that Will Monitor Computer Systems," *New York Times*, July 28, 1999, pp. A1, A16.
[65] Metz, *Armed Conflict in the 21st Century*, pp. 185, 187. [66] *Ibid.*, p. xiii.
[67] Murray, "Thinking About Revolutions in Military Affairs," p. 70. [68] *Ibid.*, p. 71.

scale of armies and battles. In the following century, the industrial revolution provided states with vast new financial and logistical resources that enabled them to fight the total war of 1914–18. RMA enthusiasts link underlying changes in modern society, notably the emergence of the "information society," to changes in the nature of warfare, and they posit change at several levels: new technologies, operational concepts, and organizational structures.

In the past, interstate warfare significantly contributed to deepening citizen identities. As Mann notes, "through wars eighteenth-century states enormously increased their fiscal and manpower exactions, caging their subjects onto the national terrain and thus politicizing them."[69] On the other hand, the effects of some postinternational forms of warfare on identities are unclear or contradictory. Certainly, low-tech warfare is associated with sociopolitical fragmentation or worse (for example, suicide bombers or ethnic cleansing), although it may also be the only available weapon of the weak. The effects of high-tech warfare on identities are equally uncertain, and we have few examples from which to draw conclusions. All other things being equal, high-tech warfare has potentially wide appeal in the United States, where technology is a cultural icon and is often viewed as a panacea for a range of problems. However, actual experience, as we have noted, has been decidedly mixed. The Persian Gulf War produced a short-lived, but intense outburst of patriotism in the United States. The overwhelming power of the allies' armored columns stirred many Americans, but their euphoria was soon tempered by the grim realization in 1991 that Saddam was still there and defiant as ever. The subsequent bloodless victory of the air war in Kosovo elicited a collective yawn from most American citizens. The Serbs, though they initially rallied around the Milošević regime in the face of the relentless pounding by NATO warplanes, afterwards began to question the foolhardiness of a conflict that devastated their country and mortgaged their future. As for the War on Terror, to be sure, there was an enormous groundswell of popular support in the United States for military retaliation against the horrific attacks of September 11, but (as in the Gulf War) enthusiasm waned when Osama Bin Laden and most of his close associates remained uncaught and unpunished. Nor did the George W. Bush administration garner enthusiastic backing for the follow-on invasion of Iraq; and, when American casualties continued

---

[69] Mann, *The Sources of Social Power*, vol. II, p. 20.

after Bush had declared the war to be at an end, public support for the president's policies steadily diminished.

Remapping, as we have observed, connotes changes in the role of territory as well as in changing identities. Here the implications of the high-tech form of postinternational violence are clearer. High-tech war contributes to deterritorializing politics in several ways, prompting even a state-centric scholar of geopolitics such as Colin Gray to speak of "anti-geography" and phenomena that are "placelessly 'beyond geography'."[70] Following on ICBMs, today's high-tech weapons further erode traditional limitations imposed by physical distance on the exercise of force. Distance still is by no means irrelevant in warfare, but it has been significantly undermined by revolutions in communication, transportation, and military delivery systems. In the 1999 Kosovo crisis, the United States dispatched B-2 stealth bombers from Missouri to strike targets deep inside Yugoslavia. In a round trip taking nearly 30 hours the bombers were able to attack the most dangerous and highest-value targets and then return to their own bases safe in the continental United States. Pilots, according to one contemporary report, were "living at home while also acting as combatants in a war in a faraway land about which their neighbors know little."[71] Even pre-Vietnam-era B-52 bombers, upgraded to carry cruise missiles, could station themselves hundreds of miles outside Yugoslav airspace and fire cruise missiles far inside Yugoslav territory. Declared one defense analyst: "Air power is very seductive to American leaders, because it combines our love of technology with our distaste for the bestial aspects of land warfare. You do it nice and cleanly. Nobody gets his or her feet muddy. A pilot flies over at 15,000 feet, kills only those people that need to be killed, flies home and has a cold beer with a beautiful young lady."[72] Contrary to this the United States effort to open a northern front in Iraq in 2003 was greatly impeded by Turkey's refusal to allow the necessary troops upon its soil.

Second, warfare is no longer likely to be conducted – if it ever was, given its perennial psychological dimension – exclusively in physical space. As we have mentioned, some commentators now propose the

---

[70] Colin S. Gray, "RMAs and the Dimensions of Strategy," *Joint Forces Quarterly* (Autumn–Winter 1997–98), pp. 53, 54.
[71] Thomas E. Ricks, "For These B-2 Pilots, Bombs Away Means Really Far, Far Away," *Wall Street Journal*, April 19, 1999, p. A1.
[72] Cited in Blaine Harden and John M. Broder, "Clinton's Aims: Win the War, Keep the US Voters Content," *New York Times*, May 22, 1999, p. A6.

need to add a new frontier of cyberspace. Information war or cyberwar – the stuff of dreams or nightmares, depending upon one's perspective – might involve the electromagnetic destruction of an enemy's command, control, communication, and radar systems, deceiving an enemy's sensors, or obtaining access to an enemy's computers. Even if military organizations can protect their own servers and files from cyberattack, it is doubtful whether other key government and civilian institutions would be able to do so.

Cyberwar potential is increasingly available not only to states but also to nonsovereign actors ranging from individuals to small networks. The relatively simple "I Love You" virus, created and disseminated globally by a single hacker in the Philippines, caused worldwide disruption.[73] In another recent case inspired by the Israeli–Palestinian conflict, a Pakistani hacker with the online name of "Doctor Nuker" defaced the Web site of a lobbying group, the American Israel Public Affairs Committee. According to the hacker, who also sold e-mail addresses and credit card numbers that he published on the Internet, his motive was "to hack for the injustice going around the globe, especially with Muslims."[74]

"Cyberattacks," declared Metz, "might erode the traditional advantage large and rich states hold in armed conflict. Private entities might be able to match state armed forces."[75] Another observer predicts: "Basically, every time there is a national crisis, Chinese hackers will challenge the other country's Web sites."[76] Such hackers, organized as the "Hacker Union of China," are among the most militant of China's nationalists. Cybertechnology is cheap and so accessible that, as Martin Libicki comments: "Most of what is needed to achieve information superiority in times of war is now available over the counter in the global marketplace."[77] Libicki argues that the diffusion of information technologies may be even more dangerous than the proliferation of WMD. "Even the smallest of countries," he writes, "can make use of a single connection, a cheap computer, and a clever hacker to disrupt or corrupt any of the

---

[73] Wayne Arnold, "Virus Brings Publicity to Computer Subculture in Philippines," *New York Times*, May 15, 2000, p. 8.
[74] Cited in John Schwartz, "When Point and Shoot Becomes Point and Click," *New York Times*, November 10, 2000, sec. 4, p. 16. The article also documents a number of similar incidents.
[75] Metz, *Armed Conflict in the 21st Century*, p. xiii.
[76] Cited in Elizabeth Becker, "F.B.I. Warns That Chinese May Disrupt US Web Sites," *New York Times*, April 28, 2001, p. A6.
[77] Martin Libicki, "Rethinking War: The Mouse's New Roar," *Foreign Policy* 117 (Winter 1999–2000), p. 39.

world's major information systems: funds transfer, transportation control, air traffic safety, phones, electric power, oil and gas distribution, and even military system."[78]

Sovereign boundaries present few obstacles to either high- or low-tech warfare, and some military specialists go so far (probably too far) as to maintain that it is no longer necessary to seize and hold territory in order to win a war. Moreover, owing to growing mass political consciousness and communications technologies that facilitate mass mobilization, it is more difficult to seize and hold territory than in the past. Still, this line of argument requires some qualification. To be sure, there are few clear "front lines" in postinternational war, and sovereign boundaries and authority are often compromised. In addition, geography plays a diminishing role in military security (with notable exceptions such as the Palestine–Israeli and Indian–Pakistani cases). However, the ability to take and hold "places," or at least to control those who live there remain important requirements for military forces in many instances. It remains as close to an axiom in the study and practice of war as the one that air and sea strategies must always be assessed in terms of their impact on land strategy.[79]

And there is no denying the connection between territory and war continues to be important in a variety of other ways. Saddam Hussein's invasion of Kuwait is a case in point. Who can doubt that if Kuwait had no oil, he would never have made the attempt and the global reaction to any such takeover would have been more muted. In addition to resources like minerals and water, territory may also host political and financial centers, communications hubs, sacred sites, or national monuments. Some low-level conflicts are mainly about national self-determination and the control of a "homeland." "Most wars," Freedman insists, "are still largely about territory." He continues: "The ability to hold on to land remains a vital test of sovereignty: even the loss of a remote, barren and under-populated province can weaken a central government's authority."[80] Nevertheless, with few exceptions, territory is no longer the sole or even most important source of wealth or security in postinternational politics.

---

[78] *Ibid.*, p. 35. Libicki also points out that what he calls the "globalization of perception" or everybody's ability to know what is going on in the world can create world opinion to protect small states from large ones (p. 41).
[79] Freedman, "The Changing Form of Military Conflict," p. 48. For a similar view, see Gray, "RMAs and the Dimensions of Strategy," pp. 50–54.
[80] Freedman, "The Changing Form of Military Conflict," p. 48.

As mention of holy and historical sites points up, territory often has additional symbolic significance, but it may symbolize something other than nation-states, as do Jerusalem's holy sites or Mecca's *Kaaba*. Kosovo is a symbol of national origin to many Serbs, just as Mecca is Islam's most revered holy site. The Panama Canal (despite its reduced economic and political importance) long remained a nationalist symbol for both the United States and Panama. New York's World Trade Center symbolized global capitalism and United States economic might. This brings us back to an earlier conclusion about the important symbolic, if lessened material, role of formal territorial boundaries, which are less frequently directly challenged today partly because they *do* have symbolic importance.

Future conflicts among different types of states

Owing to the variety of conflicts that are emerging, postinternational warfare will feature asymmetries. High-tech armies will collide with low-tech forces even as nuclear powers fought nonnuclear countries in past decades. The chink in the armor of the United States and other advanced industrial societies is vulnerability to terrorism, unconventional warfare, and other "asymmetric" threats. In part, this is a consequence of the centralization and specialization that accompanies modernization in today's societies. According to Metz, the most likely and dangerous asymmetric conflict in the future will be urban warfare. In a sort of military parallel to Saskia Sassen's views of the evolving political and economic roles of global cities, Ralph Peters foresees the "future of warfare" "in the streets, sewers, high-rise buildings, industrial parks, and the sprawl of houses, shacks, and shelters that form the broken cities of our world."[81] In such conflicts, high-tech armies that are averse to casualties may confront urban guerrillas with few scruples about casualties; and the former can improve their chances with the addition of nonmetal weapons and robotics.[82]

Metz's model of a "trisected security system"[83] is helpful for assessing asymmetries as well as the likelihood of different types of war in the

---

[81] Ralph Peters, "Our Soldiers, Their Cities," *Parameters* 26:1 (Spring 1996), p. 43. This fear dominated planning for the 2003 attack on Iraq, but the threat did not materialize to any great extent.

[82] Metz, *Armed Conflict in the 21st Century*, p. xi.

[83] Steven Metz, "Which Army After Next? The Strategic Implications of Alternative Futures," *Parameters* 27:3 (Autumn 1997), pp. 16–21.

coming years. Metz's "First Tier" of states – most of which are in North America and Western Europe – is "characterized by stability, prosperity, and multidimensional integration." These states have economies that are interdependent and that rely on "brainpower" and the creation and dissemination of information. Their military forces "will be small in terms of number of people involved, but will make extensive use of technology, robotics, information technology, and nanotechnology." There will be "widespread aversion to violence," and especially casualties, among citizens in these countries.[84]

Metz's "Second Tier" consists of states such as Pakistan, Turkey, Iraq, truncated Yugoslavia, and North Korea, the economies of which still depend on "muscle power" industrial production. In such cases, the state itself "will remain the central political and economic institution." The greatest challenge to such states is "secessionism," the demand for independence on the part of regions or groups, so that their leaders will emphasize nationalist themes and policies. Compared to First Tier states, actors in this group "will place relatively less emphasis on expensive technology and more on the blood of soldiers."[85] These are the countries that are also most likely to resort to weapons of mass destruction if they can acquire them.

Finally, Third Tier states are characterized by "economic stagnation, ungovernability, and violence." They will be left out of globalized economic and cultural systems. Their "armed forces will take the form of armed gangs, militias, the personal armies of warlords, and terrorist groups," and "there will be no clear distinction between war and peace since much of the Third Tier will experience near constant low-level organized violence."[86]

War within the First Tier is now almost unthinkable. Actors are partners in numerous cooperative formal and informal institutional arrangements such as NATO, the EU, the OECD, and the Atlantic Council. Despite disagreements such as the recent sharp one over the Iraq war, they constitute a genuine security community that reflects the supposed "democratic peace." The possibility of wars among Second Tier countries is limited by the relative incapacity of these states to project power over significant distances. Although conflicts such as the 1999 border war between Ethiopia and Eritrea – or more ominously, because of the potential use of nuclear weapons, between India and Pakistan over Kashmir – remain possible, they are also unlikely to spread beyond the

---

[84] *Ibid.*, pp. 17, 18.   [85] *Ibid.*, pp. 17, 20.   [86] *Ibid.*, pp. 18, 20, 21.

original combatants (except as nuclear fallout in the latter case). Finally, Third Tier states are largely incapable of waging organized warfare or of projecting force. Instead, they become arenas for internal or regional violence.

Generally speaking, wars among states from different tiers are more likely than wars among states within the same tier, hence the asymmetries. Metz foresees such wars as resembling the children's game "scissors, paper, rock." High-tech First Tier armies will be able to defeat the large and somewhat lower-tech forces of Second Tier states with relative ease but will find casualty aversion a serious constraint when fighting the militia, terrorists, and private armies of the Third Tier. Second Tier militaries, with their large size, ability to undertake sustained, intense operations and greater tolerance for casualties, will have success against Third Tier forces. And, while Third Tier forces will be unable to stand and face Second Tier armies, they will find that their lack of inhibition in the use of indiscriminate violence gives them some leverage on the First Tier. This all means that First Tier armies will be able to trump Second Tier; Second Tier armies will be able to trump Third Tier; and Third Tier will be able to trump First Tier.[87]

The United States' War on Terrorism in Afghanistan illustrates how complex and difficult the military and political problems confronting First Tier countries in Third Tier settings can be. So do the 1992 U.N. intervention in Somalia and the 1983–84 Western intervention in Lebanon. In both cases, Western aversion to casualties assured withdrawal following the loss of relatively few lives. "Western armies," as David Shearer argues, "designed primarily to fight the sophisticated international conflicts envisaged by Cold War strategists, are ill equipped to tackle low-intensity civil wars, with their complicated ethnic agendas, blurred boundaries between combatants and civilians, and loose military hierarchies."[88] Therefore, it is increasingly necessary to provide Western troops who are sent into areas like Bosnia with specialized training and equipment such as plows and other systems for clearing mines that is specially adapted to such settings.[89]

NATO's 1999 military campaign against Serbia suggests a more mixed verdict for Metz's prediction that First Tier forces should dominate Second Tier forces. The Kosovo campaign seemed to indicate that forces

---

[87] *Ibid.*, p. 21.   [88] Shearer, "Outsourcing War," p. 70.
[89] Eric Schmitt, "American Arsenal Honed for Bosnia," *New York Times*, December 5, 1995, pp. A1, A8.

with high-tech weaponry can attack a Second Tier state with relative impunity but that the latter's "ability to undertake sustained, intense operations" and "greater tolerance for casualties" makes it difficult for the former to achieve its objectives. As then NATO commander General Wesley Clark admitted, "you cannot stop paramilitary murder on the ground with aeroplanes."[90] And, as in current Iraq, what transpires when a First Tier force reduces a Second Tier to Third Tier status?

Privatizing violence

Political economists and pluralists have long recognized the importance of nonsovereign actors for world politics but mostly with regard to the myriad of issues contained (sometimes misleadingly) under the heading "low politics." In contrast, those like realists who see the state involved principally in providing military security to citizens and as enjoying a public monopoly of the means of coercion have little interest in nonsovereign actors. Since states are assumed to maintain a monopoly of force internally and are the only actors capable of raising, maintaining, and employing large-scale conventional armies and weapons of mass destruction, they constitute a global elite with specialized military bureaucracies. However, when states fail to provide protection to citizens, as is increasingly the case today, they "turn private security into a growth industry *par excellence* worldwide."[91]

At a time of eroding state capacity, actors such as transnational organizations and humanitarian NGOs are acquiring an expanding role in global politics, including warfare. Of these, the most important for the analysis of postinternational war are actors that provide "private" violence or security. This recalls an earlier era. Europe's religious wars were waged by "military contractors" in whose hands "war itself was turned into a form of self-sustaining capitalist enterprise that promised riches and even principalities to the most successful practitioners."[92] The mercenaries "robbed the countryside on their own behalf, even building fortified strongholds where they collected loot and held prisoners for ransom."[93] Westphalian States willingly used mercenaries, privateers, and trading companies that had their own armies to extend state influence.

---

[90] Cited in "No End in Sight," *The Economist*, April 17–23, 1999, p. 51.
[91] Van Creveld, *The Rise and Decline of the State*, p. 404.
[92] Van Creveld, *Technology and War*, p. 108.
[93] Van Creveld, *The Transformation of War* (New York: Free Press, 1991), pp. 50, 51.

In fact, as noted earlier, Thomson argues that "the state, portrayed in theory as monopolizing coercion, is distinctively modern" and "reflected a redrawing of authority claims such that authority over the use of violence was moved from the nonstate, economic, and international domains and placed in the state, political, and domestic realms of authority."[94] Europe's states did not achieve a monopoly over transborder violence until relatively late in an historical sense. States, Thomson claims, were "reluctant to exert authority and control over nonstate violence."[95] "Where princes and other military entrepreneurs used to contract with each other," predicts van Creveld, "an Amsterdam capitalist, Louis de Geer, once provided the Swedish government with a complete navy, sailors, and commanders up to the vice-admiral included – in the future various public, semi-public, and private corporations will do the same."[96]

We have already observed that in many African countries, as well as elsewhere especially in the less-developed world, "national" armies no longer are reliable instruments of state policy and, far from assuring citizens of security, are sometimes themselves *the* major threats to citizens' security. Indeed, according to Herbst, "The notion that Africa was ever composed of sovereign states classically defined as having a monopoly of force in the territory within their boundaries is false."[97] Thus, it is perhaps not surprising that one feature of Africa's violence has been what Shearer calls "outsourcing war,"[98] and it is a trend that is spreading. Shearer argues that "the increasing inability of weak governments to counter internal violence has created a ready market for private military forces."[99] One (now-defunct) mercenary company, South African-based Executive Outcomes, provided military services for the governments of Angola and Sierra Leone, and the Zairian government of President Mobutu used a variety of European mercenaries in an unsuccessful effort to prevent his overthrow. Even the US government employs private specialists in violence. "Military Professional Resources Incorporated (MPRI), a Virginia-based firm headed by retired US army

---

[94] Thomson, *Mercenaries, Pirates, and Sovereigns*, p. 11.   [95] *Ibid.*, p. 143.
[96] Van Creveld, *The Rise and Decline of the State*, p. 407.
[97] Jeffrey Herbst, "Responding to State Failure in Africa," *International Security* 21:3 (Winter 1996–97), p. 122.
[98] Shearer, "Outsourcing War," pp. 68–81. See also Muthien and Taylor, "The Return of the Dogs of War?"
[99] Shearer, "Outsourcing War," p. 70.

general . . . has hired former US military personnel to develop the military forces of Bosnia-Herzegovina and Croatia."[100] Private US contractors working closely with government agencies also play a growing role in aiding the Colombian government in its fight against its domestic adversaries.[101]

The emergence of private armies and the growing importance of private security firms, like the British company Defense Systems Limited that stands guard at embassies and provides corporations with security,[102] reflect the erosion of state institutions and their increasing inability to cope with military and criminal violence. As in seventeenth-century Europe with its bands of roving mercenaries, war is once more becoming "a form of self-sustaining capitalist enterprise." Like other private firms, military entrepreneurs emphasize profit rather than some abstract public interest or social responsibility. While such enterprises may not pose a direct security challenge to major states, they can undermine local authorities and potentially complicate crisis management, nation-building, and international efforts to restore order to conflict-ridden regions.

Outsourcing is not only a feature of low-tech wars; it also reflects the need for technical specialists in the developed world. Metz reminds us that early in the growth of the European state, "artillery and siege engineering were often handled by contractors rather than military soldiers."[103] Today, the high cost of training and maintaining a permanent corps of specialists provides incentives to subcontract for such help when needed. The soaring costs of high-tech weaponry have also fostered planning for transnational corporate mergers in order to provide economies of scale in military production.[104] There is, of course, no reason (other than government restrictions and diplomatic pressure) why such private assistance would not be available to other states and actors, including terrorists, *narcotraficantes*, mercenary groups, or rogue governments. Specialists can be hired or even kidnapped.

---

[100] *Ibid.*, p. 71.
[101] Juan Forero, "Role of US Companies in Colombia Is Questioned," *New York Times on the Web*, May 18, 2001, http://www.nytimes.com/2001/05/18/world/18COLO.html.
[102] Shearer, "Outsourcing War," p. 71.
[103] Metz, *Armed Conflict in the 21st Century*, p. 19.
[104] "Pentagon Discussing with Europeans Possibility of Mergers with US Firms," *Wall Street Journal*, July 7, 1999, pp. A2, A10.

Soldiers and civilians

We have seen how war and crime were largely indistinguishable in medieval Europe and in Europe's wars of religion and how the state imposed this distinction on global politics. Thus, during Europe's Middle Ages, war "was all but indistinguishable from simple brigandry,"[105] and civilians were the main victims of "the chaotic and roving warfare of the so-called wars of religion."[106] By contrast, Clausewitz's ideal of trinitarian warfare with its clear demarcation among government, soldiers, and civilians and, as a corollary, between war and crime, was never entirely accurate. Clausewitz himself witnessed irregular warfare during Napoleon's invasion of and retreat from Russia.

Industrialization and national mobilization made civilians very much a part of the war effort in World War I, and that war involved some atrocities against civilians. World War II, however, was qualitatively different in that respect from anything that had gone before. Both sides self-consciously waged war against civilians. The Holocaust, Dresden, Hiroshima, and Nagasaki all attested to an eroding distinction between soldiers and civilians. Thus, 65 percent of the total fatalities in World War II were civilians (in contrast to 15 percent in World War I), and "[i]n the 'low-intensity' wars of the late twentieth century – the wars of Ivory Coast, Somalia, Sudan, Liberia, East Timor, and the former Yugoslavia – civilians constitute 90 percent of the dead."[107] Today, as Freedman observes, "the circumstances of contemporary conflict imply much more interaction with civil society, and a greater difficulty in separating combatants from non-combatants."[108] Although the weaponry used in such warfare is not highly sophisticated, "these new wars tend to be very bloody because there is no distinction between armies and peoples, so everybody who gets in the way gets killed."[109]

Such trends may be accelerated by the widening gap between military personnel and civilians, even in advanced societies. Following Harold Lasswell's memorable phrase, Samuel Huntington considered the central professional skill of the modern military officer to be "the management of violence." This skill separated military officers not only from members of other professions such as lawyers and physicians

---

[105] Van Creveld, *Technology and War*, p. 108.
[106] Palmer, "Frederick the Great, Guibert, Bülow," p. 94.
[107] Barbara Ehrenreich, *Blood Rites: Origins and History of the Passions of War* (New York: Henry Holt & Co., 1997), pp. 206, 227.
[108] Lawrence Freedman, *The Revolution in Strategic Affairs*, Adelphi Paper 318 (New York: Oxford University Press, 1998), pp. 47–48.
[109] Martin van Creveld, cited in Cohen, "In Sarajevo, Victims of a 'Postmodern' War," p. 8.

but also from ordinary soldiers or enlisted personnel who specialize in the "application of violence."[110] Yet, increasingly, professional military men in the West are at least two steps removed from the relationships described by Huntington. They are not managing people but things – the technological tools of war – and the ordinary soldiers whom they are managing are not specialists in the application of violence but technical specialists trained to operate machines.

Another development is the gradual disappearance of the citizen armies that originally emerged in the wake of the French Revolution. One by one, advanced countries such as the United States, France, and Great Britain have abandoned conscription as a means of acquiring and retaining the human capital necessary to wage war. The causes of this shift vary from country to country, but its implications for global politics are more universal. We may be witnessing the emergence of a new class of mercenary. Although soldiers of fortune remain the province of failed states, drug cartels, and other transnational criminal interests, economic motivations play an important role in attracting and retaining professional soldiers in Western countries. Thus, shortly before the onset of NATO's bombing of Serbia, attention in the United States centered on the question of military retirement pay, and the nation's leading newspapers and specialized military media were filled with stories about how higher pay was necessary to attract and retain personnel.

As specialization increases, we may be seeing the emergence of an updated version of mercenary Hessians and Swiss Guards available for hire by wealthy societies that lack the manpower willing to serve as soldiers. To some extent, this trend is already evident in U.N. peacekeeping missions during which poor states, in effect, hire out their personnel in return for financial considerations and a variety of operational support services from wealthier states. Within the United States, volunteers come disproportionately from the urban poor, racial minorities, and recent immigrants who view military service as a means of social and economic advancement. Even states find themselves on the payroll. During the Gulf War and then again during the Kosovo crisis, critical voices were heard claiming that the United States and Great Britain had hired themselves out to wealthy allies – in particular, to Japan and Germany which, along with Saudi Arabia and Kuwait, provided direct payments to the United States. In the Kosovo case, several European

---

[110] Samuel P. Huntington, *The Soldier and the State: The Theory and Politics of Civil-Military Relations* (New York: Vintage Books, 1957), pp. 11, 18.

states were reluctant to commit military forces to help resolve the crisis or were unable to do so because their NATO-linked forces lacked the capabilities necessary to project power even in a region less than 200 miles from Rome. If the United States and Britain are not global policemen, they may at least be regarded by some as global security guards.

If low-tech wars collapse many Westphalian assumptions about the conduct of war by morphing civilians into combatants and back again, high-tech warfare goes in the opposite direction of maintaining the soldier–civilian distinction. Some military analysts worry that the emphasis on cyberwar will breed the warrior out of the war fighter and that temporal and spatial dislocations caused by disconnection from the fighting may create a generation of pushbutton warriors. This trend is accelerated by the "American way of war" with its focus on reducing collateral damage, including civilian casualties; minimizing "friendly" casualties by emphasizing "force protection," even at the cost of lost mission effectiveness; and insisting on the professionalization of military forces. Analysts such as van Creveld go so far as to question whether such operations are even war – since the war fighter does not risk his or her own life in battle. For better or worse, this situation is a far cry from the Greek hoplite or the foot soldier of World War II.

It is the changing relationship of soldiers and civilians and the blurring of the distinction between them that is helping to alter international law in the direction of providing individuals with standing that they lack under the "law of nations." It is, therefore, appropriate to turn directly to some of the normative implications in the shift to postinternational warfare.

Some normative implications of postinternational violence[111]

Rapidly advancing technology has, as we have seen, had major normative implications for postinternational warfare. Any discussion of violence against individuals in present-day global politics runs up against an apparent paradox. On the one hand, individuals today are probably more fully protected by international law and humanitarian norms than

---

[111] Some of the material in this section appeared in earlier form in Richard W. Mansbach and Franke Wilmer, "War and the Westphalian State of Mind," in Mathias Albert, David Jacobson, and Yosef Lapid, eds., *Identities, Borders, Orders* (Minneapolis: University of Minnesota Press, 2001), pp. 51–71.

at any historical moment since the Thirty Years War. On the other hand, the decline in interstate warfare and the dramatic growth in intrastate and transstate warfare are putting civilians at risk to a greater extent than at any time since the Thirty Years War. This leads to an additional paradox: on the one hand, human-rights activists and liberal practitioners seek to limit sovereign claims against domestic interference and humanitarian intervention, while, on the other, the erosion of state authority and sovereign capacity are accompanied by growing abuses against innocent civilians in wartime. This becomes less surprising when we recognize that the "law of nations" (as Hugo Grotius called it) is increasingly complemented by international law and custom in which individuals, as well as states, are regarded as subjects.

Changes in modern warfare are remaking international law. Although the twentieth century opened with the Hague Conferences of 1899 and 1906 where delegates celebrated a "century of peace," believing war to have become rare and "civilized," as the century progressed the actual conduct of war involved widespread inhumanity and indiscriminate violence. World Wars I and II saw the growing engagement and victimization of civilians in war whether as resistance fighters, wartime industrial workers, prisoners in concentration camps, or casualties in urban bombings. Despite efforts to maintain the distinction between combatants and noncombatants, technology and ideology conspired to erase it. The security bargain originally struck by the Westphalian polity with its citizens (more on this shortly) had begun to unravel.

The breakdown of the separation between civilians and soldiers in both world wars, the anti-colonial struggles in the less-developed world, the Vietnam War, and the many premodern and postmodern conflicts since the end of the Cold War suggested that the "law of nations" no longer provided sufficient protection for individuals in wartime. Following the Holocaust, some progress was made toward expanding the regulation of violence beyond norms pertaining to noncombatants and prisoners of war during a war, to the general protection of individuals against abuses of state coercion through the articulation of "universal" human rights. This very significant innovation for the first time extended the international regulation of violence into the shielded realm of state "domestic" jurisdiction, that is, to the use of violence by states against those within their borders. State monopoly over coercion was thus limited in principle both by an obligation to refrain from aggression against other states as well as to refrain from using force wrongly to harm civilians.

The atrocities committed by the Germans and Japanese produced the Nuremberg and Tokyo trials, both of which ignored (note well, only for defeated states) the sovereign right of states to try their own citizens and established the precedent of individual responsibility for actions undertaken even under the justification of superior orders or operational necessity. In addition to designating acts of aggression as the "crime" of war, individual agents of states could be held accountable for a whole new category of crimes – crimes against humanity and, later, genocide – in the misuse of state coercive power. The creation of the category of crimes against humanity entailed recognition of the breakdown of traditional distinctions between soldiers and civilians, and between war and crime. Thus, the concentration camps and the murder of 6 million Jews, like later "ethnic cleansing" in Bosnia and Kosovo and genocide in Cambodia and Rwanda, were regarded by the global community as the acts of common criminals without any foundation in "military necessity" (however shabby any such justification might be under any circumstances). Owing to dramatic improvements in communications, it has become more and more difficult to cover up atrocities. Vivid pictures of the dead and the dying, and of refugees in Somalia, Rwanda, Congo, Bosnia, and Kosovo created public pressure on officials to act. In this regard and in others, Jean-Marie Guehenno argues, growing access to and exchange of information has altered the legal and political features of the state system.[112]

Since World War II, UN conventions and international and regional human-rights tribunals and law have repeatedly reinforced the Nuremberg precedent. December 10, 1998, marked the fiftieth anniversary of the United Nations' Genocide Convention and the Universal Declaration of Human Rights, the most comprehensive listing of civil, political, social, and economic rights ever assembled. The year 1949 witnessed the four Geneva Conventions governing treatment of civilians and prisoners of war in wartime. The European Convention on Human Rights emerged in 1950, and the following two years brought the Convention Relating to the Status of Refugees and the Convention on the Political Rights of Women. In the ensuing years, additional conventions were adopted to deal with a variety of human-rights issues: the status of stateless persons (1954), abolishing slavery (1956), abolishing forced labor (1957), consent to marriage (1962), elimination of racial discrimination

---

[112] Jean-Marie Guehenno, *The End of the Nation-State*, trans. Victor Pesce Elliot (Minneapolis: University of Minnesota Press, 1995).

(1965), suppression of apartheid (1973), discrimination against women (1979), torture (1984), and the rights of the child (1989). In 1966, the Universal Declaration of Human Rights gained greater specificity and potentially binding character in the International Covenants on Economic, Social and Cultural Rights/Civil and Political Rights. Of course, reliably effective enforcement mechanisms have been lacking, relying in most instances upon voluntary compliance by states or the emergence of a genuine policy consensus, as happened in the cases of eliminating apartheid in South Africa or addressing war crimes in the former Yugoslavia. Nevertheless, all were violations of classical sovereignty.

In May 1996 the first international criminal court since Nuremberg – the International Criminal Tribunal for the former Yugoslavia – was convened in The Hague. Among those who were indicted for war crimes or crimes against humanity, including "ethnic cleansing" genocide,[113] were Bosnian Serb leaders Radovan Karadzić, General Ratko Mladić, and former Yugoslav President Slobodan Milošević. The United Nations also set up an international tribunal in Arusha, Tanzania to deal with the 1994 Rwandan genocide. An international court is still being discussed, as well, to try members of the Khmer Rouge for their role in Cambodia's "killing fields."[114]

An even more ambitious step was the conclusion in Rome in the summer of 1998 of a treaty to establish a permanent International Criminal Court (ICC) to try individuals charged with genocide, war crimes, and crimes against humanity. Although the ICC has been established, the United States has thus far refused to participate. The United States was one of only 7 governments (including Iraq, Libya, and China) of 127 at the meeting to vote against it and insisted – in response to concerns expressed by the Pentagon and conservative members of Congress – that the court's jurisdiction should be automatic only for those countries that had signed the treaty. American opponents of the ICC argue that politically motivated charges may be filed against US soldiers on

---

[113] Genocide is defined in the Convention on Prevention and Punishment of the Crime of Genocide that went into force in 1951 as "any of the following acts committed with intent to destroy, in whole or in part, a national, ethnic or religious group, such as a) killing members of the group; b) causing serious bodily or mental harm to members of the group; c) deliberately inflicting on the group conditions of life calculated to bring about its physical destruction in whole or in part; d) imposing measures intended to prevent births within the group; e) forcibly transferring children of the group to another group." Thus, to be defined as "genocide" violence does not need to reach the level of the Holocaust.
[114] Philip Shenon, "US Seeks War Crimes Trial of Top Khmer Rouge Leaders," *New York Times*, January 5, 1999, p. A3; "Trying Cambodia's Butchers," *The Economist*, March 13–19, 1999, pp. 19–20.

peacekeeping or regular military missions. President Bill Clinton signed the treaty just before leaving office, but the incoming Bush administration pronounced the ICC flatly unacceptable unless US personnel were specifically exempted. Indeed, the administration threatened to withhold military aid and cooperation from any ICC participant not willing to sign a bilateral agreement with the United States that provides such an exemption. Meanwhile, regional institutions such as the American[115] and European Courts of Human Rights[116] allow individuals to bring complaints to them, and, in Europe, even Great Britain has agreed that citizens can use domestic courts to enforce the European Convention on Human Rights (ECHR).[117]

The end of the Cold War and the rapid spread of democratic norms made it easier to ignore power considerations and to provide scope for human-rights concerns. European countries and at least certain judges in the US court system are prepared to extend rights and responsibilities to individuals even if doing so violates sovereignty as traditionally defined, and the new climate accelerated the efforts of international organizations like the United Nations to institutionalize human rights. An important precedent was set when a United States federal appeals court ruled that two women could use American civil courts to enforce international human-rights standards and sue Bosnian Serb leader Radovan Karadzić personally for war crimes committed against the women in Bosnia.[118] Some years later, a settlement was reached in a class action suit against the estate of Philippine dictator Ferdinand Marcos, and other civil actions have been won against human-rights

---

[115] See, for example, "Outlaw," *The Economist*, July 10–16, 1999, p. 32.

[116] The ECHR should not be confused with the European Court of Justice which also may get deeply involved in human rights if the European Union legalizes its "charter on fundamental rights." "Eventually Supreme?" *The Economist*, March 25–31, 2000, p. 50. Russian membership in the Council of Europe makes that country subject to the ECHR as well, at least in principle.

[117] "Bringing Rights Home," *The Economist*, August 26–September 1, 2000, pp. 45–46. This extraordinary shift in British legal practice implies that, at least in matters of human rights, the traditional supremacy of Parliament has been revoked. The European Court of Human Rights allows citizens to file complaints against governments once they have exhausted domestic legal channels. "Europe's Rights Court Taking on Increasingly Sensitive Cases," *New York Times*, July 21, 1999, p. A5. In one decision, the ECHR overturned Britain's ban on homosexuals in the military. Sarah Lyall, "European Court Tells British to Let Gay Soldiers Serve," *New York Times*, September 28, 1999, p. A6.

[118] Neil A. Lewis, "US Backs War-Crimes Lawsuit Against Bosnian Serb Leader," *New York Times*, September 27, 1995, p. A8; "US Court Allows Suit Against Bosnia Serbs," *New York Times*, October 14, 1995, p. 4.

abusers in Haiti, Ethiopia, Rwanda, and Indonesia.[119] In due course, Li Peng, former Chinese Prime Minister, was the target of a civil suit during a visit to New York to attend an international meeting of parliamentarians, for his role in the 1989 Tiananmen Square massacre in Beijing.[120] In addition, elderly Chinese who were forced to work for Japanese corporations or for the Japanese military during World War II have brought a suit against Japan. Although the United States later demurred on the ICC, in 1997 the US did appoint an Ambassador for War Crimes to assist the existing assistant secretary of state for human rights.[121]

The decision in 1998 of two separate panels of British Law Lords that Chile's Augusto Pinochet, though a former head of state, was not immune from extradition and prosecution for crimes against humanity as defined in the genocide convention and the 1984 convention against torture was a human-rights landmark.[122] The Spanish magistrate who sought Pinochet's arrest and extradition had previously in 1996 initiated unsuccessful suits against the military leaders of Argentina and Chile. A year after charges were brought against Pinochet, the International Criminal Tribunal for the Former Yugoslavia issued an indictment against and requested the extradition of a sitting head of state, Yugoslavia's Slobodan Milošević, and four other Serbian leaders for crimes allegedly committed in Kosovo.[123] The trial of two Libyans accused of bombing a US jetliner, finally held before a Scottish court in the Netherlands, provided an additional important reminder that individuals are deserving of international protection and that those who violate human rights will be held responsible *as individuals*. Libya

---

[119] "To Sue a Dictator," *The Economist*, April 24–30, 1999, pp. 26–27. Although it is not yet possible to bring criminal charges against foreign leaders in American courts, bringing civil suits against them if they appear on American soil can be a powerful tool. The technique was first tried in 1980 when a suit was brought against a former Paraguayan police chief.

[120] Edward Wong, "Chinese Leader Sued in New York over Deaths Stemming from Tiananmen Crackdown," *New York Times*, September 1, 2000, p. A6.

[121] "Lawyer Sam's War," *The Economist*, May 24–30, 1999, p. 30.

[122] Marlise Simons, "Pinochet Case Spurring Debate on International Laws," *New York Times*, November 22, 1998, sec. 1, p. 12; Barbara Crossette, "Dictators (and Some Lawyers) Tremble," *New York Times*, November 19, 1998, sec. 4, pp. 1, 3; "Releasing Pinochet," *The Economist*, January 15–21, 2000, p. 21. According to Human Rights Watch, other former dictators who have reason to fear this precedent include Uganda's Idi Amin (now deceased), Haiti's Jean-Claude Duvalier and Raul Cedras, Paraguay's Alfredo Stroessner, and Chad's Hissan Habre. Barbara Crossette, "Dictators Face the Pinochet Syndrome," *New York Times*, August 22, 1999, sec. 4, p. 3.

[123] "The Charges: 'An Unknown Number of Kosovo Albanians Have Been Killed'," *New York Times*, May 28, 1999, pp. A12, A13.

eventually itself agreed to pay a financial settlement to victims' families, by way of admitting responsibility and in exchange for the lifting of UN sanctions.

Violence within sovereign states has already had significant consequences for the global community. NATO's 1999 intervention in Kosovo was something of a landmark because it suggested that state sovereignty would not shield human-rights violators from humanitarian intervention (whether or not with UN approval). NATO's willingness to intervene there is only one of an increasing number of cases in which sovereignty has been ignored in the name of restoring regional peace and security. And if, as Ian Hurd argues, "[t]he stability of borders . . . is a function of the legitimacy of sovereignty rules,"[124] then UN sanctions against South Africa, UN intervention in Somalia and Cambodia, Nigeria's presence in Liberia and Sierra Leone, Tanzania's overthrow of Uganda's Idi Amin, and NATO's bombing of Serbia indicate a decline in that legitimacy. Unlike earlier centuries in Europe where the legitimacy of sovereignty rested, as Krasner argues, on "shared understanding,"[125] such consensus has largely vanished. In the case of America's 2003 intervention in Iraq, the Bush administration aimed not only to control weapons of mass destruction but also to carry out regime change.

A chasm has opened between the language and intent of the UN Charter's protection of domestic jurisdiction in Article 2, paragraph 7 and the position of UN Secretary General Kofi Annan, who declared: "As long as I am Secretary General," the United Nations, "will always place human beings at the center of everything we do." Although "fundamental sovereignty, territorial integrity, and political independence of states" continue to be a "cornerstone of the international system," sovereignty, Annan continued, cannot provide "excuses for the inexcusable."[126] Annan's view is not only endorsed by most of the world's developed states but also by an array of influential nongovernmental organizations such as Amnesty International, Doctors Without Borders, and Human Rights Watch that have emerged in recent decades as leaders in global civil society.[127]

---

[124] Ian Hurd, "Legitimacy and Authority in International Politics," *International Organization* 53:2 (Spring 1999), p. 399.
[125] Krasner, "Westphalia and All That," p. 263.
[126] Cited in Judith Miller, "Sovereignty Isn't So Sacred Anymore," *New York Times*, April 18, 1999, sec. 4, p. 4.
[127] On the question of NGO efficacy, see, for example, Wapner, *Environmental Activism and World Civic Politics*.

Historically, international law did not apply to civil wars;[128] but, as the number of intrastate wars came to be the principal statistic in global violence, the need to provide legal protection for civilians became more pressing. In addition, it has become all the more evident that in the area of human rights, the state and its agents are often the *source* of the problem rather than the *solution* to it. Increasingly, then, evolving legal practice – regardless of whether or not it violates state sovereignty – justifies humanitarian and other forms of intervention.

The technology of postinternational low-tech wars is well adapted for killing or maiming civilians. Anti-personnel mines have been especially devastating for civilians caught up in such wars. Often sown without record as to their location and without any means for their self-destruction, mines remain dangerous to civilians long after war's end. Anti-mine activists claim that there are some 110 million mines in some 64 countries, including perhaps as many as 10 million in Afghanistan alone and about 152 mines per square mile of Bosnia.[129] Roughly 60,000 Afghan children need artificial limbs as a result of mines, and some 80,000 Angolans are amputees. So widespread is the problem that an organization of former British soldiers called the Halo Trust was formed with the single task of clearing anti-personnel mines in the developing world.[130]

Statistics such as those above influenced the 1996 Conference on Conventional Weapons in Geneva to curtail the use of nondetectable plastic mines, as well as those that do not self-destruct. After additional widespread mobilization by private humanitarian groups for stronger action, in late 1997 over one hundred countries (absent, shall we say as usual, the United States, which expressed concern over defending the boundary between North and South Korea) adhered to a treaty to ban all antipersonnel mines. Those same humanitarian groups are currently involved in a campaign to end the traffic in small arms that are widely deployed with devastating results in postmodern conflicts.

In contrast to land mines, many of the high-tech innovations of recent years will, it is hoped, limit casualties and destruction in warfare. However, even these innovations have required changed rules and norms.

---

[128] Anthony Clark Arend and Robert J. Beck, *International Law and the Use of Force* (New York: Routledge, 1994).

[129] John J. Fialka, "Land Mines Prove to Be Even Harder to Detect Than They Are to Ban," *Wall Street Journal*, May 17, 1996, p. A1.

[130] Molly Moore and John Ward Anderson, "War's Young Victims," *Washington Post National Weekly Review*, May 8–14, 1995, pp. 6–7.

As Thomas W. Smith points out, humanitarian laws of war are being "recast in the light of hi-tech weapons and innovations in strategic theory." "New legal interpretations, diminished *ad bellum* rules, and an expansive view of military necessity are coalescing in a regime of legal warfare that licenses high-tech states to launch wars as long as their conduct is deemed just . . . Most striking is the use of legal language to justify the erosion of distinctions between soldiers and civilians and to legitimize collateral damage." Thomas Smith acknowledges that high-tech war "has dramatically curbed immediate civilian casualties," but he finds deeply troubling the fact that "the law sanctions infrastructural campaigns that harm long-term public health and human rights."[131]

Despite such initiatives, the incidence of violence against civilians in warfare continues to grow. This has led to even greater engagement by intergovernmental nongovernmental organizations in efforts to manage violence. Already a variety of INGOs like Doctors Without Borders provide humanitarian relief for and protect civilian victims of civil violence, and IGOs like the United Nations and its agencies, aided by regional regimes or even former colonial powers, are assuming an active interventionist role in restoring peace, promoting reconciliation in post-conflict environments, and reconstructing state institutions.[132] United Nations involvement in Somalia, Bosnia, East Timor, and Cambodia, in cooperation with INGOs, reflects the changing norm. Reluctance to take on postwar Iraqi reconstruction, in turn, again highlights US inflexibility and perhaps UN fear of its own overstretch as well.

Because sovereignty ostensibly precludes legal external interference in domestic politics, the norms regarding international responses to civil wars are much less developed than those pertaining to interstate war. They offer little more than guidelines for the variety of possible responses available to the global community to influence civil war outcomes or to remain neutral. Norms regarding the right of a state to request assistance from other states to secure itself against attack or to pursue a strategy of collective self-defense (thereby legitimating the use of force with the assistance of third parties) have left civil wars a very uncertain area of international law. This uncertainty was painfully

---

[131] Thomas W. Smith, "The New Law of War: Legitimizing Hi-Tech and Infrastructural Violence," *International Studies Quarterly* 46:3 (September 2002), p. 355.

[132] Gerald B. Helman and Steven R. Ratner, "Saving Failed States," *Foreign Policy* 89 (Winter 1992–93), advocate what they call a UN "conservatorship" in the case of failed states. William Pfaff advances the even more controversial idea of "disinterested neo-colonialism" in the case of Africa. "A New Colonialism?" *Foreign Affairs* 74:1 (January–February 1995), pp. 2–6.

apparent in the early stages of conflicts in Bosnia and Kosovo. To say the least, there remains an urgent need to articulate and establish consistent norms concerning appropriate actions for outsiders in civil wars.

It is not only the absence of institutional authority and enforcement capability that makes it difficult to achieve consensus around such norms. More serious obstacles are the absence of political will among states and the active resistance of some like Russia, China, and all too frequently the United States to allowing nonstate institutions to act authoritatively in managing the use of force during interstate, transstate, or civil violence. But there is reason for optimism. Neither human-rights norms nor the laws of war were actively enforced until the Nuremberg and Tokyo tribunals after World War II. More than a half century later, the efforts to bring war criminals to justice in Bosnia, Rwanda, and Kosovo attest to the potential for the development of sufficient political will to enforce norms and support institutional development to this end.

Conclusion: Clausewitz is history

During the Cold War, direct conflicts between the two well-armed superpower adversaries at similar levels of technological and organizational sophistication were believed to represent the greatest danger for both the participants and for humanity as a whole. The Soviet Union and the United States confronted each other with vast arsenals of nuclear weapons and large-scale conventional armies poised in potential areas of confrontation. The "standard form" battles studied in war colleges and planned for by general staffs were expected to take place in Western Europe or on the Korean peninsula. Although some prepared for regional conflicts in the Middle East or Northeast Asia, often the focus of such efforts was to limit superpower involvement, fight through proxies, and reduce the potential for escalation should US or Soviet forces become involved. High intensity, conventional war represented both the epitome of modern warfare and the least desirable possible outcome.

By contrast, for the superpowers, the "lesson" of Vietnam and of Afghanistan was, whenever possible, to avoid guerrilla wars, civil wars, and low intensity conflicts more generally. In the Persian Gulf War, the first major post-Cold War conflict, both the Iraqis and the US led coalition forces fought a set piece conventional war over territory and natural resources. The coalition was able to prosecute the war with high-tech weaponry that had been developed by the United States to fight Warsaw Pact armies in Europe under conditions for which it was ideally suited.

Yet no sooner had the Gulf War been concluded, than analysts began to argue that the nature of warfare in the 1990s and beyond was, for the most part, diverging from the models for which the superpowers had prepared during the Cold War. The Persian Gulf War was said to be an anachronism, the last large-scale conventional conflict waged between adversaries armed with Cold War era weapons. Warfare in the future would resemble the simmering conflicts in Somalia and in the former Yugoslavia that were fought between adversaries that explicitly avoided confronting one another on each other's terms. In large swathes of sub-Saharan Africa, not to mention parts of the former Soviet Union, failed states, insurgent groups, and tribal factions would, it was claimed, face off against each other largely free from the interference of the larger, better-equipped forces of the United States and Second Tier military powers.

None of these forecasts suggests that violent conflict will be less prevalent in the future. However, the interstate warfare theorized by Clausewitz is, almost literally, history. As we have observed, postinternational violence today commonly involves nonsovereign participants fighting for *anything but* reasons of state. And despite problems of coordination and the superpower role of the United States, state involvement and military planning increasingly take the form of participation in alliances such as NATO, coalitions, and/or peacekeeping and humanitarian interventions sanctioned by multilateral institutions like the United Nations. States that are lonely aggressors are even lonelier in the twenty-first century, and both low-tech and high-tech forms of violence are very different from what we used to think of as "conventional" warfare.

The developments in warfare that we have discussed will have crucial implications for global politics. Among other things, they both reflect and, more importantly, alter the relationship between governments and citizens. Soldiers may have very different ideas about how, when, and why they must fight. In short, the neat and tidy world of states, pursuing goal-directed behavior with the support of citizens is undergoing dramatic transformation. Lest we feel nostalgia, however, recall that it was that very interstate world that brought us unbridled nationalism, total war, and the threat of nuclear annihilation. Be that as it may, the erosion of state authority and the revival or intensification of identities that compete with state citizenship are at least partly responsible for the increasing frequency of warfare that bears little resemblance to Clausewitz's ideal.

8 Technology and change

Technological change has always been a factor in world history, but the rate of technological change has accelerated dramatically and especially so during the final decades of the twentieth century.[1] Such change, though crucial in producing the postinternational world, should be regarded as a *permissive* rather than a *compelling cause*; that is, it facilitates or impedes other changes like political mobilization regardless of distance.[2] Most importantly, as we have observed, technology is altering the meaning of time and space, redefining "our possible experiences of 'proximity' and 'simultaneity'."[3] Almost anyone can employ Space Imaging Inc. to take satellite photographs of any territorial space.[4] Forms of political space that are nonterritorial or are only tenuously linked to territory – like global markets, religious groupings, and professional epistemic communities – cannot be photographed but are no less real and substantial.[5] Technological change has played a leading role in devaluing territory with regard to the world economy, warfare, political mobilization, and identity formation – and thus is one of the major reasons why the task of remapping postinternational global politics is so urgently required.[6]

---

[1] It is not surprising that many IR theorists, especially those in the power tradition – given their inattention to change – largely ignore technology except for the military variety and when they do address technology, rarely treat it as an independent factor in global politics. "Technology" does not even appear in the index to Waltz's *Theory of International Politics*.
[2] Kenneth N. Waltz, *Man, the State and War* (New York: Columbia University Press, 1959), p. 233.
[3] Boyarin, "Space, Time, and the Politics of Memory," p. 13.
[4] William J. Broad, "We're Ready for Our Close-Ups Now," *New York Times*, January 16, 2000, sec. 4, p. 4.
[5] See Ferguson and Jones, *Political Space*.
[6] See also Richard W. Mansbach, "Deterritorializing Global Politics," in Donald Puchala, ed., *Visions of International Relations* (Columbia, SC: University of South Carolina Press, forthcoming).

In military affairs, distance and topography are less and less critical when real-time contemporary knowledge of a field of battle allows precision-guided munitions to locate and destroy targets such as a factory in the Sudan or a terrorist camp in Afghanistan from vast distances.[7] In economic affairs, technology fosters deterritorialized markets by enabling instantaneous transmission of information and money from almost anywhere to anywhere in the world, thereby enabling transnational corporations and banks to utilize global production and marketing strategies that, in turn, can take advantage of globalized capital markets and financial flows. The proliferation of wireless technology promises a similar impact. In identity formation, ethnic television networks carry culture and politics to their viewers in many different countries.

Van Creveld points out that there is great irony in the fact that technology, "which, between 1500 and 1945, was such a great help in constructing the state, has turned around and is often causing states to lose power in favor of various kinds of organizations which are either not territorially based, or lacking in sovereignty, or both."[8] Van Creveld argues persuasively that technological advances largely aided the spread of sovereignty *until* the spread of technologies that functioned best as networked systems – railways, telegraphs, telephones, and so forth–for which national frontiers were irrational impediments.[9] In this sense, the erosion of state authority can be dated back to the industrial revolution when networked technologies joined with the spread of education and democracy, also critical contributors in fostering a participation explosion.

What is less often recognized is the way in which technological change and a wide range of actors have always been associated, and have interacted and been somewhat mutually constitutive, throughout global history. From the humble stirrup to "Greek fire" and gunpowder, the printing press, the mechanical clock, the steam engine, the airplane, radio and television, and nuclear fission and fusion, dramatic changes in global politics have been connected with technological change and, equally important, the growth of institutions capable of effectively utilizing the new technologies.[10] The emergence of the Westphalian polity and its

---

[7] See Thomas E. Ricks, "Reliance on Cruise Missiles in Raid Signifies Weapon's New Stature," *Wall Street Journal*, August 21, 1998, p. A4.
[8] Van Creveld, *The Rise and Decline of the State*, p. 337.   [9] *Ibid.*, p. 378.
[10] For Rosenau, communication technologies have played a special role in enhancing the "skills" of people. See especially, *Distant Proximities*, ch. 10.

expansion beyond Europe's boundaries involved the exploitation of firearms and other technologies by the disciplined armies of territorial states. The technology of that epoch enabled selected secular authorities in Europe to exercise greater control over larger territorial expanses than at any time since the collapse of Rome. An "international" world emerged, featuring centralized and independent political communities whose sovereign borders constituted the most important physical and psychological boundaries among Europeans. From the steamship and modern medicines that made it possible for Europeans to penetrate previously inaccessible regions of the world to the modern armaments like the Maxim gun that they brought with them, technology was tied to the spread of the Westphalian polity. Many of the same factors, as discussed in Chapter 6, facilitated the creation of globe-girdling corporations and the emergence of genuinely global markets by the end of the nineteenth century.

The modern global transportation and communication revolutions also involved a multiplicity of actors and linkages. These revolutions have been in progress at least since the late nineteenth century, and – although state-centric theorists have failed to acknowledge this – from the outset were fostered not just by states but by other actors as well: intergovernmental organizations and firms in regimes and, increasingly, nongovernmental organizations.[11] As Liora Salter observes, the sources of present-day technology standards are almost impossible to classify and locate territorially; they are partly local, national, regional, global, and industry-by-industry. She describes the "standards regime" for communication and information technologies as a "hybrid regime": "At any moment in time, and with respect to any particular decision about a standard, it is exceptionally difficult to locate the epicenter of action, the degree to which any standard is national, local, or global in origin."[12]

The complexities of technological change

Technological change has literally shaped almost everything, from the ways in which people organize for political ends to the ways they

---

[11] Martin Hewson, "Did Global Governance Create Informational Governance?" in Hewson and Sinclair, *Approaches to Global Governance Theory*, pp. 97–115.
[12] Liora Salter, "The Standards Regime for Communication and Information Technologies," in A. Claire Cutler, Virginia Haufler, and Tony Porter, eds., *Private Authority and International Affairs* (Albany, NY: State University of New York Press, 1999), p. 117.

trade with or kill one another. It has encouraged a proliferation of nonsovereign actors that erode or share authority with territorial states. These have affected human identities and, therefore, the essential meaning of "boundaries" in global politics, and have intensified processes of political fragmentation and integration. Although we can recognize and describe some of the changes in political life wrought in part by new technologies, explaining or predicting the precise or likely impact of technology is fraught with difficulty. Luhmann captures the difficulty of making sense of the degree and implications of change from the vantage point of the present: "Every present is, as a present, sure of its own actuality. Only to the extent that the present is temporalized, that is, conceived as a difference between past and future, does a problem of securing expectations arise. The world thereby loses aspects of reliable presence and acquires aspects of mutability, aspects of 'not yet' and of 'perhaps no longer.'"[13]

There are so many timelags and contingencies. For example, we must be cautious lest we conclude that information and knowledge are the same things, because, as Edward Comor puts it, *"people learn how to select and process information into knowledge."*[14] Will genetic engineering of plants and animals be used intentionally to produce "genetic power," perhaps to sterilize an enemy's biosystem, or will it be used to create "food independence" for those for whom "food power" is a critical political concern? Will the cellular telephone prove more valuable to the enemies of global civil society, such as terrorists moving from place to place to escape detection, or to humanitarian workers in the field seeking to ease social woes? Is cyberwar the stuff of science fiction, or, as recent destructive attacks by computer hackers suggest, are we already engaged in it?

While solving some puzzles, new technologies inevitably create new ones that were not foreseen. This is highlighted in van Creveld's description of the impact of industrialization on the state:

> Dedicated to perpetual economic growth, industrial society meant change and a constant game of musical chairs as people gained or lost new employment and as fortunes were made or lost. But it also led to a vast increase in the individual's ability to move from one place to

---

[13] Niklas Luhmann, *Social Systems*, trans. John Bednarz, Jr. with Dirk Baecker (Stanford, CA: Stanford University Press, 1995), p. 310.
[14] Edward Comor, "The Role of Communication in Global Civil Society: Forces, Processes, Prospects," *International Studies Quarterly* 45:3 (September 2001), p. 392. Emphasis in original.

another; with the spread of the railroads from the 1830s on, the ties that had hitherto bound the common man to the community of his birth were broken for the first time.[15]

The uprooting process is still going on today, except that the rate of technological change has accelerated, complicating the task of making sense of what is taking place and increasing the probability of wrongheaded public policy.

Debates about the degree and novelty of globalization in today's world and the impact of technology on that process also illustrate Luhmann's point about transition and uncertainty. On the novelty question, it might be noted that the actual speed of Internet communication is not *that* much of an improvement over wireless and telephone. What has vastly changed is the cost and volume of instant communication. Likewise, most airplanes used for commerce and tourism have only gradually increased their speed, but the cost of air transport has decreased, while the number of flights and the volume of both passengers and goods has soared. Our analyses of technology are thus not only aiming at a moving target but also one that is accelerating at an almost unimaginable rate. Today, about a quarter of the world's countries do not yet have one telephone for every 100 people, let alone significant Internet service. Near-term predictions as to how quickly that situation will change are hazardous enough, let alone what the statistics will be 25 or 50 or 100 years from now. Indeed, it is almost certain that many of these now key technologies will themselves be dinosaurs long before such statistics are gathered.

Although technology has contributed to the transformation of global politics around the world and in practically all issue areas, its impact has been uneven. The postinternational world, like postmodernity itself, is more apparent in the postindustrial North (North America, Western Europe, and Japan), increasingly apparent in the Newly Industrializing Countries and Emergent Market Economies, and is least evident in the impoverished South, especially Africa and the southern periphery of the former Soviet Union.[16] But the real "digital divide" in a geographic sense, separates North America and Scandinavia, on the one hand, from the rest of the world.[17] At the same time, within Europe, Northern Europe is far more "connected" than Southern and Central

---

[15] Van Creveld, *The Rise and Decline of the State*, p. 201.
[16] See "Measuring Globalization: Economic Reversals, Forward Momentum," *Foreign Policy* 141 (March/April 2004), pp. 54–69.
[17] *Ibid.*, p. 63.

Europe, while Scandinavia and the Netherlands are well ahead of all others. The United Kingdom and Germany are coming up quickly.[18] In Latin America, Brazil, Mexico, and Argentina account for 80 percent of Internet access,[19] and there are anomalies like the fact that as of July 2001 the number of wireless telephone users in China (approaching 120 million) exceeded those in the United States.[20] By 1999 Bulgaria had more Internet users than all of sub-Saharan Africa (except South Africa), and Thailand had more cellular phones than all of Africa.[21] In Africa today, South Africa (with 2.5 million users) remains number one; all fifty-four African countries have Internet access in capital cities; and eighteen have local dial-up services nationally. There are thus significant islands of connectivity emerging even in relatively low-tech areas. While Northern and Southern Africa are experiencing some growth in access to technology, Central Africa is languishing without adequate infrastructure or any prospect for requisite economic development.[22] In the Arab Middle East most access is still only through public access terminals.[23]

Information technology and, more importantly, the capacity to make the most effective use of it are also unevenly distributed *within* societies. Cities like New York, London, Tokyo, and Singapore are information hubs and centers of information economies. However, within the United States, the divide is less geographic than a reflection of income and/or age, and the situation is changing at breakneck pace. As of 2001, 161 million persons were online, representing 58 percent of households or an increase of 15 percent in a single year. Comparable figures for African-American households are 51 percent of households and a 35 percent increase in a single year. Some 78 percent of Hispanic individuals currently use the Internet from home or elsewhere three to five times a week. In the United States (as well as Canada) female Internet users slightly exceed the number of males.[24] Only 38 percent of those persons with annual incomes less than $30,000 have Internet access versus 82 percent of those over $75.000.[25] An estimated 79 percent of

---

[18] United States Internet Council (USIC), *State of the Internet: 2001 Edition* (November 2001). Prepared by the International Technology and Trade Association Inc., p. 24.
[19] *Ibid.*, p. 40.   [20] *Ibid.*, p. 30.
[21] United Nations Development Programme, Human Development Office, *Human Development Report 1999* (New York: UNDP, 1999), p. 62.
[22] USIC, *State of the Internet: 2001 Edition*, p. 43.
[23] *Ibid.*   [24] *Ibid.*, pp. 19–20.   [25] *Ibid.*, p. 20.

18–29 year-olds have Internet access compared with a mere 15 percent over 65.[26]

Despite such variations, some further generalizations are possible and significant. The vast majority (88 percent) of the over one-half billion Internet users are in the industrialized countries,[27] and 80 percent of wireless web users are in North America and the Asia-Pacific region.[28] While English-language speakers remain the largest language group using the Internet, they declined from 51.3 percent of total users in 2000 to 45 percent in 2001. Japanese-speakers are second with 9.8 percent, and Chinese, German, and Spanish are in third, fourth, and fifth places, respectively. Chinese leap-frogged from fifth to third place in only a year (2000–01),[29] and in a few years may well be the top-ranking web language in terms of sheer numbers of users. Worldwide, not surprisingly, Internet access and other information and communication technologies are concentrated among employees of corporations, government organizations, and universities, and others with sufficient resources to purchase home computers and the services of local Internet and telephone network providers.

The consequences of technological change have clearly affected some social strata more than others, everywhere altering the lives of urban elites and expanding middle classes far faster than rural populations or those at the bottom of the economic and social ladder.[30] Differential access based on wealth and knowledge within societies, while enhancing communication among those in similar professions regardless of where they live, has had the opposite effect upon communication between rich and poor regardless of geographic proximity. But technology affects those at the bottom as well, when the media and other forms of communication make the poor painfully aware of disparities every day. In part for this reason, the poor are drawn as moths to light across the have/have not "border." Thus, it would be naïve to assume that "decentralizing and democratizing qualities of new computer technologies" will encourage users to "rise above personal, even national, self-interest and aspire to common good solutions to problems that plague the entire

---

[26] *Ibid.*   [27] *Ibid.*, p. 45.   [28] *Ibid.*, p. 55.   [29] *Ibid.*, p. 13.
[30] Edward A. Comer concludes, perhaps a bit too pessimistically: "The growing disparity in what information is becoming available to mass populations, relative to what is becoming available to elites, signals little hope that the information revolution will result in much more than the liberation of the most powerful." "Governance and the Nation-State in a Knowledge-Based Political Economy," in Hewson and Sinclair, eds., *Approaches to Global Governance Theory*, p. 129.

planet."[31] The Internet can spread hate as well as information that may facilitate cooperation.

As noted earlier, one of the most broadly observed consequences of revolutions in transportation and communication is the knitting together of the global economy. New employment opportunities have arisen in the developing world as transnational corporations move abroad and invest directly, especially in industries in which reduced labor costs and regulations offer unprecedented efficiencies. Countless new jobs have been created, albeit sometimes under "sweat-shop" conditions that, alas, often reflect traditional practices in host societies. Mexico's *maquiladoras* (mills) were globalization pioneers. Consider, too, the way in which physical distance has been overcome by new technology in India's growing role in the animation of Hollywood films and the transcription of Westerners' medical and financial records there without the knowledge of consumers. India has also used new technology to build lucrative call centers, with, as *The Economist* describes, some amusing consequences:

> Cultural distance is a bit harder to kill, especially when company and customer are talking to each other on the telephone. That is what happens at call centres, where agents handle everything from late credit-card payments to complaints about software. . . . Putting customers at their ease means talking like them and, if possible, for a few hours a day, thinking like them. For a start, you'll be hearing from Barbara (not Bhavana), even though she may be calling you at midnight her time from a cubicle in Noida, a commercial suburb of Delhi.[32]

Indeed, Thomas Friedman has asserted that it was mainly pressure from foreign IT firms and the IT ministers who now exist in every Indian state – rather than from the US government – that caused India to back away from war with Pakistan in May 2002.[33]

Modern forms of transportation and communication have facilitated the movement of persons and things, and, unfortunately, also the spread of disease, a fact brought home when in 1999 a West Nile-like virus first struck New York, killing four people.[34] That disease may have arrived

[31] Howard Frederick, "Social and Industrial Policy for Public Networks," in L. M. Harasim, ed., *Global Networks: Computers and International Communication* (Cambridge, MA: MIT Press, 1993), p. 286.

[32] "It's Barbara Calling," *The Economist*, April 29–May 5, 2000, p. 61.

[33] Thomas L. Friedman, "India, Pakistan and G. E.," *New York Times Online*, August 11, 2002.

[34] Andrew C. Revkin, "Mosquito Virus Exposes the Hole in the Safety Net," *New York Times*, October 4, 1999, pp. A1, A25.

in a mosquito hitching a ride on a jet or in an exotic bird smuggled into the United States or perhaps, as is now conjectured, might be at least partially a product of a globalized market for organ transplants. "Bioinvasion"[35] is one decidedly unwelcome consequence of globalization. In recent decades, the Asian long-horned beetle, the Mediterranean fruit fly, and the Giant African snail have made their way across great distances to the United States where they threaten major agricultural industries. In the early 1970s Newcastle disease carried by parrots from South America resulted in a giant poultry kill, and in the 1980s importation of Zebra mussels from Eastern Europe caused billions of dollars in damages to pipes and pumps, especially in the Great Lakes. And the spread of hoof and mouth disease along with the publicity given to "mad cow" disease have helped to convert numerous Europeans to vegetarianism. Most recently, the SARS epidemic highlighted both how easily new diseases can be spread and how effectively they can be identified and controlled by medical experts working in tandem with governments and the WHO.

Can anyone say with reasonable certainty which of the technological innovations of recent decades will ultimately have the greatest impact on global politics? Will it be the Human Genome Project[36] and the new science of genetic engineering? On the one hand, genetic engineering promises greater crop yields and new treatments for ancient and unfamiliar diseases. On the other, some fear that genetically modified plants or fish will eliminate native species and dangerously reduce the gene pool and biodiversity. Europeans shudder at "Frankenfood" and "Frankenfish," and seek to keep out genetically modified grain and hormone-injected cattle grown in the United States. At the same time, molecular farming or "biopharming" offers the prospect of "growing" useful drugs in plants,[37] reducing current chemical levels in the soil, and greater productivity. Or, will the most important technological innovation prove to be the science of lasers, which offers the possibility of anti-ballistic missile defenses and is already providing new forms of rapid communication and precision medical devices?

[35] Christopher Bright, "Invasive Species: Pathogens of Globalization," *Foreign Policy* 116 (Fall 1999), p. 51.
[36] See Rick Weiss, "A Brave New World in Biology," *Washington Post National Weekly Edition*, June 5, 2000, p. 9.
[37] Andrew Pollack, "New Ventures Aim to Put Farms in the Pharmaceutical Vanguard," *New York Times*, May 14, 2000, sec. 1, pp. 1, 18. See William D. Coleman and Melissa Gabler, "Agricultural Biotechnology and Regime Formation: A Constructivist Assessment," *International Studies Quarterly* 46:4 (December 2002), pp. 481–506.

What will be the eventual effect of these advancing technologies? Will they prove a boon for human progress, or will unforeseen consequences threaten new types of disasters? Some of these questions cannot be answered for decades, if at all. Thus, almost sixty years after the first and last (so far) use of nuclear weapons, heated argument continues over whether they were a blessing for mankind by preventing war among major powers or whether they should be eliminated in order to preclude some future nuclear Armageddon. Like nuclear energy, technology most of the time is potentially a double-edged sword. Karen Litfin observes that earth remote sensing (ERS) technology simultaneously gives sovereign states better data-gathering capabilities, and nonsovereign actors – monitoring state performance in the context of their own objectives and various environmental regimes – better information about what governments are or are not doing. ERS also may generate the data required to justify further global controls to secure a viable future global environment. Litfin sums up the evaluative problem:

> While the transparency and globality associated with ERS technologies very often deterritorialize state practices, they are also capable of bolstering the state's territorial control, even for developing countries. Most ERS technologies and data remain under the control of the state, not nonstate actors. Yet information is slippery, and ERS data appears to be helping local environmental and indigenous groups to reterritorialize their political practices in ways that challenge the state, thereby reconfiguring epistemic authority.[38]

As the foregoing implies, it is impossible for us to do justice here to all the ways in which technological change is involved in the transformation of an international to a postinternational world. We will, therefore, focus in the remainder of this chapter on one: the Internet or Worldwide Web.[39] The Internet is revolutionizing the ways we communicate and do business with one another, but beyond that little consensus exists. Will the microelectronic revolution help to create a more democratic world, or will it facilitate authoritarianism? Does that revolution augur an era of growing global civic society and new "thinking spaces" – or burgeoning chaos? Central to what follows is whether or not the microelectronics

---

[38] Karen T. Litfin, "Environmental Remote Sensing, Global Governance, and the Territorial State," in Hewson and Sinclair, eds., *Approaches to Global Governance Theory*, p. 90.
[39] For a history of the Internet, see Katie Hafner and Matthew Lyons, *Where Wizards Stay Up Late: The Origins of the Internet* (New York: Simon & Schuster, 1996).

revolution is, on balance, undermining or reinforcing the authority and capacity of territorial states.

The Internet and the erosion of state control

In many ways, technological developments, including the Internet, may be undermining both the internal and external faces of state sovereignty. Many of these developments, including the Internet, contribute to both globalization and localization, and pose a management problem for states.[40] Many argue that the Net diminishes the role of territory and physical location, as well as political hierarchy, because, as Paul Frissen observes, with "distributed and relational databases it no longer matters where an organisation or an administrative layer is located." "The globe is a village and the village is global. . . . The trend towards 'deterritorialisation' produced by ICTs [information and communications technologies] . . . undermines the legitimacy of a political system which is territory-bound and which receives support on the basis of elections held in a territory."[41] The foregoing, of course, makes the not always justified assumption that the political system of a state enjoys legitimacy and that effective elections are held; also, on the other side, that an organization is willing to forgo the value of face-to-face meetings and local networking.

Others agree with Martin Dodge that "the idea that the Internet liberates you from geography is a myth."[42] His conclusion arises from requirements such as fiberoptic cables, "server-farms," reliable electricity to run e-businesses, and a nearby telephone exchange in order for a high-speed digital-subscriber line connection to work. Such facilities require a territorial location and, as a result, are vulnerable to destruction. In addition, identifying users is becoming easier, and states are attempting to acquire both the legal and technological means to censor effectively what is communicated across their frontiers.[43]

Let us sift through the implications of these conflicting claims for several of the dimensions of global politics.

---

[40] Brian D. Loader, "The Governance of Cyberspace: Politics, Technology and Global Restructuring," in Brian D. Loader, ed., *The Governance of Cyberspace: Politics, Technology, and Global Restructuring* (London: Routledge, 1997), p. 9.
[41] Paul Frissen, "The Virtual State: Postmodernisation, Informatisation and Public Administration," in Loader, ed., *The Governance of Cyberspace*, pp. 114–115.
[42] Cited in "Putting it in its Place," *The Economist*, August 11–17, 2001, p. 18.
[43] *Ibid.*, pp. 18–20.

The Internet, the market, and national economies

The Internet is a major factor in economic globalization, especially the growing reach of global capital, bond, and trading markets; the instantaneous movement of funds; and the rapid reaction of markets to events. "The information revolution," write Keohane and Nye, "is at the heart of economic and social globalization" and "has made possible the transnational organization of work and the expansion of markets, thereby facilitating a new international division of labor."[44] The key, they argue, is not the growing "velocity" of information but its reduced cost. Held, too, sees global markets as reflecting "a clear disjuncture between the formal authority of the state and the spatial reach of contemporary systems of production, distribution and exchange which often function to limit the competence and effectiveness of national political authorities." Held argues that new information and communications technology "radically increases the scope of economic interconnectedness" and "enables the rapid intensification of patterns of interconnectedness."[45]

The growing role of the Internet in the global economy also undermines contemporary understandings of the distinction between what is "public" and what is "private." In Stephen J. Kobrin's view, the "major dimension of the postmodern world economy, the digitalization of commerce and the emergence of global electronic networks, also makes the public-private distinction problematic." He asks: "Is the Internet a public or private 'public utility?' It was created with public funds, but is now entirely managed – if that word is appropriate – privately. Attempts to exert public control over content . . . have been less than resounding successes."[46]

There are other significant Internet challenges to state autonomy and control of economic life. Consider just two illustrations, e-cash and intellectual property. The growing use of electronic or e-cash, Kobrin describes, involves a world of digital value units (dvus) "issued – actually created – by a large number of institutions, bank and nonbank."[47] The growing importance of cyberspace, concludes Kobrin, necessarily erodes the capacity of states anchored in territory. "The fundamental

---

[44] Robert O. Keohane and Joseph S. Nye, Jr., "Globalization: What's New? What's Not (And So What?)," *Foreign Policy* 118 (Spring 2000), p. 113.
[45] David Held, *Democracy and the Global Order: From the Modern State to Cosmopolitan Governance* (Stanford, CA: Stanford University Press, 1995), pp. 127, 128.
[46] Kobrin, "Back to the Future," p. 380.
[47] Stephen J. Kobrin, "Electronic Cash and the End of National Markets," *Foreign Policy* 107 (Summer 1997), p. 68.

problems that e-cash poses for governance result from this discon-
nect between electronic markets and political geography."[48] E-cash
does away with the need to move funds physically across borders,
whether by drug smugglers or currency speculators. E-commerce, paid
for with debit and credit cards, complicates dramatically the collection
of national taxes or tariffs imposed on goods moving across national
frontiers. And the capability of governments to trace financial flows will
be degraded as long as public-key encryption is not halted. E-cash also
makes it more difficult for central banks to monitor and control money
supply. It additionally makes foreign exchange transactions obsolete,
impedes enforcement of financial reserve and reporting requirements,
makes national income data less and less useful, widens the gap between
rich and poor, and eliminates traditional seigniorage.[49]

The Internet also undermines the ability of states to protect citizens'
and corporations' intellectual property, thereby threatening to jettison
years of arduous negotiations in the GATT and the WTO. One young
software programmer has designed a program called Freenet that he
claims will, by eliminating the need for a central database to acquire cultural material, make it impossible for anyone to control the dissemination of digital information – music, video, text or software.[50] Its designer
is intentionally trying to attack copyright law and facilitate intellectual
piracy. "If this whole thing catches on," he declares, "I think that people
will look back in 20 to 40 years and look at the idea that you can own
information in the same way as gold or real estate in the same way we
look at witch burning today."[51]

Free access to information is attractive to many individuals who
enjoy such access, but it simultaneously erodes the capacity for collective action for effective public policies even in democratic societies in
which citizens are presumed to have influence.[52] States and their agents
have few tools to protect intellectual property, just as they are unable
to prevent destructive capital flight and currency speculation, and find
their very territoriality a handicap when it comes to managing transnational economic entities. They must shudder at Cerny's provocative

---

[48] *Ibid.*, p. 75.   [49] *Ibid.*, pp. 71–74.
[50] John Markoff, "The Concept of Copyright Fights for Internet Survival," *New York Times*,
May 10, 2000, pp. A1, C23.
[51] Cited in *ibid.*, p. C23.
[52] For an analysis of this issue that focuses on multilateral economic institutions, see
Robert O'Brien, Anne Marie Goetz, Jan Aart Scholte, and Marc Williams, *Contesting Global
Governance: Multilateral Economic Institutions and Global Social Movements* (Cambridge:
Cambridge University Press, 2000).

conclusion "that the more economies of scale of dominant goods and assets diverge from the structural scale of the national state – and the more that these divergences feed back into each other in complex ways – then the more the authority, legitimacy, policymaking capacity and policy-implementing effectiveness of the state will be eroded and undermined both without and within."[53]

Information gatekeepers

The fact that states are having increasing difficulty controlling their national economies is part and parcel of a larger problem, the fact that they can no longer act as effectively as in the past as gatekeepers for information crossing their frontiers.[54] The printing press contributed to weakening the Church's dominant position in Europe and to the success of the Reformation. The ability to control the main channels of social communication subsequently became an important source of state power. For hundreds of years, for better or for worse, governments were able to influence the perceptions and beliefs of citizens by filtering much of the information available to them. Especially but not solely in wartime, governments have been able to use technologies such as the printed word, radio, film, and television to define patriotism, promote domestic unity, and encourage amity or enmity toward "others." Putschists and coup organizers knew that it was necessary to seize radio and television stations and the central post office immediately if they were to stand any chance of wresting control from those in power.

But change in communications technology is relentless. The overthrow of Iran's Shah was facilitated by the distribution of tapes with speeches by the Ayatollah Ruhollah Khomeini. The proliferation of ditto and mimeographic machines and photocopiers helped to decentralize information production and dissemination, and for this reason, the Soviet Union refused to permit the unrestricted importation of copying machines. In 1989 Chinese democracy protesters made extensive use of facsimile machines to spread the news about what was happening in Beijing's Tiananmen Square. CNN broadcast much of it. Today, the Internet further decentralizes information production, and networking dramatically empowers social groups like Mexico's Zapatistas or

---

[53] Philip G. Cerny, "Globalization and the Changing Logic of Collective Action," *International Organization* 49:4 (Autumn 1995), p. 621.
[54] For a discussion of the impact of a new generation of privately owned commercial imaging satellites in providing nonsovereign groups with direct information, see "Private Eyes in the Sky," *The Economist*, May 6–12, 2000, pp. 71–73, and Broad, "We're Ready for Our Close-Ups Now," p. 4.

Canada's Cree Indians living on James Bay in relation to their governments. Cyberspace "is especially useful in developing student movements, now that so many universities provide access to the Internet."[55]

The threat to state control of information is, of course, not new. Transborder radio broadcasts and efforts to jam them were important both during World War II and the Cold War. However, in recent decades the problem for states has been greatly exacerbated by the sheer pace of technological change, and it is especially troublesome for authoritarian regimes. Nowhere is this more the case than in China, which simultaneously wants to retain central party control over ideas and ideology, while recognizing the importance of new communications technologies for economic development. As long as television, radio, and the press were the sole sources of news, it was relatively easy for the regime to control the dissemination of information. For years, the regime worried about satellite transmissions and sought to restrict satellite-delivered TV service to hotels and residential complexes for foreigners.[56] Cable operators in China are not permitted to carry foreign satellite programs. However, an incident in which news of the death of China's director of the State Administration of Foreign Exchange was leaked in an anonymous posting in a chat room on a popular web site illustrates how the Internet can be a source of news that other Chinese media will not provide.[57]

The Internet poses unprecedented problems for state control of information in China – where there were 26 million users as of summer 2001, 17 million more than in 1999[58] – and the Chinese government has tried hard to regulate this technology. One China scholar summarizes the dilemma confronting China's leadership: "The Chinese Government has made the decision that it wants to continue to advance information technology. They recognize the challenges that it is going to pose for them, but they think that it is too important to their economic modernization to stop. What they are trying to do obviously is to control it." However: "It is important to remember that the Internet can serve

[55] "Arachnophilia," *The Economist*, August 10–16, 1996, p. 28.
[56] Chinese officials had largely turned a blind eye to the proliferation of satellite dishes and decoders, but enforcement of these laws intensified significantly with the approach of the tenth anniversary of the Tiananmen Square massacre. Mark Landler, "China Cracks Down on Foreign Satellite Transmissions," *New York Times*, May 8, 1999, p. A8.
[57] Elisabeth Rosenthal, "Chinese Monetary Official Dies in Fall From 7th-Story Window," *New York Times*, May 13, 2000, p. 17.
[58] Jennifer Lee, "US May Help Chinese Evade Net Censorship," *New York Times on the Web*, August 30, 2001, nytimes.com/2001/08/30/technology/30VOIC.html.

government's purposes, too. It's not always going to be a force for positive change from our perspective."[59] After all, in the words of a partner
at Pricewaterhouse Coopers: "The Chinese government has always had
a strong interest in managing information. And also, the government
has a strong commercial interest in the Net; it's a major owner."[60]

Chinese officials recognize that the Internet can cut more than one
way. It may serve as a government propaganda tool and has been used
to organize and publicize popular discontent, as it did at the time of
the 2001 incident in which a US surveillance aircraft collided with a
Chinese military aircraft near Hainan. Yet the Internet is also a threat to
the regime. The *People's Daily* has an Internet division that weeds out
criticisms of the Communist Party. Announcing that the government
would monitor Internet sites, China's Information Minister declared:
"We will not allow the introduction of trash that is harmful to the people."[61] An observer at the *People's Daily* captured the essence of the
official dilemma: "The Internet is very international, and with the Net
you really cannot construct obstacles to prevent people from knowing
things. So often it's better that we inform people about something rather
than have them learn about it elsewhere. But we stand on behalf of the
Chinese government, and in some areas it is better for us to keep quiet."
Chat rooms rouse special concern. "We don't worry too much about
news items. It's the chat rooms that make us really nervous. Especially
around sensitive days, like June 4 [the anniversary of the massacre in
Tiananmen Square], we have to screen very carefully, since you never
know what will appear."[62]

Government regulation of the Internet is not easy anywhere, including China. Many Chinese users know how to use proxy servers that
hide the site being served. Beijing tries to censor the Net by using filtering technologies such as that developed by Sun Microsoft to create
"intranet" in which users would have unlimited access to one another
but only screened links to the world beyond, and it has diverted viewers to "friendly" search engines.[63] China currently filters the Worldwide
Web through central computers, sometimes impeding access to selected
sites. One observer views the China Wide Web as "an attempt to create

[59] Cited in Barbara Crossette, "The Internet Changes Dictatorship's Rules," *New York Times*, August 1, 1999, sec. 4, pp. 1, 16.
[60] Cited in Elisabeth Rosenthal, "Web Sites Bloom in China, and Are Weeded," *New York Times*, December 23, 1999, p. A10.
[61] Cited in *ibid.*, p. A10.   [62] Cited in *ibid.*
[63] Joseph Kahn, "China Seems to Refine Bid to Restrict Web Access," *New York Times on the Web*, September 14, 2002, nytimes.com/2002/14/international/asia/14CHIN.html.

a Web that is isolated from the Net."[64] For its part, the United States is working with private firms through its International Broadcasting Bureau to add additional "privacy servers" (computers that disguise web sites a user is viewing) in order to impede Chinese censorship efforts.[65]

The Chinese government issued Computer Information Systems Internet Secrecy Administrative Regulations that sought to limit the release of information on the Internet, including a prohibition against disseminating so-called "state secrets." The regulations covered chat rooms, electronic mail, and Internet sites that are required to submit to "examination and approval by the appropriate secrecy work offices."[66] Whoever puts an item on the Internet, whether the original source or not, is responsible for it. "Any information provided to or issued on Internet Web sites must obtain the inspection and approval of secrecy censorship."[67] Another regulation requires those who use encryption software to register with the government. How successful enforcement of such measures will be remains to be seen.

China's government showed its teeth when it charged one Lin Hai, a computer engineer, with "inciting subversion of state power,"[68] for sending 30,000 Chinese e-mail addresses to an electronic publication in the United States called *VIP Reference*. Lin was found guilty and sentenced to two years in prison.[69] *VIP Reference* is compiled by Chinese democracy advocates in Washington, DC, providing information to about 250,000 e-mail accounts in China. Lin's prosecutors argued that the names he provided had been used to distribute "large numbers of articles aimed at inciting subversion of state power and the socialist system."[70] The case reflected how seriously Chinese officials regard the potential for disruptive electronic protest. In a comment that would resonate elsewhere as well, the publisher of *VIP Reference* declared that:

---

[64] Cited in Mark Landler, "Bringing China on Line (With Official Blessing)," *New York Times*, August 3, 1998, p. C 3. Foreign investors such as America Online and Netscape Communications oppose such isolation.
[65] Lee, "US May Help Chinese Evade Net Censorship."
[66] Cited in Elisabeth Rosenthal, "China Lists Controls to Restrict the Use of E-Mail and Web," *New York Times*, January 27, 2000, pp. A1, A12.
[67] Cited in *ibid.*
[68] Cited in Erik Eckholm, "A Trial Will Test China's Grip on the Internet," *New York Times*, November 16, 1998, p. A1.
[69] Seth Faison, "E-Mail to US Lands Chinese Internet Entrepreneur in Jail," *New York Times*, January 21, 1999, p. A10.
[70] Cited in *ibid.*

"We're posing a new problem for the Communists. I don't think there's any way they can stop us."[71]

Mobilization of political and social protest

Groups not only utilize the Internet to express political and ideological positions; they also use it to mobilize and coordinate activities, often against existing regimes. The Web is invaluable for mobilizing those with common aims who are geographically dispersed, whether anti-globalization protesters against the WTO in Seattle[72] or the remarkably successful campaign for a Land Mines Treaty. Another example is the Free Burma Coalition, consisting of Burmese exiles scattered in a host of countries. "BurmaNet" provides press coverage of events within the country and a means for the exchange of ideas among those who oppose its military junta. The regime's opponents use the information it disseminates to apply pressure on Western corporations to cease doing business in Burma. Similarly, a UN report observes: "Socially excluded and minority groups have created cyber-communities to find strength in on-line unity and fight the silence on abuses of their rights. In India DATPERS, the Dalit and Tribal People Electronic Resource Site, exposes the exclusion of 250 million low-caste people, coordinating international human rights campaigns and keeping the community in touch."[73] In a sense, the Internet makes it possible for such groups to exist in cyberspace rather than on any particular national territory – or, perhaps better, to exist in many national territories simultaneously. In the absence of the Internet, they could not exist at all. Thus: "Information and communication technologies (ICTs), primarily the Internet, have facilitated new forms of expression and connection among groups and the growth of new public spaces which are not easily controlled by states and ruling elites."[74]

---

[71] Cited in *ibid.* A second service, *Tunnel*, is written in China, sent electronically to the United States, and then returned electronically to recipients back in China. A third publication, *Public Opinion*, is produced and distributed electronically from inside China. It carries commentaries and reprinted items from the Internet.

[72] See "Lori's War," *Foreign Policy* 118 (Spring 2000), pp. 29–55. For analysis of the use of the Internet to mobilize opinion against the Multilateral Agreement on Investment, see Ronald J. Deibert, "International Plug 'n Play? Citizen Activism, the Internet, and Global Public Policy," *International Studies Perspectives* 1:3 (December 2000), pp. 255–272.

[73] *Human Development Report 1999*, p. 59.

[74] Peter J. Smith and Elizabeth Smythe, "Sleepless in Seattle: Challenging the WTO in a Globalizing World," paper presented at the Annual Meeting of the International Science Association, Chicago, February 2001, p. 3.

Technology is promoting a continually expanding array of non-sovereign actors, which constitute a more complex global civil society and play an increasing role in global governance.[75] The "world-wide web," declares Richard Falk, allows for an empowerment of globalization-from-below in a manner that seems presently difficult to subdue or ignore."[76] The effect is local as well as global. For instance, in 1998, the Environmental Defense Fund built the web site www.scorecard.org as a way of identifying industrial polluters. At the site, anyone can find out which firms are polluting a neighborhood and can protest instantly. A viewer can enter a zip code, get access to a list of the leading sources of pollution in his or her area, and obtain a draft letter to send to the polluter or to the US Environmental Protection Agency (EPA). "Ranking neighbourhood polluters is only a fraction of what Scorecard offers. You can rank offenders by industry or by type of pollution: Scorecard will generate league tables of carcinogen producers, animal-waste dumpers, and so on."[77]

The Internet obviously plays a rapidly expanding role in the mobilization and dissemination of political protest *within* as well as *across* states. In April 1999, a previously little known quasi-religious meditation and exercise group known as Falun Gong staged a massive silent protest around the Beijing compound housing China's communist leaders to protest government efforts aimed at limiting its autonomy. What frightened China's leaders was that the group had organized and coordinated its activities by means of e-mail without arousing suspicion or alerting the country's extensive surveillance system.[78] "Wednesday's demonstrators," reported the *Wall Street Journal*, "were mobilized by computer messages and loosely organized local networks of followers after Beijing began a wide-spread crackdown on the group Tuesday."[79] "China," reported the *New York Times*, "has been caught off guard by a vast, silent, virtually invisible movement (if not exactly a revolution) that came together not on the streets but on the Internet."[80] Events the

---

[75] John King Gamble and Charlotte Ku, "International Law – New Actors and New Technologies: Center Stage for NGOs?" Paper delivered to the 39th Annual International Studies Association Conference, 17–21 March 1998, Minneapolis, MN.
[76] Richard A. Falk, *Predatory Globalization: A Critique* (Cambridge: Polity Press, 1999), p. 6.
[77] "www.democracy.com," *The Economist*, April 3–9, 1999, p. 28.
[78] The Chinese state satellite-launching company recently announced that China plans to launch a television satellite that can block attempts by Falun Gong protesters to hijack its signals (NYTimes.com AP dispatch October 24, 2002).
[79] Leslie Chang, "Thousands Arrested as China Protests Escalate," *Wall Street Journal*, July 22, 1999, A20.
[80] Crossette, "The Internet Changes Dictatorship's Rules," p. 1.

previous year, when leaders of the China Democracy Party were arrested, had already alerted Chinese officials to the potential danger of the Internet. One commentator observed:

> The thing that was so threatening was certainly not the number of people, but rather that this was inter-provincial, that in over two-thirds of Chinese provinces, the China Democracy Party was able to establish branches. And this was explicitly political in the way that Falun Gong is not. The China Democracy Party still exists. It's still there, and it can emerge at any time because of the Internet.[81]

More recently, the banned Falun Gong has successfully hijacked Chinese satellite transmissions in order to transmit anti-government material throughout China.[82]

Other striking examples of reformers' use of the Internet to publicize grievances and agitate for change are in South Korea and Serbia. Koreans, of whom over a quarter have Internet access, according to reform advocate Park Byung Ok, "have realized that politicians will not bring about reforms of their own accord. Civic groups like ours are creating an avenue for people to vent their frustrations and demand change."[83] Park's Internet home page gets about 50,000 visitors each day. Reformers use the Internet to coordinate activities in ways that would have been unthinkable even a few years ago. In January 2000, more than 500 reform-minded groups merged online under the umbrella of "Citizens' Solidarity."

In Serbia, students, faculty, professionals, and journalists were pioneers in using the Internet to organize anti-government protests. When the Milošević regime closed down the independent radio station B-92 in 1996, the station's supporters launched an effective and massive online protest. No sooner was B-92's radio signal cut, than protesters flooded the mailboxes of European government officials, NGOs, and foreign media with the news of the blackout, and an Internet campaign was launched on behalf of the radio station. With the media shutdown, the Internet became a key source of information about events in Belgrade. The experience made protesters aware of the potential power of the

---

[81] Cited in *ibid.*, p. 1.
[82] Joseph Kahn, "China Says Sect Broadcasting from Taiwan," *New York Times*, September 25, 2002, nytimes.com/2002/09/25/intern . . . /25CHIN.html.
[83] Cited in Howard W. French, "Internet Recharges Reformers in Korea," *New York Times*, February 29, 2000, p. A10.

Internet.[84] Thereafter, the radio station arranged with the Amsterdam-based access service XS4ALL to broadcast its programming in digital form on the Internet, thereby allowing anyone with access to hear the radio's news over audio links. "The irony is," declared the head of B-92's Internet service, "that the Government meant to silence us, but instead forced us to build on a whole new technology to stay alive. The drive to close us down has given us a tool to vastly expand our audience."[85]

The erosion of national culture

Another of the principal means by which a state perpetuates itself is by identifying with a national cultural tradition that enhances its histori-cal and psychological legitimacy, differentiates "us" from "them," and anchors loyalties. Such traditions – built on religion, language, mythol-ogy, literature and poetry, historical events, ways of dress, and so forth – provide a normative environment and define the moral community. To the extent traditions are challenged or diluted, or are divorced from states, state legitimacy may be eroded, or at least this is what many offi-cials fear. Declares David Rothkopf: "The gates of the world are groaning shut. From marble balconies and over the airwaves, demagogues decry new risks to ancient cultures and traditional values. . . . To many people 'foreign' has become a synonym for 'danger'."[86] The reaction of tradi-tional elites to globalized culture and changing identities contribute to what Huntington believes is a larger "clash of civilizations."[87] Of course, one of the fault lines in Huntington's civilizations are the states within them, whose elites adopt different positions on the issue of challenges to tradition and what the response should be.

Quite apart from states – whether through television, radio, or, increasingly, the Internet – people learn that there are others not only "unlike themselves" but (perhaps more importantly) also "like them-selves," about whom they had known little or nothing before and with whom they can now communicate. New categories of "us" and "them" are made available for political mobilization and action. As the new microelectronic technologies provide knowledge about nonstate identities and facilitate communication among those who share these

---

[84] Chris Hedges, "Serbs' Answer to Tyranny? Get on the Web," *New York Times*, December 8, 1996, sec. 1, p. 1.
[85] Cited in *ibid.*, p. 8.
[86] David Rothkopf, "In Praise of Cultural Imperialism?" *Foreign Policy* 107 (Summer 1997), p. 38.
[87] Huntington, "The Clash of Civilizations?" p. 34.

identities regardless of physical distance, competition between transnational and subnational identities with that of citizen/national intensifies.

Canadian and French leaders were concerned about cultural invasion long before the Internet, and Chinese and American politicians have tried, with limited success, to control politically sensitive and pornographic materials sent by electronic mail. Chinese and Iranian leaders have outlawed (but not eliminated) satellite dishes that give access to material they believe to be antithetical to the political and moral foundations of their authority. Local leaders fear that women and young people are especially susceptible to the attractions of Western materialism and individualism and that the conservative and stabilizing doctrines of religion and party may be swept aside.

In Iran, debate over access to the Internet is part of the ongoing struggle between modernizers and conservative theocrats.[88] The ayatollahs fear that pornography and secularism will erode the basis of their Koranic theocracy. Western "propaganda" (especially ideas about secularism and democracy) and information from regime opponents are the special concerns of Iran's mullahs. "There is," declared Iran's Deputy Foreign Minister, "stuff on the Internet that people have access to that is as offensive as 'The Satanic Verses' and it is updated every day."[89] The fear of Iran's theocrats that cultural invasion imperils their grip on the urban young led them to ban satellite dishes in 1995, but Iranian scientists and clerics want access to the Internet for their own purposes. The government is trying to find a compromise under which all access to the Internet would be centralized through the Ministry of Posts and Telecommunications, but Iran's liberalizers resist this effort, especially university students and faculty who the mullahs fear might become a focus of opposition to their control. "The brains of the young are very impressionable," declared one official, "so the Mujahedeen Khalq might be able to brainwash people, or they might be able to influence an election."[90]

Even in Japan, the Internet is altering customary ways of doing things. Japanese women may be among the principal beneficiaries of this change. Over a quarter of Japan's 14 million Web users are women, and the Internet is especially helpful to them as regards finding child

---

[88] Neil MacFarquhar, "With Mixed Feelings, Iran Tiptoes to Internet," *New York Times*, October 8, 1996, p. A4.
[89] Cited in *ibid*. In 1989, the Ayatollah Khomeini issued a *fatwah* demanding the death of Salman Rushdie, author of *The Satanic Verses*.
[90] Cited in *ibid*.

care and care for the elderly. Even more important, according to one observer: "The business practice of face-to-face negotiation and drinking sake together into the night has made it difficult for women to advance in the business world. But as more business relationships go online, business dealings should become much more professional."[91]

Some democratic societies also fear the corrosive effects of cultural homogenization. In no region is that clearer than in North America, where democratic Canada and Mexico have long worried about vulnerability to American cultural dominance. Canada demanded and received a "cultural exemption" in its 1988 free-trade agreement with the United States. Nevertheless, American television satellites transmit signals into Canada and Mexico when beaming programs from space, and Ottawa has resisted American efforts to legalize this "gray market."[92] "Satellites," writes one journalist, "are sloppy. When they beam down television programs from outer space to home satellite dishes in the United States, they tend to spill signals all over such artificial landmarks as national borders, a bit of physics that hundreds of thousands of avid television watchers in Canada and Mexico have come to discover."[93] Consumers in both Canada and the United States have purchased small satellite dishes and have subscribed to pirated services. In November 1996, Mexican regulators agreed for economic reasons to permit US services to enter into Mexico, but Canada continues to resist, fearing the dilution of Canadian cultural autonomy. Ottawa insists that half of all television programming be Canadian, although it lacks its own satellite service. Thus, perhaps as many as 200,000 Canadians are violating Canadian law by tuning in to US satellite programming. In addition, Canada has sought to limit American advertising in split-run editions of American magazines. Other efforts to restrict the circulation of American magazines date back to 1956 when the Canadian government proposed a special excise tax aimed at *Reader's Digest* and *Time*.[94]

And in democratic Israel, the Knesset voted to require that half the songs on national radio stations be sung in Hebrew. The nationalist reasoning that lay behind this requirement was evident in the

[91] Cited in Stephanie Strom, "Use of the Internet Slowly Transforms Japan's Way of Life," *New York Times*, May 14, 2000, sec. 1, p. 10.
[92] Anthony DePalma, "Space, the TV Frontier Now," *New York Times*, December 30, 1996, pp. C1, C2.
[93] John Markoff, "US Fails to Win Global Accord on Police Internet Eavesdropping, *New York Times*, March 27, 1997, pp. A1, C3.
[94] "What You Read Is What You Are?" *The Economist*, February 6–12, 1999, p. 36.

comments of one of its advocates who declared: "We are putting up a protective wall against the flood of foreign culture. The country is 50 years old. Its culture has yet to be formed, and we thought it should be protected." "Part of the essence of setting up an independent state," he added, "was to establish our own culture here. The bill is a cultural statement."[95]

Dissemination of extremism and hate

In some respects, the free flow of opinion is a healthy sign of an existing or emerging democratic order. In the words of a specialist on free speech issues: "[The Internet is] an obvious, cost-effective way to put your material and thoughts out there, not only to communicate with the world but also to communicate your legitimacy."[96] Under some conditions, however, the Internet can become a dangerous threat to social order. For extremists and those advocating violence or perversion, the Internet provides a means of communicating views and recruiting like-minded individuals.

Racist groups, child pornographers, and others whose views go beyond offensive to intolerable have made effective use of the Internet to attract an audience. "It wasn't very long ago," declares Kenneth McVay, director of the Nizkor Project, "that Nazis and skinheads wouldn't get any mainstream press. They had to do their own dog-and-pony show. But they couldn't reach any serious market. Along comes the Internet and not only do they have access to potentially 70 million people, but they can get it for next to nothing."[97] The Internet has become "an easy, so far legal, cheap, convenient and accessible vehicle"[98] for disseminating anti-Semitism and White Supremicist ideas. Other groups including gays, Christians, and women have also have been targeted by bigots.[99] In sum, as reported by the Anti-Defamation League: "Before the Internet, many extremists worked in relative isolation, forced to make a great effort to connect with others who shared their ideology. Today, on the Internet, bigots communicate easily. . . .

[95] Cited in Joel Greenberg, "Israel Battles New Foreign Foe: Music," *New York Times*, December 20, 1998, sec. 1, p. 10.
[96] Cited in Tom Vogel and Matt Moffett, "Radical Groups Spread the Word On-Line," *Wall Street Journal*, June 6, 1997, p. A8.
[97] Cited in *ibid*.
[98] Cited in "Internet Central to Spread Anti-Semitism – Study," *The New York Times on the Web*, May 1, 2000, www.nytimes.com/reuters/international/international-inyrtne.html.
[99] "Downloading Hate," *The Economist*, November 13–19, 1999, pp. 30–31.

Extremists have found a secure forum in which to exchange ideas and plans."[100]

Radical groups use the Internet to communicate directly with supporters, publicize their views and actions, and, in general, advance their agendas. During the 1997 Tupac Maru hostage crisis at the Japanese ambassador's residence in Lima, Peru, Tupac supporters used the Internet to send out daily propaganda. Among the most electronically sophisticated of today's radical groups are Latin American guerrilla movements, including Mexico's Zapatistas and Colombia's Revolutionary Armed Forces. Some Latin American governments have belatedly tried to limit the access enjoyed by extremists to the Net. Thus, in 1996, Mexican authorities shut down a web page run through a Mexican server by Colombia's Revolutionary Armed Forces.[101]

Since 9/11, of course, the world has become increasingly aware of the extent to which the new technologies, including cell phones and Internet and even satellite television, serve terrorists and criminal interests generally. From communicating nefarious plans for money laundering and spreading hate propaganda, the result has been the construction of an evil caricature of a global village. Thomas Friedman captures the hate dimension well:

> At its best, the Internet can educate more people faster than any media tool we've ever had. At its worst, it can make people dumber faster than any media tool we've ever had. The lie that four thousand Jews were warned not to go into the World Trade Center on September 11 was spread entirely over the Internet and is now thoroughly believed in the Muslim world.... [J]ust when you might have thought you were all alone with your extreme views, the Internet puts you together with a community of people from around the world who hate all the things and people you do. And you can scrap the BBC and just get your news from those Web sites that reinforce your own stereotypes.

Friedman alludes to the "I Love You" virus that several years ago crashed computers and software, and adds: "There is another virus going around today, though, that's much more serious. I call it the 'I Hate You' virus. It's spread on the Internet and by satellite TV. It infects people's minds with the most vile ideas, and it can't be combated by just downloading a software program."[102]

---

[100] *Ibid.*, p. 30.
[101] Vogel and Moffett, "Radical Groups Spread the Word On-Line," A8.
[102] Thomas L. Friedman, *Longitudes and Attitudes: Exploring the World after September 11* (New York: Farrar, Straus, Giroux, 2002), pp. 248–249.

Societal vulnerability

Modern societies, especially their service industries, are vulnerable to cyberattacks of various kinds. Among the potential consequences are manipulation of information; destruction of information or of critical infrastructure components; disruption of communication, economic transactions, and public information; and exploitation of sensitive, proprietary, or classified information.[103] Among those critical services whose computer systems are highly vulnerable to cyberattacks are telecommunications, electrical power grids, gas and oil storage and delivery, banking and finance, transportation, water supply, and emergency and government services.[104] The Federal Aviation Administration[105] and the Internal Revenue Service[106] are among the US government agencies already shown to be highly vulnerable to cyberattack.

Regrettably, the threat – like so much in the realm of technology – seems to be accelerating, as Richard Love details:

> Coinciding with the September 11 terrorist attacks, the rate of cyberattacks in the United States . . . increased by an estimated 79 percent in the last six months of 2001. Worldwide, cyberattacks grew at an annual rate of 64 percent in the first six months of 2002, with more than 1 million suspected attempted attacks and 180,000 confirmed successful attacks. Power and energy companies were heavily targeted; 70 percent suffered severe attacks, a rate more than twice the mean of all companies.

These, together with technology, financial services, and media firms, averaged more than 700 attacks per company in the last six months of 2001.[107]

The enormous potential for creating chaos by cyberattack has led to the emergence of a new profession called "information assurance," whose practitioners, sensitive to the interdependence of modern

---

[103] See *Cyber Threats and Information Security: Meeting the 21st Century Challenge* (Washington, DC: Center for Strategic and International Studies, 2000).

[104] See William J. Clinton, Executive Order 13010 (Washington, DC: The White House, 15 July 1996), and *Report of the President of the United States on the Status of Federal Critical Infrastructure Protection Activities* (Washington, DC: The White House, 2001), p. 2.

[105] *FAA Computer Security: Actions Needed to Address Critical Weaknesses that Jeopardize Aviation Operations* (Washington, DC: General Accounting Office, 27 September 2000), pp. 3–4.

[106] *Internal Revenue Service: Progress Continues but Serious Management Challenges Remain* (Washington, DC: General Accounting Office, 2 April 2001).

[107] Richard A. Love, "The Cyberthreat Continuum," in Maryann Cusimano Love, ed., *Beyond Sovereignty: Issues for a Global Agenda* (Belmont, CA: Wadsworth/Thomson, 2003), p. 195.

societies, seek to protect networked computer systems.[108] The danger of cyberattack is multiplied to the extent that it is directed at a communications interface allowing one computer to talk to another or where there is dependency on another computer infrastructure. For example, many elements in society would be disrupted in the event of sudden interruptions in provision of water or in an energy supply grid.[109] With this in mind, the US Department of Energy's Office of Critical Infrastructure Protection offers a service to conduct interdependency exercises to identify crucial energy interdependencies, and one such exercise was conducted in Utah to prepare for the 2002 Olympic Games. Even the US Department of Defense depends on key infrastructures which rest on insecure operating systems. In September 2003 a virus temporarily shut down all of the US immigration authorities' capacity to check passports and process visas.

Unfortunately, as a computer system is made more secure from attacks, it is likely to become more difficult to use and less capable of being connected to other systems. In the end, it may be impossible to make critical computer systems entirely secure from attack because complexity, cost, and timeliness – rather than security – are the key concerns in developing operating systems and applications. Furthermore, complexity is an enemy of security. "Security engineering," declares Bruce Schneier "is different from any other type of engineering." "Most products . . . are useful for what they do. Security products . . . are useful precisely because of what they don't allow to be done. Most engineering involves making things work. . . Security engineering involves making sure things do not fail in the presence of an intelligent and malicious adversary who forces faults at precisely the worst time and in precisely the worst way. Security engineering involves programming Satan's computer. And Satan's computer is hard to test."[110]

Criminal evasion

As noted earlier, the Internet is of great value to transnational criminal groups that wish to evade government surveillance. It provides *narcotraficantes*, for example, with a relatively secure and inexpensive

[108] For the characteristics of a "system" as used in this context, see Bruce Schneier, *Secrets and Lies* (New York: John Wiley & Sons, 2000), pp. 6–7.
[109] *Electric Power Information Assurance Risk Assessment* (Washington, DC: Information Assurance Task Force, March 1997). The blackout of August 2003 that extended from New York to Ohio, New England, and Ontario made this point dramatically clear.
[110] Bruce Schneier, *CRYPTO-GRAM* (Counterpane Internet Security, 15 November 1999), p. 1.

means of communication and facilitates the instantaneous and illicit laundering and transnational movement of funds.[111] Computer "mailboxes," as a German author observes, "are a very good idea because you can communicate without the police being able to monitor."[112] Or, as a UN report puts it: the "Internet is an easy vehicle for trafficking in drugs, arms and women through nearly untraceable networks."[113]

The United States sought to deal with the problem of criminal secrecy by persuading its economic partners in the Organization for Economic Cooperation and Development (OECD) to endorse a proposal to allow computer eavesdropping by the world's law enforcement agencies.[114] The idea was to restrict private use of advanced data-scrambling technology that is used to protect e-mail privacy and other communication among computers. The proposal would have created a system in which the mathematical keys to computer-security codes would be held in escrow by agents from whom law enforcement officials could obtain them without a court-ordered wire-tapping warrant. However, commercial firms also use encryption, and they, as well as free-speech advocates, wanted no part of the US proposal.

The British and French governments have outlawed or regulated private use of data-scrambling at home, but other governments, especially those of Canada, Australia, Denmark, and Finland are loath to violate individual privacy. "The Internet," declares *The Economist*,

> has spawned a fierce war between fans of encryption and governments, especially America's, which argue that they must have access to the keys to software codes used on the web in the interests of law enforcement. . . . But given the easy availability of increasingly complex codes, governments may just have to accept defeat, which would provide more privacy not just for innocent web users, but for criminals as well.[115]

The threat of terrorism has made the essential dilemma even more apparent.

---

[111] DePalma, "Space, the TV Frontier Now," pp. C1, C2.

[112] Cited in Alan Cowell, "Neo-Nazis Now Network Online and Underground," *New York Times*, October 22, 1995, sec. 1, p. 3. See also Judith Miller, "Flying Blind in a Dangerous World," *New York Times*, February 6, 2000, sec. 4, p. 5.

[113] United Nations Development Programme, Human Development Office, *Summary: Human Development Report 1999* (New York: UNDP, 1999), p. 7.

[114] Markoff, "US Fails to Win Global Accord on Police Internet Eavesdropping," pp. A1, C3.

[115] "The Surveillance Society," *The Economist*, May 1–7, 1999, p. 23.

Reinforcing state authority

New information and communications technologies not only challenge state integrity and authority but in some respects can reinforce state power. Officials in some countries can use these technologies to extend influence at a distance and to centralize control at home.

Projecting soft power

To the extent that the Internet functions to extend "cultural attraction, ideology, and global institutions," it can augment what Nye calls a country's "soft power."[116] Nye was referring to the United States when he advanced the idea of soft power, and the Web and other innovations in information technology do help globalize America's cultural influence.

The homogenization of ideas, tastes, and fashions reflects a new and subtle imperialism. "The one country that can best lead the information revolution," declare Nye and William Owens, is the United States, owing to its dominance of "important communications and information processing technologies." This edge, they believe, is "a force multiplier of American diplomacy, including 'soft power' – the attraction of American democracy and free markets."[117] "The United States," boasts Rothkopf, "dominates this global traffic in information and ideas. American music, American movies, American television, and American software are so dominant, so sought after, and so visible that they are now available literally everywhere on the Earth." And, the United States, celebrates Rothkopf in a paean of triumphalism, "of all the nations in the history of the world . . . the most just, the most tolerant . . . and the best model for the future," should not be shy about its cultural hegemony:

> [I]t is in the economic and political interests of the United States to ensure that if the world is moving toward a common language, it be English; that if the world is moving toward common telecommunications, safety, and quality standards, they be American; that if the world is becoming linked by television, radio, and music, the programming be American; and that if common values are being developed, they be values with which Americans are comfortable.[118]

Rothkopf is enthused by America's role as "the world's only information superpower," and he declares that "the Realpolitik of the

---

[116] Nye, *Bound to Lead*, p. 188.
[117] Joseph S. Nye, Jr. and William A. Owens, "America's Information Edge," *Foreign Affairs* 75:2 (March–April 1996), p. 20.
[118] Rothkopf, "In Praise of Cultural Imperialism?" pp. 43, 45.

Information Age is that setting technological standards, defining software standards, producing the most popular information products, and leading in the related development of the global trade in services are as essential to the well-being of any would-be leader as once were the resources needed to support empire or industry."[119] Indeed, it is precisely such influence that other countries such as Canada, France, China, and Iran fear.

The United States is not the only country that can extend its cultural influence by means of the Internet. Iran, which, as we have seen, fears cultural contamination, wants to use the Internet to spread the word of Islam and Islamic law. Its Center for Islamic Jurisprudence in Qum has computerized 2,000 texts of both Shi'ite and Sunni law that can be disseminated electronically.[120] And, as in the case of China, the same states that oppose homogenizing global culture may wish to utilize microelectronic technologies to foster cultural homogeneity at home.

Some analysts like Andrew Shapiro argue that by means of old-fashioned coercion and new-fashioned technological dexterity states may capture the Internet:

> In addition to wielding an iron hand, authoritarian nations are increasingly adopting a more sly silicon touch in order to control what their citizens can read and hear online. Filtering software and protocols such as the Platform for Internet Content Selection (which, like barcodes on commercial packaging, standardize labels on Internet content) may make censorship easier than in the predigital era. Instead of confiscating underground books or pamphlets, governments can simply route all Internet communication through electronic gateways known as proxy servers. These powerful computers act as high-tech sieves, sifting out whatever is deemed subversive or offensive.[121]

Such a development would extend Orwell's authoritarian nightmare of Big Brother into the twenty-first century.

States aside, others fear the Net's power to undermine the quality of life enjoyed by individuals and society at large. Declared a physics student at Belgrade University: "The Internet is a dehumanizing addiction and the greatest single threat to human civilization.... We are working on making viruses for Unix, the system the Internet uses, but it is well protected. We know how to destroy the DOS system, that is easy. If we

---

[119] *Ibid.*, pp. 46–47. Rothkopf disagrees with those who see conflict between national and global values or between "civilizations" as inevitable.

[120] MacFarquhar, "With Mixed Feelings, Iran Tiptoes to Internet," p. A4.

[121] Andrew L. Shapiro, "The Internet," *Foreign Policy* 115 (Summer 1999), p. 14.

can't make a virus for Unix we can always cut the optical cable. This is my mission in life, to save the world from the Internet."[122] Excessive time at computers has also been associated with various health maladies like obesity, problems with eyesight, and hand disfunctions.

Cultural homogenization in heterogeneous societies

Many states routinely seek to create and maintain a single dominant culture and eliminate subcultures around which secessionist or recalcitrant minorities might mobilize. Despite the growing capacity of individuals to mobilize at a distance, this may prove difficult in a globalizing world. Businessmen "speak" to one another, as do militia extremists, effectively reinforcing one another's views while avoiding disconfirming information. Cultural homogenization is most visible among those who are integrated in the global economy and whose tastes and norms – whether in Caracas, New York, or Karachi – are similar.[123] New elites that have been largely "denationalized" are the surrogates for globalization, and they have little interest in or time for those from whom they are separated by barriers of class, knowledge, wealth, or tastes. Thus, the psychological distance between these new elites and the much larger and poorer underclass in their own country grows, even as geographic distance between these classes has narrowed owing to massive urbanization.[124]

Assimilation serves as a means of reinforcing citizen identity and loyalty. Often, it takes the form of imposing a single dominant religion and/or language upon citizens. The evolution of a single dominant "official" version of the language was central to the birth of the English and French states at the end of Europe's Middle Ages,[125] and historically the efforts of states to centralize power has involved the imposition of a single tongue. Efforts by states to stamp out linguistic competition remains a hallmark of contemporary politics as well. The Turkish effort to repress Kurdish is only one of many example of states seeking to impose linguistic unity on culturally and ethnically diverse societies.

Language autonomy is a key to national efforts to assert independence or autonomy, as in the case of the French-speaking Québécois. In Peru,

---

[122] Cited in Hedges, "Serbs' Answer to Tyranny? Get on the Web," p. 8.

[123] See, for example, Sassen, *Global Networks, Linked Cities*.

[124] Robert Reich argues that "knowledge workers" or "symbolic analysts" are conscious of a kinship to others with similar skills who may be geographically remote, *The Work of Nations*, pp. 177–180.

[125] Liah Greenfeld, *Nationalism: Five Roads to Modernity* (Cambridge, MA: Harvard University Press, 1992), pp. 69–70, 97–99.

for example, the use of Spanish as the sole language in radio and television threatens the language of indigenous peoples with extinction. Does anyone really believe the attempt to suppress Kurdish will succeed? Put alongside that example the remarkable revival of Provençal in southern France, Welsh in Wales, and even Gaelic in Scotland. Clearly, there is at least some sort of trend in the direction of linguistic diversity, including the transnational spread of English, which is all the more threatening as a special hegemonic case.

From a global perspective, cultural homogeneity, some argue, is analogous to the loss of biodiversity. As the isolation of minority communities ends, they are tied to a cultural mainstream by modern forms of communication and by migration, and are exposed to a dominant language. This is unfortunate in some respects because every language has words that alone can express concepts that are unique to that culture. "It's a cultural narrowing," declared a Yale University linguist. "It may not be plagues and pestilence, but it is a cultural disaster."[126] Within this century, as many as half the world's 6,000 languages may be lost, and only thirty are "safe," that is, spoken by at least a million people and backed by a sovereign state.[127] In fairness, some of these arguments are tinged with romanticism. Linguistic change and consolidation have been going on for millennia, and each consolidation increases the ease and thus the potential for human communication.

In some cases, those self-defined cultures that survive the Darwinian dynamics of cultural invasion may, like the Israelis, Welsh, Bretons, or Provençals, revive and reinvent their own languages. Technology attuned to localizing objectives can push that process along too. National identities are eroded and muddled as the revival of older identities and the creation of new ones produce cleavages within or across societies that had formerly prevented or repressed them in the name of national unity.

The Internet can provide states with additional capacity by fostering the formation of transnational and international knowledge or epistemic groups. The Internet facilitates the establishment of "global public policy networks" that, as Wolfgang Reinicke argues, "are meant to complement traditional public policy institutions, not replace them" and "help governments and multilateral agencies to manage risks, take advantage of opportunities presented by technological change, be more responsive

---

[126] Cited in "Cultural Loss Seen as Languages Fade," *New York Times*, May 16, 1999, p. 12.
[127] *Ibid.*

to their constituents, and promote change within bureaucracies."[128] As sources of expertise and information and as linkages between officials and advocates in different countries, networks provide a critical resource for states that seek to cope with a growing array of transnational issues and collective dilemmas. Reinicke foresees new networks "to help traditional policy makers address cutting-edge global challenges, such as transnational crime, money laundering, and the furious debate over biotechnology and genetically modified foods."[129]

Such networks perhaps provide a reason for a revival of functionalist theory. Nevertheless, an element of doublethink prevails in functionalist arguments.[130] States cannot cope by themselves, so they look to effective others to do the job for them. The long-range impact on citizens' identities and loyalties remains uncertain. Will the credit for successes or blame for failures redound to states or increasingly drift to international networks, regimes, and international institutions?

The projection of force

As described earlier, the microelectronics revolution enables some states to project force at greater distances and speed and with greater accuracy than ever before. The uses of these technologies to provide unprecedented command, control, and communication across entire battlefields first appeared in the Persian Gulf War of 1991 and again, at much higher levels, in Kosovo in 1999, Afghanistan in 2001, and Iraq in 2003. Kosovo, as a contemporary observer put it, was the first case of warfare "where a small but significant slice of the population has Internet access. The Yugoslavs, a technically savvy people for decades, have used the Web to create an entire news network consisting of E-mail exchanges, chat rooms and bulletin boards – where no rumor is too small to dissect at length and almost no hamlet too small to mention."[131] A Serbian student in Illinois declared: "Sometimes if I log on in the middle of the night, the people over there are giving me a play-by-play thing. They type things like 'The bombs are flying right over our heads'."[132] For civilians on both sides of the conflict, as we have noted, the Internet was

---

[128] Wolfgang H. Reinicke, "The Other World Wide Web: Global Public Policy Networks," *Foreign Policy* 117 (Winter 1999–2000), p. 51. See also Wolfgang H. Reinicke, *Global Public Policy: Governing Without Government?* (Washington, DC: Brookings Institution, 1998).
[129] Reinicke, "The Other World Wide Web," p. 51.
[130] See Ferguson and Mansbach, "Remapping Political Space," p. 101.
[131] Neil MacFarquhar, "For First Time in War, E-Mail Plays a Vital Role," *New York Times*, March 29, 1999, p. A 12.
[132] Cited in *ibid.*

a means of evading state-controlled media to get information. One web site in particular, kosovo-reports@egroups.com, provided a wealth of information about events.

Although it appears that, overall, microelectronic technologies provide a military advantage to wealthy advanced countries like the United States, this is not inevitably the case. When Iraq invaded Kuwait in 1990, Kuwaiti authorities were able to cable their national funds out of the country to the safety of foreign banks where they remained available to help bankroll the opponents of Saddam Hussein. In addition, the use of microelectronic facilities to publicize the aggression of large states is a significant resource for the weak. As one observer notes, "the ability of everyone to know what is happening in minute detail around the world and the increasing tendency to care about it – is another way that the small can fend off the large."[133] Osama bin Laden's image and words have frequently flooded the Internet as well as Al-Jazeera and other television networks.

Violation of personal privacy

Another potential casualty of the microelectronic and computer revolutions is individual privacy. Years ago, Supreme Court Justice Louis Brandeis feared that photography and cheap printing would threaten privacy. He would be far more concerned about electronic gathering and dissemination of data by governments.[134] Information about an individual's genetic make-up, for example, might be used to their detriment by law-enforcement officials, health insurers, or potential employers. Civil libertarians have also expressed concern about potential misuse of personal information in US and British efforts to institute surveillance of domestic cyberspace.

Technology: some normative observations

The brief discussion of privacy issues raises the more general issue of the normative implications of changing technology. For example, personal data in commercial and government databases grows whenever there is spending that involves credit or debit cards, financial transactions, telephone calls, or interactions with a local or national government. The

---

[133] Martin Libicki, "Rethinking War: The Mouse's New Roar?" *Foreign Policy* 117 (Winter 1999–2000), p. 41.
[134] "The Surveillance Society," pp. 21–23.

collection of ever-greater amounts of information by states about its citizens cannot be viewed with indifference. Governments continually seek to limit the ability of individuals and corporations to use encryption, demanding access to software codes. Such intrusion by governments does indeed have Orwellian overtones, regardless of the fact that the target may be mainly illegal activities like money laundering or terrorism. Meanwhile, individuals must face the "private" threat of "cookies" that transmit their personal Internet viewing habits to third parties, who subsequently bombard them with unwanted commercial solicitations.

Changing technology is an inescapable requirement for the growing concern about human interests rather than national interests – for the "skill revolution"[135] and the "participation explosion." A relatively few developed countries, for example, dominate the Internet, especially in terms of secure servers that are necessary for effective commercial activities.[136] Arguably, then, a major normative consequence of advancing technology has been to widen social and economic inequality among individuals and groups both within[137] and across states. Technology appears be undermining communication among groups with differential wealth and knowledge *within* societies, while enhancing communication among those in similar professions in separate societies. Despite the spread of Internet access for personal communication, sophisticated Internet use, as we have seen, has remained limited largely to those employed by corporations, universities, and government organizations or those with sufficient resources to purchase home computers and the services of a local Internet provider. Thus, Strange declared that the privileges of these "'knowledge workers' were greatly enhanced by comparison with those of manual workers in agriculture or industrial manufacturing.[138] Reich similarly argues that "knowledge workers" or "symbolic analysts" are conscious of a kinship to others with similar skills who may be geographically remote,[139] even while differential knowledge and skills separate people who may be physically close to one another. Far from being a neutral source of information and skills for individuals, "The Internet," as Claude Moisy observes, "is a fantastic tool that makes life easier for a lot of professionals. It is certainly great

---

[135] Rosenau, *Turbulence in World Politics*, p. 239.
[136] "Measuring Globalization," *Foreign Policy* 122 (January–February 2001), p. 62.
[137] Nevertheless, it appears that more highly globalized (and therefore more advanced technologically) emerging-market countries enjoy a more egalitarian income distribution that the less globalized. "Measuring Globalization," p. 64.
[138] Strange, *The Retreat of the State*, p. 102.   [139] Reich, *The Work of Nations*, pp. 177–180.

for global stocks and for global smut. But it represents in no way the miraculous advent of the much heralded 'global village'."[140]

Rather than exposing large numbers of people to diverse information, "two of the Internet's main characteristics – interactivity and virtuality – can have strongly negative effects on an individual's knowledge of and concern for the rest of the world" because its "news groups" "generally cater to the primal yearning to be heard and to reinforce one's biases by sharing them with like-minded persons. From one perspective, the Internet has become the haven for a myriad of one-issue chapels estranged from the rest of the world."[141] Hence the *diversity*, if not the total amount, of information is auto-limited as individuals communicate only with those with similar ideological proclivities and are no longer exposed to different perspectives, as would have been at least more the case with traditional mass media. Businessmen "speak" to one another, as do militia extremists, and the messages they exchange tend to eliminate disconfirming information and to reinforce "groupthink" on a much broader scale than the originator of that concept intended.[142]

Even as the vertical divisions separating citizens in different states soften, new horizontal divisions based on knowledge and skills are becoming more pronounced in global politics. A networked class of managers and technocrats is emerging that is linked globally by language (English and "techno-jargon"), jet aircraft (First and Business classes are the ultimate symbols), and e-mail. At the top of the status and wealth heap are often those who own or manage those new technologies. This "new class" of technocrats is more often than not to be found outside of government. However much he may be disparaged, Bill Gates, not George W. Bush, is the greater role model for increasing numbers of young people around the world.

For those who think of themselves as members of this new class, and who perceive themselves to be distinct from fellow citizens who lack the same knowledge and skills, normative issues like accountability may assume a different hue than for those who give greater weight to their identity as citizens. For the former, democratic accountability of the sort thought to be desirable in the West after the hardening of

---

[140] Claude Moisy, "Myths of the Global Information Village," *Foreign Affairs* 107 (Summer 1997), p. 78.
[141] *Ibid.*, p. 84.
[142] See Irving L. Janis, *Victims of Groupthink: A Psychological Study of Foreign-Policy Decisions and Fiascoes* (Boston: Houghton Mifflin, 1972).

national boundaries and the mobilization of the masses may have little relevance. Instead, members of this "new class" may see themselves as accountable first to others – family, business elites, bankers, shareholders, customers, and clients around the world. Or, sometimes, as recent corporate scandals in the United State reveal, to no one and nothing, except personal greed.

Conclusion: a mixed verdict

On balance, then, what has been the impact of the Internet on state integrity? One of the most challenging of the tasks before students of global politics is to make sense of how rapidly changing technology is rendering many of our most cherished theories of global politics increasingly irrelevant. This task is growing harder as rates of technological change accelerate and link individuals together in new and more complex ways that are fundamentally altering the nature of political association and communication. At the start of the twenty-first century we are opening new battlegrounds between and among non-sovereign and state actors.

As we have seen, at the same time as the authority of many states is declining and their boundaries are becoming more porous, transnational authorities and processes, sustained by new means of instantaneous communication and rapid transportation, are proliferating. Nongovernmental organizations with members around the world can mobilize at the drop of an e-mail to campaign for a cause; political dissidents with no territorial focus can organize their activities; hedge funds can bring national economies to the brink of catastrophe by the virtually instantaneous movement of funds from one country and currency to another;[143] and criminal groups and terrorists can launder and move funds using computers and e-cash.

As new technologies overwhelm old political structures, they also erode the normative foundations of those structures that had anchored identities and provided citizens with prescriptive guidance. Stripped of norms such as sovereignty that had helped to provide individuals with a definition of who they are and of their "proper" place in the cosmos and that had served as filters for mediating and interpreting "external" information and ideas, people now question practices and

---

[143] See especially Strange, *Mad Money*; and Cohen, *The Geography of Money*.

institutions that they previously had regarded as legitimate.[144] A "crisis of authority" ensues, and citizens become available for competing norms that enhance other identities. In the words of Metz:

> The information revolution is both a force for stability and for instability. On the positive side, it complicates the task of old-style repression and facilitates the development of grass roots civil society. But the information revolution also allows organizations intent on instability or violence to form alliances, thus making the world more dangerous. Some of the most complex struggles of the twenty-first century will pit polyglot networks against states. Hierarchies and bureaucracies face serious disadvantages when pitted against unscrupulous, flexible, adaptable enemies.[145]

It is hardly surprising, but more than a little ironic, that technological change should contribute to the erosion of state capacity and to the declining importance of territory at the beginning of the twenty-first century. Centuries earlier, when gunpowder and cannon smashed stone fortresses and longbows and crossbows wielded by yeomen and peasants brought down armored knights, technology placed a premium on territorial expansion and contributed to the triumph of the state as a political form. Europe, the birthplace of the Westphalian polity, is now pioneering the construction of new political forms based on "transnational microeconomic links."[146] As we have stressed, we might even turn to a much older world with little technological innovation, medieval Europe, in order to make better sense of the cartography of our new high-tech world.

At the end of the day, the revolutions in information and communication seem more likely to speed the erosion of the territorial state than to reinforce its power and authority. The Internet, in particular, is a further step in creating non-sovereign sources of norms, economic power, and political ideologies. As two observers contend: "Since so many of the institutions of the nation-state are hierarchical and so many of the transnational organizations are networked, the net flow of power today tends to be out of the nation-state and into nonstate actors."[147] The fact

---

[144] As we saw in Chapter 1, among the most articulate adversaries of this position is Stephen D. Krasner, who argues that sovereignty has always been an aspiration to a greater or lesser extent.

[145] Metz, *Armed Conflict in the 21st Century*, p. viii.

[146] Ruggie, "Territoriality and Beyond," p. 172.

[147] Carl H. Builder and Brian Nichiporuk, *Information Technologies and the Future of Land Warfare* (Santa Monica, CA: Rand Corporation, 1995), p. 35.

that the Internet, like other microelectronic innovations, can overcome the limitations of distance and time suggests that, on the whole, it will diminish the role of territorial boundaries, while contributing to new identity boundaries uniting and separating people on bases other than geographic location.

9　The future

The central theme of this book is that the capacity, legitimacy, and authority of sovereign states are decreasing and that we have entered or are entering a new postinternational epoch of global politics. Evidence is to be found in all dimensions of political, economic, and social life, even, as van Creveld points out, in "the field of sport," where "[f]rom the Olympics down, the most important competitions have become commercialized."[1] Nevertheless, it must be acknowledged that it is also possible that future historians may look back on the decades after the end of the Cold War as a brief interlude before a return to security-business-as-usual; that is, intense and dangerous rivalry among major states. History reminds us of the euphoria that follows many wars and of the accompanying expectations for major change and a benign future. History is not a one-way street, and political forms and practices may evolve in different directions.

Were a new era of interstate tensions to begin, it would strengthen the governments of some states *vis-à-vis* their own peoples, again highlight military preparation and alliances, and encourage us to dust off all the old realist literature.[2] Such literature tells us about a world that thinks like Hobbes, Morgenthau, and Waltz, one quite different from that of Rosenau or Rosecrance. More debatable is whether the sort of "political crack-up" sketched in sensational fashion by Robert Kaplan – terrorists with nuclear weapons in suitcases, snipers on street corners, bioterror outbreaks, and so on – is, as he insists, "just beginning to

---

[1] Van Creveld, *The Rise and Decline of the State*, pp. 411–412.
[2] According to Condoleezza Rice, this was the agenda of the George W. Bush administration when it came to office. See Condoleezza Rice, "Promoting the National Interest," *Foreign Affairs* 79:1 (January/February 2000), pp. 45–62.

occur worldwide." Such a trend might have been heralded (although we certainly hope not) by recent events like the apocalyptic terror attacks of Osama bin Laden and Al-Qaeda, waves of suicide bombers in Israel, the Washington, DC Beltway sniper, the anthrax murders in the United States, the Bali nightclub bombing, the Chechen rebel seizure of a Moscow theater, the train station bombing in Madrid, and other bomb attacks in Saudi Arabia and Casablanca not to mention official speculation about the possible acquisition of nuclear, biological, and chemical weapons by Iran and North Korea. Should a genuine and widespread political crack-up occur – a contemporary Dark Age – it might usher in an extended period of almost-unimaginable "Mad Max" chaos and surely would drastically raise popular anxiety, encourage authoritarian "solutions," and thereby make for at least a limited reinvigoration of those governments that could seem to offer any form of protection.

While there is little more disciplinary consensus about global processes than about structure, there is general agreement about some trends. It appears, for instance, that we are witnessing at least a temporary shift toward greater democratic rhetoric and mass participation globally (despite the democratic deficit), broader but possibly slowing acceptance of free markets, an upsurge in ethnic identity and religious fundamentalism, and a changing definition of "security" to encompass collective threats to survival and well-being such as terrorism and transnational crime, the proliferation of weapons of mass destruction, global warming, additional environmental degradation, and new or resurgent diseases. The danger of interstate war has declined even while that of postinternational violence has grown, contributing to a rash of "failed states."[3] There has been also a proliferation of IGOs, INGOs, and NGOs, formal and informal regimes, regional institutions and movements, TNCs and business alliances, and networks of various kinds. The language of globalization encompasses revolutions in telecommunications and transportation, the declining efficacy of state frontiers, cultural diffusion, increased migration of people and microbes, and the growing impact of global markets, trade within and among giant transnational corporations, "hot money," and currency speculation.[4]

---

[3] Gerald B. Helman and Steven R. Ratner, "Saving Failed States," *Foreign Policy* 89 (Winter 1992–93), p. 3.

[4] Deregulated financial trading has created a "virtual world" of currency markets. Cf. Peter F. Drucker, "The Global Economy and the Nation-State," *Foreign Affairs* 76:5 (September–October 1997), pp. 159–171.

If so, then what?

But if sovereign states become feebler, nonterritorial identities grow in importance, and the distinction between the foreign and domestic policy arenas diminishes, what then are the options for developing more effective strategies to manage global violence? Three possibilities suggest themselves, all of which assume a truncated state; and there may be more. The first entails a substantial restructuring of the state, in response to the challenges posed by one or more versions of neoclassical liberalism. The second involves restructuring the global system and providing a greater role for nonsovereign and interstate institutions. The third and last is one of escalating chaos because of the incapacity of the present system to cope. *In actuality, the world will probably feature elements of some or all of these patterns, with different countries and regions reflecting more of one or another of them.* As Rosenau says, it is a "messy" world[5] and likely to get even messier. The first two would require some kind of redrawing of the boundaries of moral community within the state and with regard to the state system, which would entail both reconceptualizing state sovereignty and a struggle for the inclusion of non-Western perspectives in the construction of world order.

In the first scenario, the state assumes a purely utilitarian role, maintaining and trying to improve basic infrastructure, attempting to enhance economic competitiveness, defining jurisdictional boundaries, and making an effort to assure citizens of equality of opportunity in the manner of an institutionalized referee impartially enforcing the rules of the game. Here, the link between state and identity is weak, and citizens make growing use of a rich universe of civic associations that are subnational and sometimes transnational. The state principally has the limited function of managing the distribution of some economic and educational resources within an environment of equal opportunity and so would (in theory) distribute public goods according to the rules of majoritarian democratic discourse while protecting the right of dissent. Since allocating resources presumes agreement over values, this version of the limited state requires an informed citizenry with access to multiple channels of political discourse and a pluralistic constellation of mediating associations.

Supportive of this possibility are the shift from national to civic culture in the Western liberal tradition and the growing emphasis in Western political life on regarding politics mainly in terms of allocating resources

---

[5] Rosenau, *Distant Proximities*, p. 9.

according to consensual norms. One might conceive this tendency less as a change in the state itself than as a movement from state sovereignty in the direction of market sovereignty or the hegemony of "transnational liberalism."[6]

In this first scenario, what it "means" to be American, or Canadian, or French, or Chinese becomes less important than that individuals are entitled to more or less equal life chances, which the state (aided by the market) is bound to establish and protect, coupled with majoritarian democracy and minority rights. Under these conditions, Westphalian polities will evolve in a direction akin to that followed by the states within the United States. These were once major expressions of local authority and identity, but increased economic integration and mobility across state lines relegated them, eventually, to a lesser role of managing particular resources.

This model already exists to some extent in the developed world, especially the OECD. Neoliberals regard war as a waste of resources that disrupts the market; theirs is the world of Norman Angell, albeit more than eight decades later. In this perspective, where the threat of violence remains high – as in Northern Ireland or in some American urban centers – the causes can be traced to the extent to which those societies have failed to satisfy the requirements of the liberal model.[7] As in the case of race relations in the United States, minorities perceive that the state does not provide equal life chances. In Northern Ireland, citizens do not agree that participatory rules are fair and equal. More importantly, the Irish case points to a serious problem with the liberal model, its failure to take account of the persistence of identity as the basis for transforming power into political authority. As a result, it cannot cope effectively either with the integrating forces of globalism or the fragmenting impact of subnational and transnational identities. Thus, Sandel deplores the disappearance of civic virtue in defining citizenship:

> The growing aspiration for the public expression of communal identities reflects a yearning for political arrangements that can situate people in a world increasingly governed by vast and distant forces. For a time the nation-state promised to answer this yearning, to provide the link

[6] Agnew and Corbridge, *Mastering Space*, pp. 164–207.
[7] The case may be made that racial conflict reflects the problem that certain identities generate fundamentally different values regarding resource allocation. Majoritarian rule cannot satisfy resulting grievances. This is also the case in conflicts between settler and indigenous peoples. See Wilmer, *The Indigenous Voice in World Politics*.

> between identity and self-rule . . . The nation-state laid claim to the allegiance of its citizens on the ground that its exercise of sovereignty expressed their collective identity. In the contemporary world, however, this claim is losing its force . . . As their effective sovereignty fades, nations gradually lose their hold on the allegiance of their citizens.[8]

If citizens perceive that the rules allow for fair and equal chances to influence allocation, the threat of civil violence will be reduced. However, the problem of external and transnational violence remains. The prospect that the liberal state can manage external violence lies in the Kantian hope that all states can be simultaneously restructured along liberal lines. Research on the incidence of wars between democracies and nondemocracies and between states with market and nonmarket economies is not reassuring.[9] In sum, the liberal solution is, at best, a very long-term one and makes the dubious assumption that individuals will abandon subnational and transnational identities in favor of republican citizenship. The model also makes the unlikely assumption that the liberal state can or will accommodate identity groups for whom there exist irreconcilable differences regarding the values that underlie resource allocation.

A second possibility is a world in which international organizations such as the United Nations, the IMF, and NATO, aided by a variety of nongovernmental organizations and wealthy states, actively intervene to restore peace or provide for the welfare of citizens living in states that have failed or are in imminent danger of doing so.[10] This is a world in which sovereignty has come to mean even less than in the liberal model, and violations of sovereign boundaries have become routine. In this scenario – reminiscent of the UN Trusteeship system – international organizations, along with regional regimes or even former colonial powers, attempt to restore order, promote reconciliation in postconflict environments, and reconstruct state institutions. Here, although states are restructured, the impetus for restructuring arises from the global system, from the norms and institutions of interstate and transnational collaboration. Examples include international and NGO efforts to help East

---

[8] Michael J. Sandel, "America's Search for a New Public Philosophy," *The Atlantic Monthly*, March, 1996, p. 74.
[9] Etel Solingen, "Domestic Legitimacy and International Cooperation," paper presented at the International Studies Association (Acapulco, Mexico, March 1993).
[10] See, for example, Gareth Evans, *Cooperating for Peace: The Global Agenda for the 1990s and Beyond* (St. Leonard, Australia: Allen & Unwin, 1993).

Timor prepare for self-rule and to reconstruct working institutions in Afghanistan and Iraq.

The second model is in some ways a variation of the first, with intervention legitimated by norms compelling states to construct majoritarian institutions, protect minority rights, and take responsibility for establishing rules of distributional fairness.[11] It assumes that the norms, which already exist for the management of external violence in the form of *jus in bello* and *jus contra bellum*,[12] are still in force.

Because sovereignty legally forbids interference in domestic politics, the norms regarding global responses to civil and transnational wars are to date much less developed than those pertaining to interstate war. They offer little more than guidelines to the international community with regard to influencing civil-war outcomes or remaining neutral. Existing norms concerning the right of a state to request assistance from other states to secure itself against attack or to pursue a strategy of collective self-defense (and therefore the legitimate use of force with the assistance of third parties) have left civil wars a gray area of international law. This was apparent in the early stages of conflict in the former Yugoslavia. Hence, there is an urgent need to articulate reasonably consistent norms that might be translated into practical guidelines for appropriate actions by outsiders in civil wars.

It is not only the absence of institutional authority and enforcement capacity that make it difficult to realize this model. More serious obstacles are the absence of political will among states to allow nonsovereign institutions to act authoritatively to manage the use of force during war, especially transnational conflicts or civil strife. Human-rights norms and the laws of war, to say the least, have rarely been consistently enforced. To date, such legal regulation has relied on the existence of sufficient political will to enforce norms and support institutional development – a fact illustrated on repeated occasions such as the US refusal to ratify the ICC and the United Nations' faltering enforcement of weapons inspections in Iraq after the 1991 Gulf War. Doctrines like the supposed right to "pre-emptive self-defense" asserted by the George W. Bush administration also obviously undermine the building of collective capacity to deal with security issues.

A variant of the second model involves providing a greater role for nongovernmental organizations in efforts to manage violence. Already

---

[11] To some extent these are the aims of the two UN International Covenants on Civil and Political Rights and on Economic, Social, and Cultural Rights.
[12] Laws during war, and laws against war.

a range of NGOs like Oxfam provide humanitarian relief and protection for civilian victims of global violence. One proposal to reform the UN Trusteeship Council as a Forum for Indigenous Peoples would make available to the nongovernmental representatives of indigenous peoples a forum to discuss their status and seek redress for their grievances against states without violence.[13] Proposals such as this aim to increase NGO participation as a way of preventing conflict or reducing its consequences. Another way in which NGOs might be involved is by utilizing strategies of conflict management and resolution that are being developed in academic settings such as the Carter Center. Unfortunately, NGO involvement in civil conflict almost always entails an appearance of "taking sides" as it did in the refugee camps of Congo.

A third scenario is that of an extended period of chaos that will raise popular anxiety and encourage authoritarian "solutions" of the sort imposed in Uruguay and Argentina in the 1970s. As states are forced to share authority with or surrender it to other polities, what will the world look like? Kaplan describes an apocalyptic nonterritorial "last map" drawn from travel amid the ruins of "failed states" and "postmodern wars."

> Imagine cartography in three dimensions, as if in a hologram. In this hologram would be the overlapping sediments of various group identities such as those of language and economic class, atop the two-dimensional color distinctions among city-states and the remaining nations, themselves confused in places by shadows overhead, indicating the power of drug cartels, mafias, and private security agencies that guard the wealthy in failing states and hunt down terrorists. Instead of borders, there would be moving "centers" of power, as in the Middle Ages. These power centers would be both national and financial, reflecting the sovereignty of global corporations. Many of these holistic layers would be in motion. Replacing fixed and abrupt lines on a flat space would be a shifting pattern of ecoregions and buffer entities . . . To this protean cartographic hologram one must add other factors, such as growing populations, refugee migrations, soil and water scarcities and . . . vectors of disease. Henceforward the map of the world will never be static. This future map – in a sense, the "Last Map" – will be an ever-mutating representation of cartographic

---

[13] For a variation of this proposal, see Mark Nerfin, "The Future of the United Nations System: Some Questions on the Occasion of an Anniversary," in Richard A. Falk, Samuel S. Kim, and Saul H. Mendlovitz, *The United Nations and a Just World Order* (Boulder, CO: Westview, 1991).

chaos . . . On this map, the rules by which diplomats and other policymaking elites have ordered the world these past few hundred years
will apply less and less.[14]

There is some evidence for all three scenarios, and they by no means
exhaust possible futures; nor – it is crucial to stress again – are they
necessarily exclusive. Jan Aart Scholte, for example, offers a mixed version of the first two: "Largely owing to globalizing capital, states of
the late twentieth century have on the whole lost sovereignty, acquired
supraterritorial constituents, retreated from interstate warfare (for the
moment), frozen or reduced social security provisions, multiplied multilateral governance arrangements and lost considerable democratic
potential."[15] Kaplan's apocalyptic vision captures some of the uncertainty of the present but falls short of depicting how much "governance"
would exist even if Westphalian polities were to disappear tomorrow.
There are a host of international functional regimes; the European exper-
iment and other regional schemes continue to evolve by fits and starts;
NGOs are proliferating; corporations and markets have their own shifting structures; most religions have church hierarchies of one form or
another; tribes still have chiefs and elders; more autonomy arrangements for certain minorities are almost certain to emerge; and, for that
matter, already existing within many present Westphalian polities are
numerous other "public" entities like the states of the United States,
the republics of Russia, cities, counties, and so on. There is plenty of
room for maneuver, for redistribution and modification of authority
and responsibilities in response to changing circumstances.

The political forms they used to teach – unitary, federal, or confederal,
and so forth – now seem hopelessly inadequate to describe the possible
variations on these forms, not to mention the sort of complexity that
is day-by-day reality in a world of layered, overlapping, and interacting polities. But, we must contemplate other forms of governance than
the Westphalian polity, because already there are a wide range of such
forms – past and future – converging in the present. In an immediate
and pressing sense, they are part of the reason we are witnessing both
history's revenge and future shock.

---

[14] Robert D. Kaplan, *The Ends of the Earth: A Journey to the Frontiers of Anarchy* (New York: Random House, 1996), pp. 336–337.
[15] Jan Aart Scholte, "Global Capitalism and the State," *International Affairs* 73:3 (1997), p. 452.

A disconcerting era

The transformation of political communities and patterns of authority in *any* era is likely to be accompanied by unpredictability, anxiety, instability, and conflict. The postinternational world is certainly no exception. Accelerated fission and fusion of political communities involve the redrawing of psychological maps, and the proliferation of new identities, as well as new forms of governance, that defy the "sovereign" psychology of recent centuries and that mock physical distance. Global authority is in the midst of rapid but ambiguous distribution and redistribution, and, even as people grow more and more complexly interdependent, they find it more and more difficult to discern and hold responsible the sources of their well-being or the threats to that well-being. This diffusion of authority is accompanied by the emergence of ever more boundaries separating "us" from "them" and therefore potential conflict sites. Complexity augurs misunderstanding; misunderstanding promises unpredictability; and unpredictability threatens political instability.

Additional reasons for anxiety and instability include intensifying concern about a democratic deficit and the growing wealth gap in global politics combined with expanding awareness of that gap. Large gaps in wealth also hobble democratic institutions by encouraging corruption and producing nodes of economic power that are unavailable for collective ends. State weakness makes it difficult for governments to carry out the wishes of electorates or for citizens to identify the sources of lost jobs, shrinking markets, or declining competitiveness. The growing role of anonymous authorities, in turn, produces a search for powerful scapegoats like transnational corporations and interstate organizations.

From one point of view, the traditional interstate system was reasonably stable. Notwithstanding the myth of equality, the system was anchored by hierarchy among its members, and tacit rules among leading states generally provided stability, managed violence, and enabled them to "govern" the system as a whole. Just as Europe's balance-of-power system was subject to norms such as the demand that states join flexible alliances when one or a group of them threatened preponderance,[16] so the Cold War system evolved norms between the superpowers such as permitting conflicts among pawns while forbidding direct

---

[16] See Edward Vose Gulick, *Europe's Classical Balance of Power* (New York: Norton, 1955).

violence between the superpowers themselves. By contrast, the erosion of states sharply reduces the role of one set of authorities without substituting others that enjoy an equivalent range or scope of authority over persons and things. Norms associated with the state (for example, some traditional features of international law) decay, at least in the short run, and the polities that emerge are more highly specialized than the multifunctional leviathans that characterized Europe after Westphalia.

Complexity is further heightened in the postinternational world because the boundaries of states become less important barriers among moral communities. Other identities with their own boundaries are recalled to life, reconstructed, or invented. Just as "Hellenic," "Roman," and "Chinese" had powerful cultural connotations that meant more than residing within a state's political boundaries, so today "American" means more than residing within the sovereign borders of the United States. Today, a host of overlapping identity boundaries not only separate inside from outside, but also mark discontinuities in spheres of authority and, therefore, the authoritative allocation of values. A globalized world exhibits boundaries among networks of authorities that overlap with, enclose, and transcend the sovereign boundaries of states in an international world. Also, a globalized world is one of highly specialized spheres of authority or polities that are often unconnected with territorial space or are "out of place."

The proliferation of identities and actors and the growing role of individuals constitute disintegration in the capacity of *any* single type of collective authority or set of authorities to undertake governance or manage global affairs. "Networking" (like subcontracting), the skills revolution, and institutional proliferation further disguise the sources of authority. Theorists used to write of balances among several powers, bipolarity between two, and states without visible societies. How blissfully simple it all seems in retrospect. Practitioners believed that sort of thing then, and unfortunately many still do. Compared with the story of the archetypal eighteenth-century balance-of-power epoch in Europe with rule by a few diplomats who chatted in French, bartered brides and tendered bribes among one another, and had little in common with their own subjects, the postinternational world seems utterly bewildering. Analysts and policymakers alike hardly know how to begin to make sense of it, let alone what to recommend or do in response to its many challenges.

The return of norms to global politics

We have pointed up selected normative aspects of issues discussed earlier. Partly, this flows from our conclusion that the "scientific" separation of facts and values cannot be sustained. In addition, the retreat of the state, the increasingly porous nature of state boundaries, shifting conceptions of time and space, and the growing autonomy of markets have altered what Strange called "the mix of values in the [global] system as a whole."[17] There is a new interest in and debate over global norms. In theory, this new preoccupation with norms was most apparent in postpositivism in general and in postmodernism in particular. Postmodernism, though by its nature offering little in the way of a serious research agenda, was a radical break in all respects from science and its goals of cold objectivity and accumulation of knowledge. The postmodern movement powerfully reaffirmed the central inevitability and importance of normative analysis. Unlike scientists who objected to "reflexivism," postmodernists enthusiastically endorsed the aims of feminists, environmentalists, and workers, among others.

Normative consciousness plays a key role in postmodernists' self-image as "dissidents." It was in this spirit that Ashley denounced the "technical rationality" that underpins much of international relations theory, especially that reflecting the assumptions of "science." Theorists who advocate "means-ends rationality," with its claim of being "inherently objective, value-neutral, void of normative or substantive content," Ashley argued, have abandoned politics. And in inhabiting "the domain of the 'is' rather than the domain of the 'ought'," where no "normative defense" of truth is necessary,[18] social scientists implicitly disparage the capacity of human beings to alter their own fate. In this, Ashley was on the mark. Moreover, failure to focus on norms necessarily meant failure to focus on those aspects of politics that push people to act in the first place, thereby violating the behavioral ethos that underlay the scientific project.

There were exceptions to Ashley's criticism, including Rosenau. Although a spokesperson for and advocate of the separation of facts and

[17] Strange, *The Retreat of the State*, p. 34. Strange identifies four central values – wealth, security, justice, and freedom.
[18] Richard K. Ashley, "The Poverty of Neorealism," in Robert O. Keohane, ed., *Neorealism and its Critics* (New York: Columbia University Press, 1984), p. 282.

values in the 1960s and 1970s,[19] he implicitly betrayed a profound normative commitment by rejecting the power of impersonal structures and placing people and their well-being squarely at the heart of his analyses. Even in his early work, one can sense a tension between the individual as a cog in a larger system and the individual as a flesh and blood, autonomous being. His work, for instance, went beyond a mechanical assessment of what later came to be called the "agent–structure" question.

Writing of the impact of race in global politics, for example, Rosenau warned readers not "to exaggerate the potency of individual variables" because of the "limits set by role, governmental, societal, and systemic variables." To be sure, the particular experience and personality traits of officials produce different reactions "to the fact and symbolism of skin color."[20] "Our values stress the dignity of the person, the inviolability of the human spirit, and normative responsibility for one's own actions." Nevertheless, he then concluded: "Individuals need to be treated . . . as complexes of roles and statuses" so that there is little scope for the "unique person."[21] By contrast, Rosenau more recently, in "mixing micro-macro," has argued that it is people's growing skills and escalating participation in world politics that have helped to produce the postinternational world.[22] Highlighting once again the tension created by the juxtaposition of human beings as autonomous and moral beings and as the pawns of larger structural forces, he now insists that "individual actions can cumulate into system-wide outcomes" and that "people are becoming ever more powerful as galvanizers of global change."[23]

Rosenau's succinct version of the "skill revolution" is that "recent years have witnessed citizens becoming more analytic, active, committed, and wiser."[24] "To become more skillful," he declares, "is to be able to construct more elaborate scenarios, to discern more causal relationships, and to be readier to accept complexity."[25] These words echo John Stuart Mill's earlier enthusiastic endorsement of the relationship between education and democracy, as well as the work of scholars of nationalism like

---

[19] The terms "norm" and "normative" do not appear at all in Rosenau, *The Scientific Study of Foreign Policy.*
[20] *Ibid.,* pp. 359, 360.   [21] Rosenau, *Turbulence in World Politics,* pp. 115, 117.
[22] *Ibid.,* pp. 141–177. See also Rosenau, *Along the Domestic-Foreign Frontier,* pp. 275–298, and Rosenau, *Distant Proximities,* pp. 18–49.
[23] Rosenau, *Turbulence in World Politics,* p. 142.
[24] Rosenau, *Along the Domestic-Foreign Frontier,* p. 278.   [25] *Ibid.,* p. 280.

Ernest Gellner. And like Mill, Rosenau holds a liberal perspective that sees improving the well-being of individuals as a principal objective of political life. Nowhere is the growing liberal emphasis on individuals more apparent than in the increasing focus on human rights and on individual responsibility for violating those rights. As Rosenau puts it, "the more people in diverse countries converge around similar orientations, the more are core values spreading on a global scale."[26]

There is, of course, another side to this. As we shall see shortly, many individuals are bewildered about the sources of change in their lives. Whether an Argentinian factory worker who loses his job because of the collapse of the national economy, a Balinese hotel owner whose hotel remains empty owing to an act of terrorism, a Russian whose savings are halved by currency devaluation, or an Enron employee whose pension vanishes because of corporate wrongdoing, there are growing numbers of people who discover that their well-being is in the hands of faceless others and that their governments are powerless to cope with these impersonal forces or, worse, are in cahoots with them. Inevitably, this produces immense frustration, a dangerous legitimacy crisis for governments, and a decline in the authority of states.

The democratic deficit

Many of the most important normative concerns raised about the postinternational world, including those opposed to globalization, are explicitly or implicitly linked to the broad concern that people, including those in democratic societies, are losing their ability to control their own lives or to choose how to live them. There is, in other words, a growing democratic deficit.

The essence of democratic citizenship is participation in government and the accountability of elected officials. The weakening of states in the postinternational world in some ways entails a reduction in the rights and responsibilities of citizenship, ranging from democratic participation to contributing to public welfare. Historically, "citizenship can then range from thin to thick: thin where it entails few transactions, rights and obligations; thick where it occupies a significant share of all transactions, rights and obligations sustained by state agents and people living under their jurisdiction."[27] As it already appears that the social dimensions

---

[26] *Ibid.*, p. 283.   [27] Tilly, "Citizenship, Identity and Social History," p. 8.

of citizenship associated with the welfare state are under attack, is there a possibility that political rights might thin as well?[28]

Important normative issues arise if the meaning of citizenship changes alongside shifts in the nature of states, markets, and boundaries, whether states initiate this shift in authority or not. If decisions are made by transnational or international institutions, where will individuals turn with claims based on fairness, equity, and freedom? Some argue that older forms of citizenship may, or perhaps should, revive. Echoing Rousseau, philosopher Sandel, for one, has championed republican notions based on "small and bounded places," deliberation, participation, and public spiritedness; in short, to notions of citizenship associated with the ancient Greek polis.[29] Others have suggested the need for more "cosmopolitan" notions of belonging and rights-bearing status based on notions of "global citizenship" and shared humanity.[30] While there is little historical evidence supporting the long philosophical tradition associated with Kant that espouses cosmopolitanism, the proliferation of influential transnational, international, and supranational authorities may one day give lie to pessimists, especially if we take seriously constructivist claims about the malleability of human allegiances.

Meanwhile, the proliferation of identities and boundaries places a strain on democratic institutions, most of which currently function in a state context.[31] When democracy works, it makes it easier to encompass within the system those with other important identities than citizen. Cleavages cross-cut; a rich pluralism exists; and the system remains moderate. However, the proliferation of strong identities and alternate authorities endangers the consensus in favor of democratic state institutions that evolved in the West to mediate the tension between majority rule and minority rights. New moral communities that may not coincide with sovereign boundaries and resulting "outsiders" may no longer be deemed deserving of democratic rights and protections. Ethnic, racial,

---

[28] See, for example, Jeffrey C. Isaac, *Democracy in Dark Times* (Ithaca, NY: Cornell University Press, 1998).
[29] Michael J. Sandel, *Democracy's Discontent: America in Search of a Public Philosophy* (Cambridge, MA: Belknap Press of Harvard University Press, 1996), pp. 317–351; and Anthony Giddens, *The Third Way: The Renewal of Social Democracy* (Cambridge: Polity Press, 1998), pp. 138–141.
[30] Sandel, *Democracy's Discontent*, p. 341. See also David Held's advocacy of "cosmopolitan democratic law," *Democracy and the Global Order: From the Modern State to Cosmopolitan Governance* (Stanford, CA: Stanford University Press, 1995).
[31] Rosenau, *Along the Domestic-Foreign Frontier*, pp. 335–336.

and religious self-consciousness are especially threatening in this regard, and advocates of a secular society in countries such as Turkey, India, and Israel are conscious of this danger.

Those who applaud economic globalization perhaps underestimate its psychological and political consequences and overestimate collective rationality. Rosecrance, for example, recognizes the possible rise in personal insecurity as states fail to protect citizens from external economic forces, although he believes that those with education[32] and talent will succeed. By freeing markets from state intervention or even regulation – the other end of a continuum extending to the expropriation or nationalization of private property – rational economic man guided by the norm of efficiency (often translated as corporate profit) may finally triumph. Giddens, for his part, sees the "radical modernity" involved in globalization as creating a "dialectic of powerlessness and empowerment in terms of both experience and action."[33] In his view, much of the technology that allocates power and control to transnational corporations, regional and global markets, and supranational institutions also provides individuals with access to unprecedented amounts of information and connects them to others with similar skills and interests around the world. For this reason, Giddens optimistically concludes that "coordinated political engagement" may be "possible and necessary, on a global level as well as locally."[34]

Even in an era during which individuals are better educated and trained than ever before and have become politically conscious, more and more voices are, nonetheless, being heard that individuals are pawns of globe-girdling institutions and processes that deprive them of democratic rights. Contrary to Rosenau's view of matters, a sense of political efficacy does *not* necessarily flow from the skills revolution. Anxiety rather than a sense of efficacy drives foes of globalization and those protesters who gathered first in Seattle and then in Quebec and Genoa to oppose the World Trade Organization (WTO) and later in Prague and Washington to denounce the IMF and World Bank. Their basic claims are that, as citizens of sovereign states, they have enjoyed a voice in making policy or in punishing leaders who betray their trust, and that today their well-being is increasingly determined by

---

[32] Rosecrance, *The Rise of the Virtual State*. Rosecrance emphasizes the critical importance of education in becoming a successful virtual state (pp. 205–207).
[33] Anthony Giddens, *The Consequences of Modernity* (Stanford, CA: Stanford University Press, 1990), p. 150.
[34] *Ibid.*

institutions (including global markets) that are not accountable to them. In their gloomy vision, unresponsive TNCs scour the world for labor, shifting job opportunities from country to country, often placing employees in sweatshop conditions, and destroying the environment and local cultures as they expand operations. And as the global market acquires its own form of sovereignty, transnational violence, exotic diseases, and dangerous pathogens travel globally with trade.[35] The IMF, World Bank, and other giant financial institutions, critics insist, place harsh conditions on loans against which populations impotently protest. Prying emerging markets open to trade and investment and enforcing austerity, in this view, not only often reduce the welfare of local populations but also reduce the autonomy of democratically elected leaders and heighten the likelihood of civil unrest and violence.

One might shrug off such protests by responding that international organizations like the WTO and IMF are and have always been unaccountable to individual citizens. Whether the League of Nations, the European Union, or the UN Security Council, international organizations are under no obligation to account to individuals for their activities. But their sovereign member states legally represent those individuals, and any effort of international organizations to ignore major states seeking to protect individual citizens would invite institutional suicide. However much they have a degree of autonomy and collective perspective that is broader than the sum of their member parts, IGOs are to a substantial extent the creatures of sovereign states with primary obligations to those states. And, as the creatures of states, they have been approved by elected state institutions (where there are elections) and have been legally incorporated into national legal systems. In this sense, the WTO is no different than any international organization before it, except perhaps as regards a lack of transparency in its dispute settlement mechanism.

There have always been those who protest against international organizations because of fear of the loss of state sovereignty. Such fear motivates right-wing American groups today. It also lay behind America's refusal to join the League of Nations or to add a proposed guarantee of "racial equality" to the Treaty of Versailles, join the International Trade Organization after World War II, ratify the Genocide Convention for many years, or accept the International Criminal Court today.

---

[35] See Christopher Bright, "Invasive Species: Pathogens of Globalization," *Foreign Policy* 116 (Fall 1999), p. 50.

Nevertheless, the proliferation of transnational or networked organizations (especially labor unions, environmentalists, and neo-Marxists), liberal church organizations, cultural nationalists, loose networks of Internet chat groups, anarchists, and angered citizens – some of whom showed up in Seattle, Prague, Geneva, and other globalization venues – suggests we may be witnessing the emergence of a broad new anti-globalization movement and ideology.[36] Whatever the almost ridiculous variations in motives and aims of affiliated groups, most feature opposition to the erosion of sovereignty, free trade, deregulation, and reduction of national welfare programs, and support for higher global environmental and labor standards, and defense of local cultures. Such a conglomerate ideology obviously combines elements of both nationalism and globalism.

A paradox is apparent here. First, the alienation reflected by protests against globalization grows even as state sovereignty weakens, yet previously the state was regarded as the "problem," not the "solution," to individual powerlessness and *anomie* and as the major source of human-rights violations. Until the French Revolution, the monarchies of Europe allowed individuals to have virtually no impact on state policy, and much of the liberal tradition in political philosophy was preoccupied with limiting state interference and arbitrariness in the lives of citizens and in increasing individual autonomy and political efficacy. Theorists like John Locke and Adam Smith sought to limit state impediments to individual economic happiness. More recently, moving in an opposite direction, theorists such as T. H. Green have sought to persuade states to assume greater responsibility for citizens' welfare.

Even today, those who fear the democratic deficit rarely recognize or acknowledge how restricted democracy actually is globally. Those living in an OECD country forget how small a minority functional democracies constitute among the world's roughly 200 sovereign states. Although many countries have political parties and elections, few have an institutionalized democratic political culture or a tolerance of political diversity. In much of the developing world, particular ethnic, racial, religious, or regional groups control the organs of government at the expense of

---

[36] See, for example, Robin Broad, ed., *Global Backlash: Citizen Initiatives for a Just World Economy* (Blue Ridge, PA: Romman & Littlefield, 2002); Jackie Smith and Hank Johnston, eds., *Globalization and Resistance: Transnational Dimensions of Social Movements* (Blue Ridge, PA: Romman & Littlefield, 2002); Barry K. Gills, ed., *Globalization and the Politics of Resistance* (London: Palgrave, 2001).

other groups and use government institutions to repress and exploit. These are hardly democracies worthy of the name.

The incompatibility between a system of states and global governance has progressed furthest in the economic realm and, not surprisingly, anti-globalization protests have focused on this sphere. One of the great contributions of Marxism was recognition that economics and politics were inseparable. Marx recognized that this might happen because of the globalization of capital. The idea that states would become the tools of global capitalism, especially after the merger of industrial and bank capital, remains a stock feature of Marxist analysis. And the possibility that states would "wither away" presumed the global triumph of an alternative economic system. Unfortunately for Marx, he was right about the "withering" but wrong about the economic system that would triumph.

Two normative stories about globalization and its effects

Just as international and postinternational scholars tell different stories about global politics generally, so do those who favor globalization and those who oppose it. Again, there is some truth in both stories. Much of the difference turns on views of the sovereign state.

If the state is losing pride of place in global politics, then we have to seek a new unit of analysis around which to focus research. As this book has repeatedly emphasized, postinternational theory revolves around individuals and groups associating with one another, whereas international theory focuses on a system of states. In a globalized world of few relatively strong states, many weakening states, and still others that are failing, the essential definition of self (and logically also of others) no longer conforms to the givens of the state system. Even a modest call for better data on contemporary loyalty shifts and identity changes risks perpetuating the conceptual blindness aggravated by the yearning for "hard" data that has consumed our discipline for over two decades. It is not simply the facts/values dichotomy that is unsustainable but that there are all that many "true" and "false" facts. For example, if we define wars as interstate phenomena, there have been few to study in recent years. Yet surely we would not want to conclude that these years have been peaceful. Nevertheless, international relations has been slow to keep pace with change in part because of the preference by empiricists for data that are easily available in neat geographic pigeonholes, and do not overlap, thereby facilitating the comparative method. None of this suggests that we reject empiricism. What we reject is the idea that "facts speak for themselves." Fact selection, their arrangement, and their meaning – the chief functions of theory – are dangerous tasks. All are conditioned by necessary and inevitable prejudices; to a substantial extent we perceive what we look for and we are often conditioned to ignore what is in front of our noses. Moreover, like the Cheshire Cat, the world is constantly in the process of rapid construction and reconstruction, even as we are constructing and reconstructing our understandings of that world.

Consider the "backlash" against globalization. Some of this is just media hype and the predictable response to media attention, linked to the sort of youthful idealism and energy that in the 1960s fueled hippie happenings as well as opposition to the war in Vietnam. In reality, however, now as then, there are also powerful undercurrents at work. Our "fragmegrating" world touches wellsprings of human emotion and attachment to the imagined stable state-centric political universe and exposes limitations to envisioning any other sort of world. Fear of the unknown, of allegedly ruthless corporate conglomerates and faceless bureaucrats, encourages not only an embrace of the local, near, and familiar – the neighborhood or village, kith and kin, ethnic traditions – but also nostalgia for "country" and romanticization of the state's record of accomplishment. There is more than a germ of truth in the anti-globalization story. Let us examine it more closely – and also offer a pro-globalization alternative that is less nostalgic about the past and more optimistic about a globalizing future.

The anti-globalization chronicle

The anti-globalization story begins with the emergence of the state from "tribalism" and the segmentary society that characterized the Middle Ages. In this version, as we have noted, states established clear and secure boundaries, formed legal systems, reduced brigandage, and encouraged markets. Order within a "domestic" realm was created and defended against enemies in the external anarchic world. To be sure, many of the early kings and nobles were pretty rude characters – one had to be in the context of those times – but over the years in the transition from king's domain to sovereign state, many of the regimes were rationalized and depersonalized. Monarchs became constitutional rather than absolute rulers, themselves subject to the law and more respectful of traditional liberties and "the rights of man." Representative assemblies became more powerful, and democracies began to evolve.

Although the notion of a "people" harked back in some cases to folk memories and the "realm" of the king, a healthy sense of "nation" and "nationalism" came to fruition in the early nineteenth century. "Citizen" took on a new element of dignity, more like that associated with ancient Athens or the Italian cities of the Renaissance. Conscription and regular drill created proud and patriotic citizen armies that gave young men a sense of participation in the defense of their country and nation – not like the venal mercenaries relied upon (for lack of an alternative) in earlier times. War and diplomacy both had their own rules that eventually became enshrined in international law. States began to regulate commerce with greater care and gradually began to assume more responsibility for the health and welfare of citizens. From the late nineteenth century through World War II full-blown welfare or "nanny" states developed. The Westphalian State gave the citizen a sense of belonging to something greater than him- or herself, a patriotic identity that did not depend on religious belief in everyone's being a "child of God." Citizenship was also a badge of identity that was not inherently incompatible with church, loyalty to family or village, or most other identities.

The great accomplishment of the Europeans and their enduring political gift to the rest of the world was the sovereign territorial state, and it is therefore not surprising that that state became the model to which all came to aspire. In addition, since the end of the Cold War, more and more states have made strides toward democratization. At this juncture, however, what is destabilizing are the many ways the state is being undermined by contemporary globalizing trends. There is widespread *angst* and growing resentment on the part of those who believe that their state represents and protects their interests, and has been responsive, however incompletely, to their preferences. Globalization in some respects entails a reduction in the rights and responsibilities of citizenship ranging from state contributions to public welfare to democratic participation.

In the closing years of the twentieth century, resentment began to coalesce in the form of a growing anti-globalization movement. Some analysts began to speak of the movement as part of an emerging global "civil society," which perhaps somewhat contradictorily defended national workers and local-culture "olive trees" (Friedman's term) against neoliberal economic "reforms" and the cultural cosmopolitanism of McWorld. The movement as it developed, however, enlisted a strange and uncoordinated collection of political bedfellows. In fact, its very diversity was at once its greatest strength and liability. The anti-globalization banner was adopted by political liberals *and* democratic socialists concerned about democratic deficits and an erosion of the welfare state. It also attracted labor unions worried about foreign competition for jobs and investment, environmentalists fearing a flight of economic production to countries with poor environmental standards, human-rights activists troubled by sweat-shop and child-labor practices, xenophobic nationalists, cultural preservationists ranging from advocates of a "slow Europe" or a "little England" to fanatical Islamic fundamentalists, anarchists whose only creed is individual freedom and social chaos, and late-blooming flower children who were willing to enlist in any protest march on offer.

The anti-globalization movement reached a crescendo, however reprehensible, in 1999 when large demonstrations at the WTO Seattle meeting ended in violent riots. The protests – and probably more importantly, grave differences of opinion among the official delegates – caused the meeting to end in stalemate. Analysts began to write of a possible stillborn WTO, and governments learned two fundamental lessons: there must be some recognition of and at least a nominal response to the plight of the "losers" in a globalizing world economy; and future meetings of neoliberal international economic institutions must be held under much tighter security.

"Public" authority, according to the anti-globalization story, is moving to the "private" sectors of huge networks, corporate alliances, banks, and hedge funds which are motivated strictly by competitiveness and unfettered greed and not even genuinely responsible to their stockholders. International organizations like the United Nations, the EU, or the IMF may comprise sovereign governments, but national interests get submerged in voting blocs (sometimes weighted voting) in such institutions and their bureaucracies operate with no real constituency or accountability. Transnational NGOs may do some good, but it is not apparent who many of them actually represent and speak for. Democratic choice and participation, then, is one of the victims of globalization.

There are other concerns as well. National cultures are being overwhelmed by the homogenized culture of globalization, which is often seen as predominantly the "Coca-Cola/McDonald's" culture of the United States hegemon. Television programs, movies, radio, pop music, and the Internet all carry a glossy message of nihilistic and narcissistic self-gratification, the decline of moral standards, and violence that is antithetical to any sort of public or community spirit.

The rapid growth of economic enterprise is, according to globalization's environmental adversaries, also menacing the planet with uncontrolled development. Not only are human working standards under threat but so is the very future of humanity, with the pollution of the air we breathe, the loss of rainforests and irreplaceable species, energy exploration in the earth's last wild places, overfishing, and the contamination and exhaustion of oceans, streams, and subterranean aquifers. Growing migrations of people are disrupting communities, creating more cultural ghettos, and providing more opportunities for a host of new mafias and trafficking in humans, from illegal aliens to women to slaves. Nor is the new global technology completely innocent and constructive. The computer and Internet that enable us to get our bank balance and buy sports tickets on line also provide an opening for money laundering, drug lords, hate groups, terrorists, corporate expansion, and reckless financial speculation at the expense of countries, by what Friedman has labeled the Electronic Herd and the Supermarkets. Finally, on an individual level, the computer permits its user to withdraw in cyberspace from society and social responsibility, and interact only with persons of his or her own peer group(s).

A new global elite plays the game of globalization for its own benefit, increasing the psychological as well as material-welfare distance between its members and the great mass of citizens at home and abroad. We are dividing into a bipolar world of the few who benefit, often outrageously, from globalization and the many who do not or even have their lives made far worse. The cohesion traditionally provided by the state and by national identity is giving way to a numbing sense of alienation from large anonymous institutions and a homogenized high-tech global marketplace that can only end in Big Brother on a scale heretofore unimaginable – or in political and social fragmentation of equally unthinkable proportions.

The proglobalization chronicle

The pro-globalization story begins by emphasizing the highly tentative nature of the state's rise and its shared authority and identity from the very outset with other polity types. In this version, however, the state's creators – rather than liberators from primal segmentary backwardness – were often "thugs" whose primary "virtues" were guile, a sense of self-preservation, and pugnacity. Rulers and nobles were exploiters who extracted heavy taxes from an impoverished peasantry and borrowed from prosperous merchants to finance continual wars of aggrandizement. To be sure, monarchs and aristocrats were forced to become more "constitutional" and less arbitrary over time, but the best of the "representative democracies" until well into the twentieth century were narrowly elitist. Among other things, it is hard to regard as a true "democracy," any system that excluded all women (half the population) from voting and office holding. Even in America, one of the world's leading democracies, women did not get the vote until 1927. Blacks were systematically excluded from political participation in the South until the 1960s, and minorities today are still seriously underrepresented at the polls and in the corridors of power.

On the other hand, radical attempts to reduce elite control and broaden mass participation in states resulted in authoritarianism or even totalitarianism. The French Revolution was a bloodbath and ended with the egomaniacal Emperor Napoleon on the march to conquer Europe. The overthrow of the Tsars brought the Bolsheviks to power and ultimately the monolithic brutal dictatorship of Stalin and his successors. Mao's peasant revolution degenerated into the ideological excesses of the Cultural Revolution and the massacre of young freedom-loving Chinese at Tiannamen Square.

The nineteenth-century shift in Europe to citizen armies, and close-order drill, coupled with new myths of the nation and its destiny, signaled a change from limited wars fought by mercenaries to potentially total wars waged for patriotism. Far from a virtue, the invention of nationalism divided rather than united and gave callow youths with too much testosterone a more convincing cause to fight for. The fact that they were dressed in uniforms and fought under the rules of war made them no less lethal to themselves and others, including the civilian populations who happened to get in the line of fire or whose worldly goods were seized for military provisions. When loyalty to state fused with the essentially tribal or atavistic idea of nation, and patriotism was touted as the highest fulfillment of self, the world was bound to be in for a bad time.

Now after a few hundred years and a twentieth century that pushed interstate conflict to the brink of nuclear annihilation, humanity seems better able to get the state in perspective and under control, and to cultivate higher callings. There is a marked decline in interstate wars. Although identity with country is slow to erode around the world,

334

public opinion polls in nearly all countries indicate that most govern-ments and politicians are held in low esteem. Attentive publics seem to be increasingly aware that states simply cannot deliver on many of their promises and that, like it or not, citizen welfare is caught up in wider global processes.

Fortunately, a desperately needed expansion of global governance is already well under way, exercised by more diverse groups of actors, at and across many levels. There has been a veritable explosion of inter-national law, nonstate actors, transnational firms, and financial institu-tions – and regimes and networks combining some of these selfsame actors – that are beginning to address interdependence issues that no state has the capacity to deal with alone. At long last, international law and institution-building are also advancing – sometimes rapidly, and sometimes slowly – to wrestle with urgent collective problems such as gross violations of human rights, peacekeeping, environmental protec-tion, organized crime, terrorism, refugees, telecommunications, ship-ping, aviation, disease, monetary instability, barriers to trade, corporate malfeasance, and so on.

To say the least, the activities of transnational firms and banks often do not meet high ethical standards. However, the tremendous growth of the world economy that they have engendered – notwithstanding some turbulence that reflects mainly growing pains – has been almost entirely good news for human welfare. Globalization has brought count-less workers around the world new jobs and better living standards. The consumer has also benefited with a wider range of less expensive prod-ucts to choose from. NGOs and attentive publics are having consider-able success in persuading governments that are negotiating neoliberal rules, as well as firms who do business abroad, to agree to and to enforce improved working conditions and environmental standards. The going is slow in these issue areas, but far more is being accomplished than if the foreign firms had never ventured abroad in the first instance. Demon-strators at WTO, World Bank, IMF, and Davos meetings who want to stop globalization are thus putting their own selfish interests and some-times anarchism or xenophobic nationalism ahead of the preferences of responsible consumers and the crying needs of the poor in emerging market countries. In any event, the processes of globalization are inex-orable and can only be in modest ways guided and tamed. As Thomas L. Friedman observes: "[T]oday there is no more First World, Second World or Third World. There is now just the Fast World – the world of the wide-open plain – and the Slow World – the world of those who either fall by the wayside or choose to live away from the plain in some artificially walled-off valley of their own."[37]

The alleged threat of Western-style cultural homogenization is vastly overrated, so resilient are local cultures. As Latin American novelist Mario Vargas Llosa writes:

> [C]ontrary to the warnings of those who fear globalization, it is not easy to completely erase cultures – however small they may be – if behind them is a rich tradition and people who practice them, even in secret. And, today, thanks to the weakening of the nation-state, we are seeing forgotten, marginalized, and silenced local cultures reemerging and displaying dynamic signs of life in the great concert of this globalized planet.[38]

It is also simplistic to think of cultural globalization as equivalent to American cultural hegemony. After all, Chinese food, pizzas, and sushi are all increasingly to be found throughout the world. Global cities offer a veritable cornucopia of different cuisines that is reflective of their cosmopolitan populations. In the end, concern for cultural threats often involves either romantic sentimentality and condescension ("aren't they quaint"), or a blind eye turned to local practices and conditions that *should* go the way of the dinosaur, such as the treatment of women in conservative Muslim circles and the grinding poverty of preindustrial villages.

The Internet and other improvements in telecommunications can be abused, but their impact has been generally positive. Those improvements have provided the technological foundation for much of the tremendous expansion in the world economy and in the ranks of skilled individuals. Citizens around much of the world are getting more and more information, and hence are much harder for governments to propagandize effectively. Governments can use some of the same technology to curb access to information and monitor the affairs of citizens, but typically users and technology stay several steps ahead. Far from encouraging users just to play computer games in lonely rooms, computers and the Internet have opened up to individuals not only vast stores of information but also a new means of communication and organization that is the driving force behind an emerging global civil society. Globalization critics are quick to point out that those "wired"

---

[37] Friedman, *The Lexus and the Olive Tree*.
[38] Mario Vargas Llosa, "The Culture of Liberty," *Foreign Policy* 112 (January/February 2001), 66–71.

into the new technology are often those closest to the business sector, and they tend to be predominantly urban and young. But technology is becoming cheaper and moving further into less affluent urban neighborhoods and even into the countryside at a rapid pace. Twenty-two-and-a half million Chinese had access to the Internet in 2001. Would anyone care to wager what that figure will be ten or twenty years from today?

Finally, like cultural homogenization, the democratic deficit problem that some believe grows out of globalization is also exaggerated. Most states have long had a monumental democratic deficit problem of their own. By far the majority of states in today's world are either outright authoritarian or very imperfect democracies at best. In much of the developing world, some parochial ethnic, racial, religious, or regional group controls the organs of government at the expense of other groups and uses government institutions to exploit and control groups other than themselves. There was a considerable expansion of aspiring democracies at the end of the Cold War, but, as Samuel P. Huntington reminds us, every previous democratic wave has been followed by a partial retreat.[39] To be sure, there are some countries that are genuine and stable democracies, but the politicians in charge in many of them are not doing at all well in public opinion polls.

In an earlier era, the boundaries of Westphalian polities, internalized in the form of identities tied to territory and citizenship, gradually took precedence over, and in many cases erased local boundaries delineated by regional, religious, or ethnic identities. Being an American, as an identity, replaced Virginian, New Yorker, and so forth at the top of identity hierarchies. To be French first meant that one was no longer primarily Burgundian, Breton, Norman, or Alsatian. In similar fashion, recent decades have witnessed erosion in state authority accompanied by a proliferation of new identities and dramatic changes in individuals' identity hierarchy. These trends may be dated from the mid-nineteenth century and the growth in political participation, literacy, and democracy, but they were disguised by state control of historical meaning. The reemergence of prestate identities and their manipulation by a generation of leaders who see their access to power blocked by states have helped to rip off this disguise. More important, new identities with new potentialities are being formed.

---

[39] Samuel P. Huntington, *The Third Wave: Democratization in the Late Twentieth Century* (Norman: University of Oklahoma Press, 1991).

Conclusion: maps for an uncertain future

This chapter has reviewed some of the major questions of remapping global politics in our time. The rapidly evolving normative temper of an era, during which a state system is in transition to a more complex postinternational world, is an "unruly time" with "ungovernable globalization, turbulent governance, and disorderly geography."[40] To date, insufficient consideration has been given to the normative issues raised by shifts in authority and the impact on individuals living in an increasingly polyarchical global society.[41]

From the perspective of the field of global politics, facts and values are being reunited. As we have seen, the erosion of state authority and advancing globalization raise critical normative issues. Declining state autonomy in the face of technological change, market exigencies, and other factors have reduced state commitment to citizens' welfare (where such commitment exists). Growing reliance on the anonymous decision-making of global markets and, more broadly, on governance rather than government, also means a declining commitment to state-level democratic norms and to the norm of accountability (where such commitment exists). These trends additionally reflect a reduced ability of states to protect citizens from a range of external threats (where such commitment exists). Yet, arguably, individuals and groups now have many more options in terms of the polities with which they can identify, to which they give their allegiance, and through which they expect to receive psychological and material benefits or to advance the values they hold dear.

As we said at the outset of this book, more than one story can be true, but not all are necessarily equally true, and some may even be false. The authors are more sympathetic to the pro- than anti-globalization narrative and believe that globalizing trends are less and less reversible, and hold more promise than threat. This conclusion, however, is tempered by recognizing that the pro-globalization story, like all stories, ignores or plays down significant factors. Thus, recalling our relatively brief allusions to the idea that globalization is itself the result of and remains under the control of the policies of a group of leading states, especially

---

[40] Gearóid Ó Tuathail, Andrew Herod, and Susan M. Roberts, "Negotiating Unruly Problematics," in Andrew Herod, Gearóid Ó Tuathail, and Susan M. Roberts, eds., *An Unruly World? Globalization, Governance, and Geography* (London: Routledge, 1998), pp. 2, 3.
[41] Robert Dahl, *Democracy and its Critics* (New Haven, CT: Yale University Press, 1989). See also, Rosenau, "Citizenship," pp. 284–291.

the United States, forces us to face the possibility of a benign hegemon that is viewed by many others as increasingly malign.

If the United States hegemon not only fostered the forces of globalization in the past but today retains the capacity to reverse them, then that country's growing unilateralism in recent years should raise concerns. Recent events like the invasion and occupation of Iraq in spring 2003 despite the opposition of most of the U.N. Security Council have forced even the most optimistic of the pro-globalizers to pay attention. Other actions, largely but not entirely associated with the presidency of George W. Bush, also provoke rethinking: unilateral cancellation of the 1972 ABM agreement and commitment to build a limited anti-ballistic missile shield, refusal to join the International Criminal Court, rejection of the Kyoto agreement on carbon emissions, imposition of illegal steel quotas, among others, seem to reflect a rejection of the web of international institutions such as the United Nations, the European Union, the World Trade Organization, and even NATO that the United States was so important in building after World War II.[42] What if Washington turns its back on these institutions and adopts long-term policies aimed at ending selected aspects of globalization? Is the United States likely to pursue such policies in the long run? Is the American "hyperpower" sufficiently powerful to do so, or are globalization processes sufficiently embedded as part of global structure to resist such efforts? These are questions that merit thoughtful consideration by even the most liberal of theorists.

Other stories also help to illuminate part of today's complex reality, help us envision other possibilities and possible problems, and, insofar as they continue to condition the behavior of those who tell and believe them, justify and provoke political action and tend to be self-confirming. Even those stories that are false or seriously misleading, which we believe most of the realist chronicle and radical anti-globalization tales to be, have undeniable consequences and, like it or not, are part of the normative context of today's global politics. Taken together, the stories suggest some of the contradictions with which we all must wrestle, and they provide a foundation for what needs to be continued discourse and dialogue.

Beyond that is the central and extraordinarily difficult question of what the future holds, and here the alternate stories on authority and

[42] Madelaine K. Albright, "United Nations," *Foreign Policy* 138 (September/October 2003), pp. 16–24.

its redistribution are important. If globalization is dispersing authority, the future may augur greater conflict and less capacity to cope with collective dilemmas, even while eroding state capacity makes it more and more difficult to protect citizens against negative externalities. On the other hand, if peoples are complexly interdependent as never before, the pressure to cooperate in order to cope with transnational and global issues and solve collective goods puzzles will become more intense. And if the proliferation of polities, rather than dispersing authority, is creating centers of transnational and global expertise, we may anticipate a more hopeful problem-solving future.

Rosenau's spirited challenge to political scientists in 1986 is even more relevant today as we enter a postinternational world: "[T]his is not a time for nit-picking, for finding fault with vague definitions, imprecise formulations, and skewed data. We need, rather, to . . . build upon the work of those among us who do not shrink from taking on the whole world and its underlying patterns as their theoretical problem."[43] Instead, it is time to take seriously his advice: "One way of unearthing the bedrock premises of metatheory is to play a game with one's reasoning. By asking the same question – 'Why do I make that assertion about the fundamentals of world politics?' – and then endlessly repeating it in response to every substantive answer one offers, eventually the string runs out and one comes upon the answer, 'Because that is what I believe!'"[44] At that point we can get beyond the unchanging and false parsimony in much of international relations theory and turn instead to the rich and dynamic tapestry of human identities and loyalties, thereby bringing human beings back into the analysis. Our task will be to "investigate . . . how preferences are formed and how identities are shaped."[45]

The shape of post-Westphalian global politics remains obscure. Maps that portray the world divided into exclusive sovereign states tell only part of the tale and, for many issues, not the most important part. The classic distinction between "domestic" and "international" means less and less; the role of state frontiers as walls between "us" and "them" continues to erode. This by no means signals the end of such cleavages;

---

[43] James N. Rosenau, "Before Cooperation; Hegemons, Regimes, and Habit-driven Actors in World Politics," *International Organization* 40:4 (Autumn 1986), p. 850.
[44] *Ibid.*, p. 856.
[45] Goldstein and Keohane, "Ideas and Foreign Policy: An Analytical Framework," p. 6. See also Goldstein, *Ideas, Interests, and American Trade Policy*. Goldstein and Keohane are interested in "world views, principled beliefs, and causal beliefs" (pp. 7–8) and regard loyalties as the products of world view (p. 8). The present authors are concerned with loyalties and their impact on other beliefs and ideas. See Ferguson and Mansbach, *Polities*.

instead, it means that the criteria for those cleavages are changing, sometimes issue by issue. In the end, it may make less sense to continue debating whether or not sovereignty is eroding, as if this were a discoverable truth, than to acknowledge that Westphalian polities are less and less able to accomplish their basic tasks. This shifts the discussion from a purely theoretical to a more practical realm, thereby linking the abstract question of "what is happening to the state?" to the investigation of policies and institutions to cope more effectively with the monumental challenges and opportunities that lie ahead.

Recent events reflect that one state, at least, the putative hyperpower, can still throw its weight around and defy world opinion by invading and conquering Iraq.[46] Continued resistance in Iraq, the difficulties confronted in reconstructing that country as well as Afghanistan, and earlier events that go back to France's war in Algeria in the 1950s, the United States in Vietnam, and the Soviets in Afghanistan point up the limits of power. Pacification of areas inhabited by hostile and politically mobilized populations is a virtually impossible task, and not least in today's world in which the protection of civilians, human rights, and democratic values have become important norms.

The United States' ability and propensity to act unilaterally in recent years and to control, impede, weaken, or even destroy international institutions tempts one to conclude that it alone could reverse many of the trends of postinternationalism. This would be a premature and, in our judgment, unwise conclusion because much of the United States' unique unilateral capability seems better adapted to resisting change than to guiding it, moving it in different directions, or managing it. And, even if the United States had the capability to reverse contemporary trends, it has few incentives to do so, at least in the long term. Unilateralism breeds isolation and fear, which are antithetical to the secure neoliberal world that Americans recognize is a prerequisite for them to remain physically and economically secure. Of the three possible global futures presented earlier in the chapter, American norms, interests, and identities would suffer most in the event that the third – a world of chaos – were to materialize. Therefore, in our view, the current extreme "neoconservative" period in US policy is likely soon to pass and be replaced by what has been a traditional posture of at least moderate internationalism.

[46] Carnegie Endowment for International Politics, ed., "The World After Iraq," *Foreign Policy* 137 (July/August 2003), pp. 49–72.

However, given the message of this book, we cannot stress too strongly that "internationalism" is an orientation to governance and policymaking that is still rooted in a familiar and limited conception of interstate relations. In contrast, the postinternational world features an increasingly variegated universe of polities, identities, and loyalties. Buffeted both by history's revenge and future shock, patterns of authority are only going to get messier.

Index

CAMBRIDGE STUDIES IN INTERNATIONAL RELATIONS